The RETURN *of the* OYSTERCATCHER

ALSO BY SCOTT WEIDENSAUL

A World on the Wing: The Global Odyssey of Migratory Birds

Peterson Reference Guide to Owls of North America and the Caribbean

The First Frontier: The Forgotten History of Struggle, Savagery, and Endurance in Early America

Of a Feather: A Brief History of American Birding

Return to Wild America: A Yearlong Search for the Continent's Natural Soul

The Ghost with Trembling Wings: Science, Wishful Thinking, and the Search for Lost Species

Living on the Wind: Across the Hemisphere with Migratory Birds

Mountains of the Heart: A Natural History of the Appalachians

The Return of the Oystercatcher

Saving Birds to Save the Planet

SCOTT WEIDENSAUL

PICADOR

First published 2026 by W. W. Norton & Company, New York

First published in the UK 2026 by Picador
an imprint of Pan Macmillan
The Smithson, 6 Briset Street, London EC1M 5NR
EU representative: Macmillan Publishers Ireland Limited, 1st Floor,
The Liffey Trust Centre, 117–126 Sheriff Street Upper,
Dublin 1 D01 YC43
Associated companies throughout the world
www.panmacmillan.com

ISBN 978-1-0350-1651-8 HB
ISBN 978-1-0350-9101-0 TPB

Copyright © Scott Weidensaul 2026

The right of Scott Weidensaul to be identified as the
author of this work has been asserted in accordance
with the Copyright, Designs and Patents Act 1988.

All rights reserved. No part of this publication may be reproduced,
stored in a retrieval system, or transmitted, in any form, or by any means
(including, without limitation, electronic, mechanical, photocopying, recording
or otherwise) without the prior written permission of the publisher.

Pan Macmillan does not have any control over, or any responsibility for,
any author or third-party websites referred to in or on this book.

1 3 5 7 9 8 6 4 2

A CIP catalogue record for this book is available from the British Library.

Printed and bound in the UK using 100% Renewable Electricity by CPI Group (UK) Ltd

This book is sold subject to the condition that it shall not, by way of
trade or otherwise, be lent, hired out, or otherwise circulated without
the publisher's prior consent in any form of binding or cover other than
that in which it is published and without a similar condition including this
condition being imposed on the subsequent purchaser. The publisher does not
authorize the use or reproduction of any part of this book in any manner
for the purpose of training artificial intelligence technologies or systems.
The publisher expressly reserves this book from the Text and Data Mining
exception in accordance with Article 4(3) of the European Union
Digital Single Market Directive 2019/790.

Visit **www.picador.com** to read more about
all our books and to buy them.

*In memory of Thomas Brodie Johnson,
who reveled in birds*

Contents

	Introduction	1
One	Rebound	5
Two	Paying Sufficient Attention	30
Three	Mullet Hawks and the Witches' Walk	56
Four	The Nightingales of Knepp	85
Five	From the Carpathians to the Delta	114
Six	Rescuing the Unlovely	143
Seven	Guano-Bombed on Egg Rock	166
Eight	Islands of Sanctuary	193
Nine	Tastes Like Chicken	220
Ten	Prairie Ghosts	248
Eleven	Good for the Bird	276
Twelve	Land of the Ancestors	306
	Acknowledgments	335
	References	339
	Bibliography	345
	Index	373

The RETURN *of the* OYSTERCATCHER

Introduction

This is a book about optimism.

Optimism may seem badly misplaced these days, especially to those of us who have been battling for years on behalf of conservation. As I write this, it is still the early months of an administration that has unleashed a ferocious and profoundly shortsighted attack on federal environmental policy, protection, funding, and staffing (among many other things), against which only the first concerted pushback, mostly through the courts, has begun. Where it will lead I cannot say, beyond: nowhere good.

Even before President Donald J. Trump reclaimed office and began defenestrating resource and science agencies like the EPA, the US Forest Service, the National Park Service, the US Fish and Wildlife Service, the National Oceanic and Atmospheric Administration, and a host of smaller facets of the federal government many never heard of until they'd been all but wiped clean, the news for birds was generally gloomy.

I remember how my stomach sank in 2019 when I first heard about a paper soon to appear in the journal *Science*, all then still very hush-hush, the result of years of work by a cadre of the top ornithologists in North America who, after poring through decades of bird survey results, aerial waterfowl censuses, Christmas Bird Counts, and careful analyses of Doppler radar data, had concluded that the continent had lost one-third of its birds since 1970—there were 2.9 billion fewer individuals than 50 years before.

It was a gut-punch, though only because it finally quantified what any birder older than perhaps 35 already knew; if you'd been birding for a decade or two, you'd seen the erosion of bird numbers firsthand: the hollowing out of the springtime dawn chorus, the withering away of once-great migration multitudes. Still, for the wider public that *Science* paper was a bombshell, thanks in part to a masterful outreach campaign among the many partner organizations designed to finally raise the profile of the avian population crisis among non-birders and policymakers.

Understandably, almost all of the press coverage then and since (and there's been a lot of it) has focused on the grim statistics, showing catastrophic declines in guilds of birds dependent on various habitats—western forest birds, down almost 30 percent; birds of the boreal spruce forests of Canada and Alaska, down by 30 percent; and grassland birds, the worst-faring of all, down by 53 percent since 1970, with three-quarters of all grassland species in decline.

Yet the news, while awful, was not entirely bad. In some respects, given the way humans have run roughshod over the planet for the past half-century, maybe the wonder is that we still had fully two-thirds of North America's birds left. But more remarkably, a few groups of birds had actually done very well over the previous half-century. For example, while most forest songbirds showed steep declines, one group, the vireos, had increased by more than half, while populations of gnatcatchers, which look like miniature, frenetic mockingbirds, rose by about 15 percent. Why? No one really knows. Vireos for the most part inhabit the canopy or edges of mature forests, where they feed overwhelmingly on insects, although for some species like red-eyed vireos, fruit and berries can be important in late summer and autumn. They are mostly long-distance migrants, traveling to Latin America or the Caribbean. But the same can be said in terms of habitat, diet, and migration for other groups of songbirds like warblers, whose numbers are crashing. The paper offered no explanation for the difference, and scientists still have no idea why these two families are an exception.

On the other hand, there was no mystery about why two other groups of birds identified as winners in *Science* had come out ahead in the previous half-century. Waterfowl like ducks, geese, and swans were up by more than 50 percent, thanks to decades of wetland protection and restoration. As a group, raptors like hawks, eagles, falcons, and vultures had increased by 200 percent, thanks to better protection, bans on harmful pesticides like DDT, and targeted reintroduction programs that brought back species like peregrine falcons that had essentially vanished from huge areas of North America.

As a species, we're more attuned to bad news than to good news, and bad news often motivates us to action. There has been plenty of action since 2019. The following year, many of the authors of the *Science* paper launched a huge, concerted, privately funded initiative dubbed Road to Recovery. R2R, as it is known, began as a series of three multiday virtual workshops during and after the Covid-19 lockdowns, and eventually transitioned to in-person meetings, assembling hundreds of ornithologists and other scientists to begin to identify the critical gaps in our knowledge of bird populations, how to fill them as fast as possible, and how to act most effectively on that new information. They identified more than 110 "tipping point" species of birds that have lost at least half of their population in the past fifty years, like evening grosbeaks, rufous hummingbirds, and eastern whip-poor-wills, birds at the greatest risk but which offer the best chance for a reversal of fortune.

Yet we don't have to wait for good-news stories. All around the world—from a tiny island on the coast of Maine to the middle of the Pacific Ocean, from a hereditary estate in England to the deep Carpathian Mountains in Romania, from the middle of the Canadian boreal forest to a watery wilderness where you can hear the air raid sirens in Ukraine screaming at night—people are mapping avenues to recovery if we choose to follow them, making progress for birds. Which means they are making progress for us, too, because a world that works for birds, in all their complexity of movement and ecological need, will work for everything else, including people. The stories that follow aren't meant to mask harsh reality, but rather to offer a glimpse of what is possible, even in the face of what can seem insurmountable odds.

This may seem like the worst possible time to be writing an optimistic book about bird conservation, because I expect hope and optimism will be hard to come by in the months and years ahead. Resignation and despair may be all too easy to find, but maybe for that reason it's the best possible time for this book.

Because the far end will come, and the work of recovery will continue. For those of us to whom the natural world is more than just a pretty backdrop, reaching it with our sanity and souls intact will require a careful emotional balancing act. We cannot withdraw and cede the field to the destroyers, nor can we completely burn ourselves out with endless fury and grief that consumes us from within while the juggernaut grinds relentlessly forward. For each moment of justified rage, we must remember to take a moment of calm and recharge.

There is no better way to do so than in the company of birds.

So, if the news today was a stab to the heart, seek them out. It doesn't matter where you are, or what kind of birds you find; there is solace among them. Maybe you'll be able to immerse yourself in the great hemispheric dance of migration, and see here-today-and-gone-tomorrow travelers whose invisible paths through the night sky connect some of the farthest reaches of the planet. Maybe you'll be at a time and in a place where the air is full of birdsong, that sweet and vivid expression of an evolutionary tenacity that survived the great Cretaceous-ending asteroid and will, with a little help, survive us.

Whatever the bird, wherever the place, just watch. Listen. Breathe. Feel the clenched fingers around your heart and gut relax a little. Whatever we give back to birds—our passion, our voices, our resources, our righteous anger that motivates us to action—it is a small repayment for the gifts they unknowingly offer us, the chance to step out of ourselves for a time and inhabit their world, to slip inside the miracle of their extraordinary migrations, to see in their eyes more than 150 million years of avian evolution that makes this earth so much richer and lovelier and worth living in than would otherwise be the case.

Then back into the fray, reenergized, because if we secure their future, we secure our own.

One

Rebound

Up here in New England, March is an iffy month. Some years it remains locked in snow and ice for the duration; other years the south winds arrive early with a thaw that we welcome until it turns to mud season, when the frost comes out of the suddenly spongy ground and the gravel road at the end of our lane becomes enough of a quagmire that sometimes the school buses sink to their hubcaps.

But most years, no matter how hard the winter has been, by the end of March the rivers are running and the ice is going out of the lakes. As the first openings appear where the ice-fishing huts once stood, the ducks and geese arrive, the earliest of the spring migrants.

There is something definitive about the earliest waves of northbound waterfowl each year. Perhaps no one has ever put it more beautifully than Aldo Leopold, the visionary mid-20th-century ecologist who, in *A Sand County Almanac*, wrote, "One swallow does not make a summer, but one skein of geese, cleaving the March thaw, is the spring. . . . a migrating goose, staking two hundred miles of black night on the chance of finding a hole in the lake, has no easy chance for retreat. His arrival carries the conviction of a prophet who has burned his bridges."

It was an early March evening, and my wife Amy and I were walking quietly along the Ipswich River north of Boston, which meanders gently through expansive marshes of cattails and reeds. The woods on this Massachusetts Audubon sanctuary were mostly quiet, though earlier in the day the first, still-tentative choruses of birdsong had filled them: northern cardinals, tufted titmice, the *Fee-bee-bee* songs of black-capped chickadees. For now, we wanted to see what the warm front had brought in the way of ducks.

Out on the water, rippling reflections caught our eye, which our binoculars showed were clusters of diving ducks, plunging and popping back to the surface, breasting the current. There were buffleheads, comically small, rotund birds not much more than a foot long, which old-time duck hunters called butterballs; the drakes, the males, wore white wrap-around patches across the backs of black heads that seem too large for their bodies. Monochrome was the color scheme of the day; the bufflehead hens were all dark gray, save for a streak of white behind each eye. Common goldeneyes, the drakes mostly white-bodied with large, dark-green heads that looked black at this distance, held themselves apart from a flock of male common mergansers, big, similarly patterned in blackish-green-and-white, each merg just one long, streamlined taper starting with its bright red serrated beak. When the goldeneyes spooked and flushed, the males' wings made a high, thin sound: one old country name was "the whistler."

There would soon be waves of so-called puddle ducks arriving, mallards, northern pintails, green-winged teal, and the extravagantly attired wood duck drakes whose more understatedly colored mates would, by April, be incubating large clutches of eggs in the many nest boxes around the sanctuary. The Canada geese—well, they're always around; the twice-a-year spectacle of their migration has been somewhat diluted by the resident flocks that remain winter and summer, at most moving grudgingly south if there's a big freeze-up, and returning the moment the ice quits. Yet the true migrant geese, the Canadas that still travel to the subarctic to breed, continue to keep faith with the North, and some days the flat, overcast March skies are filled with their many thousands.

It's easy, on a mild March day, to take this all for granted, but it very nearly was not so. For a continent that once held almost unimaginable flocks of waterfowl, the 19th and much of the 20th centuries were a disaster for ducks, geese, and swans. Overshooting for the market before the 1920s, then the Dust Bowl drought in the 1930s, then rampant habitat destruction in the decades after World War II, drove their numbers to the floor. As recently as the late 1980s, when prolonged drought seemed poised to hammer a final nail in the coffin, biologists all but despaired of restoring waterfowl to even the modest numbers of the 1950s.

Yet today, one could argue that waterfowl numbers, overall, are higher than at almost any time since the market guns fell silent. The trumpeter swan, North America's largest native waterfowl weighing as much as 30 pounds, was all but given up for extinction in the early 1900s, but by 2024 numbered an estimated 63,000, thanks in part to reintroduction programs in the Great Lakes and eastern Canada. For that matter, one subspecies of Canada goose, likewise the largest of the species, was thought to have been lost a century ago, but now numbers in the millions. In fact, there have likely never been as many Canada geese and snow geese as there are today, and their numbers pose not just a nuisance for parkgoers stepping around gooey turds, but in the case of millions of hungry snow geese, an ecological problem reshaping the far-northern breeding grounds they share with many other species.

Little of this happened by accident. The dramatic increase in waterfowl populations in the last fifty years was largely the direct result of conservation efforts that entailed groundbreaking legislation fundamentally changing the way Americans treated their wetlands—along with a boatload of money, both public and private, and an unusually potent political will to restore and enhance waterfowl habitat.

North America in precolonial days was a waterfowl paradise, as early European accounts readily attest. "The rivers from August, or September, till February, are covered with flocks of Wildfoule: as swannes, geese, ducke, mallard, teal, wigeons . . . in such abundance as are not in all the world to be equalled," said the Councell for Virginia at Jamestown in 1610. More than two hundred years later, and on the other side of the continent, a guidebook written for emigrants to California in the 1840s lamented the sheer racket caused by migrant waterfowl:

When passing down the Sacramento River, or crossing the bay of St. Francisco, I have been greatly annoyed by the almost deafening, tumultuous and confused noises of the innumerable flocks of geese and ducks, which were continually flying to and fro and at times blackening the very heavens with their increasing numbers and making the aerial region ring with their tumultuous croaking and vehement squeaking. During the winter season California is truly a noisy, turbulent region; all the northern world seems to have given up its millions of the feathered tribes, which are here in universal convention, having complete possession of the entire country.

Such overwhelming abundance did not last. The latter half of the 19th century was an orgy of market shooting, with no seasons or bag limits. Many of the commercial gunners used what were known as punt guns, basically cannon-sized, muzzle-loading shotguns, some of them ten or twelve feet long and weighing more than a hundred pounds, mounted to the bows of low-riding boats and charged with several pounds of black powder. The gunner, lying prone in the boat and quietly poling into position near a resting flock, usually at night, could with one blast kill fifty to one hundred birds at a time; the punt-gunners often worked in teams, multiplying the carnage, but even a single punt-gunner could kill and sell as many as 10,000 ducks and geese in a winter season.

Nor were waterfowl the only birds coming under the gun; shore-birds like plovers, curlews, and sandpipers taste good and come to decoys as readily as do ducks, and were shot in such numbers that the populations of many species approached the brink of collapse. One, the Eskimo curlew—dubbed the "prairie pigeon" because its flocks were said to have been as immense as those of passenger pigeons—was like the wild pigeons eventually driven completely to extinction. Wading birds like herons and egrets, and seabirds like gulls and terns, were slaughtered for their feathers to decorate hats. Even songbirds like American robins were commonly shot in the millions for the market and the table. By some estimates, Americans were killing 100 million to 200 million birds a year for sale.

In addition to these direct attacks, waterfowl were losing their homes: the marshes, bogs, seasonal prairie lakes, and other wetlands on which they depended. A 1990 US Fish and Wildlife Service (USFWS) report to Congress concluded that in the two centuries from the 1780s to the 1980s, the United States destroyed more than half its wetlands—a relentless pace of ruination that wiped out, on average, sixty acres an hour *every hour for two hundred years*. Just as the great flocks were being decimated for the market, the very land that produced such bounty was being drained, filled, and farmed out of existence.

The market hunting assault ended first. Earlier attempts to marshal public opinion against the feather trade, led by a magazine editor and sportsman named George Bird Grinnell who created the first Audubon Society in the 1880s, fizzled. A decade later, two determined, upper-crust cousins from Boston, Harriet Hemenway and Minna Hall, resurrected the idea and linked it to the burgeoning women's club movement in the United States. This second coming of the Audubon societies—first in Massachusetts and then across the country—provided much of the societal pressure on state agencies and the US Congress to pass a raft of bird-protection measures. These laws ranged from bans on punt guns, spring hunting, and the use of live decoys, to the eventual outlawing of market hunting of any sort. Most notable among them was the Migratory Bird Treaty Act of 1918, which remains the bedrock legislation under which wild, native birds are supposed to be protected from harm and harassment.

That stopped the worst hemorrhaging, but the loss of habitat continued, and hit its lowest ebb during the Dust Bowl years of the 1930s, when drought gripped much of North America's heartland even as the Great Depression eviscerated the economy. Farms, many of them on land that should never have been plowed in the first place, failed as the dry topsoil literally blew away, creating epic dust storms.

Waterfowl populations, already low, crashed further. Some conservationists spoke soberly about the once-unthinkable extinction of previously common species of ducks and geese; after all, passenger pigeons and Carolina parakeets, once both in uncountable abundance, were already gone. By 1930 duck hunting seasons were slashed in length, and some of the most vulnerable species, including wood ducks, brant, canvasbacks, and redheads, were given complete protection. But with so much Depression-era land abandoned or foreclosed upon, the government also seized an opportunity to buy up tens of thousands of acres at fire-sale prices and use it for conservation. The money came from several visionary sources, including the federal Migratory Bird Hunting Stamp, better known as the Duck Stamp, which since 1934 any US waterfowl hunter over the age of sixteen has been required to buy. All but 2 percent of the purchase price (originally one dollar, now twenty-five) goes into the Migratory Bird Conservation Fund, which since its inception in 1929 has underwritten the purchase, lease, or easement acquisition of more than 6 million acres of bird habitat, much of it now part of the National Wildlife Refuge (NWR) system.

The end of the Dust Bowl droughts, tighter regulations, and the establishment of the NWR system (along with myriad state and provincial wildlife management areas, many aimed at enhancing waterfowl populations) brought a resurgence in duck and goose numbers. Here, simple biology worked in the birds' favor; waterfowl are an amazingly fecund group of birds, with females laying up to a dozen eggs in a single clutch. They have in many ways evolved to take advantage of rapidly changing environmental conditions. After all, drought is part of a natural cycle, and their high reproductive potential allows waterfowl to quickly boom once a drought-induced bust is over. By the 1950s, banding data had shown how different regional waterfowl breeding populations used four very broad pathways, quickly dubbed "flyways," north and south across the continent; while the birds' movements scribble well outside these neat lines, the flyways became the organizing structure for more precise management decisions regarding seasons and limits. The final piece was the creation in 1955 of the Waterfowl Breeding Population and Habitat Survey, which each year covers some

2 million square miles of the northern United States and Canada by aircraft, boat, and foot, estimating the number of nesting waterfowl and providing a benchmark against which to set fall hunting seasons.

The beating heart of North America's waterfowl world is the prairie pothole region, the area of the northern Great Plains stretching from Alberta, southern Saskatchewan, and Manitoba to northern Montana, much of the Dakotas, and parts of Minnesota, Nebraska, and Iowa. Covering more than 240,000 square miles, this expanse of once-native grassland, much now converted to agriculture, is studded with tens of millions of shallow, glacially dug depression marshes and ponds known as potholes. Dependent on snow melt and rainfall for their existence, these potholes are biologically rich, full of insects and other invertebrates that newly hatched ducklings, which emerge from the egg wide-eyed, fluffy, and chasing down their own food, need to

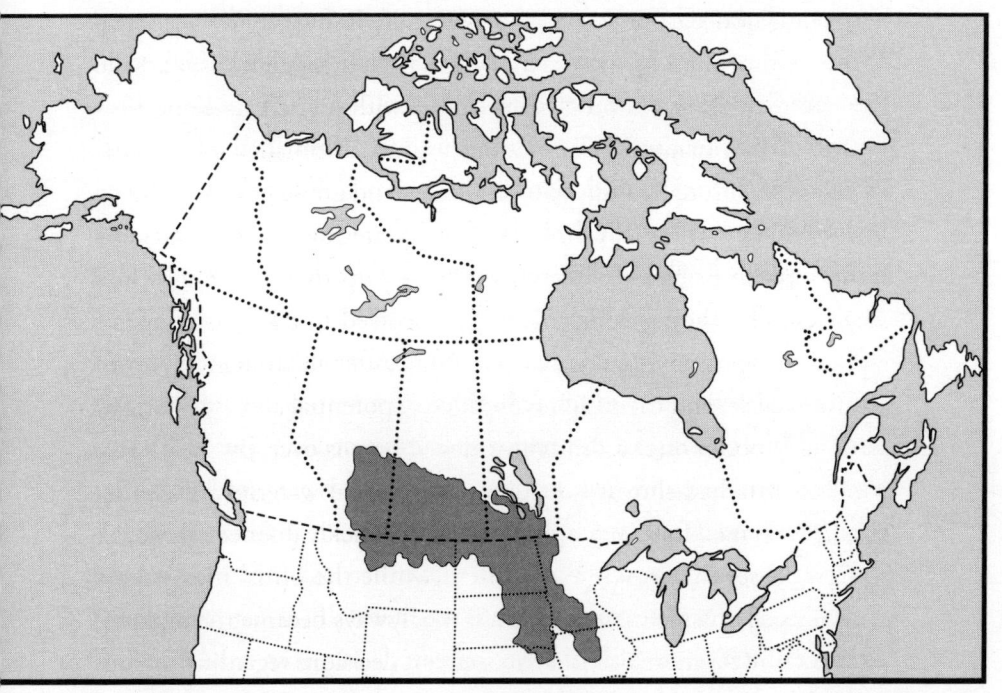

The prairie pothole region of the northern Great Plains is one of the most productive duck-breeding areas in North America.

thrive. In wet years, up to 70 percent of the continent's ducks nest in the pothole region.

But ducks need more than water and wetlands; they also need drier, grassy uplands in which to nest. Many ducks lay their eggs quite some distance from the water's edge, hidden in the prairie grasslands, a tactic that dramatically reduces a predator's chances of finding the nest. In parts of the pothole region, like the Prairie Coteau of the eastern Dakotas and southwestern Minnesota, the soil around the potholes is rocky and dry, unsuitable for plowing, and still retains its native northern tallgrass prairie. (*Coteau* is an old French Canadian term for a hilly plateau.) But in other sections of the pothole region where the soil is deep and plowing is easy, many farmers tilled right to the edges of ponds and wetlands, leaving ducks with few safe places to nest, and making it easy for nest predators like skunks, foxes, and raccoons to find them.

Because the potholes have no perennial source of water, drought is a particular danger that never goes away for good. After the bountiful 1950s, the early 1960s were extremely dry, and waterfowl numbers in the pothole region plummeted from 45 million to 25 million. They bounced back in the 1970s, if not quite to 1950s levels, but starting around 1980 the midcontinent entered another unusually deep and prolonged dry spell. Millions of potholes vanished; in some cases farmers plowed right over the dusty soil of what once had been a rich and vital ecosystem.

Duck numbers cratered; in 1985 the USFWS reported the lowest continental population estimate in thirty-one years of record-keeping, with all but one out of ten major species in decline. But 1985 was also the turning point, thanks to a revolutionary piece of legislation: the 1985 Food Security Act, better known simply as the Farm Bill.

Congress passes a new Farm Bill—another legacy of FDR's New Deal—every five years or so. Each is a behemoth package of a dozen or more sections, or "titles," covering everything from rural development to farm loans and federal crop insurance, to the Supplemental Nutrition Assistance Program (SNAP, formerly known as food stamps), price and income support for commodities farmers, to food research. One of those titles focuses on conservation, and the 1985 Farm Bill, coming in the midst of the collapse in duck populations and a belated recognition that agricultural policies had helped to disembowel wetlands, staked out bold new strategies to stem and eventually reverse the losses. Its conservation title was designed to accomplish three goals: prevent the further loss to agriculture of existing wetlands; prevent the further loss of highly erodible land to ill-conceived farming; and encourage the restoration of marginal lands that had already been plowed up in the past. These three provisions, a combination of sticks and carrots, became known as Swampbuster, Sodbuster, and the Conservation Reserve Program (CRP).

The Swampbuster provisions denied agricultural support to farmers who convert, drain, or alter protected wetlands. Those who did so would lose a host of farm bill benefits, including commodity payments, and subsidies for farm loans and crop insurance premiums, among other federal agricultural support. Sodbuster worked along similar lines, preventing farmers from converting easily erodible land that supported native grassland or woodland into crops. Both were intended to halt the loss of existing habitat, while CRP was a voluntary incentive program to restore habitat, paying farmers who had already plowed marginal land an annual rental fee and other perks to replant that acreage with an approved mix of grasses or trees; contracts are ten to fifteen years in length.

And goodness, did they work. Swampbuster and Sodbuster dramatically slowed the destruction of sensitive habitat, while CRP quickly became the largest private-land conservation measure in US history, with an average of roughly 20 million acres enrolled each year in CRP or its more recent cousin, the Conservation Reserve Enhancement Program.

The other major step in setting the continent's waterfowl on a better course came the following year, 1986, when Canada and the United States signed the North American Waterfowl Management Plan, the first major transnational bird conservation effort of its kind, and pledged up to $1.5 billion over the following 12 years to implement it. (Mexico, where many ducks and geese winter, became a signatory in 1994.) NAWMP created 22 regional, habitat-based "migratory bird joint ventures"—partnerships that brought together state, provincial, federal, local, and tribal governments, along with conservation NGOs, businesses, and private individuals, to work collaboratively on habitat conservation. The JVs, as they are known, initially focused mostly on waterfowl, but eventually expanded to encompass all migratory birds.

All of this came very much at the eleventh hour, and no one was at all sure it would be enough. In fact, many assumed it would not be. "Urgent Effort to Save Ducks Begins in U.S. and Canada," the *New York Times* announced in February 1988, calling the plan "a last-ditch effort to rebuild the flocks of the migratory birds." The newspaper quoted Harvey K. Nelson, the respected American waterfowl biologist who had been tapped to serve as the plan's first executive director, as saying there was no hope of bringing back the peak numbers of ducks seen in the 1950s; the "realistic goal," Harvey said, was a return to the middling levels of the 1970s. Optimism was hard to come by.

So was money, because NAWMP itself had no funding mechanism. But help for ducks, geese, and swans kept coming. At the end of 1989, President George H. W. Bush signed the North American Wetlands Conservation Act, or NAWCA, which provides federal grant money to public-private partners who bring matching funds to the table.

The effects have been enormous. Since the waterfowl management plan's establishment, its partners have conserved or restored almost 16 million acres of waterfowl habitat, while NAWCA has generated more than $2 billion in grants (matched by more than $4 billion in partner contributions) to protect or enhance 32 million acres of wetland and surrounding upland habitat in Canada, the United States, and Mexico. NAWCA is funded in part by fines levied against those who damage or destroy wetlands, or cause serious harm to birds, such as a $100 million fine under the Migratory Bird Protection Act on British Petroleum following the Deepwater Horizon oil spill in the Gulf of Mexico in 2010, as well as congressional appropriations. (Soon after taking office for the second time, President Trump's Department of the Interior changed its interpretation of the MBTA in such a way that a similar spill today would likely result in no fines at all under the bird protection law for a similar polluter.)

So, how well did this decade or so of transnational planning and extraordinary financial investment on behalf of wetlands and waterfowl pay off? Astoundingly so. By the early 1990s, duck numbers were climbing rapidly, soon exceeding even the glory days of the 1950s. In the droughty years of the early 2000s, waterfowl populations fell, but only to the same level as the rain-rich 1970s, which had recently been considered the best-chance "realistic" target for the NAWMP. Once the rains returned, the ducks were really off to the races; waterfowl numbers in the heavily surveyed prairie pothole region surged to a peak of almost 50 million by 2015, a population likely not seen since before the market hunting era.

Would that every group of beleaguered birds saw the cavalry riding to rescue the way waterfowl did. Getting anything through Congress is a slog, and trying to pass big, expensive initiatives like NAWCA is usually an exercise in frustration. But ducks, of course, have a singularly potent constituency behind them, one that bridges typical political and economic divisions, and has historically been willing to put its money and considerable influence where its collective mouth is: waterfowl hunters. Thanks to that influence, the money has continued to flow.

Duck hunters are an unusual breed. Like fly fishing, waterfowling is very process-driven. It is a complex sport, requiring arcane knowledge and skills that take years to master—how to read the weather and wind, how to build a blind that merges seamlessly with the background, how to set a seductive decoy rig that mimics a natural flock, or play a mouth call like a virtuoso. It requires specialized and frequently expensive gear like boats, good shotguns, foul-weather clothing, and highly trained retrieving dogs, and occurs in lovely and fragile habitats like marshes and coastlines. There are a lot of steps to be taken before one can pull the trigger and down a duck. I would argue that for a lot of waterfowlers, this complexity isn't a barrier, but the very point.

Most waterfowlers I've met take a lot of pride in their conservation ethic. During that period in the mid-1980s when duck populations were at historic lows, seasons were shortened and shortened again. Bag limits were cut. Ducks Unlimited called for "voluntary restraint," asking hunters to take even fewer birds than the legal limit allowed, or none at all—but not to stop buying their annual federal duck stamp, as well as a state duck stamp if one was offered, and to contribute to waterfowl and wetlands conservation in other ways.

Ducks Unlimited—DU, as it is universally known—was founded in 1937, part of the desperate Dust Bowl push to create habitat and salvage waterfowl populations. It counts some 670,000 members in the United States, and in 2024 brought in a record $333 million, at least 80 percent of which the organization pledges to spend on conservation and education; in 2024, the figure was 83 percent, spread across more than 1 million acres of habitat work.

Most of the funding comes from government grants, philanthropic gifts, and partnerships, but in 2024, $99.5 million came from some 5,200 fundraising events, often annual banquets organized by volunteers with local chapters that invariably end with raffles and auctions featuring guns, sporting artwork, decoys, and including a few high-end items like guided hunting trips and boats, and more objects decorated in camouflage than one can possibly imagine. In my days as the outdoor editor for the state capital newspaper in Pennsylvania in the early 1990s, I attended a lot of DU banquets, which was an expensive assignment on a reporter's meager salary. The money just gushed at DU dinners; it wasn't unusual for the attendees at a small, rural event to leave tens of thousands of dollars in the kitty by the end of the night, and rare was any auction item that didn't bring far more than its retail value. It was a point of pride for the attendees. Most of the DU'ers came with a chunk of money, often hundreds or even thousands of dollars, that they intended to spend that night on something. Anything. The merchandise was just an excuse to hand over the cash to a cause they believed in.

DU has not been without its controversies. It has taken—or failed to take—positions on important issues, from public stream access in Montana to predator control in Alaska, that at times set it apart from many other conservation organizations. It has been accused of being too cozy with major corporate donors, and critics wish DU would always live up to its ideals. These are not irrelevant concerns, but they are stacked against one of the more remarkable legacies in wildlife conservation. In its nearly ninety years of existence, DU and its partners—Ducks Unlimited Canada, founded in 1938, and Ducks Unlimited de México, started in 1970—have funded conservation on nearly 20 million wetland and grassland acres in the three countries.

And they have helped to ensure that NAWCA is reauthorized every few years, regular as a metronome, by even the most bitterly partisan Congress. The biodiversity dividends extend well beyond waterfowl. For example, when US and Canadian researchers analyzed data from exhaustive surveys conducted between 2011 and 2021 at nearly eight hundred wetlands along the shores of all the Great Lakes, looking at how populations of eighteen species of marsh birds—coots, rails, gallinules, terns, and more, many of them rare species of particular conservation concern—had changed, they found that not only had none of those species declined during that period, but nine had shown remarkably strong increases. Common gallinule numbers had risen by more than 37 percent, black terns by 26 percent, pied-billed grebes and least bitterns each by about 18 percent. The scientists surmised that unusually high water in the Great Lakes system was partially responsible for the positive trends, but also noted that coastal wetlands protection was essential because as waters continue to rise with a warming climate, wetlands must be able to migrate away from the current shoreline.

Up to this point, we've been talking mostly about ducks, but there are other kinds of waterfowl, of course, including geese. Which brings us to the question: What happens when bird conservation is *too* successful?

In April 1805 along the Missouri River, the Lewis and Clark expedition encountered an odd sight—a goose sitting in a nest some sixty feet above the ground in a big cottonwood tree. Capt. William Clark shot the bird, and one of the men shinnied up to the nest, finding in it a single egg. Because geese normally nest on the ground, the incident was unusual enough for Clark and several other members of the expedition to mention in their journals, and Capt. Meriwether Lewis noted again a few weeks later that all but one goose nest they'd seen had likewise been in trees.

Not only were the geese of the Missouri unusual in their nesting habits, we now know they belonged to the largest subspecies of Canada goose in the world, *Branta canadensis maxima*, the giant Canada goose. Found on the eastern prairies from southern Manitoba down the Mississippi Valley to Missouri, they were giants indeed, averaging more than twelve pounds, versus a more typical six or seven pounds for other Canada geese. One behemoth allegedly tipped the scales at twenty-two pounds, which if true would have made it nearly as heavy as some trumpeter swans. At best weakly migratory, flying south only as far as winter cold and ice would force them, giant Canadas were fat and tasty and ready to the gun, and by the 1930s were assumed to have been driven to extinction.

In 1963, however, the USFWS announced (on April Fool's Day, no less) that the giant Canada goose had been rediscovered. The year before a sharp-eyed state waterfowl research supervisor named Forrest B. Lee had noticed a flock of unusually big Canada geese on Silver Lake in Rochester, Minnesota, that didn't migrate south in winter. Intrigued, he reached out to goose expert Harold C. Hanson from the Illinois Natural History Survey, who with a number of equally experienced colleagues went to Silver Lake to see for themselves. Hanson, Lee, and the others trapped more than two hundred of the geese for banding, carefully weighing and measuring each one. The geese weighed so much that the team, assuming their scales were malfunctioning, went to town and bought bags of flour and sugar, checking them on a certified grocer's scale before comparing those results with what their own equipment showed. The weights were accurate, and the giant Canada goose had risen from the dead.

Once scientists knew what to look for, several other remnant populations were also discovered, and a captive breeding program overseen by Lee, who became known as "Father Goose" for his work with this and other endangered geese, was soon producing thousands of pen-reared giant Canadas at a new federal facility in North Dakota. These birds were reintroduced to areas from which they'd been extirpated a generation or more earlier, and experts developed new techniques to help the restored populations, such as building predator-proof artificial nest structures consisting of a wide tub mounted on a tall pole in the marsh—a throwback, perhaps, to those tree-nesting geese Lewis and Clark saw.

Soon, giant Canada geese were thriving in dozens of locations. Because geese, like all waterfowl, molt all of their flight feathers at once after the breeding season, becoming temporarily flightless, they are at that time easy to round up, crate, and ship off to somewhere else. For years, if a state had too many geese in its waterfowl management areas it would call up the game agency in a neighboring state and say, Hey, you want to start your own nonmigratory goose flock? But with time it became harder and harder to find any takers, because giant Canada geese were on the march to what today seems like complete, continental domination. By some estimates, this once "extinct" bird now numbers more than 4 million individuals in North America. When Forrest Lee died in 2013 at age 93, his obituary noted that each of those 4 million geese could trace their ancestry back to an egg or gosling Lee had held in his hands.

Through no fault of his, that's a mixed legacy. As anyone who has scraped green goose droppings off their shoes knows, Canada geese have become a serious nuisance problem on thousands of parks, golf courses, and suburban office complexes across North America and beyond. Hardy and adaptable, they are capable of staggering rates of growth. In Maine, the original breeding population of a different subspecies of Canada goose was wiped out in the early 1800s, leaving only twice-yearly migrants that nest in the eastern Arctic, and which passed through in fall and spring. But state game officials started reintroducing geese in the 1950s, including giant Canadas in later years. Initially slow to establish themselves in New England, by the early 2000s their numbers mushroomed, increasing a mind-bending 46,000 percent in Maine between 1966 and 2017. It's hard to find a place south of the Canadian border, and north of Texas and the desert Southwest, where Canada geese haven't experienced similar increases. (The same can be said of the United Kingdom and much of western Europe, where introduced Canada geese have become a seriously invasive threat to wetlands and a stiff competitor to native waterfowl.)

To understand why Canada geese have done so well, look at 21st-century North America from a goose's perspective. Canada geese are grazers; they love tender grasses and sedges in spring and summer, and grains like waste corn in winter, feeding wherever they have wide sight lines to spot approaching predators, and within easy flight of ponds, lakes, or marshes. But because they don't necessarily depend on the resources of the wetland itself, the way many ducks do, any bit of water will serve, be it a municipal reservoir, a decorative suburban pond, or a city park lake. We keep the grass mowed, so the geese can easily see what few natural predators there may be, and no one usually hunts in such densely populated areas. Highly intelligent, even where they are hunted geese get the lay of the land quickly, flying complex routes when leaving waterfowl management areas and neatly side-stepping the scattered, permanent blinds occupied by disappointed hunters. In sum, it may be impossible to design a world more perfectly suited to Canada geese than the one we've accidentally created.

Nor are giant Canada geese the only hyper-successful species in North America. At the same time that Canada geese were on the rise, so too were snow geese, whose vast, swirling flocks, often numbering in the tens or even hundreds of thousands, invariably invite awestruck comparisons with blizzards. There are two major populations: the somewhat larger "greater" snow geese that nest in the eastern Canadian Arctic and winter along the Atlantic coast; and a mid-continental population of the smaller "lesser" snow geese nesting in the central Canadian Arctic, and wintering from the central Plains to the Gulf of Mexico. (A third, smaller population of lessers breeds in Alaska and the western Canadian Arctic, and winters from California and the desert Southwest into Mexico.)

While Canada geese are strictly grazers, nipping off vegetation, snow geese are also grubbers, using their short, serrated bills to dig below the surface and yank up roots and tubers. In precolonial days, it seems likely that snow goose numbers were kept in check by a lack of nutritious food on their coastal wintering grounds, where largely indigestible cordgrass provided much of their diet and where high overwinter mortality may have been a serious constraint on population size. That is no longer the case, however, thanks to agriculture. By one calculation, only 25 percent of a cordgrass rhizome is digestible to a goose, while 87 percent of a grain of corn is. As farming, especially large-scale industrial farming, spread in the middle of the 20th century, the table was set and snow geese chowed down, moving away from the coasts in winter and into the endless ag-land buffet.

Like most wild birds, snow geese suffered during the market hunting era, and at the turn of the 20th century the greater snow goose population on the Atlantic flyway was probably only about 3,000 birds. By the 1960s that had risen to about 40,000, but this was still considered small enough to be of concern, especially because most of those geese used a few concentrated areas on migration and during the winter—in bulrush marshes on islands in the St. Lawrence River in Québec, for instance, and cordgrass salt marshes along the mid-Atlantic coast. A single oil spill or other environmental catastrophe, it was feared, could doom them. Hunting for greater snow geese in the eastern United States remained closed from 1931 until 1975, when surveys showed about 100,000 of the birds, a number of managers felt could withstand some limited hunting pressure.

That's about when the cork popped. Biologists noticed significant changes in snow goose behavior and migratory patterns; they were not only forsaking coastal marshes for farm fields, they began "short-stopping," not migrating as far south as they once did, taking advantage of increasingly mild winter temperatures and a lack of snow cover. More calories means a healthier goose heading back to the Arctic to breed, and breed the snow geese did—and continue to do. On Baffin Island in the Canadian Arctic, surveys showed 446,000 greater snow geese in 1973; by 1997 that number had quadrupled to 1.8 million. Through the 1980s and most of the 1990s, the number of greater snow geese doubled every eight years. Continent-wide, the overall snow goose population rocketed from 5 million in 1997 to 15 million in 2017, though getting an accurate handle on their population has been tricky.

Snow geese have for the most part not become an urban-park nuisance like Canada geese, but they have posed their own set of thorny problems, both in the Arctic and on their wintering grounds. Waterfowl in general are social, but snow geese are hypersocial. They nest in enormous, densely packed colonies that range in size from a few thousand to several hundred thousand birds, migrate in great synchronous waves north and south, and spend the winter in close-packed concentrations. For someone new to birding, the sight of one of these snow goose storms can be difficult to comprehend. About 15 years ago I was guiding a small group to the Platte River in central Nebraska to see migrating sandhill cranes, one of the world's preeminent migratory spectacles. It had been a late, cold spring, and the crane numbers were well below their peak of 600,000 or more—but there were still perhaps 2 million lesser snow geese in the region that had not yet moved north.

Our group had spent the windy day exploring the network of shallow playa lakes that make up the Rainwater Basin south of the river, scoping dozens of species of ducks, grebes, and other waterbirds. But the red-letter climax came, ironically, as we drove back to our big-box hotel in a commercial strip along I-80 near Kearney, behind which was a couple-of-acres gravel pit that I suspect had been dug out to provide fill for the interstate. As we pulled into the parking lot near sunset, we realized that thousands and thousands of snow geese were spiraling into the pond from every direction, the raucous, confused gabble of their doglike barking honks and the torn-cloth sound of wings slicing the chilly March air. The guests stumbled from our van, their mouths hanging open and eyes wide, as we stood at the center of this titanic in-rushing of birds bathed in low, yellow light. Soon there seemed to us no more room on the tight-packed surface of the pond, not a spot where a single additional goose could shoehorn in, but they kept coming until it was almost too dark to see. We pulled ourselves away, hungry for dinner, and still the geese poured down. If I'd been forced to guess how many birds were jammed into that relatively small pond, I would have said somewhere north of 15,000 or 20,000. That's just a middling gathering of snow geese.

As the mass of snow geese continent-wide has risen, so too has their impact on their environment. Along the St. Lawrence River, where the eastern birds pause to rest and feed on their spring migration north, native bulrush marshes have suffered, and damage to hay fields in the surrounding farmland has become severe. Similarly, along the Atlantic coast snow geese—which feed, as they do all other things in life, in tightly packed flocks—have entirely grubbed away whole sections of once-healthy cordgrass, one root at a time, creating what are known as eat-outs, converting hundreds of acres of marsh into open water and further exacerbating the consequences of sea-level rise.

The impact of snow geese has been most damaging on the Arctic and subarctic breeding grounds, however. Greater snows breed in and near freshwater marshes in places like Bylot Island in Nunavut in the eastern Canadian Arctic, where researchers have been studying their interaction with the land, vegetation, and other species for years. The scientists have found evidence of habitat degradation from intense goose feeding, but such marshes seem fairly resilient. Coastal salt marshes, where truly enormous colonies of lesser snow geese breed, have fared much more poorly. One 2006 study from the University of Toronto and the Ontario Ministry of Natural Resources found that snow geese at several study sites along Hudson and James Bays had turned more than 86,000 acres of intertidal marsh into mudflats, and had inflicted similar damage at countless other places along more than 1,200 miles of coastline.

The consequences for some species have been severe. Arctic-nesting shorebirds, which include some of the longest-distance migrants in the world, share the coastal saltmarsh and tundra habitat with snow geese, and this competition and habitat loss are among the causes blamed for the continued and accelerating decline in many North American shorebirds, especially those that use the Atlantic flyway.

There have been similar goose explosions in Europe, where waterfowl populations were slammed by market gunning between the wars in the early 20th century, and again after World War II; market hunting for geese was not banned in the United Kingdom until 1967. But with protection came rising numbers. Of 17 species of geese in western Europe, 14 have shown large increases, especially barnacle, pink-footed, and white-fronted geese, and as in North America, the driver seems to be the ready availability of agricultural waste grain and pasture.

And as in North America, there have been negative consequences, both economic and ecological. The rising population of pink-footed geese that nests in the Svalbard archipelago in the Norwegian Arctic have caused friction with farmers on their wintering grounds in Belgium and the Netherlands, and habitat degradation on Svalbard itself much as snow geese have been damaging the Canadian Arctic.

It's not that waterfowl managers were blind to the problems caused by too many geese. The simplest way to reduce their numbers would be to extend open seasons and expand bag limits, which for snow geese the USFWS and Canadian Wildlife Service did. But snow geese pose particular challenges. You can attract a flock of Canada geese with a few dozen decoys in a field, but a hunter needs hundreds of decoys to get snow geese to pay even a passing glance, and to be consistently successful may require 1,500 or more. (The definition of "decoy" is loose; some hunters bulk up their rigs with an army of disposable diapers, white rags or some other cheap, easily packed visual substitute which, from a distance, gives the impression of a horde of geese.)

As careful and conservative initial approaches seemed to be having limited effect, federal managers in the United States and Canada got progressively more liberal with snow goose hunting restrictions, with a goal of at least stabilizing the snowballing population. In 1999, the USFWS issued a Light Goose Conservation Order ("light goose" referring to both snow geese and smaller but otherwise identical Ross's geese). Once-banned hunting techniques like the use of electronic callers were allowed, and spring hunting, which had been forbidden since 1916 for anyone other than Indigenous hunters in Alaska and Canada, was authorized. Hunters, who are usually required to plug their shotguns so they hold no more than three shells, were permitted to load to the max, and during this special hunt in late winter, the bag and possession limits were either boosted enormously or lifted entirely. In many cases, a hunter could shoot as many snow geese as he or she was able to, and stockpile as many as they had freezer capacity to store. But for all the aggressive action, some old approaches remained beyond the pale; the conservation order still specifically prohibited the use of punt guns.

The results have been mixed. The greater snow goose population that nests in the eastern Canadian Arctic, which had been at about 1 million birds, seems to have stabilized at around 600,000–700,000, and has even dropped a bit below its 10-year average, partly from hunting but also because the eastern and central Canadian Arctic has, thanks to the weirdness that is global climate change, become significantly colder and snowier in late winter and early spring, reducing nest success for snow geese and other migrants that breed there. (Midsummers have become increasingly warm, though, so birds are getting the worst of all worlds.) The mid-continental population has seen similar declines starting around 2005, although it was enormously larger to start with. At the time the conservation order was issued in 1999, winter surveys suggested the mid-continent flocks numbered about 3 million; in hindsight, biologists now think the true number may have been closer to 8 million, and some put it as high as 20 million. Hunters were taking 2 million geese a year from that population, which, while an enormous number in its own right, didn't do much to slow such a big train quickly. One Ducks Unlimited biologist calculated that before the conservation order, hunters killed one adult snow goose out of 40 from the mid-continental flyway. After all the changes, that ratio inched up to one out of 37.

But with time, the flocks have thinned somewhat. By 2023, biologists estimated the mid-continent snow goose population was about 4.8 million birds, with another 1.2 million Ross's geese. That put the snows pretty close to the abundance target set by wildlife managers (Ross's geese were still four or five times higher than the goal), but the reason for the decline probably has little to do with the liberalized hunting regulations. Instead, goose specialists said, the fall was due to lower productivity caused by nesting ground crowding, competition for food resources, the changing Arctic climate causing a disconnect between when the goslings hatch and when their insect food reaches its peak, and more frequent rain during the peak hatching season when the fluffy goslings are at greatest risk of hypothermia.

But while snow geese in the eastern and mid-continent regions may have leveled off or dropped, the western population, which breeds in Alaska and Wrangel Island off the coast of Russia, has seen rapid growth, fueled by the rich pickings in the Central Valley of California where many of the birds winter. In the Colville River delta on Alaska's North Slope, part of the National Petroleum Reserve-Alaska, snow goose numbers went from a couple of thousand in 2005 to more than 30,000 in 2022, with no signs of slowing down.

Of course, one risk for any species that packs such huge numbers into tight spaces is disease. Since its emergence as a global wildlife pandemic in 2021, the H5N1 strain of highly pathogenic avian influenza (HPAI) has killed millions of waterbirds, including waterfowl, around the world. In the case of some colonial seabirds, the population-level losses have been severe. In the United Kingdom, for example, northern gannet numbers had fallen by 2023 by 25 percent, common terns by 42 percent, and great skuas by 76 percent. In North America, thousands of snow geese have been killed by this strain of HPAI (as have predators like bald eagles, snowy owls, foxes, and even seals that feed upon them), but it is unclear what additional effect that has had on the species' overall populations.

It's important to bear in mind that there are seven species of wild geese that breed in North America, and not all of them have seen the kind of boom times that Canada geese and snow geese have enjoyed. Greater white-fronted geese, which nest from western Hudson Bay to Alaska and winter from Louisiana and Arkansas south through Mexico and up central California to western Washington, are abundant and have been fairly stable since the early 2000s, with an estimated mid-continental population of 3.14 million, although the Pacific population appears to be growing fast. But other species have had a harder time. The emperor goose, a small, pudgy bird with a white head and neck offsetting a body covered in beautifully scalloped gray feathers, and which spends most of its life year-round in the intertidal zone of coastal Alaska and the Russian Far East, has suffered serious declines from overhunting on the nesting grounds and possibly oil pollution. Its numbers fell from 139,000 in 1964 to just 42,000 in 1986, at which point all hunting, including subsistence hunting by Alaska Natives, was closed. There has been some measure of recovery, but the 2024 population was just 19,000.

And while most ducks have fared very well since the NAWMP and NAWCA were put in place, there have been some worrisome exceptions. The North American population of northern pintails, among the most graceful of waterfowl, has dropped by more than half from its long-term average, and in 2024 was 1.9 million, an 11 percent drop from the year before, and far below the long-term average since 1955 of 3.8 million. Should pintail numbers fall to 1.75 million, it's likely pintail hunting, already restricted to a one-bird limit, would be closed entirely.

A prairie-nesting specialist, pintails seem to be suffering to an unusual degree from habitat issues in the Canadian portion of the prairie pothole region, because pintails nesting on the US side appear to be holding their own. The issue may be less the loss of native grassland to crops, than a switch by Canadian farmers away from allowing large areas of cropland to rest fallow for part of the year, providing cover for pintail nests.

Scaup are another exception. While still among the most abundant ducks in North America, the two species of scaup (the more widespread and common lesser scaup and the almost identical greater scaup) have likewise seen a dramatic slide, from a combined population of about 8 million in 1972 to an estimated 4 million or so in 2024—and that was a 16 percent increase over the previous year, though still below their long-term average of nearly 5 million. Despite decades of research, no one is still sure exactly where the problem or, more likely, multiple problems lie. Among the possibilities suggested have been the loss and degradation of wetlands in the Midwest that once provided critical stopover habitat on the northbound migration, or environmental contaminants including heavy metals like selenium, which accumulate in the tissues of invasive zebra mussels that now swarm important stopover sites like the Great Lakes and are a favored scaup food. Others have pointed to the loss to pollution of once-important prey in some regions, like fingernail clams, or the possible spread of blood parasites like avian malaria because of climate change.

A warming climate is also sparking perhaps the strangest and most unsettling threat to Arctic-nesting waterfowl, including scaup: the disappearance of the very lakes and wetlands on which they nest. From the air, the Arctic and subarctic can at times seem more water than land, with millions of lakes, ponds, and bogs. In reality, these regions receive relatively little annual precipitation, but what falls cannot drain into the ground because the layer of permafrost ice just below the surface forms a seal. Yet as the climate warms—and in the far North it is warming faster than anywhere on Earth—that permafrost barrier is vanishing, allowing thousands of bodies of water to simply drain away, leaving dry mud and eventually tundra vegetation in its place. In parts of Alaska, an important nesting ground for both scaup species, one-quarter of wetlands have disappeared since the 1950s, with the greatest loss coming in the past two decades, even though precipitation patterns have not changed significantly. Wildfires, which are increasing in scope and frequency in the region, also seem to be reinforcing the trend.

Finally, there is politics. In May 2023, the US Supreme Court dealt an indirect body blow to waterfowl, and all the other species that depend on wetlands, in a ruling, *Sackett v. EPA*, that drastically curtailed the US Environmental Protection Agency's authority to enforce long-standing regulations under the Clean Water Act protecting wetlands from pollution and destruction. Critics of the court—and they included almost every major environmental and conservation group—called the 5–4 decision a singularly disastrous turn for wetlands, the species that depend on them, and the human communities they protect from floodwaters and other dangers. Regulations from the EPA revised by the Biden administration in August 2023 to comply with the decision removed federal protection from almost two-thirds—63 percent—of US wetlands. That was followed in 2024 by the Supreme Court jettisoning half a century of precedent that directed federal judges to defer to the expertise of agency personnel when interpreting ambiguous laws, something known as the Chevron deference, and most recently by a Trump EPA that is openly hostile to a wide range of clean water and other environmental protections.

The warning signs are flashing. The USFWS in 2024 announced that wetland losses in the lower 48 states have increased by 50 percent since 2009, and in just the decade prior to 2019 the nation experienced a net loss of 670,000 acres. That's having an effect on waterfowl. The 2025 State of the Birds report, compiled by seventeen of the largest bird conservation groups including National Audubon, DU, the Cornell Lab of Ornithology, and the American Bird Conservancy, noted that while duck populations remain 24 percent higher than they were in 1970, until recently they had been more than 40 percent higher. The trends are going the wrong way, especially in crucial places like the prairie pothole region, where duck numbers are now 10 percent below long-term averages. Whether the next 50 years will be as bright for waterfowl as the last have been is more of an open question than it should be.

Two

Paying Sufficient Attention

It was a perfect, late October migration day. The night before a cold front had passed through eastern Pennsylvania, and a chilly wind was gusting out of the northwest. With two good friends by my side I climbed a rocky path up the spine of the Kittatinny Ridge, a trail our feet know so well they could follow it in the dark, until the track broke out of the oak and hemlock forest onto a view that, similarly, I know as well and intimately as my wife's eyes. Below us, on either side of this sinuous, thousand-foot-high mountain that runs from the New York border most of the way to Maryland, lay farm valleys whose fields were ochre with drying corn. Before us was a bouldery rock field jammed with people, most holding binoculars and watching the sky.

This was North Lookout at Hawk Mountain Sanctuary, a place that has been central to my life since I was a kid. I became a bird nut, a hawk nut, a bird bander, and a migration researcher, largely because of this mountaintop and the people like me caught in its orbit. It was also the first place in the world to boldly declare itself, in the autumn of 1934, a refuge for birds of prey, which were in those days almost universally scorned even by those professing to be conservationists, birds that until the year before that declaration had been gunned from the sky by the thousands here. That is, until a formidable woman put an end to the slaughter and sparked what became a global movement recognizing the importance, ecological and spiritual, of raptors, some

20,000 of which—hawks, eagles, falcons, vultures—still migrate past this overlook each autumn.

We faithful come to pay homage. Seth, Holly, and I found a place for ourselves among the crowd, gravitating by long habit and experience to a sweet spot on the lookout, close enough to the windy north side on our left, from which we could see any passing birds that swung below eye level, but within ear shot of the counter's pit to our right. There two staff biologists and a couple of volunteers tallied every passing raptor, an annual fall census that has carried on, unbroken but for a few seasons during World War II, for ninety years, the longest-running such migration count in the world.

We'd barely time to pull out our binoculars. "Bird high over Five, looks good for a buteo," staff biologist Bracken Brown yelled, pitching his voice over the wind and calling out one of the local landmarks so visitors could spot the hawk for themselves. "A second bird behind it, a little lower, looks like both are redtails. A much bigger bird below horizon on Four—looks like a bald eagle."

For the next several hours, the parade did not flag. Scores of raptors—red-tailed and red-shouldered hawks, sharp-shinned hawks, Cooper's hawks, northern harriers, merlins—flowed by like a river. The morning was punctuated with repeated hails announcing yet another passing bald eagle, or the frequent appearance of three local adults, which unlike the migrants, passing resolutely down the ridge from northeast to southwest, often circled lazily overhead, white heads and tails glinting.

After the ninth or tenth bald eagle of the day had passed, I cocked an eye at Seth and said, "You know, I don't think sufficient attention is being paid, do you?" He knew what I meant. Fresh from college in 1976, Seth Benz had been the first intern at Hawk Mountain, at a time when bald eagles were all but gone from the East. Peregrine falcons, like the chocolate-brown juvenile that had flashed over our heads moments earlier, playing on the wind with a fluidity and grace as only the fastest creature on the planet can do, had been entirely wiped out as a breeding species east of the Rockies. I'd graduated high school the same year as his internship, and we both remembered how the season's count for the unofficial national bird* during that Bicentennial year was a pathetic 18. Yet so dramatically have bald eagles recovered from centuries of persecution, and the near-death knell of 20th-century pesticide poisoning, that in 2023, the sanctuary set a new all-time record for bald eagles passing North Lookout: 639, 48 of them on a single day.

So Seth and I certainly understood why, on this blustery day, so many people were chatting with their friends or nibbling snacks, instead of watching, rapt, as another adult bald eagle sailed by at eye level. But I'll confess to the urge to grab a few of them by the collar and shake, to say, *Look, this is important. This almost didn't happen. We almost lost them.*

Such is the price of success; what once seemed incomprehensibly optimistic becomes humdrum. Maybe that's an advantage of getting older. You know what's priceless.

Raptors are, with waterfowl, the other broad guild of birds that have bucked a half-century-long declining trend in North America and elsewhere. While there are still places in the world where direct persecution remains a serious problem—like Batumi in the Republic of Georgia, where gunners shoot many of the nearly 1 million raptors of 32 species that migrate along the eastern edge of the Black Sea, and even parts of the United Kingdom, where some driven grouse-shooting aficionados

---

* It's true. Until an amateur eagle fanatic named Preston Cook started digging into the subject, everyone just assumed that at some point in the nation's nearly 250-year history Congress must have officially declared the bald eagle the national bird. After years of searching archives and nagging everyone in an official capacity that he could think of, Cook could find no evidence that Congress had ever actually done so. Yes, the bald eagle has been on the Great Seal of the United States since 1782, but that's not quite the same thing. Finally Cook himself drafted a bill to correct the oversight, which was passed by Congress in 2024.

can hold a deadly grudge against birds of prey—the picture in North America is dramatically brighter than it was when I was a kid.

My life, with birds at its core from an early age, has overlapped the steep collapse and spectacular recovery of North American raptors. I was born in 1959, which marked not only the waning years of the Baby Boom but also the last throes of America's blind love affair with seemingly miraculous chemical insecticides like dichlorodiphenyl trichloroethane, or DDT. If by my arrival the headiest days of chemical infatuation had passed—for example, women's magazines no longer carried ads, as they had in 1947, for Trimz DDT-impregnated wallpaper, made specifically for a child's nursery and decorated with Donald Duck, Bambi, and Mickey Mouse ("Protect Your Child from Disease-Carrying Insects!")—still, grocery and hardware store shelves remained chockablock with highly persistent organochloride pesticides like DDT, dieldrin, heptachlor, lindane, and endrin.

As my parents were adjusting to life with a newborn that spring, a marine biologist and best-selling author named Rachel Carson was apologizing to her editor at Houghton Mifflin for being far behind on a book she'd been laboring over for several years, synthesizing the vast and mounting evidence against pesticides like DDT and their danger to wildlife and humans. When *Silent Spring* appeared, first serialized in *The New Yorker* in June 1962 and then in book form that September, birds of prey stood out among Carson's many strands of evidence. She noted that Hawk Mountain's curator, Maurice Broun, had seen the disappearance of young bald eagles from the migratory population he counted every fall from the lookout. (Because it takes five years for a bald eagle to achieve its white head and tail, distinguishing youngsters is simple.) When the sanctuary's fall migration count began in the early 1930s, juvenile bald eagles made up 40 percent of the species' total. By the late 1950s, the ratio had dropped to as low as one young eagle for every 32 adults.

Nor was the problem confined to a single ridgetop in Pennsylvania. In Florida, the number of active bald eagle nests fell from roughly 125 in the 1940s to barely a third of that, 40 nests, in 1957, only seven of which produced any chicks. In 1958, Carson noted, only a single bald eagle chick could be found anywhere in Florida, despite an extensive search.

Silent Spring was a bombshell, and the chemical industry leveled a ferocious attack on its author, who was by that point seriously ill with what would soon prove to be terminal breast cancer. They faulted her science and maligned her intelligence, personality, integrity, and patriotism, but the evidence was only growing more stark. In June 1962, as the first installment was appearing in *The New Yorker*, scientists realized to their shock that not a single peregrine falcon nest anywhere in the northeastern United States was still active. Similarly disturbing reports were coming from Great Britain, France, Germany, and Scandinavia. In 1964, having mounted an ambitious survey across 14 eastern US states and one Canadian province, ornithologists found all 133 known falcon eyries (as their cliff nests are known) abandoned. In a decade or less, one of the most widespread raptors in eastern North America had been snuffed out, and the eastern subspecies, *Falco peregrinus anatum*, was functionally extinct east of the Rocky Mountains. The only peregrines seen in eastern skies were Arctic-breeding birds of the subspecies *P.f. tundrius*, whose numbers had slumped badly but which had not yet vanished entirely.

Eagles and peregrines attracted the earliest and most alarmed attention, but in fact a wide variety of raptors and fish-eating birds, from ospreys, golden eagles, and Cooper's hawks to various gulls, white pelicans, brown pelicans, and double-crested cormorants, were suffering similar reproductive failure and population declines, often unnoticed at first. By the late 1960s, scientists had puzzled out the especially insidious way in which DDT and its chemical relatives caused this damage. DDT can be quickly and directly toxic to birds if applied at high levels, but even at low rates, once in the environment these very persistent, long-lasting compounds *bioaccumulate*—that is, at each step up the food chain, from microorganisms to invertebrates, then through, say, several ascending levels from minnows to larger and larger predatory fish, and finally into long-lived, fish-eating birds like ospreys and bald eagles, the concentration of the pesticide in body tissues increases. Eventually the bird has stored so much of the toxin that it interferes with a host of physiological functions, including reproduction, interrupting the calcium cycle in the female bird's body, preventing it from creating the normal, thick shell that protects the embryo inside. In extreme cases, as with some brown pelicans in California, the eggs were laid with no discernible shell at all.

I had just turned 11 when the first Earth Day occurred in 1970, and "Ban DDT" was the watchword of an increasingly assertive environmental movement. Pressure was building on the newly created US Environmental Protection Agency to severely restrict DDT, and I did my part, reading an impassioned essay on the subject to my thoroughly bemused eighth-grade classmates in 1972, who mostly rolled their eyes that that weird Weidensaul kid was off on one of his bird rants again. But just as school let out that summer, EPA administrator William Ruckelshaus announced that by the end of the year, DDT would be banned for almost all uses in the United States. The announcement came almost exactly a decade after *Silent Spring* first hit the pages of *The New Yorker*, and eight years after Rachel Carson's death.

I was, by that point, thoroughly obsessed with raptors. It was not always a healthy fascination; I got knocked out of an oak tree on the mountain ridge behind our house one early spring day, trying to shinny up the trunk to see the great horned owl chicks huddled in an old crow nest thirty feet above. The blow from one of the unusually aggressive adults felt as though I'd been smacked on the back of the head with a piece of firewood, and I lost my grip and fell backwards fifteen feet to the bouldery ground in just such a way that my head and neck lay cushioned in leaves between a couple of large rocks that might have ended my bird career before it really started. I was wise enough not to tell my parents.

At 16 I was old enough to drive, and able to borrow the family car to visit Hawk Mountain myself on fall weekends, less than an hour from our house. I climbed the three-quarters-mile trail to North Lookout, feeling as though I had found my tribe. But the eagle migration we saw was a shadow of what the old-timers whom I befriended there recalled from earlier days.

I grew up at the end of a long nadir for raptors in North America. It wasn't just pesticides; there had been a literal war on birds of prey since colonial times, when shooting a "chicken hawk" (and to most people, they were *all* chicken hawks) was a civic obligation. Those pre-DDT bald eagle numbers were no great shakes, but rather a reflection of hundreds of years of people with guns aiming for any big raptor. My native state is as good an example as any. In 1885 Pennsylvania passed what was officially (and with grim accuracy) known as the Scalp Act, which set a 50-cent bounty on the heads—literally—of almost all hawks, falcons, and owls, along with foxes, mink, weasels, and the handful of wolves remaining in the state; the only raptors exempted were barn, northern saw-whet, and screech-owls. Before it was hastily repealed two years later, mired in allegations of fraud and waste, bounties had been paid on 180,000 raptor scalps.

Nor, despite their obvious faults, was that the last time bounties were offered. Indeed, it was the unusual number of American goshawks being turned in for bounty from a particular mountaintop in southeastern Pennsylvania in the late 1920s that finally began to tip the balance toward conservation. George Miksch Sutton, later a renowned ornithologist but at the time a young biologist working for the state Game Commission, published a dry article in an ornithological journal in 1927 noting the large number of migrating goshawks, among many other species, being shot each autumn along what is locally known as the Blue Mountain, north of Reading; in a follow-up article he reported that a single gunner, in one afternoon in 1926, had killed 67 of the large, gray raptors.

By this point, what had been a local secret, frequented by a few dozen farmers from the surrounding valley, had been plastered all over the Reading and Philadelphia papers, and some days there were 400 or more gunners jammed along the escarpment where an old sand-mining operation and gravity railroad had opened the forest and provided a clear shot at the passing hawks. So many rounds of shotgun ammo were fired that after busy weekends, scrap collectors shoveled up the discarded shells to sell for the brass bases. (They missed many; on my office shelf are a few somewhat corroded shell bases that I found in the 1980s, buried deep beneath the leaf duff on the slope below the old railroad landing.)

Sutton's goshawk article, and a previous one describing Sutton's own visit to the gunning site, caught the attention of a 24-year-old photographer in Philadelphia named Richard Pough. In the fall of 1932, Pough visited the ridgetop and witnessed the slaughter, then came back on subsequent weekends with several others. They spent hours gathering hundreds of dead hawks, falcons, and at least one eagle, arranging the stinking carcasses in macabre rows and photographing them. These graphic images formed the core of Pough's campaign over the next two years to get someone—anyone—to take action. The Game Commission basically shrugged; Pough was at one point reduced to lobbying the Lord's Day Alliance because some of the shooting took place on Sundays. The National Association of Audubon Societies (NAAS) made some noises about purchasing the mountaintop, which was available for back taxes, but never made a decision; unknown to the conservationists, a local gun club was considering the same thing to keep the ridge open permanently for hawk-shooting. Apathy and inaction reigned, until Rosalie Edge stepped into the fray.

A famously prickly New York City activist, Edge had already earned the ire of "professional" conservationists like the directors of the American Ornithologists' Union and NAAS president Gilbert Pearson, whom she considered weak tea at best when it came to protecting birds and other wildlife. She had tangled with Pearson and the Audubon leadership over fur-trapping on Audubon refuges in the South, for example, and the sweetheart relationship the NAAS maintained with ammunition manufacturers. She endlessly badgered J. N. "Ding" Darling, the famed political cartoonist who was running the US Bureau of Biological Survey (forerunner of today's US Fish and Wildlife Service), about reining in federal efforts to poison predators. When she learned, in the summer of 1934, that NAAS had made no moves to remedy the situation in Pennsylvania before another autumn of carnage, Edge's characteristically direct approach was to sign a $500 lease for the nearly 1,400-acre property with an option to buy it outright for about $3,000. That she did not have the money, needing to raise it quickly from a handful of longtime supporters, did not stop her for a moment.

Purchase made, Hawk Mountain Sanctuary, the world's first refuge for birds of prey, was born. Edge next reached out to Maurice Broun, a skinny, 28-year-old Romanian-born ornithologist living on Cape Cod who had been sending modest donations to Edge's Emergency Conservation Committee. Could she hire him to serve as warden that fall? Broun agreed, declining a salary and asking only for room and board for himself and his wife of a few months, Irma. Posting "No Trespassing" signs and advertising in local papers the closure of the mountain to hunting, they got immediate pushback. When threats from gunners grew too heated, Broun hired a deputy sheriff carrying a pistol to back him up—although in retrospect, perhaps the wisest move they made was to routinely post petite Irma, barely five feet tall, at the trailhead off the rutted dirt road to turn away shooting parties. It's unlikely the gunners would have backed down to a man had Broun or the deputy tried to stop them, but reflexive respect for a woman was baked into these otherwise iron-hard Pennsylvania German farmers and rough-necked coal miners. The posted signs were torn down as fast as they were nailed up, and someone famously hung a dead red-tailed hawk from a nearby bridge, a photograph of which proved a powerful fundraising tool for the new sanctuary, but the shooting stopped.

Stopped there, at least. Edge, Broun, and other conservationists would spend further decades trying to safeguard raptors elsewhere along the ridges of the Appalachians. In 1937, Pennsylvania granted legal protection to all hawks except the accipiters, the three species of agile forest hawks: the sharp-shinned and Cooper's hawks, and the American goshawk. Given that raptor identification is challenging enough even for moderately experienced birders with good binoculars, it is no surprise that an open season on a few species was functionally an open season on every raptor, even those few like American kestrels and ospreys that had long been granted some measure of legal protection. The $5 goshawk bounty remained on the books until 1950, and Maurice Broun and other hawk proponents dreaded the bloodbath they knew was happening elsewhere along the ridge on windy autumn days when the migration was heavy.

"You'd get a good hawking weekend shaping up," Broun told author Michael Harwood, whose 1973 book *The View from Hawk Mountain* captures the dichotomy that time, "and everybody would be calling in and saying, 'How's the hawking, Maurice?' and I'd say, 'It looks great.' . . . But those nights I never slept, because I knew what was happening up the ridge. It just *killed* me." Broun told Harwood that he'd drive east to Bake Oven Knob, another high overlook along the Kittatinny Ridge, "and there'd be half a dozen guys lined up with guns, shooting the birds as fast as they came. You'd see them drop on the road, drop in the woods, there was nothing you could do about it because they'd always make sure to shoot sharpshins when I was there."

There was progress, however halting, at other levels. The federal Bald Eagle Protection Act, passed in 1940 a decade after first being introduced, brought belated federal protection to that species—except in Alaska, which was exempted on the theory that bald eagles ate too many salmon. Even zoologist William T. Hornaday, president of the Wildlife Conservation Society, argued in 1931 that bald eagles in parts of Alaska were too abundant and needed to be "thinned out"; indeed, bounties were paid on Alaskan bald eagles until the exemption was revoked in 1952. Golden eagles, which Hornaday similarly thought needed to be "kept down to a low point," didn't receive similar federal protection until 1962. By then they had been essentially driven from the East anywhere south of the Canadian subarctic, and were on the ropes even in remote parts of the West. For example, in the 1940s sheep ranchers in west Texas banded together to hire professional hunters to shoot golden eagles. One such man, wielding a sawed-off shotgun from the cockpit of his tiny plane, killed an astounding 1,875 goldens in just two years in the area around the Davis Mountains of west Texas.

It wasn't until 1972 that the Migratory Bird Treaty Act was amended to provide protection to great horned owls and a few other raptors that had been purposefully excluded from earlier safeguards. I knew a few old game wardens in rural Pennsylvania who, years later, reminisced fondly about passing the long, cold nighttime hours on autumn patrol for deer poachers by "hooting up" great horned owls, fixing the responding bird in the beam of a spotlight, and shooting it with their service revolvers.

In the early 1980s, I was working for a local newspaper as a general assignment reporter, a job I had fallen into after I had started writing a weekly natural history column for them a few years earlier. At the time, there were very few wildlife rehabilitators in the state, and so—with more enthusiasm than experience—I started taking in injured raptors, working under Hawk Mountain's state and federal permits and learning on the job. It was a time when the older, more seasoned rehabbers were seeing a shift; instead of a large measure of their patients coming in with gunshot wounds, the problems, while still overwhelmingly caused by humans, tended to be more indirect and accidental: vehicle collisions, birds ill from eating poisoned rodents, people "rescuing" perfectly healthy raptor chicks that had, as is their nature, left the nest before they were really able to fly.

Rehabbing is tough work, because you may invest weeks or months in a bird only to realize it will never *quite* be healed enough to go back into the wild. If it's a rare or unusual species, if it has a mellow personality and its injuries are unlikely to cause chronic pain, as would, say, a joint break that will turn arthritic, you may be able to place it in a zoo or nature center as a captive educational bird. But most of these almost-but-not-quite cases were common species, like red-tailed hawks or eastern screech-owls; every institution that wanted one likely already had one. And then the only option was euthanasia, which for me got harder every time, until it became too much.

About the time I gave up raptor rehabilitation, I moved into another, even more direct intersection with the changing fortunes of North America's raptors. Hawk Mountain had hired its first fulltime director of research, a newly minted PhD raptor biologist named Jim Bednarz, who had established a couple of raptor-banding sites a few miles upridge of Hawk Mountain. I was still working as a reporter, and after weeks of nagging (since to Jim's mind a nosy reporter, even one with a raptor background, was an unwelcome distraction) he reluctantly agreed to let me tag along.

The idea was to lure passing raptors—redtails, Cooper's hawks, sharp-shinneds—with the promise of a meal, a pigeon or domestic dove dressed in a heavy, protective leather "flak jacket" sitting in the middle of a large, spring-loaded bow net like a giant mousetrap. It was like fly fishing in the sky, and while I was initially alarmed for the lure bird, I soon discovered that injuries were rare thanks to the leather armor. It took no time at all for me to become hooked and enter one of the most exciting and obsessive periods of my life. Within a year or two I was a licensed subpermittee bander, allowed to run the station in Jim's absence, banding hundreds of hawks and falcons every year, and helping to deploy radio transmitters on dozens of birds so chase teams from the sanctuary could attempt to follow them by car or small plane as they migrated south hundreds of miles. When Jim left Hawk Mountain for a raptor job out west, I organized volunteers to help me run the sanctuary's banding program; when Bednarz's replacement decided to close the banding stations and focus on different study questions, I took over one of them with a friend and continued banding several days a week through each autumn.

Thus, I had a front-row seat to the renaissance of raptors that was occurring in the 1980s and '90s. The combination of slowly falling DDT levels in the environment, coupled with active reintroduction and translocation programs for species like bald eagles, peregrine falcons, and ospreys, began to pay off increasingly hefty dividends on an almost year-to-year basis. Pioneering work in the 1960s and '70s learning to breed peregrines in captivity, spearheaded by scientists (and ardent falconers) like Heinz Meng at the State University of New York and Tom Cade with the Peregrine Fund, initially based at Cornell University, took a process that would otherwise have required generations for natural recolonization and compressed it to a few decades of intensive restoration work. Once they figured out the kinks and streamlined techniques like artificial insemination, captive propagation of peregrines at the Cornell "Hawk Barn" grew to an almost industrial scale. The chicks they produced were placed in so-called hack boxes, a modification of an old falconry technique in which the nestlings were kept in protected, grate-fronted enclosures mounted in high, secluded sites, and into which food in the form of quail and other dead birds could be slid down a long tube without the falcon chicks ever seeing a person. When the young were old enough, the barred door would be opened, and the chicks allowed to emerge and exercise their wings; food would be provided for weeks thereafter until they had learned to hunt for themselves.

Not everyone was convinced it would work, or that Cade and the others were taking the right approach by using a mishmash of peregrine subspecies from all around the world. And like a lot of groundbreaking science, it was trial and error. For understandable reasons, the first hack attempts were made at some of the old historic nest sites that peregrines had used before the DDT crash. But at those wooded cliff locations up and down the Appalachians, the young falcons, with no parental protection, were summarily killed and eaten by great horned owls, forcing the Peregrine Fund and their partners to switch to urban rooftops, or hack towers built amid the salt marshes of the Atlantic coastal plain, where there were no large owls. (In the West, predation was still an issue but for the most part one that could be managed, and most peregrine hack sites there were near historic eyries.)

Between the spring of 1975, when the *New York Times* buried a small story on page 10 announcing "an ecological experiment devised by Cornell scientists and the United States Fish and Wildlife Service to re-establish a species in its native region," and 1998, some 7,000 young falcons were released. Those that survived their first, dangerous months of freedom proved to be remarkably resilient. A few purists grumbled that captive-reared falcons weren't "real" peregrines, but if the measure of a peregrine is its ability to hunt—and no other raptor can equal its speed or aerial flair as it hunts its avian prey on the wing—a tiercel (male) peregrine raised at Cornell that nested on the salt marshes of New Jersey silenced many of the naysayers. Most peregrines succeed in capturing their quarry one time out of three. This bird, nicknamed the Red Baron, was seen to make 95 successful captures in 102 attempts, a 93 percent success rate. A real peregrine, indeed.

Once they were back in the wild, and with DDT levels falling, peregrines began breeding ever-more successfully near release sites. But like many birds, the young falcons tend to imprint—that is, gravitate toward—the kinds of nest sites where they were born. That initially meant a lot of urban falcons in the East nesting on buildings and under bridges, or on artificial structures in coastal marshes, and far fewer using historic cliff sites, even though urban locations proved much more dangerous for fledglings leaving their eyrie for the first time, winding up on busy city streets, crashing into office building windows, or falling down rooftop air ventilation shafts.

As eastern urban populations have reached saturation levels, though, younger falcons seeking unoccupied territories have moved farther and farther out, up and down river valleys and throughout the mountains, reclaiming cliff sites that, in some cases, haven't seen a nesting falcon since the 1950s. By 2024, the population of peregrine falcons in North America was pegged at about 72,000 birds, and the two subspecies that had been listed under the federal Endangered Species Act, the Arctic *tundrius* and the eastern *anatum*, were delisted in 1994 and 1999, respectively.

In 1975, as the nation's bicentennial approached, the US Department of the Interior asked Cade to oversee an attempt to replicate those early successes with bald eagles. No one was intentionally breeding eagles, but there were a few populations in the Great Lakes and upper Midwest that hadn't been as badly mauled by DDT poisoning, which served as a source of chicks. The first eagle hacking took place in 1976 at Montezuma National Wildlife Refuge in the Finger

Lakes region of New York, where a young undergrad named Tina Morris—one of very, very few women in the then-testosterone-soaked, male-dominated world of raptor biology—figured out how to apply the lessons of peregrine restoration to the nation's unofficial symbol. It worked, and by the 1980s many eastern states were conducting their own eagle restoration projects, with chicks sourced from nests as far away as Manitoba and Nova Scotia. Similar projects translocated osprey chicks from, say, the tidewaters of the Chesapeake, where ospreys had already begun a strong recovery, to places like the glacial lakes of the Pennsylvania Poconos.

The proof of the pudding was in the watching; every autumn saw increasing numbers of these once-rare raptors at hawkwatches up and down the Appalachians and beyond. As hawk-watchers, we had to recalibrate what we considered common and what we considered rare. The Cooper's hawk, one of the bird-eating accipiters known to old-timers as "blue darters" for their gun-metal coloration and flash-and-grab ambush attacks, was an underappreciated victim of DDT. By the late 1990s, though, Cooper's hawks were roaring back, adapting especially well to nesting in suburban backyards and plucking prey (particularly mourning doves) from feeders.

At Hawk Mountain, whose long-term counts served as pivotal evidence for Rachel Carson's arguments against DDT, the change has been nothing short of miraculous. It took until 1995, when 137 were counted, for the autumn bald eagle tally to exceed the pre-DDT record of 116 eagles in 1950, but it has only continued to climb. In 1963, at the height of the organochloride era, only 417 pairs remained in the entire lower 48. (Alaska's eagle population never suffered the same degree of pesticide damage.) By 2009, the USFWS estimated there were 72,000 eagles in the contiguous 48 states, a number which by 2019 had more than quadrupled to roughly 324,000 birds, including more than 73,000 nesting pairs.

I still enjoy seeing a bald eagle—and it's a rare week, driving around rural New England where we now live, that I don't see at least a couple—but I have to admit, these days my reaction is less ebullience and more a small, quiet smile. Yet the eagles are not entirely out of the woods. A 2022 study by dozens of eagle biologists found that the blood of nearly half of the dead bald eagles tested had lead levels indicative of chronic poisoning, while 25 percent of the birds had levels showing acute poisoning leading to death, toxins they pick up scavenging gut piles and carcasses of animals shot with lead ammunition. (The situation was only slightly less grim for golden eagles.) The authors concluded that the population losses from lead alone are enough to suppress the continued growth of bald eagle numbers.

Lead poisoning in bald eagles was found to be especially severe in the Central Flyway, and seasonally worst during autumn hunting season. That's why conservation-minded hunters use nontoxic ammunition, not just for waterfowl, as mandated by federal law, but for big-game hunting as well. California has banned all lead ammunition statewide, but for the rest of the United States and Canada, it's up to individuals to make the switch. I did some years ago, and the nontoxic copper .30-30 shells I use for white-tailed deer are just as effective as traditional lead rounds, without the wider environmental effects (or those on human health—I don't want to eat a toxin, either). The last time I killed a buck, I pointed a game camera at the gut pile, and was treated to videos of red-tailed and red-shouldered hawks, crows, ravens, chickadees, and blue jays cleaning it up in the days that followed, as well as gray foxes, coyotes, bobcats, opossums, and even flying squirrels and deer mice picking clean the carefully butchered bones. I could rest easy knowing none of them would suffer from their meal.

Not every reintroduction attempt has been an immediate, barnburning success. Conservationists have struggled for decades to restore the aplomado falcon, a strikingly beautiful bird with a blue-gray back (one meaning of *aplomado* in Spanish is "lead-colored") with a dark cummerbund separating its cream chest from rusty belly, and bold white eyebrow slashes on each side of its black, mustached face, that is widespread in Latin America, but reached its northern range extent in the Mexican borderlands of Texas, New Mexico, and Arizona. They disappeared from the United States by the 1950s, probably first as a result of habitat conversion from the open grasslands where they hunted smaller birds to brushland and agriculture, and then from the introduction of DDT, and are federally listed as endangered. After more than 40 years and multiple reintroduction attempts, hampered by drought, hurricanes, and owl predation, the only modestly stable population is in south Texas, where more than 900 chicks were released, but barely more than two dozen pairs were breeding in 2024.

Then there is the raptor that made lemonade from what at first appeared to be some dangerous ecological lemons, and literally grew its way to a better future: the snail kite. Another widespread tropical raptor with a distinct subspecies found only in central and south Florida, snail kites were named for their utter dependence on the Florida apple snail, a golfball-sized mollusk that the kites pluck from emergent vegetation and shallow water in sawgrass marshes and other wetlands. After the massive destruction and reengineering of Florida's wetlands in the first two-thirds of the 20th century, the kites had all but vanished; one estimate in the 1960s put their numbers at fewer than 20, and the first attempt to make a range-wide count in 1972 came up with just 65.

Snail kites are mid-sized raptors, a bit smaller than red-tailed hawks, with wide, somewhat paddle-shaped wings and white tails tipped with a single broad, black band. Males are slate gray, juveniles and females brown, but their most noticeable feature regardless of age and sex are their bills—long, thin, and deeply curved into almost a full half-circle. This is the tool they use to pry open the snails on which they feed; the curve of the bill slides neatly beneath the operculum, the plate that a snail pulls tight to seal itself inside, and having removed the door slips in to extract the meat from the shell like a key fitting in a lock. The kites are loose-limbed in the air, with a slow, floppy flight that looks careless but allows them to drift and hover easily, long legs dangling, then drift gently to the water's surface to snatch a snail before the snail's surprisingly sharp vision detects the hawk and the mollusk drops into deeper water.

Snail kites have ridden a population rollercoaster for years, its ups and downs driven by water levels and drought. By 1999, thanks to more consistent rains and better water management, the future was looking very bright for the Florida snail kites, their population totaling about 3,400 individuals. But then the bottom fell out; persistent drought conditions reduced the number of apple snails, and by 2002 the number of kites had dropped by about half, to 1,700 birds. After a slight recovery it fell by half *again* between 2006 and 2008, to just 700 to 800 kites. "Population models predict that if current trends continue, this iconic Florida species could become functionally extinct in a matter of 20 to 30 years," Audubon of Florida warned in 2011.

Then, worse news. In 2004, the invasive island apple snail, originally from South America and four or five times as big and heavy as the native apple snail, showed up in Lake Tohopekaliga, near Kissimmee. Lake Toho, as it is known, was at the time home to the healthiest remaining snail kite population in Florida, hosting 40 percent of all the successful nests in the state, and producing nearly 60 percent of all its fledged chicks.

The number of island apple snails exploded there. The exotic snails were dramatically more fertile, laying up to 10 times as many eggs as the natives; they can breathe air and tolerate seasonal drought that Florida apple snails can't, and occur at densities up to 200 times higher than the smaller natives. And they were just too big for the snail kites, especially young ones, to easily handle.

Chris Cattau, then a PhD candidate at the University of Florida, documented how poorly the young kites in particular handled this new food source; overall, the kites fumbled and dropped the invading snails eight or 10 times as often as they dropped natives, and even if they hung onto their prey it took them up to four times longer to open one to eat it, because a beak that evolved to open a small Florida apple snail wasn't the right tool to pry open one of these monsters.

While adult snail kites seemed to be holding their own with the new food supply, the juveniles were struggling—and no juveniles, no future for the species. "[W]e hypothesize that wetlands invaded by [island apple snails] . . . may function as ecological traps for the snail kite in Florida by attracting breeding adults but simultaneously depressing juvenile survival," Cattau and his coauthors warned. An ecological trap, in this sense, is a place that draws in a species but prevents it from successfully reproducing—a population sink, rather than a source.

When they made that prediction, the island apple snails were only found in Lake Toho; perhaps, these researchers and others hoped, the kites could shift to uninvaded wetlands. Soon, though, the exotic snails had spread almost everywhere across central and southern Florida, appearing wherever snail kites nested. There was no escaping them; the ecological trap had become universal, and the jaws were closing.

But then the snail kites pulled one of the more remarkable surprises in recent ornithology. They are a fairly long-lived species, with some birds making it to age 24 or more. Such organisms, with a relatively long generation time, are assumed to have poor flexibility in the face of rapid environmental change. But no one told the kites. The University of Florida team was able to show that, in less than a decade, Florida's snail kites had developed significantly larger, heavier beaks for opening the island apple snails, somewhat longer legs, and overall heavier body mass—an astonishingly rapid response that probably reflected the intense selective pressure young snail kites were facing. If you were too small, you died. If you were at least a little bit bigger, you might survive.

And you thrived. Far from being a death trap for young kites, within a few years invaded marshes were a boon; thanks to a population that now averaged larger and heavier-billed, juvenile kite survival in invaded wetlands *increased* 50 percent over marshes with native snails. Breeding rates and the number of young produced per nest also went up. What's more, the kites exhibited what the biologists called a "silver spoon," or carryover effect. Those born in invaded marshes, eating exotic apple snails, gained an advantage that carried over for up to the first 10 years of their lives, compared with kites from marshes without invasive snails. The result has been a spectacular recovery by snail kites, which by 2022 again numbered some 3,000 birds in Florida.

It wasn't evolution, not exactly. Scientists had physical measurements of kites from the pre-invasion years, which showed that snail kites had always exhibited a wide range of variation in bill size and other attributes. With the arrival of the larger snails, those individuals that by the luck of the draw were born with bigger beaks, legs, and body size survived more easily, while those that were too small did not, quickly shifting the kite population as a whole to a bigger, heftier level. And this plasticity, with time, could indeed become baked into the species' DNA in a true evolutionary fashion.

The invasive apple snails have moved very far from Lake Toho, and are now found west as far as Texas and north to the Carolinas. In the past few years, snail kites, too, have begun popping up far from their peninsular Florida home—in Pennsylvania in 2019, in North Carolina for the third time in 2024, in Louisiana and Tennessee for the first time that same year. Maybe this is just normal, occasional vagrancy, but until the 2010s snail kites had almost never strayed north of the Georgia border. Is something else at work, and could their always-tiny range increase? Some experts are skeptical, noting the kites' fussy taste in nesting habitat, but when the invasive apple snail colonized marshes on the Pacific coast of Mexico, snail kites followed north in its wake. Only time will tell.

The idea of a southern species moving north is old hat in this day of climate change; dozens of species of birds are pushing rapidly north, including many raptors. In the 1980s, it was a big deal when the first nesting black vultures were discovered in the central Appalachian Mountains, or in southern New York in the late 1990s; by the early 2020s, though, these ostensibly southern scavengers were regular summer visitors in Atlantic Canada. Meanwhile turkey vultures—which have always been better adapted to colder climates—have occupied much of the Maritimes and have begun appearing in Labrador and Newfoundland.

And while vultures were heading north, merlins—midsized, hyperaggressive falcons that specialize in hunting birds, and which are the living embodiment of the word *sizzle*—were heading south, and into town. Originally restricted in summer primarily to Canada and Alaska, they began nesting in Canadian prairie towns like Saskatoon, Saskatchewan, in the 1970s, using old hawk, crow, or magpie nests. Soon urban merlins were common across western Canada, and by the 1980s merlins from eastern Canada were moving south into Maine, occupying essentially all of the state by the early 2010s, again often using backyards and urban woodlands. From there, merlins just kept marching, nesting in New Hampshire, Vermont, and New York by the 1990s, in Massachusetts by 2008, and Pennsylvania by the early 2000s. West Virginia and the southern Appalachian Mountains beckoned thereafter, and by 2020 there was evidence merlins were breeding in the highlands of North Carolina—a range extension of almost 2,000 miles in less than 40 years.

Still, occasionally a raptor makes such an unexpected leap into new terrain that even when the evidence is plain as a nose on one's face, the experts refuse to believe it. Mississippi kites, which are slim, aerobatic, pale gray, red-eyed insect eaters only distantly related to snail kites, have long been a primarily southern raptor. They had disappeared from the upper Mississippi Valley in a dramatic range contraction in the second half of the 19th century, perhaps driven by shooting and the felling of the old cottonwood and oak forests along the rivers of the Great Plains.

The kites' fortunes started to change after the Dust Bowl years as millions of trees were planted on the Plains. By the middle of the 20th century Mississippi kites had reclaimed most or all of their lost ground, and were starting to spill north and west from their core range in the southern Great Plains, lower Mississippi Valley, and southeastern United States, and in the 1960s and '70s to the southwest into New Mexico and Arizona. They also moved increasingly into towns, whose shade trees provided nest sites and backyards provided insect food, often supporting colonies of up to 40 nesting pairs.

Mississippi kites had by the early 2000s already cemented a reputation as a raptor on the make, but the rising tide had by then reached no farther east and north than the Carolinas, with a few pioneering pairs in the Washington, DC, area. Which is why in 2004, when a wildlife biologist from Maine named Robert Roy was fishing along the Lamprey River in the town of Newmarket in southeastern New Hampshire and reported seeing what he identified as a Mississippi kite fly into a tree, snap off a branch in its feet and fly off with it, as though building a nest, the reaction from the birding cognoscenti was a scoffing laugh.

"I mean, a Mississippi kite in New Hampshire? Building a *nest?* C'mon," Steve Mirick told me, waving his hand in dismissal. Mirick and his wife Jane are a local birding power couple, and he served on the state bird records committee that considered, and rejected, Roy's carefully described observation. It was just too ridiculous to be true. That's where the matter lay for four years, until in 2008 when another birder posted an online report of a pair of kites in Newmarket, quickly followed by an account from two birders with impeccable credentials of a pair of kites copulating and building a nest. Ridiculous or not, the red-eyed bug hawks had come to the Granite State and have stayed, while the Miricks have become their unofficial chroniclers, chasing down nesting reports every summer, in years past documenting as many as five pairs. The numbers have remained low, and it may be that the kites have pushed the envelope as far to the north as they can. Unlike southern nests, which routinely hold two or three chicks, the New Hampshire birds never raise more than one baby, if that. In 2024, for example, the only nest the Miricks knew about failed.

But the kites' march north may not be over. In the years since the New Hampshire colony established itself, Mississippi kites have become much more frequently seen in the mid-Atlantic and Northeast, and have started breeding in Illinois, Iowa and, in 2016, in Wisconsin. Certainly no one was expecting them to show up in Winnipeg, Manitoba, a province where the species had never even been seen until a pair raised a chick there in 2014.

Oh, Canada. In the summer of 2022 Mississippi kites stormed into

Nova Scotia. Until then, only five had been reported in the province; that summer, as many as 19 were documented. Clearly there are a lot of Mississippi kites being hatched out there somewhere. Down in Veracruz, Mexico, the hemispheric chokepoint through which most of the world's Mississippi kite population funnels on its migration to South America, the annual count for this species has risen from 200,000 two decades ago, to 300,000 ten years ago, to nearly 700,000 in 2024, with no end in sight.

If Mississippi kites represent a raptor that is thriving, for reasons that aren't immediately apparent, American kestrels are the reverse of the coin: a once-abundant species that has fallen on inexplicable hard times.

One of the prettiest, most widespread, and familiar of the Western Hemisphere's raptors, American kestrels have long been a ubiquitous presence in farmland and open country from the Alaskan Arctic to the southern tip of South America. The size of a jay, kestrels are unique among North American falcons for being strikingly dimorphic—while both sexes share a basic color scheme including prominent black "mustache" marks on the face, the male's wings are blue-gray and his tail solid brick-orange with a single black terminal band, while the female's wings and tail are brick-colored and heavily barred.

Kestrels, which feed on large insects, small mammals, and birds, were one of the few raptors to be granted early legal protection (however imperfectly it was observed) because of their evident inoffensiveness to any human activity. But since the 1960s their numbers have been decreasing in many parts of North America, and by almost any measure—Breeding Bird Survey (BBS) data, Christmas Bird Counts, and migration records at places like Hawk Mountain in Pennsylvania and Cape May, New Jersey. The declines have been especially severe in regions like the Northeast, the prairie pothole grasslands, coastal California, and the southern Rocky Mountains; a few regions like the

Southwestern borderlands of the Chihuahuan Desert, or the southern Mississippi River valley, have seen increases.

There have been a raft of possible explanations floated for the kestrel's still-mysterious problems, from habitat degradation on the breeding or wintering grounds, to pesticides like neonicotinoids that may directly affect the birds or decimate their prey, or climate change effects. For a time, one plausible explanation was the recovery of the Cooper's hawk, which as we've seen preys heavily on birds. Female Cooper's hawks in particular (which like most raptors are the larger of the sexes) can kill kestrels with ease if they catch them. Perhaps, kestrel researchers wondered, the growth of Cooper's hawk populations, combined with rural development that created more of a patchwork of homes and shade trees favoring ambush hunters like the Coop in what had been open agricultural land, tipped the balance from the small falcons to the larger, bird-hunting accipiters.

Big raptors can have an outsize impact on smaller raptors. One especially well-documented example comes from the Kielder Forest of northern England, where Eurasian kestrels were once common. Eurasian goshawks, which had been extirpated from Britain in the 19th century, recolonized the forest in 1973—as they did many other parts of the United Kingdom—as falconers lost or released theirs. As goshawk numbers climbed, kestrel numbers plummeted; based on prey remains in nests, the scientists estimated the 20 or so pairs of Kiedler goshawks were killing some 115 kestrels a year. That's far more than had previously nested in the forest, and probably represented successive waves of kestrels trying to move into repeatedly depopulated territories. The Eurasian kestrels were eventually all but extirpated from Kielder.

So the notion that Cooper's hawks, which are related to and only somewhat smaller than goshawks, might be having a similar effect on American kestrels wasn't outlandish. But when kestrel experts analyzed BBS and Christmas Count data, they found only minimal evidence for direct predation like that seen in England. Perhaps, they thought, it's a "landscape of fear" situation, in which a predator needn't kill another species to displace it. To take another example involving goshawks in the United Kingdom, the British raptor ecologist Ian Newton has pointed to how the mere presence of goshawks, and the threat they pose, has forced smaller Eurasian sparrowhawks to abandon more open woodlands where they were once abundant and nest only in the thickest, densest stands where the bigger accipiters have more trouble hunting.

So that's one possible explanation. Researchers at Hawk Mountain, and at more than 50 other collaborating agencies, organizations, and academic institutions, have mounted a continent-wide investigation with federal funding to finally find the root cause, or causes.

There's no conclusive proof yet, like those falcon eggs in the 1960s with their thinning shells, but there is growing evidence that a key stumbling block for kestrels may be juvenile survival in late summer. "If I'm only allowed one word: grasshoppers," a prominent kestrel researcher told the *New York Times* in 2023, speculating on the cause. Insect abundance has tumbled in many parts of the world, and big, juicy grasshoppers are an ideal prey for newly independent young kestrels—and one that may be harder and harder to find as agriculture becomes ever-more mechanized and chemically dependent. As history has shown, the first step in bringing back a flagging raptor is understanding the threat.

The wind raking North Lookout did not falter, and neither did the hawk flight that day. But by late afternoon other commitments pulled me, very reluctantly, off the rocks, where I bid my old friends Seth and Holly goodbye. There's an assumption among hawk watchers, among birders in general, that as soon as you leave you'll miss the best bird of the day, so I joked about being the human sacrifice, though in truth the day hadn't needed any supernatural help. It had already benefitted, however little most of the casual visitors realized it, from half a century of forward-thinking raptor conservation.

As I picked my way back along the rocky trail, I could hear behind me

Bracken's voice raised again, calling out another approaching bald eagle for the crowd. By the time the 2024 autumn migration count ended in late December, Hawk Mountain had set yet another high count record for bald eagles, 653 this time. Nor was it alone. Hawk Ridge, a count site near Duluth, Minnesota, marked its own all-time bald eagle record in 2024 as well—a stunning 6,200 of the great birds, a reflection of the fact that Hawk Ridge sits below the vast Canadian boreal forest where huge numbers of bald eagles nest.

A few days after Hawk Mountain announced its new tally, outgoing president Joe Biden signed the new law that formally designated the bald eagle as the national bird of the United States. I was driving not far from home when I heard the news on the radio. A mile or two farther down the road, passing the local lake still unfrozen in a December thaw, my eye caught that unmistakable silhouette: wings like wide planks, and a prominent white head with a massive beak sticking out as far in the front as the white tail did behind. I pulled over and watched. Attention needed to be paid.

Three

Mullet Hawks and the Witches' Walk

I was asked to remain quiet, and to follow the path from the car park carefully, keeping hidden as much as possible.

I was in Dorset, on the southern coast of England, at a once long-abandoned and now restored Victorian walled garden where I was hoping to see the latest example of the ongoing recovery of one of the United Kingdom's most storied raptors. I followed Liv Elwood up through a grove of trees, passing out of the woods to an elaborate, multistory viewing platform not far from Poole Harbour on the English Channel. The final approach was screened to prevent our appearance from spooking the objects of our interest—the first pair of ospreys to nest in southern Britain in nearly two centuries.

Elwood, 29, is the charity manager for the Birds of Poole Harbour, which since 2017 has partnered with the Roy Dennis Wildlife Foundation to bring these fish-eating birds back to this huge and ornithologically important area. In that time, here at this restored Victorian attraction known as Carey's Secret Garden, they'd released 43 young ospreys drawn from nests in Scotland, where the species has made a slow but steady recovery since the mid-20th century. The young ospreys now join massive white-tailed eagles, themselves reintroduced just a few years earlier to the nearby Isle of Wight, feasting on the abundance of fish in Poole Harbour's sheltered bay.

In many ways, the broad history of raptor declines and rebound in the United Kingdom and Europe mirrors that in North America, yet the stories differ in significant ways. In the British Isles in particular, the nadir was a much deeper hole of population collapse and local extinction; persecution began centuries earlier, and many species were driven out of Britain and Ireland entirely. The threats of the modern world, like pesticide contamination, only exacerbated that earlier damage. For some raptors, thanks to legal protection and bans on some persistent toxins, recovery has come relatively quickly and almost completely, while others need a helping hand to reestablish themselves. And sadly for some, the present has proven no safer than the supposedly less civilized past.

White-tailed eagles, the larger Eurasian close cousin of the bald eagle, were found throughout Britain in the medieval period, but with time they became ever rarer, disappearing from England after 1780, and from Scotland by 1918. Ospreys lasted a bit longer, with the last one to nest in England meeting its end in 1847, shot by a gamekeeper in Somerset, and the last pair in Scotland disappearing after 1916. Red kites, which had been widespread and abundant across Britain during the Middle Ages, and so valued for their role in cleaning up urban waste that they were granted legal protection in London, were driven farther and farther west in later centuries until by the early 20th century they remained—just barely—in Wales, where only about 10 pairs survived.

By the late 1700s, common buzzards* were already being targeted by gamekeepers for their alleged sins against gamebirds, and by the

---

* To Americans, "buzzard" is a slang term for a vulture, but it more correctly refers to soaring hawks in the genus *Buteo*; technically, a red-tailed hawk is a red-tailed buzzard. Similarly, what North Americans once called a "sparrowhawk" is the small falcon now known as an American kestrel, its name changing in the 1960s and '70s to align with UK usage and prevent confusion with the unrelated Eurasian sparrowhawk. Many other North American raptor names changed then as well: pigeon hawk became merlin, duck hawk became peregrine falcon, and marsh hawk became northern harrier.

early 1900s there were barely 1,000 pairs in all of the United Kingdom, mostly in western Britain. During the 1950s and '60s, buzzards suffered a double blow from pesticides like DDT coupled with the collapse of wild rabbit populations from myxomatosis, a viral disease. Eurasian goshawks were driven to extinction in the United Kingdom in the 19th century, victims of deforestation and persecution, while peregrine falcons fell victim to DDT poisoning just as they had in North America—in fact, the first recognition that organochlorides were causing eggshell thinning came from British ornithologists.

With a little help from falconers, goshawks recolonized many parts of the United Kingdom, especially in Wales, the north of England, and parts of Scotland; by 2011, the British Trust for Ornithology (BTO) estimated, their population had increased by 1,300 percent. The breeding range of peregrine falcons has almost doubled since 1970, with the UK population climbing to nearly 1,800 pairs by 2014.

Merlins, unlike their North American cousins, have struggled in the United Kingdom, where they largely inhabit moors and other open uplands, with earlier population increases eroding in recent years. But Eurasian hobbies, trim falcons with rusty-red "trousers," have occupied all of southern and central Britain and keep expanding north, with some nesting in Scotland. Golden eagles, which are essentially restricted to Scotland, have remained stable at around 500 pairs for many years.

Mark Thomas has had a front-row seat to the resurgence of British raptors. Now 52, he knew even as a kid growing up in South Yorkshire, not far from the Peak District in northern England, that he wanted to someday work for the Royal Society for the Protection of Birds. After a series of positions, from guarding beach-nesting colonies of little terns to working for the National Trust in the Farne Islands off the Northumberland coast, he found himself at the RSPB.

I spoke to Thomas some months before I was leaving for England, seeking his guidance on a specific aspect of British raptor conservation that we'll turn to a bit later. He remembers a time when hawks or owls of any sort were scarce in England. "You're quite right to say there's far more birds of prey, generally speaking now than what there was 20, 30 years ago," he told me. "As a kid in Sheffield, I never saw a buzzard. I remember the first pair of buzzards at the headquarters for RSPB [in Bedfordshire, north of London], which was probably 15, 18 years ago, and people would go outside and look at them when they were in display flight. Now there are probably 50 pairs in the area."

In fact, the common buzzard has been perhaps the biggest raptor success story in Great Britain, and is now its most common bird of prey, with an 80 percent population growth between about 1985 and 2022. By 2011, buzzards were found to be breeding in 94 percent of England, absent only from sites along the coast that were more water than land, or urbanized areas with little suitable habitat. In all, the most recent estimate from the British Trust for Ornithology (BTO) in 2016 put the UK population at 63,000 pairs, and it has almost certainly grown since then.

The ledger is more mixed in regard to owls, which, being nocturnal, are also harder to survey. Barn owls, which are very popular with the public and have benefitted from direct action like placing nest boxes in suitable farmland habitat, more than doubled their population between 1995 and 2020, while little owls have shown a nearly 80 percent decline since the 1960s, possibly due to agricultural changes affecting their invertebrate prey. Long-eared owls likewise seem to be on the decline, though this is an especially secretive species whose numbers are hard to track. Tawny owls, totaling an estimated 50,000 pairs in the United Kingdom, appear relatively stable.

As in North America, not every raptor can make an unassisted comeback. Red kites had been extirpated from England, Scotland, and Northern Ireland by the 1870s, but in 1989, chicks from Sweden were released in the Chiltern Hills of southern England, and on the Black Isle peninsula in northern Scotland. By 2013, almost 1,000 young kites had been released in England and Scotland, sourced from wild nests in Wales, Germany, and Spain, in addition to Sweden.

As I drove south from London toward Poole, I had plenty of evidence of the red kite's success. I quickly lost count of the number of red kites I saw along the way, though I never grew tired of spotting their instantly recognizable silhouettes in the air—long, gracefully tapered wings, their tails with a shallow fork, which these buoyant raptors twist and angle for maximum aerial maneuverability. And I was south of the regions of their greatest abundance; red kite densities are even higher to the north and west, and a 2017 BTO Breeding Bird Survey showed a staggering 19,000 percent increase in red kite numbers in the preceding 22 years. (Recovery has been slower in Scotland due to a stubbornly embedded hostility to birds of prey.)

Ospreys recolonized Scotland on their own beginning in 1954 and ever so slowly increased there, under constant threat of pesticide contamination, illegal shooting, and egg-collecting, this last a scourge that has never fully died out in the United Kingdom. With time, vigilant nest-guarding, and a broad public enthusiasm for ospreys, the Scottish population now numbers between 250 and 300 breeding pairs, with spillover into an increasing number of nesting pairs in northern England, especially in Northumberland.

But southern England long remained bereft of ospreys except as passage migrants. In the 1980s artificial nest platforms, which ospreys in many parts of the world will readily adopt, were installed at the famed Rutland Water Nature Reserve in the east Midlands. Hopes were raised in 1994 when two ospreys oversummered there, until observers realized both birds were males. At that point, Tim Appleton, the Rutland reserve's storied director, reached out to Roy Dennis, an equally renowned expert on raptors, and they hatched a plan to bring Scottish osprey chicks to Rutland. The project began in 1996 and resulted in the first successfully nesting pair there just five years later. From that small nucleus, a growing British osprey population has been building across England and into Wales, supported by nearly 300 chicks fledged at Rutland itself.

To jump-start a wider English recovery requires applying the same techniques used at Rutland elsewhere in the country, which is why the Poole Harbour effort began in 2017. Before we headed to the

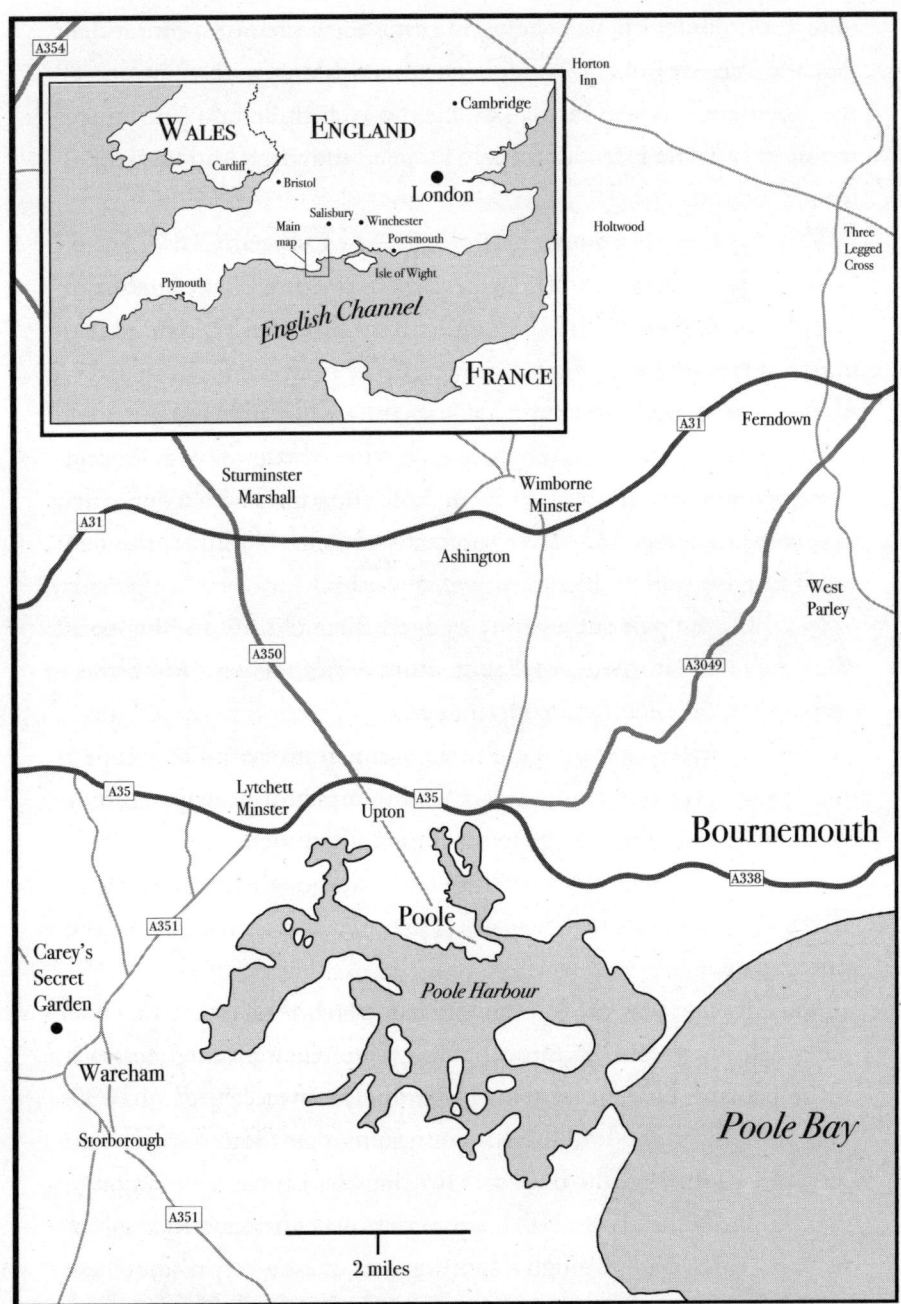

Poole Harbour, in southern England, is home to reintroduced ospreys and white-tailed eagles, the latter nesting again after an absence from southern England of nearly 250 years.

observation hide, Liv had shown me around the release cages, which perch at the edge of the floodplain—cages that were then empty, as the global outbreak of highly pathogenic avian influenza had caused the Birds of Poole Harbour folks to suspend moving additional chicks from Scotland.

Thus far there is a single nesting pair of ospreys at Carey's Secret Garden. The female, known by her ring number CJ7, fledged from a wild nest at Rutland in 2015 and, after the usual two-year hiatus in Africa growing to maturity, showed up at Poole Harbour in 2017. After a false start in 2019 with a young male who failed to return the following spring from migration, and clutches of infertile eggs she laid while mateless in 2020 and 2021, in 2022 she paired with a two-year-old male known as 022. They hatched two chicks in 2022, the first south English ospreys in almost two centuries.

In 2023, the pair successfully fledged three chicks, and by April 2024 they had returned on schedule from Africa and resumed housekeeping. By the time I visited in mid-May, CJ7 was broody and incubating her first-ever four-egg clutch, about the maximum number this species ever lays, and a sign that the highly productive harbor environment was providing plenty of food. Their one surviving 2022 chick, a female, had also returned from her juvenile sabbatical in Africa, Liv told me, further reason for optimism on the part of the osprey team.

And although new chick releases remained on hold, the nesting pair draws a steady stream of visitors booking carefully monitored sessions in the viewing hide, accompanied by one of several Birds of Poole Harbour guides who lead three such sessions a day, four days a week. Liv and I slipped on the deck as Mya Bambrick, the guide on duty, was talking about CJ7 and 022, with everyone's attention focused on the nest, which even through a spotting scope was a very distant view indeed, perhaps half a kilometer away. It was clear that no one was taking any chances with disturbance that might spook the ospreys.

The pair had just done a nest exchange, the female slipping off for a short while as 022, the male, settled down to keep the eggs warm in her absence. "This male is quite good," Mya said. "He'll fish over on the Wareham Channel, which is about just two kilometers from nest, but he also fishes on the River Piddle," which runs through the estate. One of the main food fish for Poole's ospreys, Liv had mentioned earlier, is gray mullet, a species on which both the birds and the local fishing industry depend. Hereabouts, ospreys were known as "mullet hawks" in the old days because of their taste for this long, gracefully tapered schooling fish, but some have worried that steadily declining commercial landings suggest the mullet stocks may be overexploited.

Another small band of visitors arrived, and someone expressed polite disappointment that the nest was so far away, but Mya said it was a criminal offense to approach an osprey nest any closer than 200 meters. I learned some time later that this is not, strictly speaking, true; while it is an offense to disturb a nest, there is no firm buffer zone radius. But when Liv asked what the restrictions were in the US for approaching an osprey nest, she and Mya both were stunned when I said there were none.

"None at all?" Liv asked.

"No," I said. "If there were, some people would never be able to enter or leave their homes." Shock was written all over both women's faces, but in North America ospreys nest literally in backyards, right next to houses or in the middle of busy marinas, and the edges of shopping mall parking lots, all without a bit of bother. That's because they've had generations of ospreys living cheek-by-jowl with people, decades of habituation. Those in the United Kingdom, both in Scotland and elsewhere, have grown up in a more sheltered, carefully protected, less human-impacted world, and would probably react with panic to the kind of activity at which an American or Canadian osprey wouldn't bat an eye.

As osprey reintroduction gathers steam across England, so too does the restoration of an even more impressive bird, the white-tailed eagle. This is a raptor that benefitted from one of the earliest translocation projects anywhere, though not initially a successful one. Three chicks were brought from Norway to the Scottish Highlands in 1959; one disappeared, one wound up back in captivity, and the third, after a year of freedom, was caught in a leghold trap. Another attempt in 1968 by Roy Dennis, releasing four chicks on Fair Isle in the Shetlands, also failed, but the effort finally gained traction beginning in 1975 when eaglets from wild nests in Norway were hacked out on the Isle of Rum off the west coast of Scotland. By the time translocations ended in 2012, more than 200 eaglets had been released in Scotland, where the breeding population is now estimated at more than 130 pairs. Another 100 have been hacked out in Ireland, where they now breed in limited numbers, but until recently the eagles were still absent from England.

That changed in 2019, when the Roy Dennis Wildlife Foundation and Forestry England began a translocation project on the Isle of Wight, where the eagles last nested in 1780. Over the next five years, 37 eaglets from nests in Scotland were released, with rapid results. By 2023 the first successful English eagle nest in 243 years fledged a single chick, and by 2024 there were four territorial pairs on Wight and just to the west at Poole Harbour.

So successful has the Isle of Wight work been that the foundation is now turning its attention to Exmoor National Park in the southwest of England, while across the Bristol Channel, a similar project has been proposed to restore not only white-tailed eagles but also golden eagles, both of which disappeared from Wales by the mid-1800s.

You can be forgiven for thinking this is a new Golden Age for British raptors. It is, for many species in many places. But in the interests of fairness, we need to turn away from all the good news to take a hard look at the bad, and especially what can be done to change it.

I first searched for hen harriers along the Witches' Walk.

It runs through the high, windswept moorland of Lancashire, in the north of England, the route along which, in August 1612, a group of 10 women and two men accused of witchcraft were taken for trial; eight of the women and both of the men were convicted over the course of a two-day trial and executed the following day by hanging. The key witness for the prosecution was a nine-year-old girl, Jennet Device; among those whom she accused to their deaths were her grandmother, mother, brother, and sister.

Today, along the 51-mile route on which the hapless captives were marched to Lancaster Castle, a series of waist-high iron waymarkers was installed in 2012 to mark the 400th anniversary of the trial, each inscribed with the name of one of the supposed witches, and three-line tercets from a poem about the trials and executions by then-poet laureate Carol Ann Duffy.

These days, the moors of northern England and Scotland see persecution of a different sort. I was hiking up the slopes of Waddington Fell following Steve Downing, whose long career in law enforcement

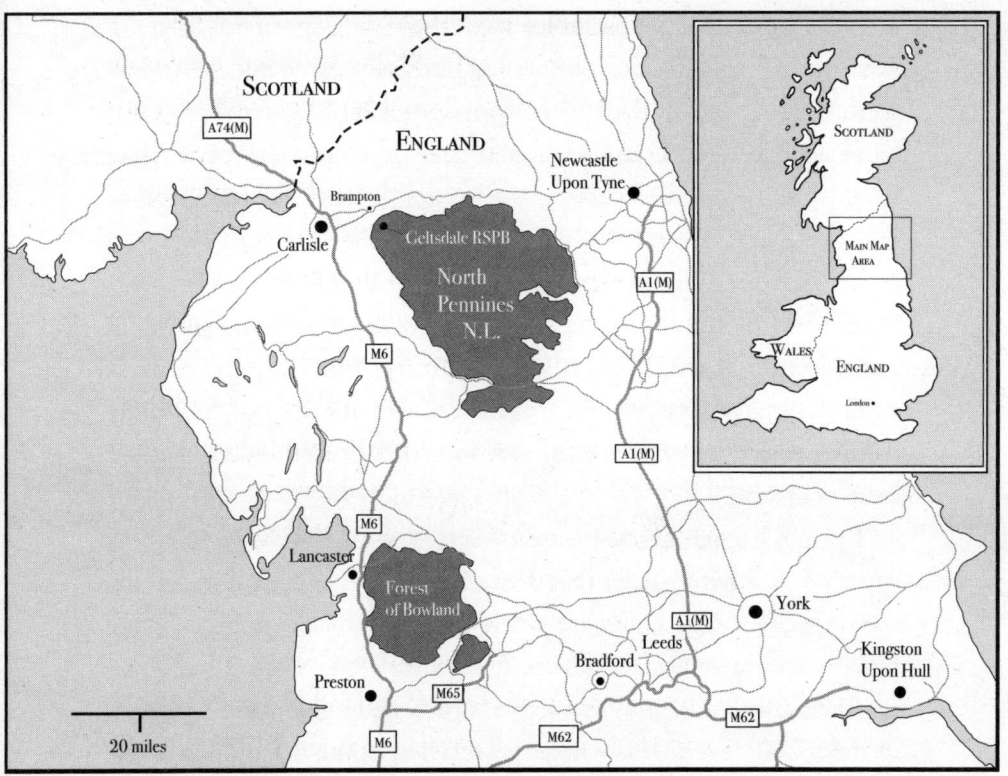

Northern England, ground zero for the fight to protect hen harriers from persecution.

grew ever more tightly bound with raptors. He spent 37 years on the West Yorkshire police force, 10 of them directing a 17-person staff as force wildlife crime officer. He was eventually tapped to head up the first UK-wide task force aimed at wildlife crime, Operation Artemis, which ran from 2004 to 2008, after which he joined the RSPB's investigations team for another 10 years. Along the way he also took the lead role on ringing and satellite-tagging young hen harriers, a responsibility he still holds and which keeps him active and in the field at 74. With us was Howard Jones, 36, a senior investigations officer with the society, because despite years of effort by Downing and others, the fate of those harriers is still rarely a happy one.

The reason I had called Mark Thomas at RSPB months earlier wasn't just to hear his reminiscences about the return of buzzards to England. Thomas heads up the 15-person investigations team at RSPB that includes Jones, and whose office faces the daunting, uphill battle to save one of England's most imperiled birds of prey. While the overall picture for raptors in the United Kingdom is far brighter than it was half a century ago, there are still pervasive problems with entrenched hostility and continued persecution in rural Britain toward raptors of any sort. Every year, the RSPB publishes what's known as its *Birdcrime* report summarizing the depressing litany of illegal killing of raptors from buzzards and goshawks to eagles and falcons. But the species at the epicenter of the toughest fight to protect birds of prey in Great Britain is one of its rarest, the hen harrier, which finds itself in deadly conflict with a lot of very rich, very influential stakeholders over the issue of grouse.

The hen harrier, *Circus cyaneus*, is a close enough relative to North America's northern harrier that they were until recently considered the same species. Adult males are pearly gray with black wingtips, while females and juveniles are brown. It is a lithe, long-winged hunter of marshes, grasslands, and, in much of northern England and Scotland, of moorlands—which is where the rub lies. Some 4.1 million acres, fully 8 percent of the United Kingdom's land area, are managed with fire and other means specifically for red grouse, generally considered an endemic subspecies of the same bird North Americans know as the willow ptarmigan, for the peculiarly British sport of driven grouse hunts, which occur on roughly 450 managed grouse moors in Scotland, northern England, and Northern Ireland.

The kind of gamebird hunting I knew growing up in the mountains of Pennsylvania, chasing ruffed grouse in the hills and ring-necked pheasants on the farms, working behind a dog on foot or flushing the birds ourselves, is known in Britain as "walked up" shooting, but the epitome of British grouse gunning is a driven shoot. Born of the Victorian era and both enormously expensive and exceedingly exclusive, driven shoots feature a line of eight or 10 "guns" (as the shooters are known) arrayed in a line across the landscape behind butts, or waist-high hides traditionally made of stone and turf; there's usually a loader for each gun, someone to switch and reload shotguns because once the grouse start roaring past, there is little time to do more than swing, shoot, and grab a fresh gun at the ready. The sport is infused with ritual and etiquette, and routinely costs many thousands of pounds per hunter per day. The opening day of the grouse season, August 12, has been enshrined in English law since 1831, and is known as the "Glorious Twelfth."

By most accounts, driven grouse provide one of the most challenging forms of wing-shooting there is. Flushed by a long line of beaters marching slowly across the heather waving cloth flags, the grouse do not appear singly but rather in packs, as they're known, dozens (or many more) barreling toward the guns at up to 70 miles per hour, hugging the terrain like radar-evading planes in a twisting, chaotic, confusing mass of speed and motion. The hunter has bare seconds to isolate a target in the melee, swing, aim, and fire before the birds have raced past.

This kind of shooting depends on enormous numbers of grouse. To be commercially successful, an estate's moorland must produce thousands of grouse each year—a typical single day's bag is often 75 to 150 two-bird "braces."* And unlike the pheasants, ducks, or partridge that are pen-reared for similar driven-bird shoots in the United Kingdom, red grouse cannot easily be raised in captivity. But to call them "wild" may strain the meaning of that word, since the grouse moors are managed to such an extent that the birds are really as much a crop as a field of grain would be.

The heather moors are burned regularly, providing fresh, new plant shoots for the grouse and removing encroaching woody vegetation, creating a crazy-quilt pattern on the uplands. Many estates provide the grouse with medicated grit treated with an antiparasitic drug to control a threadworm that causes periodic population collapses in the birds. And the grouse moors have a very long history of ruthless predator control. Weasels, stoats, foxes, and crows can be legally killed on grouse moors, but birds of prey may not. Yet as the RSPB's investigations show, that clearly does not stop those who see raptors as vermin to exterminate. From 2009 to 2023, 75 percent of all individuals convicted of raptor-persecution offenses were connected with the gamebird shooting industry, according to the 2023 *Birdcrime* report. While according to the RSPB's 2022 *Birdcrime* report, almost two-thirds of all the confirmed raptor deaths in the UK that year occurred on land managed for shooting, a proportion that has remained roughly constant for several years.

Hen harriers, which hunt predominantly for birds and small mammals, also nest on moorland, and they are large enough to take young

---

* If that seems a lot, consider that the Forest of Bowland holds the record for the largest one-day grouse bag in British history, a staggering 2,929 killed by eight guns at the Abbeystead estate on Aug. 12, 1915. That's more than 350 birds per hunter, but in terms of single-handed slaughter—and that really is the only word for it—the record is held by Thomas de Grey, 6th Lord Walsingham, who *by himself* on Aug. 30, 1888, shot 1,070 grouse on his estate in Yorkshire. He is said to have begun a little after 5 in the morning and ended just before 7 that evening, killing the final 13 grouse on the walk home. By one calculation, that works out to one grouse every 13 seconds for more than 12 hours. All but 500 of the birds, which he gave to friends, were shipped to market for sale.

red grouse. That makes them an especially tempting target for those who begrudge any grouse not available for the gunners, and it has pushed hen harriers to the brink in many parts of the United Kingdom.

Thomas said it was a shame my visit would come a few weeks too early to help Steve Downing with the satellite tagging, because I would miss the emotional gut-punch that affects every one of the hen harrier team.

"You'd be looking at a juvenile harrier, staring it in the eye knowing full well in about three months' time there's a strong chance that bird's going to be shot dead. And that's the absolute cold face of what we're dealing with," he said.

Steve and Howard had picked me up in Clitheroe and driven north beyond the town of Slaidburn to Waddington Fell, following up on telemetry data showing that a male hen harrier had been in the area. This is more or less in the heart of the Forest of Bowland—which is not, in point of fact, a forest; the ancient term refers to a royal hunting ground, and while Bowland may once have been wooded, today it is mostly open moorland and bog, a designated National Landscape covering more than 300 square miles, almost all of it privately owned land. Along the way we stopped on the old Roman-built road, today a dirt track along which the accused Pendle witches were marched. Nearby was one of the white-painted iron witches' waymarkers, number six of the series. Along one narrow edge of the oddly shaped post was the name Elizabeth Device, the mother of the accusatory young Jennet. It was a chilly, cloudy, gusty evening, but that was not the only reason the hair prickled on my neck.

At Waddington Fell, sheep scattered as we hiked up Sadler Hill, our boots squishing in the wet, mucky peat, past a few weathered grouse-shooting butts just below the knoll of a heather-covered hill. Skylarks spiraled high overhead in their mating flight display, their long, complex trilling songs spilling across the landscape. We flushed slim, streaky, olive-brown meadow pipits, which Steve said were, with voles, a major prey species for hen harriers, but his practiced eye had already sized up the area and found it wanting—too wet, too small and, despite the pipits, too prey-poor to hold a pair.

The symbol of the Forest of Bowland National Landscape is the hen harrier, which is ironic, because Lancashire and some of the surrounding counties are as rough a place to be a hen harrier today as they were to be an accused witch in the 17th century. The average life expectancy of a harrier chick, fledgling on the moors in the English north, is about four months, according to a peer-reviewed study analyzing tracking data from 148 satellite-tagged hen harriers in the UK.

Raptor persecutions via gun, poison, and trap by and large map directly onto the areas with the largest gamebird shooting activity, and since 2009, 75 percent of those convicted of offenses related to raptor persecution have been connected with the bird-shooting industry, 68 percent of them gamekeepers, according to the 2023 *Birdcrime* report, summarizing 15 years of RSPB investigations. Any raptor may become a victim. For example, in October 2021 and again in January 2022, newly reintroduced white-tailed eagles died of poisoning in England, one from an acutely toxic pesticide called bendiocarb that, RSPB investigators say, is a favored chemical for killing raptors, the other from a lethal dose of rat poison. Two young white-tailed eagles, one of them among the very first reintroduced to the Republic of Ireland, also died from bendiocarb poisoning in May 2023 on Northern Ireland's only grouse moor. No prosecution was brought in any of the three cases.

A 2017 study by Scottish Natural Heritage concluded that of 131 young golden eagles fitted with satellite tags, 31 percent (41 birds) disappeared and presumably died "under suspicious circumstances significantly connected with contemporaneous records of illegal persecution. . . . Some, but not all, areas managed as grouse moors were strongly associated with the disappearance of many of the tagged eagles."

Still, hen harriers face the most focused threat, since they nest on or near the grouse moors themselves. Between just January 2022 and October 2023, 39 satellite-tagged hen harriers either disappeared suspiciously or were confirmed illegally killed in England. The previously referenced 2023 analysis of harrier tracking data from 2014 to 2021, encompassing 148 satellite-tagged harriers, found that just 14 percent of males and 30 percent of females lived past their first birthday. An earlier study from 2019 found an almost perfect correlation between the final week's location for dead and suspiciously disappearing harriers and the percentage of land there in grouse moors, regardless of whether that land was part of a recognized protected area like a national park or designated "area of outstanding natural beauty," now known as a national landscape.* In fact, the study found that several protected areas, including the North York Moors and the Peak District national parks, had the highest rates of such "terminal week fixes," the last time a harrier's transmitter checked in before going dark.

"I could take you to one 10 kilometer square in Sheffield in the Peak District National Park. And that square is the worst 10 kilometer square in the whole of the United Kingdom for raptor persecution incidents. There's six or seven grouse moors that intersect within that square and over time it's just incident after incident after incident. It's really difficult to prove who's doing it," Mark Thomas had told me.

That is the nub of the problem—proving who's pulling the trigger or setting out the poison. Thomas's RSPB team is exceedingly careful. They face vocal pushback from the countryside lobby to only count as a confirmed persecution incident a bird whose killing has been backed up by corroborating evidence like post-mortem forensics, toxicological analysis, eyewitnesses, video recordings, or the conclusions of a police investigation.

Arrests are rare. The 2024 *Birdcrime* report, summarizing 15 years

---

* "National park" means something very different in Great Britain than it does in the US or Canada, where national parks are public land, at best lightly inhabited, and stringently regulated. In Britain, most of the land in national parks, which were created following World War II, is privately owned, farmed, or timbered, and includes some quite large towns and villages, though with some degree of regulatory oversight. British parks were created not so much to preserve wild and largely untouched landscapes as to encourage public access and outdoor recreation.

of RSPB investigations, found that of 1,529 "confirmed" incidents, just 62 resulted in prosecutions and only 57 in a conviction; five of those ended with a suspended sentence. Exactly one person in the United Kingdom has been jailed in recent years for killing a raptor. But even that is the tip of the iceberg, because there is evidence that those shooting raptors intentionally target hawks without "boxes," that is, transmitters, knowing they can't be tracked. Even so, the RSPB counts more than 5,400 incidents during that period that it classifies as probable or unconfirmed, cases where, for instance, a satellite-tagged raptor has mysteriously disappeared, its transmitter signal cut off in the midst of sending location data, and no trace of it ever found.

The society is also exceedingly careful with its public statements because Britain's defamation laws allow someone claiming slander or libel to bring suit, forcing the defendant to prove that the disputed statement was in fact true. That can be ruinously expensive even if one mounts a successful defense.

The next morning I rode with Steve to the Stocks Reservoir, not far from where we'd been the evening before. Howard Jones had other commitments, but we met Ludwig, the RSPB's species and habitat officer for Bowland, who before we left kenneled her two very friendly black Labs, which she uses at local hunts to find lost birds. It was a connection to the shooting community I had perhaps narrow-mindedly not expected from someone in the RSPB. I later learned she had worked as a senior scientist for the Game and Wildlife Conservation Trust, a UK charity closely associated with the shooting and countryside lobby. Sonja thinks there is room for common ground between bird conservation groups and the hunters, an attitude which I must in honesty say is viewed with some skepticism by the more veteran members of the harrier team. Sonja completed her PhD studying common terns, but had been working in the Bowland area with RSPB for a couple of years, where monitoring hen harriers is a major part of her job.

We rode in her white RSPB truck deep into the countryside, rolling and pitching up some rough dirt tracks past small farmsteads. Sonja and Steve wanted to check on several harrier nest locations, about which the less said, the better. Our first stop was on a windswept hill, parking near a trim and tidy, wood-lined shooting butt, though Steve said the gunning on this estate was mostly for stocked pheasant and red-legged partridge. "The grouse are just a nice extra for a day or two," he said.

We were watching a high, empty fell a mile or more away—they were taking no chances with disturbing any of the precious nesting pairs. It took some time, but eventually a tiny speck of pale gray appeared; the male harrier, quartering the landscape in typically low and somewhat wobbly flight, his wings angled up in a shallow vee.

This was a male nicknamed Dynamo, whom Sonja said was two-timing—he had a secondary female nesting about four kilometers away. Such bigamy is not uncommon in hen harriers, but the distance between Dynamo's two nests was very unusual, she explained. More typically, the two nests would be within sight of each other, because for the first 10 days or so after the chicks hatch, the male is the sole supplier of food to them and the female, as well as their main protector against other predators.

Hen harriers are oddly individualistic birds in several respects. For example, Dynamo wears the satellite tag he was fitted with as a chick in 2019, and so the RSPB knows he's never traveled more than 50 miles from Bowland. But his brother Apollo, similarly tagged, made two winter migrations to precisely the same spot in Extremadura, in southwestern Spain, roughly 1,000 miles each way, something only about one in 10 British harriers do. Why? No one really knows. But it's dangerous. Apollo was the first British harrier to make it back alive from Spain; the previous nine that made that migration all disappeared.

Not that the United Kingdom is necessarily safer, though certain times of the year are worse than others.

"The dangerous periods are just after fledging, and just before breeding for the first time," Steve said. "It's worst for the males—they wander a lot, they're light-colored, and they have to hunt every day." Dynamo has made it safely to adulthood. But no one on the harrier team ever takes the survival of their nesting birds for granted, even on property like this one, managed as a drinking water catchment by United Utilities, which like Forest England and the National Trust manages huge areas of land and has an enlightened attitude toward harriers.

Dynamo had vanished from sight as we spoke, but then he reappeared and zeroed in on the hidden nest site, from which the female emerged, flying up to meet him. It was hard to be sure at this distance, but they seemed to connect for a moment, most likely as he transferred prey to his mate. Then he was off again, perhaps to go check on his second nest.

"I think that's it for a while here," Steve said. "Let's go see where Dagda was born."

In making the plight of hen harriers more real and meaningful to the broader British public, the RSPB and its allies have a powerful tool: the personalization of the victims. Every year, the society fits between 20 and 25 harrier chicks with satellite tags and, more importantly, gives each one a name. Some might dismiss this as needless anthropomorphizing, but to know a bird as, say, Dynamo or Apollo carries more emotional weight than referring to it by a band number or transmitter ID.

For most of the 18 or 20 chicks Steve Downing tags with transmitters each year, he also chooses their names. His go-to sources are deities, gods and goddesses from around the world and across the span of history. Who can blame him? With the odds stacked so steeply against them, the young raptors need all the divine protection they can get.

Dagda, named for one of the great gods of pre-Christian Ireland, was a male harrier hatched in 2022 in the Bowland Hills, and fitted with a transmitter before he fledged. Once he was independent, his satellite signal showed Dagda ranging widely, up into Scotland, then back to Bowland, into the Yorkshire Dales and Lake District National Parks, then to what is now North Pennines National Landscape. Those are all places dominated by grouse moors, and dangerous ground for a harrier.

The following April, Dagda had moved into one of the few spots where a hen harrier has an unconditional welcome—the RSPB's Geltsdale Nature Reserve on the Cumbria-Northumbria line, barely 20 miles from the Scottish border. Less than a year old, he wasted no time, pairing up with a female who laid a clutch of eggs. But Geltsdale, while itself a sanctuary, is all but surrounded by driven grouse moors. RSPB staff noted early on in the nesting period that Dagda's tail had been damaged in a way suggesting he'd survived a gunshot, and so they were especially concerned when on May 8, 2023, he moved onto a private grouse moor.

"Sometime between 9 and 10 May he was shot dead," the RSPB reported in its 2023 edition of *Birdcrime*. "The RSPB located his body which was recovered from Knarsdale Moor by Northumbria Police and the [National Wildlife Crimes Unit] on 12 May. An expert post-mortem confirmed that Dagda's body contained recent shot (from a shotgun), confirmed to be the cause of death. The post-mortem also indicated that the bird had recovered from an earlier, unknown shooting incident. It also identified damage to his tail, consistent with damage caused by a shotgun. . . . All these injuries prove that Dagda [had] been shot on at least two separate occasions. The last was fatal." He was one of 39 satellite-tagged hen harriers to be killed illegally or die under suspicious circumstances between January 2022 and October 2023, most of them clustered in the same fairly small area on the Cumbria–North Yorkshire border, and up into the neighboring counties of Durham and Northumbria.

"Some places are just the Bermuda Triangle for harriers. The birds go in and never come out," Steve had told me.

No one was ever prosecuted for Dagda's shooting, and Mark Thomas told me that the RSPB had filed an official letter of complaint with the police, which had taken no further action in the case. "It would be difficult to find a more clear-cut case of raptor persecution requiring enforcement," the society argued in its *Birdcrime* report, though it noted: "There is no evidence as to who may have been responsible for the death. For the avoidance of doubt, there is no suggestion that the landowner, their agent or any of their employees was involved in any way."

We circled around through the hills, up one small dirt track after another, parking in a deep, narrow valley and then scrambling, at times almost on all fours, up the steep slope to the left. At length we sank down gratefully with the hill at our backs, our knapsacks as cushions, nibbling snacks, sipping water, and waiting, watching across the valley to where I was assured there was another harrier nest, the one that Dagda and his siblings had come from two years earlier. I followed Steve's instructions—find that big rock, follow the dark draw to the left and up a few hundred meters, the nest is hidden in that large area of heather—but if the female was incubating she was out of sight.

It gave us a chance to talk, and I was especially interested in hearing how Steve handled the relentless bad news, frustrations, and disappointments that come with immersing himself in this work. It must exact a hell of an emotional toll, I said.

"Each one of these cases is a little chip"—he snapped his fingers lightly—"off of you. And another. And another. You have to investigate the case, then move on, or it will just kill you."

"Like a trauma surgeon losing a patient?" I asked?

"Exactly right. You move onto the next case. But that's why a lot of surgeons drink heavily. And police officers, too," he said, with a nod to his former life in the force.

Our patience was eventually rewarded, when the male came swooping in, though this time there was no sign of a prey exchange; the female, if she was down in the heather on the nest, remained there. In touch with Steve some months later, I found that both nests we'd checked in that day had been successful. Dynamo and his mate (well, one of his mates, the one with whom we'd seen him do the prey exchange) had fledged three chicks, two of which were tagged: a female Steve named Sita after the Hindu goddess known for purity and sacrifice, and a male he named Shango, after the Yoruba sky father and thunder god. There were only two males in Dagda's old nest, whom he dubbed Teshub, for the chief deity and god of the weather among the ancient Hurrians of the Bronze Age Near East, and Binbeal, the god of rainbows among the Indigenous Wurundjeri of Australia.

At the same time that the chicks were tagged, they also had a mouth swab taken to collect their DNA. Steve told me he hoped that someday the samples they've collected might be used to explore the lineages and genetic diversity of the country's harriers, but for now they have a more practical and morbid purpose: to confirm the identity of a carcass should it be recovered without bands or a transmitter. Such is the sorry state of harrier conservation in the United Kingdom.

It was time to follow Dagda. Having seen where he was born, I was headed next to where he died—and where life is still perilous for even the boldest harrier.

The Geltsdale RSPB reserve lies on the northwestern edge of the North Pennine Hills, near the small Cumbrian village of Brampton, seven or eight miles east of the city of Carlisle. My guide on this quiet Sunday morning was Ben Dymond, a young and enthusiastic RSPB warden who was assigned temporarily to Geltsdale, which encompasses two old hill farms that the RSPB is managing to create the best conditions for birds, particularly rare species like European golden-plovers, common redshanks, black grouse, ring ouzels, and Eurasian curlews—and for hen harriers, one of Geltsdale's marquee species.

A close, nearly constant, eye is kept on the harriers, as I found when we met a volunteer named Craig manning a tented, camouflaged watch post, spotting scope at the ready, that overlooked one of the two harrier nests at Geltsdale that year. Craig had started helping the previous nesting season, and got immediately hooked on harriers. "The more I've spent time with them, I just sort of fell for them, I suppose. It's a strange thing to say, but I love the way they fly," he said.

But harriers are not timid hunters. Craig said the female of the nest he was watching had been bringing in venomous adders to feed her chicks. Craig was part of the day shift. Between the roughly 15 volunteers like Craig, as well as Ben and two seasonal staff, the RSPB has someone watching the nests 24/7 because the organization has learned the hard way that some people will go to great lengths to kill harriers. The previous year, 2023, was the first time since 1999 that harriers had successfully produced chicks at Geltsdale, although after Dagda was killed, his mate abandoned their nest and its chicks, only one of which fledged thanks to supplementary feeding by the reserve staff. Fortunately, another pair at Geltsdale fledged four babies, though one of them, a female named Saranyu, was among two dozen tagged hen harriers that wound up missing or dead that year.

"This is the first time I've worked with a species people are actually trying to kill. I was watching Dagda in May when he disappeared—that hit me hard," Ben said.

The second nest was a long, leg-stretching hike to the top of Haltonlea Fell, climbing straight upslope, then along a rough path through wet sphagnum moss that sucked at our boots. At length we reached a hide on the flat top of the fell, with yet higher slopes beyond rising to the summit of Blackburn Head. We settled in, and Ben took me through the usual find-the-rock-and-go-up series of directions until he got me more or less focused on where this nest was hidden, about three-quarters of a mile away.

It was, I could see, frighteningly close to the reserve boundary, marked by a fence, beyond which lay Knarsdale Moor, the property on which Dagda had been found dead. Of course, to a bird, fences and property lines mean nothing, and the society had hoped to create more of a buffer. A large lowland property to the north had come up for sale the previous year, Ben said, a place that harriers use for their communal roosts, and the RSPB had tried to acquire it to expand Geltsdale, but it was instead snatched up by one of the estates for commercial pheasant hunts, further reducing the zone of safety for the reserve's harriers.[*]

It wasn't long before the ghostly, almost white male came into view;

---

[*] In early 2025 the RSPB announced that it had secured the purchase of land at Geltsdale that it had long been only leasing, expanding the size of the reserve by one-third to almost 13,600 acres, making it the largest RSPB holding in England.

he is unbanded and has no transmitter, and so does not have a nickname. We watched him passing prey to the female, and he was a watchful guardian, for when two buzzards soared into view, the male went on the immediate attack, harassing one of them mercilessly until both buteos had fled the area. I expressed surprise at how visible he was, even at that distance, all but glowing against the dark green-gray of the heather.

"I guess that's why they're so easy to shoot," Ben said quietly.

Desperate times call for desperate measures. In addition to supplementary feeding if one of the adults disappears, the RSPB has tried diversionary feeding, putting dead, captive-reared quail carcasses on fence posts where the adult harriers can find them. Not every pair will take the offerings, but those that do may not be forced to hunt as far, or to go off the reserve. Even if the food isn't shared with the chicks, it may mean the male doesn't have to go off hunting for himself.

It's a huge investment to protect a bird that should, like many other British raptors, be thriving. Based on how much suitable habitat is available, experts say there's room for roughly 300 pairs of hen harriers in England, were they not being killed. When I later asked Mark Thomas for an estimate on what the society spends each year to safeguard the hen harriers it watches over, he guessed that between the investigations costs and satellite tags, it's more than £375,000 a year (roughly $460,000 at this writing), which wouldn't include staff time for, say, a reserve employee like Ben Dymond.

Proponents of intensive red grouse management often point to other upland birds that benefit from the moors, including declining species like European golden-plover, Eurasian curlew, and northern lapwing, which are among the few that prefer to nest in burned and heavily managed, predator-controlled heather uplands. They also stress the economic benefits of grouse moors, which provide employment in rural communities for gamekeepers, ghillies (hunting guides), beaters, loaders, and others.

It's an argument many on the conservation side dismiss. Naturalist and author Benedict Macdonald, in his 2019 book *Rebirding: Restoring Britain's Wildlife*, did a deep dive into the employment and economic figures surrounding driven grouse moors and found a stark difference when compared with nature tourism.

Macdonald quotes reports from the grouse-shooting industry and its supporters that place the total number of full-time jobs or their equivalent on both English and Scottish grouse moors at 2,592; of these, 1,520 are in England and 1,072 in Scotland. Spread across almost 6,500 square miles (more than 16,700 square kilometers) of British grouse moors—an area, Macdonald notes, that is twice the size of Yellowstone National Park—that equates to one job for every 2.5 square miles (6.5 square kilometers). The economic impact of those roughly 1,100 Scottish grouse-moor jobs was estimated by industry allies at £23.3 million in 2016, catering to roughly 40,000 shooters.

"Millions always sound like a lot, if taken out of context," Macdonald writes. "The UK, however, the fifth-largest economy in the world by GDP, was worth, in 2016, $2.647 trillion, or £1.88 trillion at the time of this writing. . . . In England, the Moorland Association estimates that the economic value of the grouse-shooting industry is £67.7 million. . . . That brings the combined contribution of grouse shooting, in England and Scotland, to less than 0.005% of the United Kingdom's GDP, a contribution made from 8% of its land!"

By contrast, Macdonald notes that National Parks England during the same period produced 48,000 full-time job equivalents, while osprey-watching sites alone attracted 290,000 people a year. Nature tourism in England was worth £21 billion annually, and another £1.4 billion in Scotland.

Rebirding is a book shot through with a simmering sense of righteous indignation at what he sees as the long mismanagement of Great Britain's land and wildlife heritage, but that anger rarely flares hotter than in Macdonald's attacks on the grouse-shooting industry. "Eight percent of a nation's land, burned by 0.0003% of its population for 0.0008% of its jobs and under 0.005% of its economy, is a destructive national embarrassment," he writes.

Yet in the end the wildlife, especially raptors, pays the heaviest price. Overall, 2024 was another poor year for hen harriers in England. Only 34 pairs nested, down from 53 the year before and 49 in 2022. Of those 34 pairs, only 25 fledged any chicks.

I have to admit, I held my breath every time we watched that unnamed male harrier drift toward the Geltsdale boundary line, and I released it each time he veered off and headed in a different direction. What I didn't yet know is that he and his mate had four chicks in their nest, as did the pair that Craig was watching across the valley, and that both would bring off their large families successfully. It's a remarkable achievement in the face of so much opposition, and a bright spot in a dark year. But it was made all the more astounding when Steve Downing emailed me photos of the male with what appear to be in my eyes the perfectly round holes of bird shot in the flight feathers of both his wings.

"You can see how much damage there is on the grey male's feathers. It's inconceivable that he is not carrying shot in his body, too," Steve wrote. The same thing had happened to Dagda, before that bird was shot a second time and killed; it's incredible how these hawks soldier on despite their wounds. A bird this tenacious, which perseveres against such odds even with buckshot in its body, deserves a decent chance. The question is, what can be done to stop the killing? For a while it appeared Scotland might finally have shown the way.

Law enforcement has clearly failed hen harriers, golden eagles, and the other persecuted raptors of the United Kingdom. Even when the RSPB and its allies obtain what they would consider to be incontrovertible evidence of wrongdoing, up to and including videos and eyewitnesses, the official police response is often seen to be sluggish or nonexistent. I'm an ex-reporter and thus a cynic, and I realize much of that inaction can almost certainly be chalked up to what I see as the degree to which wealthy and well-connected landowners influence the behavior of local officials; it was ever thus. Without proof of an individual's direct involvement in a shooting, trapping, or poisoning case, prosecution is almost never pursued, and even when it is, the penalties are often laughably light. Estate owners can easily shrug off and deny any involvement, though I can imagine none would be anxious to welcome investigators who might actually solve the crimes.

British conservationists have for years argued that the simplest solution is to hold grouse moor managers and owners responsible for what happens on their properties through a licensing system. Estates would need a government license to offer commercial driven shoots, but that license could be revoked in the face of incidents like raptor deaths. If, as the estates routinely swear, they have no involvement in such persecution events, they would presumably have a powerful interest in patrolling their own lands to see that no one is killing birds of prey there, or trespassing to do so, if only to preserve their license to shoot.

While my focus to this point has primarily been on England, Scotland has a long and equally unenviable record of raptor persecution, too, much of it similarly focused on land managed for grouse shooting. The targeted species are a bit different—hen harriers, certainly, but especially golden eagles and buzzards, along with goshawks and red kites. Ironically, Scotland also holds the largest population of British hen harriers, which the RSPB's 2023 hen harrier survey put at 529 territorial pairs, a 15 percent increase since the previous survey in 2016. Those harriers, however, occur in parts of Scotland where there are red grouse but no grouse-shooting moors, like the Orkney Islands off the northern coast, the Hebrides off the west coast, and parts of the western Highlands. The story is far different in places where commercial driven hunts occur; in the Southern Uplands, the region north of the English border that includes the Cheviot Hills, harrier numbers have fallen 32 percent since 2016, and across four "special protection areas" ostensibly maintained for harriers by the government agency NatureScot, only a single pair could be found.

The 2017 Scottish Natural Heritage study I mentioned earlier, which found that roughly one-third of 131 satellite-tagged young golden eagles had disappeared under suspicious circumstances, prompted the Scottish government that year to convene an expert panel to consider whether more stringent steps were needed to protect raptors. Two years later the committee, the Grouse Moor Management Group, issued its findings.

The panel unanimously recommended the institution of a licensing scheme "if, within five years from . . . publishing this report, there is no marked improvement in the ecological sustainability of grouse moor management, as evidenced by the populations of breeding Golden Eagles, Hen Harriers and Peregrines on or within the vicinity of grouse moors being in favourable condition." The report also called for tighter controls on the practice of muirburn, the seasonal moor burning, which has been harshly criticized for damaging peatlands that are critical carbon sinks, and for killing wildlife when land managers ignore best-practice codes and burn during the nesting season.

By 2022, it was clear there had been no such marked improvement in raptor persecution, and the legislative wheels began to turn. In March 2023, the Wildlife Management and Muirburn Bill was introduced in the Scottish Parliament, eventually passing in March 2024 over the objections of conservatives and the shooting lobby. The bill instituted licensing for grouse moors, and it expanded the authority of officers of the Scottish Society for the Prevention of Cruelty to Animals (SSPCA), which unlike the RSPB has statutory power to enter premises and search for evidence, to investigate wildlife crimes—an alternative to local authorities who might be otherwise occupied or choose to ignore or slow-walk investigations.

Conservation groups, which have been pushing for grouse-moor licensing for years, hailed the decision in Scotland, and renewed their efforts to pressure the English Parliament to follow suit. But before long, closed-door efforts were under way in Scotland to drastically water down the new law, and by late 2024 the enforcing agency, NatureScot, announced that any estate applying for the license could also specify—meaning limit—the area to which the license would apply. NatureScot might say it would "expect" that the license would apply to the full grouse moor, but that decision would be left to people with a strong incentive to restrict the license to the smallest possible area, potentially leaving thousands of acres of the same estate unregulated.

In England, where a petition drive to outlaw driven grouse shooting has been slowly gaining ground and may eventually force a parliamentary debate, initial hopes that the Labour government would be more sympathetic to raptor conservation than the Conservative government that preceded it proved unfounded.

Still, the last time I spoke with Mark Thomas he, like the harriers, is soldiering on. "One day it will change," he said. "I know one day it will change." British raptors aren't the only tenacious ones in this fight.

Four

The Nightingales of Knepp

It's one thing to protect a bird like hen harriers where the problem is clear, and for which the solution is in some respects fairly straightforward: vigorous enforcement of the laws already on the books. But for dozens of other species of declining birds, the problems are more diffuse—the intersections of habitat loss, international agricultural policy, changing land use, development, demographic shifts, and more.

Yet all across Europe, people are trying to harness the power of nature to heal itself. On a journey that took me from the British Isles to the wildest mountain range in southern Europe, from the edge of Ukraine's war zone to remote Bulgarian forests, people are trying to restore functioning ecosystems at landscape scale, and in doing so throwing a lifeline to the continent's increasingly beleaguered birdlife. It's a growing success, but still, I did not expect that the first bird I would see on the English leg of my travels would be a species that had last lived in Great Britain in the 15th century.

And yet as I exited the A24 near the village of Dial Post, in West Sussex in southeastern England, I glanced up to see an enormous white bird with black flight feathers and the wingspan of an eagle, a bright red rapier of a beak, and long, trailing red legs, gliding serenely past me not all that far above the windscreen of my rental car—which in my shock I very nearly drove off the macadam.

There is remarkably little known about the history of white storks in the United Kingdom. The last generally accepted record comes from the 1410s in Edinburgh, Scotland, where a pair reportedly nested on St. Giles Cathedral. For the better part of six centuries, it appears the only wild storks in England were the occasional wanderers from across the English Channel in Europe, where they have remained relatively common, nesting on chimneys, street lamps, and yes, church roofs. But their successful return to England, where in just a few years they have reestablished themselves in thriving colonies, is just one example of how the movement known as rewilding is transforming parts of the United Kingdom and Europe for the betterment of birds, and a great deal more.

There are layers of irony enmeshed in rewilding. It's a word that means many different and at times highly divisive things to different and often highly divided people. It is a movement centered in Europe but a term that meant something very different when it was coined in North America, and where I have been surprised by how little awareness there is, even among US and Canadian conservationists, of how powerful a force it's become across the Atlantic. In its most frequently articulated European form, rewilding's goal is to create functional, sustainable natural systems that support rich, wild biodiversity that do not require intensive human management. In order to do so, however, it often relies on domestic livestock—feral, free-ranging, and usually heritage breeds—that serve as analogues for now-extinct species like the wild ox of Europe, the aurochs, or the extinct Pleistocene horse, the tarpan—or, in some cases, uses iconic native species themselves, animals that had become extinct in the wild or were extirpated for centuries.

Rewilding has had many parents, but one can make a good case that its current notoriety and momentum owes much to the place I would be visiting for the next few days—the Knepp Wildland, which started as one couple's Hail Mary attempt to stave off agricultural bankruptcy but which has become a globally famous example of how a badly bruised and depauperate farming landscape can recover, in shockingly quick order, to become an oasis of life and diversity. That this happened in England, which by some measures is the most nature-deficient part of the United Kingdom, which is in turn arguably the most nature-deficient country in Europe and one of the nature-poorest in the world, makes that success all the more dazzling.

Keeping my eyes firmly on the road, I made a few turns and drove back a long gravel lane that brings visitors to what Knepp has become today. The car park was filled with vehicles, lots of day-trippers and dog-walkers, and one or two organized groups of visitors. The shop sold books and mugs and many of the usual gifty-tchotchke things, but also the estate's free-range beef and venison and produce from its market garden. Beyond and down some steps, a new Wilding Café had opened, though that term seemed insufficient to the lofty building with exposed, repurposed wooden beams that housed it.

I'd have time for that later; now I wanted to see how almost 25 years and the application of some then-revolutionary approaches, using the teeth and hooves and hunger of large mammals, had transformed marginal and profitless farmland into an ark of recovery for some of Britain's rarest and most beloved native birds and other wildlife. Despite the hour—it was early afternoon on a warmish, mid-May day—the thornscrub and woodlands along the loop trails were thrumming with birdsong and movement: Eurasian robins and Eurasian blackbirds were ubiquitous, chiffchaffs were common, and my walk was enlivened by an entertaining mix of chaffinches with their blue-gray heads and orange breasts, dull brown dunnocks, Eurasian blackcaps, frenetic greater whitethroats flitting through the underbrush, and song thrushes, one of these last perched on a dead oak branch, singing constantly changing phrases that put me in mind of a northern mockingbird back home.

The trail passed through fields gone fallow, grazed by the estate's herds of free-ranging Old English Longhorn cattle, many of which were suckling new calves. I passed along dense hedgerows, many of them anchored by heavy-trunked oaks, the most quintessentially English of trees. I rounded a bend and found a huge pig, a Tamworth

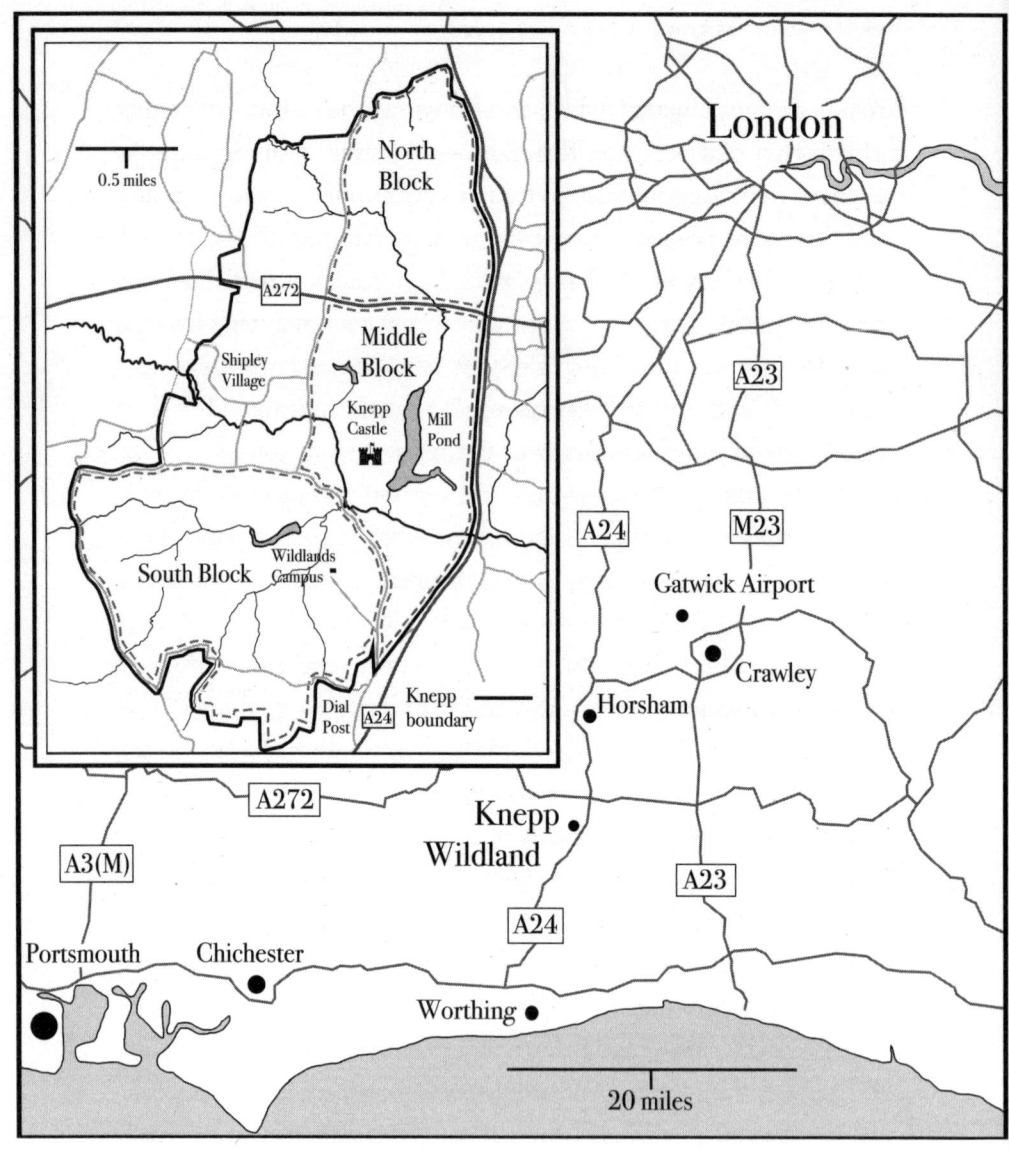

The Knepp Wildlands, where what had been marginal farmland has become a beacon for British rewilding and the recovery of rare species.

sow brick-orange and solid as a boulder, quietly grubbing for food just off the path while three or four of her piglets lay in a contented heap in the grass, soaking up the dim sunshine.

The cows, the pigs, and the red, roe, and fallow deer, and Exmoor ponies that I knew were somewhere around if not immediately in sight, have been foundational to creating Knepp. Since the early 2000s

Knepp's owners, Charles Burrell and his wife Isabella Tree, have transformed what had been Charlie's failing ancestral family farm into a mecca for wildlife enthusiasts. Turning away from intensive agriculture, and from heavy-handed management of any sort, they fought for years for the chance to show that working with nature, giving it the reins, can be both ecologically and economically rewarding, a story Issy Tree told in her best-selling 2018 book, *Wilding*. The Knepp Wildland Project is the proof of that groundbreaking pudding.

But the Knepp Wildland's success grew out of desperation, and a growing recognition on Issy's and Charlie's parts that something was deeply, deeply wrong with Britain's relationship with its land. How wrong? An exhaustive 2023 "State of Nature" report compiled by a collaboration of 70 British conservation and research organizations found that for each of the four countries that compose the United Kingdom (England, Scotland, Wales, and Northern Ireland), as well as overseas territories and Crown dependencies, there has been a general erosion in biodiversity from top to bottom, vertebrates to lichens. Despite lofty goals, like the 30x30 initiative to set aside 30 percent of any given country's land and water for conservation by 2030, just 11 percent of the land in Great Britain is in some form of legal conservation protection—and in 2024 the amount judged "effectively protected" in England itself had actually fallen, to less than 3 percent.

For birds, the news has been mixed. Rare or newly colonizing bird species like Eurasian spoonbills, Eurasian bitterns, and common cranes have increased, in some cases dramatically, thanks to wetlands restoration. But the report also notes that those rare and colonizing species make up only one tenth of 1 percent of Britain's birdlife. The populations of 125 common breeding species fell 14 percent overall since 1970, while farmland birds specifically declined by almost 60 percent—figures distressingly similar to what's happened in North America. In all, 43 percent of Great Britain's 243 native bird species are to some degree threatened, endangered, or are already extinct there. This includes species that were once so abundant, widespread, and beloved, like common nightingales and European turtledoves, that they and their songs are essentially synonymous with rural England. Yet these are among the species now most at risk of disappearing entirely from the country, as once-abundant red-backed shrikes have all but done.

Turn back the clock about 25 years, and the 3,500-acre Knepp Castle Estate wasn't part of the solution, it was part of the problem. Since the late 18th century Knepp and the hereditary baronetcy that went along with it—Charlie is Sir Charles Burrell, 10th baronet—has been in the possession of Charlie's family, which had roots in Sussex back to at least the 15th century. Issy, a respected nature and travel writer, and Charlie took over operation of the estate's dairy and cropland operations in 1987 when he inherited it from his grandfather. (Because Charlie's father made an alternate farming life in Australia, the inheritance skipped a generation.) He and Issy spent more than a decade trying and failing to make mechanized, industrialized, chemically dependent agriculture pay for itself on land that should never have been plowed. In the end, rewilding was born out of despair.

There are in places more than 300 meters—almost a thousand feet—of clay under most of Knepp, the worst possible stuff to farm, which is why most of West Sussex was pasture land or deer park time out of mind. Despite that, during and after World War II, when food independence and security were considered vital national interests, Charlie's great-grandfather set an example. Knepp's thorny thickets were chained flat into fields, its ancient oaks cut to open still more land for planting, and what had been deer park or grazing land for thousands of years was plowed for row crops. But the soil forms an impervious layer. When it rains, the water sluices off instead of percolating down; when it doesn't rain, the ground becomes cracked hardpan. Any gardener knows what a nightmare it is to try to raise things in clay. Even for someone with Charlie's experience and savvy, having grown up on his parents' farm in New South Wales, Australia, and studied at the Royal Agricultural University, there was no way to make the farm work. When they took over, Charlie found to his shock that the only thing giving it the appearance of solvency was the rapidly dwindling family money that had plugged the disparity between income and expenses for generations.

Still, for most of the next 15 years he and Issy tried to make Knepp a paying proposition, progressively intensifying their operations, experimenting with new crops and approaches, trying to create new markets, but only digging themselves deeper into debt. By 1999 it was clear: if they continued on this course they would utterly bankrupt themselves. In 2000, they swallowed hard and sold off their dairy herds and farm machinery to try to stanch the financial bleeding, and set about trying to do something very different with some of the land.

Just as Charlie and Issy closed the book on intensive farming, the UK government was rolling out a new program to underwrite the costs of restoring land like Knepp's 350-acre former deer park that had been cleared after World War II. With that funding, they planted the old park with native meadow seed collected locally. As it blossomed, literally and figuratively, they fenced it and brought in fallow deer—not native to Britain, but present since at least the time of the Romans—to graze and browse.

But these were preliminaries to the seminal event in Knepp's transformation, when Charlie and Issy met Frans Vera, a Dutch biologist whose controversial research and writing had upended the conventional wisdom about Europe's ecology after the ice ages—and thus, what constitutes "natural" for much of the continent. Rather than the deep, closed-canopy forests long assumed to be the original postglacial, pre-Neolithic condition of central and western Europe and the British Isles, Vera hypothesized that even after the Pleistocene megafauna like mammoths and woolly rhinoceroses became extinct, the remaining large European mammals—among them red deer, moose (elk, in European terminology), European bison, European beaver, aurochs, tarpan, and wild boar—maintained through their grazing, browsing, chewing, and rooting a generally open mosaic of woodlands, marsh, and grassy savannahs.

Vera was instrumental in the late 1970s and early 1980s in the creation of a unique nature reserve in the north of the Netherlands,

Oostvaardersplassen, where he and others were able to put his theory into practice. The 14,000-acre tract was a polder, an area of land reclaimed from the sea (or, in this case, what had once been an inlet of the sea, itself dammed off to make a freshwater lake), originally slated to become farmland and industrial sites. But when marsh vegetation established itself and tens of thousands of migrating geese began using it, it became a reserve, and the perfect place to see whether Vera's ideas about the impact of large herbivores on the landscape had any merit.

While the aurochs and the tarpan are extinct, their descendants (domestic cattle in the case of the aurochs) or close relatives (domestic horses in the case of the tarpan) are still around. So Vera and his colleagues turned to the nearest equivalents to those lost species—what are known as Heck cattle, a hardy breed established in the 1930s by, and named for, two German brothers who back-crossed varieties of heritage cattle to approximate something of the size and form of the wild ox.* They also acquired Konik horses, small, sturdy ponies from Poland once thought to be descended from the tarpan, though DNA testing has more recently dispelled that notion. Red deer from Scotland completed the trio of large mammals brought to the reserve between 1983 and 1992 (roe deer were already present).

The newcomers flourished, creating the conditions Vera had predicted, preventing the incursion of woody plants, helping maintain a mix of habitats for many of the birds. Easily accessible (a rail line

---

* The politics of the elder Heck brother, Lutz, is the enduring stain on Heck cattle, given that Lutz was an enthusiastic Nazi supporter and party member, a friend of Reichmarshall Hermann Göring and propaganda minister Joseph Goebbels. His younger brother Heinz was not, and in fact was interned in the 1930s at Dachau (not yet an extermination camp, but built initially to hold political prisoners) under suspicion he had Communist ties, and for his earlier marriage to a Jewish woman. While the Heck cattle project is sometimes cast as a Nazi effort to promote an ur-Aryan primeval Germany, the backcross work began in the 1920s, from what seems to have been a purely zoological curiosity by the brothers. But the Heck cattle never more than vaguely approximated the size and build of the original aurochs.

runs along the edge of the preserve, and Amsterdam is just half an hour away), it attracted more and more visitors, and more and more international attention. Oostvaardersplassen became known as "the Serengeti behind a dike."

As we'll see, the bloom did not remain on Oostvaardersplassen permanently, but when Charlie Burrell and Issy Tree first saw it with Frans Vera in the early 2001 it seemed both like a glimpse of an earlier epoch in European history and a peek at what might be possible at Knepp. Inspired, they mapped out an audacious plan to create, as they said in their 2002 letter of intent to English Nature, "a biodiverse wilderness area on the Low Weald of Sussex." ("Weald" is a Saxon word meaning "forest.")

As Issy later admitted, they were shooting for the moon, seeking funding for their own mini-Oostvaardersplassen complete not only with Heck cattle and feral horses, but also European bison, European beavers, and wild boars. Government bureaucrats initially took a rather jaundiced view of their enthusiastic plans before eventually signing off on a staged rewilding, using British equivalents for missing Neolithic herbivores—not Heck cattle but Old English Longhorns, and Exmoor ponies that grow thick, shaggy coats and are as tough as nails. Red deer joined the fallow and roe deer already on the estate, with the Tamworth pigs substituting for wild boar.

It took years of slowly, painfully convincing bureaucrats and funders, but with time Issy and Charlie installed large perimeter fences and pulled down endless miles of interior fencing, culverts, and other remnants from the farming era to create what became three great habitat blocks: Northern, Middle, and Southern. In stages, with fits and starts and headaches and hiccups along the way, they let the land relax, molded into something new by the constantly shifting tension between herbivores and plant succession. Among the most important components of the new landscape were species like blackthorn and hawthorn, the kind of habitat denigrated as "scrub," which not only provided sheltering habitat for myriad species of birds and invertebrates, but within whose needled thickets, guarded from nibbling teeth, young oaks sprouted and grew.

They learned the hard way to trust nature. When Knepp was hit with a multiyear explosion of creeping thistle (known as Canada thistle in North America) that overran more and more of the property, local naysayers felt vindicated, as the stuff is reviled as a pernicious weed, and critics had already savaged the Knepp effort in public and private for encouraging other species like common ragwort that are considered noxious by farmers. But just as Issy and Charlie were about to throw up their hands, millions of painted lady butterflies swarmed north to Britain from their wintering areas in northern Africa, laying eggs on the thistles, one of their prime host plants. The ravenous painted lady caterpillars soon made short work of the thistle infestation, which was entirely gone in short order. Providential? Perhaps, or perhaps just a case of nature doing what nature does, swinging a pendulum.

By the late 2000s, Knepp was building a richer and richer living library of diversity. Rare birds like skylarks and wood larks appeared in growing numbers, as did other species more widespread but still in nationwide decline. The number and diversity of bats grew, feeding as they did on the rising diversity and abundance of invertebrates, 60 species of which were considered of conservation importance, most notably the rare purple emperor, a gorgeous and elusive butterfly, the second-largest in Britain. At Knepp this butterfly, which draws lepidoptera enthusiasts like a magnet, has formed what is by far the largest colony in Britain, and is now the symbol of the Knepp Wildland Project.

While all this was happening at Knepp, the rewilding movement was gathering steam elsewhere in the United Kingdom and across Europe, aiming not at single estates but expansive landscapes, although in a form that those who first coined the term more than 30 years ago and an ocean away would not necessarily have recognized.

Ironically, given the still rather low profile European-style rewilding has in the United States and Canada, it was an American who first coined the term. The late Dave Foreman, the sometimes polarizing founder of the direct-action, self-described radical environmental group Earth First!, wrote in a 1992 essay, "It is time to rewild North America; it is past time to reweave the full fabric of life on our continent." Foreman and others in the 1980s and '90s saw what he called rewilding as a way to connect existing disjunct natural lands through corridors and buffer zones, an outgrowth of a desire to facilitate what some called wilderness recovery, restoring large carnivores that would sit at the pinnacle of expansive, functioning ecosystems.

But in the decades since then, the term "rewilding" has come to hold almost contradictory meanings depending on location and context. To some people it means reintroducing top-level predators to reorder the local food chain and carnivore hierarchy, much as happened in Yellowstone when gray wolves were returned in 1995. To others, rewilding refers to a more hands-off approach, passively letting nature reassert control over landscapes being abandoned by humans—a situation playing out across immense areas of Europe, for example, where rural depopulation and mass land abandonment affects millions of hectares of former small-scale farmland and pasture. Some people think rewilding is accomplished by allowing hedgerows and field margins to revert while maintaining commercial agriculture; others see it as a complete turn away from almost any human management of the landscape.

In 1998, an essay by the renowned conservation biologists Michael E. Soulé and Reed F. Noss encapsulated what can be thought of as the North American approach to rewilding, boiling it down to what became known as the Three Cs: Cores (large, protected reserves), Corridors (protected or restored habitat connecting the cores), and Carnivores (the apex predators like grizzly bears and gray wolves that are most often missing from protected wildlands). Perhaps the most audacious example of this approach (and one that actually preceded their call to action) is the transnational Yellowstone to Yukon Conservation Initiative, known as Y2Y, envisioned as an interlocking ribbon of cores and corridors running along the northern Rocky Mountains between Yellowstone National Park in the United States and ending more than 2,000 miles to the north in the Yukon wilderness of western Canada. In the more than 30 years since it was proposed in 1993, Y2Y has made significant progress, including a near-doubling of the area of protected land within its aspirational boundaries, one-quarter of it managed by Indigenous communities.

In 2006, Foreman and Soulé joined nearly a dozen academics and government scientists to propose "Pleistocene rewilding," an attempt to recreate North America's Ice Age assemblage of large mammals—or as close as possible, given that most of the continent's megafauna became extinct 12,000 or more years ago. This is the aurochs-Heck cattle idea on steroids. In the absence of North America's five vanished species of mammoths and mastodons, they suggested using Asian or African elephants; instead of the two species of extinct American cheetahs, they suggested substituting African cheetahs. Noting that some taxonomists consider all lions, including the huge extinct American variety, to belong to the same Holarctic species, they recommended using African lions as a proxy. To feral domestic horses already roaming the West, they would add several species of camelids like Old World dromedaries and South American guanacos and vicuñas, as well as Bolsón tortoises, a 180-pound species historically widespread across the Southwest but today critically endangered and restricted to parts of the Mexican Chihuahuan Desert.

The plan would not be without potential pitfalls. "Risks of Pleistocene rewilding include the possibility of altered disease ecology and associated human health implications, as well as unexpected ecological and sociopolitical consequences of reintroductions," the authors admitted—presumably including the sociopolitical consequence of, say, African lions eating people.

So far, the only step toward Pleistocene rewilding in America has been the reintroduction of Bolsón tortoises to private land in New Mexico. But in northern Siberia, even before the American paper was published, a Russian scientist named Sergey Zimov was trying to make the same concept a reality. The founder of the Northeast Science Station along the Kolyma River, Zimov had as early as 1988 been experimenting with a small herd of burly Yakutian horses endemic to that part of Siberia, believing that the restoration of large herds of grazing and browsing mammals could re-create conditions for the grassy "mammoth steppe" that once covered the area in the Pleistocene, but which was replaced by shrub-dominated tundra and taiga after the megafaunal extinctions. Reestablishing the mammoth steppe, Zimov thought, would serve as barrier to permafrost melting and the release of vast quantities of soil-bound methane that could dangerously exacerbate climate change; grasslands reflect more sunlight than shrubs and trees, and he believed grazing animals trampling the snow would allow the ground to freeze much more deeply, preserving permafrost.

The collapse of the Soviet Union in 1991 brought that initial effort to an end, but by 1996, Zimov had acquired about 35,000 acres from the Russian government and launched what he called Pleistocene Park, a deliberate nod to the movie *Jurassic Park*. Fencing off about 5,000 acres, he and his son Nikita, who now runs the park, eventually introduced Yakutian horses, Kalmykian cows (another winter-hardy heritage breed), yaks, both European and American bison, moose, sheep, goats, and musk oxen. The results have been mixed at best; many of the animals have struggled to survive without supplemental feeding, but the father and son believe the grazing is shifting the steppe to more and more grass.

The notion of releasing elephants on the shortgrass prairie of Montana may seem silly on its face, but these Pleistocene rewilding concepts are arguing for at least doing *something*, and doing it big. Conservation has for more than a century been a game of rearguard actions, delaying tactics, managed retreats, and an occasional small advance or victory. Really big ideas that engage the imagination of the general public have been rare, and rewilding—whether it means creating a connected network of protected land across thousands of miles, like Y2Y, or re-creating a pseudo–Ice Age megafauna—offers undeniably big ideas. In fact, the subtitle of the 2006 paper calling for an American Pleistocene Park was "An Optimistic Agenda for Twenty-first Century Conservation." Optimism is in awfully short supply, and a vision of a richer, wilder, more complete natural world, growing in diversity and stability alongside us, instead of steadily diminishing in the face of humanity, is a powerful one.

Ironically, one of the most damaging reversals to that optimism in Europe came at Oostvaardersplassen itself, the "the Serengeti behind a dike" in the Netherlands. The reserve quickly gained notoriety for its birdlife, attracting huge numbers of breeding and migrant waterbirds. White-tailed eagles, once extirpated from western Europe, began nesting, and tens of thousands of migratory geese settled in. In 1989, it was designated a globally important wetland under the international Ramsar Treaty. But given its fairly restricted size, complete isolation, and lack of predators, there was no control on the ever-growing population of grazing mammals. No control, that is, other than starvation, and the reserve's management, including Frans Vera, was determined to let nature run its course.

The result was foreseeably grim, with repeated winters of mass mortality starting in 2011–12. The worst occurred during the winter of 2017–18, when only about 2,000 of the more than 5,200 animals in the reserve were still alive the next spring, most of the rest having been shot by the Dutch state forestry department to prevent further suffering by the emaciated beasts. The ill-feeling generated by the debacle continues to this day in some quarters, with critics arguing that a fourth rewilding C was needed along with the original three: compassion.

The Dutch forestry service Staatsbosbeheer now manages Oostvaardersplassen as part of Nieuw Land National Park, and after the most recent starvation incident plotted a new course for the reserve, based on recommendations from international commissions in 2005 and 2010, and an external steering committee in 2018, brought in to evaluate the reserve's operations. The ungulate herds today are regularly reduced by relocation or culling to keep the number at a much lower level which does not require artificial feeding, and in late 2024 the forestry service decided to remove all of the remaining 70 Konik horses. Vera has condemned the changes to the press, but is no longer involved with the reserve.

That's just one way in which the term "rewilding" has become a lightning rod. There is a lot of tension in the United Kingdom between rewilding advocates and traditional agricultural interests, ingrained ideas in the public mind about what constitutes a "natural" landscape, and how to balance nature conservation with food production. The flip side of the coin are arguments that the small-scale changes that places like Knepp represent are too modest to warrant the term. Even Issy and Charlie, and the advisory team of experts they had assembled to help guide the Knepp project, struggled initially with the polarizing terminology. "Should we, perhaps, just call it 'wilding'?" she wrote, looking back on those arguments. "Could we really describe what we were doing on a relatively small parcel of post-agricultural land sandwiched between the creeping conurbations of Horsham and Worthing, under the Gatwick [Airport] stacking-system, crisscrossed by roads and with no apex predators as 'wild?'"

Controversies aside, serious momentum behind rewilding was building across continental Europe, springing (ironically enough) from the same small country that was wrestling with the Oostvaardersplassen. In 2008, an array of nature NGOs convened in the Netherlands to discuss pursuing rewilding on a serious scale. In 2011, Rewilding Europe was formally established as a Dutch charity, its work coalescing around 10 rewilding "landscapes," as their focus areas are known, ranging from Swedish Lapland and the Affric Highlands in Scotland to the central Apennine Mountains in Italy, the Oder River delta on the German-Polish border (where moose have returned from Poland), and the immense and bird-rich Danube River delta shared between Romania, Ukraine, and Moldova. In-country affiliates run the restoration work on the ground with support, funding, and direction from the Dutch head office.

As in Knepp and many other rewilding schemes, most of the work on these landscapes revolves around the return of large herbivores, either wild species, as in Swedish Lapland where the goal is to eventually supplement the carefully managed reindeer herds of the Indigenous Sami people with wild forest reindeer, European bison, and musk ox. European bison have already been reintroduced in places like the eastern Rhodope Mountains of Bulgaria and Romania's southern Carpathian Mountains (a region Charlie has long been involved in through a different charity, Foundation Conservation Carpathia, although he is now also on a supervisory board for Rewilding Europe). Red, fallow, and roe deer are also commonly reintroduced or their historically low numbers reinforced with additional stocking.

On other rewilding landscapes, domestic analogues are being employed. Rather than Heck cattle, most rewilding projects today use a different, more recent back-bred form of pseudo-aurochs known as Tauros cattle, descended largely from ancient Iberian and eastern European breeds, as well as a variety of semiwild, heritage horses and ponies like Koniks, Carpathian ponies known as Huculs, Karakachan ponies from Bulgaria, and the Exmoor ponies used at Knepp and at rewilding projects in the Netherlands. In a few places, rewilders have turned to the two remaining wild equids, the Przewalski's horse or takhi of central Asia, which became extinct in the wild during the late 20th century, and the kulan, a wild ass that, like Przewalski's horse, was originally found on the Eurasian steppe, but until recently had been restricted to parts of Turkmenistan. Przewalski's horse and kulan have been used for rewilding in the Iberian highlands of Spain, while kulans have been reintroduced to the Tarutino Steppe in Ukraine, part of the Danube Delta rewilding landscape.

What do all these large grazers have to do with birds? In part, as at Knepp, they are expected to create a mosaic of habitats with their appetites, hooves, and wallowing bodies. But for some especially threatened larger birds, their dead bodies will be the main attraction. Vultures are among the most endangered group of birds in the world, and vulture restoration is a primary rewilding goal in places like the Iberian highlands and the Rhodope Mountains, where reintroductions of missing apex scavengers like huge cinereous vultures are underway. One obstacle to their recovery, however, is a lack of food, since game populations tend to be fairly sparse, and under EU regulations meant to curb the spread of mad cow disease, farmers have long been required to bury or incinerate dead livestock. Rewilded herbivores, on the other hand, can remain after death as vulture food. In other places, like the Danube Delta, the second-largest wetland in Europe, bird conservation and restoration is a primary goal, with grazing animals providing the necessary means of habitat alteration.

Rewilding Europe is by no means the only game in town. There is a rapidly expanding network of other, unaffiliated rewilding projects working at many levels, from a single property like Knepp to entire regions. Conservationists in Scotland have set as a goal of theirs becoming the first rewilded nation by 2030, with efforts like Cairngorms Connect in the Highlands, the largest rewilding project in the United Kingdom, uniting large land-owning partners like RSPB Scotland and agencies including NatureScot and Forestry and Land Scotland on 600 square kilometers (230 square miles) of land within Cairngorms National Park.

In Sussex, there are plans to magnify the impact of smaller rewilding projects like Knepp through an initiative called Weald to Waves, in which Issy and Charlie are deeply involved with dozens of other partners. It's the first two Cs of Soulé's and Ross's trio, cores and corridors. The idea is to link protected parcels like Knepp, RSPB sanctuaries, private farms and estates (some covering more than 11,000 acres), designated natural areas, and parts of South Downs National Park, creating an interlocking, 150-mile-long system of corridors along three rivers that flow from the High Weald to the English Channel. By the end of 2024 the initiative had more than 20,500 hectares (50,600 acres) registered, toward a goal of 100,000 hectares (almost 250,000 acres). That's the kind of connection that turns an island into a stepping stone, allowing isolated populations of birds and other wildlife to spread beyond the bounds of a place like Knepp and effect real recovery.

That third C, carnivores, is one that British and European rewilding has for the most part steered clear of, other than the still-quixotic talk of returning wolves to Scotland, and the somewhat more realistic discussions about bringing Eurasian lynx back to the Highlands.* (Captive-reared wildcats, which are much the same size as their domestic cousins, were released in Cairngorms National Park in 2023 to bolster flagging wild populations.) Lynx reintroductions are planned for some Rewilding Europe landscapes, as in the Iberian Highlands, and wolves have reclaimed so much of Europe on their own, recolonizing Germany, France, and regions of Italy from which they'd long been absent, as well as expanding from Russia across most of Scandinavia, and into new areas of southeastern Europe, that at the end of 2024, the committee that oversees the Bern Convention, the EU law regulating wildlife conservation, voted to significantly loosen their previously absolute legal protection. The kind of predator relocation that's been carried out in North America, like reintroducing wolves to Yellowstone, has been conspicuous by its absence, in part because mainland Europe's large predators haven't needed the help.

The scale between European and North American rewilding is also vastly different. While the Rewilding Europe strategy has been to aim at the landscape level, in the United States especially, rewilding is generally small in scope. That's understandable, because unlike most of Europe, North America still has enormous areas of relatively intact wild land, many with their full (or nearly full) sweep of big mammals—and where there are biotic gaps, the missing pieces tend to be large carnivores. The ungulate management issues on that side of the Atlantic more often revolve around too many deer or elk or other browsers, not too few, and the absence of predators is painfully obvious.

One of the few exceptions to the generally limited extent of North American rewilding has been American Prairie in northeastern Montana, a private nonprofit that has set a goal of acquiring 700,000

---

* In January 2025, four Eurasian lynx were illegally released in the Cairngorms, an act of so-called guerilla rewilding that infuriated both opponents and supporters of lynx restoration. All four cats were relatively tame, clearly unsuited for life in the wild in the middle of winter, and were quickly captured, though one died shortly thereafter.

acres of private land that would connect immense areas of protected federal land to create a 3.1-million-acre grassland preserve on which American bison and other native species—including gray wolves and grizzly bears—would roam. The preserve now encompasses more than 140,000 acres of purchased land and another 380,000 acres of associated federal or state grazing leases, and has raised the hackles of local ranch communities that see it as a threat to their way of life.

Thus far, though, American rewilding has tended to focus on restoring what had been urbanized, industrialized, or overly manicured land, usually on the order of a few dozen to several hundred (occasionally several thousand) acres—places like old golf courses, capped landfills, and cemeteries. One of the most remarkable examples is 2,200-acre Fresh Kills Park on Staten Island, which was until 2001 the world's largest landfill, receiving 29,000 tons of household trash a day. (Wreckage from the Twin Towers was also brought there after the 9/11 attacks.) Today the old trash is buried beneath layers designed to keep the material contained, and covered with soil and vegetation. Fresh Kills has become a haven for grassland wildlife including birds like grasshopper sparrows, upland sandpipers, and American kestrels whose populations have been in wide and long decline. The restoration is occurring in stages, with much of the place still off-limits to visitors, though the whole of Fresh Kills is slated to open as a park by 2036.

Cemeteries, which birders have long known to be excellent if unintentional birding hotspots, are also embracing this small-scale form of rewilding, converting some of their grounds into pollinator gardens, meadows, and thickets featuring native flora, sometimes over the objections of visitors for whom the untidiness of nature in that setting is an affront. But some cemeteries have so thoroughly embraced the transition that a few, like Mount Auburn Cemetery in Cambridge, Massachusetts, a storied birding hotspot, now employ staff ecologists to guide the process.

The waning American obsession with golf has also offered small-scale rewilding opportunities. According to the National Park and Recreation Association, the number of 18-hole golf courses in the

United States peaked at almost 15,000 in 2005, two years after the number of golfers hit its own high-water mark. By 2018 there were 6.8 million fewer golfers than 15 years earlier, and an average of about 200 courses a year have been closing. Although golfing has seen a modest bounce-back in participation since then, many courses continue to go on the auction block—and more and more are being purchased by land trusts and other conservation groups for rewilding as natural habitat and open space.

I scraped the mud off my hiking boots, changed into a more presentable pair of shoes, and drove the short distance from the preserve car park, past an electronic gate and up the long lane to Knepp Castle to meet Charlie and Issy, who were generously squeezing me in for a two-night visit between their own peripatetic travel schedule.

There are, I should note, not one but two castles at Knepp. There is Old Knepp Castle, the remains of a Norman motte-and-bailey built sometime before 1210 on a *cnæp*, a mound in Old English. Then there's the sprawling modern castle, turrets and crenelations and towers, built between 1809 and 1812. It was gutted by a catastrophic fire in 1904 that took with it a fine assortment of Renaissance masterpieces by Holbein, Raphael, and Vandyke, but which also allowed the family to rebuild with more modern conveniences.

Let's get this out of the way, because as an American I can't think of how else to put it except by cliche: Staying at Knepp felt like being dropped into a *Downton Abbey* episode, though without the below-stairs service staff bustling all around answering summoning bells and dressing the gentry for dinner. Charlie and Issy have none of those vibes, fortunately. He's a bluff man of 62 with an easy laugh, his hair a thicket of brown curls. Issy, a few years younger, is slender, her brown hair worn short and sensible, and there is no moss gathering on either of them as they're in near-constant motion. Their daughter Nancy, 29, who stopped in briefly as her parents got dinner preparation underway, is finishing her PhD at Oxford, her dissertation focused on calculating how much carbon the rewilded landscape is storing, both above and below ground—an enormously greater amount, she told me, than anyone had suspected. Their 27-year-old son Ned was running the Wilding Kitchen, so the Wildlands project is very much a family affair.

Dinner was relaxed and delicious, the conversation flowing around the wide kitchen table through a variety of rewilding topics, including their long-standing work to bring Eurasian beavers back to southern England, a restoration effort that has faced significant pushback from those who fear beavers will destroy property. Charlie also discussed the challenges of managing the estate's deer population, which can grow much too large, much too fast, but is crucial to creating the habitat they want. Each of the three enclosed blocks of land on the estate are managed differently. The North Block, for example, currently has only a small population of roe deer, permitting the land to "scrub up," as Charlie put it, for the next five years with no browsing; they are tracking the results using LiDAR, which uses lasers to create extraordinarily detailed 3D maps of vegetation. The Middle Block has about 150 fallow deer and about 30 red deer. In the Southern Block, which has all three species of deer (fallow, roe, and red), they set a goal of 280 animals, conducting twice-yearly surveys on foot with about 30 people, and culling as needed toward that goal. But over the course of eight years, Charlie noticed that less and less grass was making it through the winter. They hired a professional with a thermal imaging drone at night in midwinter, a time when the leaves were down and the animals weren't moving around in response to survey-takers, and they discovered there were actually 570 deer present.

But because Knepp is fenced, they were able to quickly address the problem by bringing in sharpshooters with night-scopes and paring the herd back to size. (That's the source of the venison I saw for sale in the estate shop.) My experience in the United States, where overbrowsing by white-tailed deer is easily the most pervasive forest health issue virtually everywhere east of the Great Plains, with profoundly negative effects on other species like forest-nesting birds, makes me especially sensitive to the delicate balance between just enough and too much pressure from hungry herbivores. Many American land managers might be envious of the latitude Charlie enjoys, since in the United Kingdom deer are considered property, and Knepp needs no special license (other than the permit hurdles required to possess a rifle) for Charlie to cull as needed, when needed. Knepp's is not an approach that would be legal in the United States or Canada, even leaving aside the fact that fully fenced tracts where such population fine-tuning is possible are very few and far between there.

The next morning I was up and out early. There's a bird hide along the mill pond below the castle, and on the walk down the lane to get there I passed through an avenue of old oaks, and an avenue of birdsong that wrapped me in sonic layers: Eurasian wrens, chiffchaffs, wood pigeons, Eurasian blackbirds, blackcaps, song thrushes, great tits, robins, common chaffinches, all in full throat. I slipped into the hide and spent a glorious hour watching the world go by. Gray herons and great egrets flapped on wide wings to land, thigh-deep in water, to hunt. There were several families of Eurasian coots feeding in the emergent vegetation close to the blind, the chicks fuzzy and black with bright orange-red faces, as though they had bad sunburns, while what I took to be two males mixed it up aggressively, charging together with harsh calls and vicious, splashing attacks, kicking their lobed feet and striking with their bills. While the coots were raising hell, two great crested grebes glided by in elegant calm, paying no mind except to flare their rusty cheek patches as if in polite disapproval.

I would have stayed longer, but I had a meeting back at the castle with Charlie and Penny Green. At the time Green was the lead ecologist at Knepp Wildland. As head of monitoring and research she had her finger on the pulse of many of the resurgent birds on the estate, especially those like European turtledove and common nightingale that are of particular conservation concern as they disappear from the wider English landscape outside the reserve. She also shouldered responsibility for the guided wildlife safaris that attract close to 10,000 visitors to Knepp every year, a large part of the financial success of the estate's rewilding business model.

Nightingales, justly famed for their nocturnal song, historically reached the northwesternmost edge of their range in England, though they are widespread in the breeding season across Europe and east as far as western China and Mongolia, migrating to sub-Saharan Africa for the winter. This is, of course, a bird once so deeply entwined with British—especially English—identity that it's hard to overemphasize the connection. But where they once nested as far north in England as Lincolnshire and west to Shropshire on the Welsh border, nightingales have suffered a catastrophic population collapse of 92 percent since the 1970s, even as their range has contracted to the south and east by more than 40 percent. Only about 5,500 singing males (the easiest to count) remained in the country by 2011, almost all of them concentrated in just three southeastern counties, including Sussex where Knepp is found. Abundance mapping using current eBird data suggests an even more recent contraction to largely coastal areas in that region. There have been similar, if not quite as severe, declines in western and southern Europe, while nightingales have actually increased in number farther east on the continent, where their habitat is in much better shape.

Turtledoves have had an even rougher time of it in the United Kingdom. The British Trust for Ornithology estimates a 99 percent decline in their population since 1967. "These trends, unless halted or reversed, would bring the species close to extinction in the U.K. within the next two decades," the BTO has warned. In 1970, there were roughly 125,000 territories in Great Britain, while the first-ever national turtledove survey in 2021 found that the entire British population numbered just 2,100 pairs in eastern and southeastern England, two-thirds of them in only three counties: Kent, Suffolk, and Essex.

The causes are myriad, including hunting (both legal and illegal) on their 3,000-mile migration route to and from Africa. Roughly 1 million turtledoves had been shot legally each autumn in Spain, Portugal, and France, although that hunt was at least temporarily suspended in 2021 to give the beleaguered population some breathing room, which appears to be working; over the next two years the European population increased by 25 percent, and there is hope that the moratorium will continue for the foreseeable future.

But for both nightingales and turtledoves, the loss and degradation of nesting habitat are near the top of the list of the threats they face. Which is why the resurgence of nightingales, and the reappearance of turtledoves after years of absence, were signal moments in Knepp's rewilding journey, and a marker of how its thorn and scrub habitat benefits these rare birds. Penny Green told me that the nightingales are relatively easy to census, given the way the males sing at night when no other songbirds are active; in 2024 the estate held at least 48 singing males. Research at Knepp has shown that the birds depend on Knepp's deep blackthorn hedges, which are all but impenetrable fortresses for shelter and foraging.

The turtledoves are more mobile and more secretive, Green said, making counting them more challenging, but their numbers had risen to at least 21 territories that year—which may not sound like many, but a countywide survey in 2019 found that about 1,000 acres on Knepp held roughly one-quarter of all the turtledoves in all of Sussex, and the estate is the only place where their numbers appear to be increasing.

Later, as we bounced down dirt tracks in the Middle Block in his Land Rover, then got out to walk, Charlie returned to the subject of turtledoves and habitat. "They need scrubby willows, blackthorn, they need water and arable weeds, especially after fledging. Having all those things close together doesn't seem like rocket science, does it?" he asked. By letting the land relax away from farming, and under the varied influences of big mammals like cows, ponies, pigs, and deer, microcosms form. "Each animal is taking from the landscape with different mouth structures, to fill different stomachs, eating different plants," he explained.

A common buzzard flew by; the reserve has an abundance of raptors, including goshawks, Eurasian hobbies, common kestrels, and Eurasian sparrowhawks. Peregrine falcons nested in the North Block, using an old tree nest one year before moving to an electrical pylon, and honey-buzzards have been seen in courtship display. There are five species of owls at Knepp—barn, tawny, little, short-eared, and long-eared.

As we turned a corner in the path, two red deer with their antlers in velvet, one an especially fine, big stag, jumped to their feet, but stood their ground as I sank slowly to a crouch and took a few photographs. Charlie started to say something, then froze in mid-sentence; we both heard the distinctive "purring" song of a male turtledove, coming from deep within a thicket of blackthorn at what sounded like my very elbow. I so wanted to see the bird; turtledoves are lovely, their black wing feathers boldly edged in tones of raw sienna, their necks marked with slashes of black and white. Yet no matter how we carefully shifted and peered and craned our necks, we couldn't see it. "It is literally *there*," Charlie whispered, as he pointed, but the bird remained a ghost.

There was no similar difficulty finding the other headliner species at Knepp. Charlie took us back to an area of the estate away from the public footpaths where we saw a number of white stork nests clustered in big oaks; one pair stood side by side on their immense stick platform, their heads thrown back in synchronous display as they clacked their bright red bills loudly like castanets.

As we watched a dozen or so storks thermaling overhead and others coming and going on the nests, I asked Charlie how long it had been since such a sight had been seen regularly in England. He explained that when Knepp and its partners drew up the proposal for what in 2016 became the White Stork Project, they found very few references to storks in historical literature, but they assumed it had been at least 600 years since storks were a regularly occurring species in Britain. But their former presence echoes through local place names like Storwood and Storgelond that stem from the Saxon root word for stork; Storrington, a lovely village just a few miles from the estate, was listed in the 11th century Domesday Book as "Estorchestone," from the Old English *Storca-tun*, "homestead with the storks."

White storks never completely abandoned Britain; throughout the 18th and 19th centuries there were consistent reports of the species appearing in England, presumably overshoots by migrants heading back to continental Europe from Africa, though almost all of them were shot. By the 1980s such arrivals, usually a couple dozen a year, were more or less annual. Some even attempted to breed, but without success; they were often inexperienced and not fully mature juveniles, and they lacked the critical mass of a colony to provide protection from predators.

When it became clear that natural colonization was unlikely to happen, Knepp and others hatched their plan to reintroduce them to Sussex. With support from the ever-busy Roy Dennis Wildlife Foundation, permanently injured, nonreleasable white storks were provided by the Warsaw Zoo to form a captive breeding colony at the Cotswold Wildlife Park starting in 2016. Each summer at fledging time, chicks from that flock are brought to Knepp, as well as to Wadhurst Park 30 miles to the east, where they're released.

Naysayers raised a variety of yes-but criticisms of the initial attempt to restore storks in southeast England, including arguing that the birds wouldn't develop the correct migratory instinct to travel to northern Africa. That proved to be completely unfounded, and only a small percentage of the released chicks have elected to winter in southern England. Each summer the newly freed juveniles prove so anxious to spread their wings that they immediately lift off to join wild storks overhead, always a stressful moment but never more so than when the Knepp team freed their first cohort in 2019.

"Off they go, up and up, until they all but disappeared in the blue. The first time we did this we thought, 'My God, what have we done, we'll never see them again,' but it's the first time they've flown, and after a while they start crashing back down again, exhausted, not knowing how to land—coming down in the scrubland, and we were running around collecting them all," Charlie said. Now the stork team knows what to expect, and the released chicks adapt rapidly to life in the wild.

Breeding at Knepp also happened much faster than anyone expected. In 2019, the first pair built a tree nest and in 2020 it and another pair fledged three chicks during the pandemic lockdown. In just four years the number of nesting pairs jumped to 30 and began to coalesce into a colony, building their bulky stick nests within a short distance of each other in huge oaks close to the pen, while the remaining nonflighted storks in a large, open-topped, fenced enclosure have begun to nest on the ground, yet another surprise. In 2023, Knepp fledged 26 chicks, a number that shot up to an impressive 53 fledglings the following year. A number of Knepp's nests produced three or four chicks each, suggesting there is plenty of food on the reserve for the growing population. The wild-born chicks were supplemented in both 2023 and 2024 by 33 young storks from the Cotswold Wildlife Park. All the youngsters, wild or captive, were ringed, and every year eight or nine of the youngsters are fitted with satellite tags to monitor their movements.

Two months after I saw them, the 2024 chicks fledged, and a couple of weeks later began responding to the tug of migration. The first sat-tagged Knepp bird, a wild chick from a ground nest, made it to Morocco by the middle of September, with five others arriving in the weeks that followed, reinforcing the newly restored connection between southern England and northern Africa. It seems clear the White Stork Project will smash through its goal of producing 50 breeding pairs in southern England by 2030.

Buoyed by the storks' success, Charlie and Issy have been contemplating other reintroductions. One that is high on their list is the red-backed shrike, which has virtually disappeared from the United Kingdom, with only a handful of pairs of these handsome, predatory songbirds still clinging to existence in parts of England and Scotland. A single male set up a territory for some weeks at Knepp in 2017 but did not stay. Given the species' habitat requirements—scrubland and thorn thickets amid diverse grassland habitat full of large bumblebees, grasshoppers, beetles, and dragonflies—Knepp would seem to be an ideal site, and a feasibility study for the potential reintroduction suggests the property could support at least 25 pairs. But until the Weald to Waves initiative gains some traction, or a proposed "Shrike Conservation Landscape" program to create other Knepp-like oases takes off, the preserve remains an island in a sea of intensive agriculture.

Another potential candidate for reintroduction that has been batted around for years in British rewilding circles is the Dalmatian pelican, the world's largest pelican and one that occurred rather commonly in coastal Britain during the Bronze and Iron Ages, but appears to have vanished sometime after the Romans arrived in Britain. Today, these hulking waterbirds are found no closer to the United Kingdom than southeastern Europe in places like Serbia, Montenegro, and Greece, which form the westernmost fringe of a range that extends to western China and Mongolia. But given the rapid success of the stork project, there have been growing calls for Dalmatian pelicans to be returned to the wetlands of Britain, especially since 2016, when a wild pelican showed up in Cornwall to the delight of twitchers.

My last night at Knepp was a busy one. Issy had asked if I would give a presentation about bird migration in the cafe, to be followed by a sit-down meal, which passed in a happy blur of good food and more conversation. By the time the event was over and the last of the guests had gone, it was getting quite late. When Charlie suggested we take our own, wee-hours safari, Issy begged off, but I was game.

Along with their tall, lanky friend Harry Barton, the former director of the Devon Wildlife Trust, which pioneered the legal reintroduction of beavers to the wild in England, Charlie drove us into the estate under the light of a quarter moon to listen for nightingales singing through the darkest portions of the early summer night as they try to attract a mate.

What we experienced wasn't a silent, wildernessy kind of night—jet traffic into Gatwick about 15 miles away periodically drowned out the singing birds. But hearing three or four males chorusing at once, each one riffing and improvising on some of the hundreds of liquid song phrases that a male nightingale has in his repertoire, did have the flavor of magic, even for an American like me who lacks the deep emotional and cultural connection to nightingale song that many older Brits possess. Knepp runs midnight nightingale safaris for visitors. "We have a lot of people cry, because it's the sound of their youth," Penny Green had told me earlier in the day.

Above us, the sky was at last free of Gatwick-bound planes, and the nightingales were in full voice. "God, that's lovely," Charlie said with a sigh. "Do you have anything as beautiful in the US?"

I assured him we do, because this nocturnal choir had made me a little homesick for the vesper songs of the hermit thrushes in the deep woods around our house. I pulled up the Merlin app on my phone, with which I'd been recording the nightingales, and played for Charlie and Harry a song that is, in its own way, as dear to me as the nightingales are to them, the ethereal fluting notes that we hear drifting out of the woods at twilight back home in New Hampshire. In the pale light of the phone, I could see by their expressions that they weren't expecting something so strange and otherworldly. Then I shut down that reminder of New England, and we sat in contented silence, listening to the night-voices of Knepp, growing in strength like the recovering land that surrounds them.

Knepp is rewilding's promise of what Great Britain could return to. But there are places where the aim of rewilders is not to restore but to maintain, to find a way to keep what is already a bird-lavish landscape, full of species that are but a memory in the United Kingdom, thriving in an uncertain future. I'd had a chance to see that for myself the previous year, in one of the wildest places left on the European continent—as well as another, even birdier place existing cheek-by-jowl with war.

Five

From the Carpathians to the Delta

It was hot. My shirt clung to the small of my back, plastered there by sweat. Not far ahead I could hear the sound of large bodies moving through the summer-dried grasses—a herd of bison, shaggy and brown, just visible when I raised myself from a belly-crawl to my knees: huge, shaggy brown animals less than fifty yards away. The lead cow sensed me and turned, staring back over her shoulder.

But I wasn't scrambling through a sagebrush flat on a Montana prairie—I was more than 5,000 miles to the east, in densely forested mountains more closely associated with mythical bloodsuckers than huge grazing animals. These were European bison, the far less famous cousin of the American bison, and I was in the southern Carpathian Mountains of Romania to learn about another approach to rewilding that takes what Issy Tree and Charlie Burrell are doing at Knepp in England and transplants it to one of the most intact ecosystems in Europe.

After an absence of about 250 years, these bison have been returned, in large measure, in the hope that they will maintain an ecological balance that humans have created over thousands of years, but one which they are abandoning along with their residency on rural landscapes. Unlike in much of western Europe, and especially the United Kingdom, where rewilding aims to reverse a staggering loss of birdlife, here in part of the old Eastern Bloc of formerly Communist countries the goal is to harness the power of large ungulates to create self-sustaining natural systems that will maintain what is already in place. The fate of one of the most bird-rich regions in Europe hangs on whether this experiment succeeds.

It's a lot to place on the back on one species, but the European bison, also known as the wisent, has broad shoulders. The bison came within a whisker of following the aurochs into extinction. From a prehistoric range that once encompassed most of Europe and Britain, by the beginning of the 20th century they remained in the wild in just two places, the Białowieża Forest of what is now Poland and Belarus, and the Caucasus Mountains of Russia. In 1914, there were more than 700 bison in Białowieża, but just five years later they had been all but wiped out by German soldiers and locals desperate for food during World War I. The last three wild Caucasian bison were killed in 1927, leaving just 54 captive individuals in the world, all descended from 12 founder individuals, 11 from Białowieża and just one male of the smaller Caucasus race.

From this meager parental stock the European bison has made a slow but remarkable comeback. They were returned to Białowieża in 1929, protected by the occupying Nazis (to whom they, like the aurochs, represented Aryan mythos) and survived World War II. It wasn't until 1952 that the first wisent were released into the wild in Białowieża, the initial steps toward restoring this species more widely. In the nearly 75 years since then, wisent have been freed in more and more places, so that by the early 2020s there were more than 6,000 free-living individuals in 10 European countries. Yet with the exception of Białowieża, where the bison number more than 1,000, the herds are generally quite small, and all are geographically isolated, with little room to truly roam.

Unlike American bison, European bison are creatures of the forest-grassland ecotone. To an eye raised on American bison, the wisent looks more delicate and gracile; the hips are narrower, the head less massive, the legs longer. Where an American bison's head hangs low, to more easily crop prairie grass, a wisent's neck is longer and more

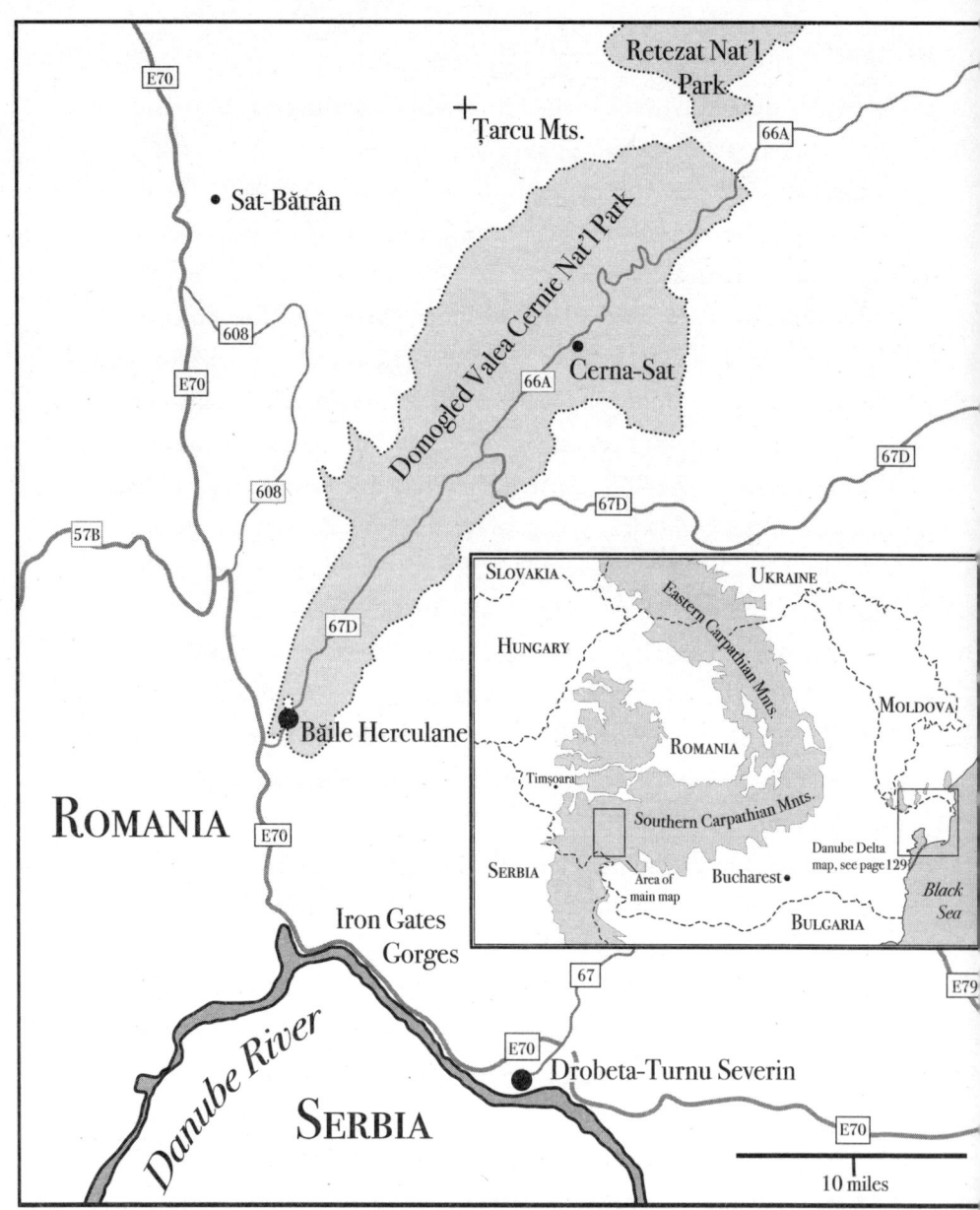

The Southern Carpathian Mountains in Romania, one of the wildest regions of Europe south of the Arctic.

horizontal, built for browsing. Still, these are massive beasts; even the cows can weigh up to 1,400 pounds, while bulls can reach one ton in weight and seven feet at the shoulder—the heaviest land mammals in Europe, and thanks to those long legs, even taller than American bison.

From a post-market-hunting low in the 1920s and '30s, populations of geese in North America, Europe, and the UK have exploded. There may now be as many as 20 million lesser snow geese like these, which, like geese in many regions, are having serious effects on their own habitat. (© SCOTT WEIDENSAUL)

(*Left*) The carnage of the market hunting period of the late 19th and early 20th centuries decimated waterfowl populations, driving many species close to extinction. (US FISH AND WILDLIFE SERVICE NATIONAL DIGITAL ARCHIVE)

(*Right*) O. M. Pinkerton of the Pennsylvania Game Commission with some of nearly 500 American goshawks turned in for bounty in 1937. Bounties were an expensive, fraud-prone waste of both money and wildlife. (© PENNSYLVANIA GAME COMMISSION)

Images of ranks of dead hawks, falcons, and eagles, taken by Richard Pough and Henry Collins in 1932 at what later became Hawk Mountain Sanctuary, galvanized the beginning of the raptor conservation movement. (COURTESY HAWK MOUNTAIN SANCTUARY ARCHIVES)

Rosalie Edge, left, was a ferocious advocate for conservation. Realizing that no one else was doing anything to stop the annual slaughter of migrating raptors in eastern Pennsylvania, she simply bought the mountain for back taxes and created the world's first sanctuary for birds of prey. (COURTESY HAWK MOUNTAIN SANCTUARY ARCHIVES)

By 1964, peregrine falcons had vanished as a breeding species from hundreds of historic nesting sites in eastern North America, the victims—along with dozens of others species of bird- and fish-eating raptors—of DDT poisoning. Similar population collapses happened throughout the UK and Europe after World War II as pesticide use became commonplace. (© BILL MOSES)

With bans on DDT and other organochloride pesticides in the 1970s, and innovative reintroduction techniques based on ancient falconry methods, bald eagles have made a spectacular recovery in the contiguous 48 states, from a low of 417 pairs in 1963 to a population of 324,000 today.
(© BILL MOSES)

Steve Downing, who has been involved in wildlife law enforcement for decades, holds a hen harrier chick that faces a bleak and likely abbreviated future.
(© STEVE DOWNING)

The hen harrier nicknamed Dagda, fitted with a satellite transmitter as a chick, was found shot dead a year later, after he strayed off the Geltsdale RSPB sanctuary where he had nested.
(© STEVE DOWNING)

His flight feathers peppered with what appear to be pellet holes, the untagged male hen harrier the author watched at Geltsdale soldiered on despite having apparently been shot. (© CONRAD DICKINSON)

Heads thrown back and red bills agape, a pair of white storks display on their immense nest at Knepp Wildland. They had been absent from Great Britain for as long as 600 years, but dozens of pairs now nest in southern England.
(© SCOTT WEIDENSAUL)

Mature oaks and expanding thornscrub at Knepp provide habitat for a host of birds that are otherwise declining across the UK, especially nightingales and Eurasian turtledoves.
(© SCOTT WEIDENSAUL)

(*Left*) It was economic necessity that drove Charlie Burrell and his wife, Isabella Tree, to embrace rewilding at Knepp, helping to spark national interest in restoring wild, functioning ecosystems in southern England and beyond. (© SCOTT WEIDENSAUL)

(*Below*) In Romania's Southern Carpathian Mountains, conservationists hope the teeth, hooves, and appetites of European bison will help maintain one of the most bird-rich regions in Europe. (© CĂTĂLIN JOSAN)

(*Above*) Morning mist lifts in the Southern Carpathians, a landscape that has been formed and maintained by small-scale farming and grazing for millennia, but which is being abandoned as people move abroad or to the cities. (© SCOTT WEIDENSAUL)

(*Right*) A squacco heron flies over a small part of the Danube Delta, the second-largest wetland in Europe and, despite a century of ecological abuse, still one of the most important areas in Europe for birds. (© SCOTT WEIDENSAUL)

A lone Dalmatian pelican rests in a marsh on the Danube Delta, a stronghold for this otherwise endangered species. (© SCOTT WEIDENSAUL)

Crest flashing, a hoopoe races away from its nest hole after delivering a big insect to one of its chicks. (© SCOTT WEIDENSAUL)

(*Left*) Even though the war in Ukraine grinds on nearby, conservationists with Rewilding Romania and Rewilding Ukraine continue to work on habitat improvement for species like this whiskered tern. (© SCOTT WEIDENSAUL)

(*Right*) A young cinereous vulture brought from Spain to Bulgaria relaxes in an acclimation aviary, preparing to join earlier cohorts of this huge, newly reintroduced species. (© SCOTT WEIDENSAUL)

The Arda River flows through the eastern Rhodope Mountains of Bulgaria, home to a resurgent population of vultures growing thanks to intensive conservation. (© SCOTT WEIDENSAUL)

A big mammal needs a lot of room, and that's where the Southern Carpathians come in. The Carpathians as a whole are Europe's largest mountain range, encompassing more than 80,000 square miles (210,000 square kilometers) across primarily six countries, from the Czech Republic, Slovakia, and Poland in the east and north, to Romania, Ukraine, and Serbia in the east and south. In Romania, the Carpathians form a huge reversed L shape, cutting west-to-east across southern Romania—the Southern Carpathians—and then turning sharply to the north and west, eventually passing into western Ukraine and Slovakia. The Southern Carpathians offer the kind of expansive habitat that could provide space for an ecologically and genetically robust herd of bison, which in turn could serve as landscape engineers whose teeth and appetites shape ecosystems. That's the plan, at least.

Between 2014, when the first group of 17 bison were released in the Southern Carpathians, and 2023, the herd had grown to at least 190 animals, ranging over forest, farmland, and mountain slopes, with hopes that the area could eventually support as many as 450 animals. The reintroduction began as a project of Rewilding Europe and WWF-Romania, with Rewilding Romania—a fairly new addition to the Rewilding network, founded in 2022—stepping in more recently as a partner in managing the bison.

I'd taken a red-eye flight from the United States to Timișoara, the regional hub in western Romania. Sebastian Ursuța—Seba, as he's known, the communications officer for Rewilding Romania, lanky and heavily bearded, a cigarette usually at hand—picked me up at the airport. Our destination was Sat Bătrân (*sat* meaning "village" in Romanian, *bătrân* meaning "old"), part of the five-village commune of Armeniș in the foothills of the Țarcu Mountains, more than two hours' drive to the southeast in the southern Carpathian Mountains, sometimes known as the Transylvanian Alps.

The Southern Carpathians are often described as the largest wild area in Europe south of the Arctic, with peaks more than 8,000 feet high looming over deep river valleys and gorges, many still cloaked in old-growth forests of beech. Its populations of large carnivores have remained strong in the post-communist era, with estimates of as many as 8,000 brown bears and 3,000 wolves—former Communist dictator Nicolae Ceaușescu, before his toppling and execution in a 1989 revolution, liked to hunt bears and had forbidden anyone else to do so. In fact, aside from the long-extinct aurochs, the only large mammal that had been missing from the Southern Carpathians was the bison.

These mountains had drawn my curiosity for years. The bison reintroduction was itself an intriguing element of the rewilding plan, but the more I read about Romania's birdlife, the more certain I was that I needed to go there. Benedict Macdonald, the naturalist and author of *Rebirding*, raved about avian abundance and diversity on Romanian farms, especially species like red-backed shrikes that have all but vanished from the United Kingdom. Romania also offered a second rewilding bird story, the transnational Danube River delta on the Black Sea, shared by Romania, Moldova, and Ukraine, and home to one of the most important (albeit sadly battered) wetlands on the continent, alive with tens of thousands of marsh and waterbirds. So: to the Southern Carpathians first, then east to the delta, where conservation continued despite the war raging on its doorstep.

We arrived in Sat Bătrân near dusk. The restored farmhouse where we were staying, managed as a guest house by a local family, was low-slung, a single story of freshly painted plaster above dry stone half-walls, its orange ceramic tile roof weathered to a soft brown splotched with lichen and moss, along the peak of which a common redstart, black-masked and orange-breasted, flitted. Despite the thick stone walls, the intense heat of the day had permeated the room, for I had arrived during an epic heat wave across southern Europe.

Waiting for us when we finally arrived was Ioan Simescu, known as Nelu, the Romanian diminutive of his given name. He was a trim 52-year-old with tightly cropped gray hair, one of the Rewilding rangers who monitor the restored bison herd in the Țarcu Mountains. As we waited for our hosts to bring the evening meal, Nelu produced a plastic soda bottle filled with a pale yellowish liquid; this was *țuică*, a plum brandy that is rural Romania's moonshine, distilled in backyards and sold along roadsides throughout the country. He poured a round for the three of us into small shot glasses; the liquor had a sweet nose, a sharp, not-unpleasant burn, and as I had been warned, quite a kick.

Nelu poured another round as two more companions arrived. Vali Petru Miculescu—Petrișor to his friends—was like Nelu a bison ranger, a burly fellow in his thirties with a five-o'clock shadow and heavy muscles under his black tee-shirt. Anghel Drasovean followed him in the gate; the field operations manager for Rewilding Romania, Anghel was a young-looking 36, with a thatch of unruly dark hair and a heavy stubble that wasn't quite a beard. He'd been in the field for more than a week and was short on sleep. As I learned in the coming days, he is a keen birder and sharp ecologist, and it was thanks to his and Seba's patient answers to my many questions that I came to understand how Rewilding Romania is trying to preserve what is one of the most diverse bird communities remaining anywhere in Europe, using bison to do it.

The reason rural Romania had retained such a wealth and diversity of farmland and woodlot birds, Anghel and Seba explained, was the centuries-old traditions of small-scale farming and grazing, which maintained a complex mosaic of habitats and successional stages, and which carried on through the Communist era long after farmers in the West had industrialized. The Southern Carpathians aren't wilderness, and haven't really been since the Neolithic. It is a landscape that has been shaped and modified by people for thousands of years, and one with which its birds had evolved.

The problem, Anghel said, is that rural Romanians are fleeing the land for the cities, or abroad. It's happening all over Europe; rural land abandonment is rampant as competition with highly mechanized, intensified agricultural systems in western Europe drives small farmers out of business. The European Parliament has estimated that almost one-third of the agricultural land in the EU is at risk of abandonment, and Romania has some of the highest abandonment rates in the union. Take people out of the equation and the landscape changes in ways that no longer favor the birds that thrive with small-scale farming, the same ones that have all but disappeared in western Europe and the United Kingdom.

The next morning the heat had receded enough to be comfortable. We ate a quick, pre-daybreak breakfast, listening to a golden oriole's sweet, gurgling song in the trees across the quiet lane, then climbed into a couple of four-wheel-drive vehicles and headed out as the sun rose. The hay harvest was at its peak, and we passed farm families already scything, raking, and stacking it to create the traditional conical hayricks known in Romanian as *căpițe de fân*, "heads of hay," though to my eye they looked more like squat, golden-yellow Christmas trees. Farmland birds were everywhere—Eurasian robins, wagtails of several species, blackbirds, swarms of swallows. Common buzzards sailed over the fields looking for prey.

While the centuries-old approach to haymaking remains strong in this part of Romania, other agricultural traditions are fading. As we drove up into the hills, we passed old, abandoned houses, the remains of "summer villages," to which farm families once moved themselves and their horses, sheep, and cattle in spring, driving the free-ranging herds higher and higher into the Carpathians as summer went on, right to the grassy summits of the Țarcu peaks. Today, though, Anghel said machinery is replacing horse-power, and it's harder and harder to find shepherds willing to spend the summer following sheep across mountain pastures; easier to get rid of the sheep, fence off some of the land and add a few cows.

As a result, Anghel said, the intensity of grazing and browsing that shaped the Carpathians for hundreds of years is rapidly fading, and what had been a patchwork of habitats is turning into a uniform expanse of young, regenerating forest. That's obviously good habitat for some species, but without a diversity mosaic, many of the farmyard and pasture species that have remained abundant in many parts of Romania will fade away. The hope is that the bison, which browse and wallow and kill trees by stripping their bark, will maintain habitat complexity, and thus overall biodiversity.

The reintroduced bison range over more than 500 square kilometers (about 190 square miles), climbing in summer high into the Țarcus, so our chances of encountering them in the few days I had with the rangers were slim. Therefore, they were taking me to the nearly 300-acre enclosure where the newest cohort of bison, being readied for eventual release, were allowed to acclimate to the landscape. We parked at a locked gate, shouldered our packs, and felt some relief from the sun when we reentered the shade of the forest. Bison weren't the only animals around; Petrișor pointed out a couple of places where brown bears had flipped large rocks to expose ant colonies beneath.

Even in a fenced area, it took us nearly an hour to locate the bison, creeping behind Nelu and Petrișor as we circled first one way, then backtracked across deep ravines before finally crawling the last 50 yards through brambles and grass to see the small herd of young adult cows, some wearing GPS collars. They were dusty (we were all dusty, in this dry, unrelenting heat), and while the rear cow obviously knew we were close by, casting a periodic eye back at us as she and the others grazed, they seemed unconcerned.

Not surprisingly, there have been conflicts with landowners since the bison have been released. As they strip bark to eat, a herd of hungry bison will not distinguish between young trees encroaching on a former pasture, or prized plum or apple trees in an orchard, which can generate a lot of animosity in a hurry. There is a compensation plan, Anghel and Seba told me, but the payments offered are often insultingly inadequate, just enough to buy a spindly fruit tree sapling to "replace" a mature, possibly centuries-old tree that produced an annual bounty of fruit.

Rewilding Romania, and WWF before it, have tried to build connections between the communities and the newly arrived bison. For those like our hosts at the guesthouse who are making a financial wager on increasing tourism, the bison are a significant plus. There is also a clearly evident sense of local pride in the bison. But to a farmer who will realize no gain from increasing tourism, they're simply a large, occasionally hungry nuisance.

The next morning was a foggy one, after overnight rain that knocked back the heat and washed clean all of the dust. We rode up a different valley than the previous day, stopping along Pârâul Alb—"White Creek"—frequently so Anghel could scan the margins of the fast-flowing water for white-throated dippers, those odd, rotund songbirds that plunge into frothy rapids and half-walk, half-fly underwater across the stony bottom, probing for aquatic insects. He was ultimately disappointed, but the morning was thick with other birds—a Eurasian wren bubbling its unceasing trills and whistles; flocks of marsh tits that, not surprisingly given their close relationship, reminded me of chickadees back home; great spotted and green woodpeckers calling or flying across small meadows; male yellowhammers whose heads all but glowed lemony in the morning light; and an abundance of blackbirds and wagtails, the latter seeming to struggle into flight as though they carried the weight of the world on their long tails. As mist wraiths rose from the forest, a buzzard flew across the shallow valley below eye level, giving a single, piercing cry again and again.

There were plenty of bison signs, if not the bison themselves—old tracks in the mud, some even older droppings. The sun rose behind Țarcu Mountain, the highest peak in its namesake range, silhouetting the tiny weather station on its summit, miles away. With the sun, the bird activity ratcheted up yet another level, especially once we reached an old orchard. There were red-backed shrikes everywhere, from what I could see mostly recently fledged youngsters, gray and brown and lightly barred above, but there were plenty of adult males, snappy-looking birds six or seven inches long with blue-gray heads, black robbers' masks and rusty backs, and adult females that were a rich brown with pale gray vermiculation below. Regardless of age or sex, all had heavy, slightly hooked beaks, the hallmarks of the shrike family.

Red-backed shrikes are shrub-grassland specialists with a huge range across Europe and western Asia, songbirds that, like all shrikes, have taken to a predatory lifestyle, feeding on large insects. They need a landscape that combines orchards or dense thickets, especially of thorny shrubs like blackthorn or hawthorn, with open areas where they can pounce on large insects like grasshoppers and beetles, small vertebrates like mice, frogs, and even smaller songbirds—hence the old name "butcher bird" applied to many shrikes.

The most recent European Breeding Bird Atlas, completed in 2017, found some of the highest densities of red-backed shrikes on the continent in Romania, especially in the southern Carpathian Mountains, where a 50-by-50-kilometer (31-by-31-square-mile) block may hold more than 100,000 pairs. The farther west one goes, however, the bleaker things look for this species. It has suffered from a litany of ills including habitat loss, agricultural intensification, and pesticide use. That likely reduces the abundance of the large insects on which it feeds, along with small vertebrates. The near-universal practice of worming cattle with the drug ivermectin leaves their droppings toxic to the dung beetles that once recycled it into the soil, and which became prey for shrikes themselves. Once widespread in the United Kingdom, red-backed shrike numbers slipped through the late 19th and 20th centuries, and the shrike has been all but functionally extinct there since the 1980s, with no more than three pairs known in recent years.

In the Carpathians, though, the shrikes were everywhere. "When people come here from the Netherlands they're excited by all the shrikes, but people from the United Kingdom simply can't believe how many there are," Anghel said. I had a hard time believing it myself, so used had I become to reading about this shrike as a bellwether of farmland bird decline. Even Anghel was rethinking a few things as he watched dozens of shrikes chasing each other and dropping on insects, along with a dozen or more other species of flycatchers, tits, chaffinches, and thrushes. "Because of the conflicts with the bison in their orchards, I was thinking of trying to convince the local community to remove the orchards and turn them into pasture. But now, seeing these shrikes, I realize what good habitat these orchards are for birds," he said.

Midday found us back at the guest house, dozing through the heat, but after lunch Seba and I drove south toward the ancient spa town of Băile Herculane, squeezed between the Mehedinți Mountains to the east and the Cerna Mountains to the west, and just north of the famed Iron Gates of the Danube, the dramatic gorge that forms the boundary between Romania and Serbia. Seba's academic background is actually architecture, not conservation, and he was eager to show me Băile Herculane; its hot springs attracted the Romans as early as 153 CE (spawning a legend that Hercules bathed there), and it has been a destination ever since, reaching its zenith in the 19th century, when the Austro-Hungarian emperor Franz Josef I and his wife, Empress Elizabeth, often came.

That glory is gone. The Hapsburg-era grand hotels and old baths are in a state of sad neglect, gutted and many of their windows open to the elements, great streaks of iron rust staining their rooftops, facing soulless hotels built during the Communist era, monolithic slabs with garish signage. The town is still a tourist hub, though, and was bustling even though it was midweek. I quickly realized everyone was of a certain age, however, and the only young people I saw were being towed around by their grandparents, often with sullen looks on their faces. Still, the bones of the place remain striking, and an architectural renovation of the hotels, baths, and other landmarks could make Băile Herculane once again a destination worthy of its past. But it was not our real destination.

We followed the Cerna River toward its headwaters, deeper and deeper into the mountains and the river's canyon in Domogled Valea Cernei National Park. We turned off the main road onto an ungodly potholed track that made me deeply worried for the suspension on the rental car, even though we moved at a crawling pace. The scenery was breathtaking—high cliffs rising above the hardwood-forested lowlands and bracketing the valley, which was already in late-day shadow.

At one time, those cliffs and the surrounding landscape would have been the haunt of several species of vultures, including griffon vultures, the second-largest and once most widespread of Europe's five species, and the continent's largest, the cinereous or Eurasian black vulture. Griffons have broad wings with deeply emarginated flight feathers that look like long-protruding fingers as they soar, their wings more than seven and one-half to eight-and-one-half feet across. Yet as huge as the griffons are, a cinereous vulture, with a wingspan of more than nine feet and weighing 15 to 25 pounds, easily eclipses them.

There was no point in scanning the skies here for those vultures, or for the other two species that once nested in Romania, the huge bearded vulture or lammergeier that once lived in the high reaches of the southern Carpathians, or the smaller Egyptian vulture, pure white as an adult, with inky black flight feathers and a face of bright orange skin. Aside from rare and often unsubstantiated reports, there has been no evidence of any vultures of any kind breeding in the country since the late 20th century.

That had been the case across much of Europe, where during the preceding century or more vulture populations crashed continent-wide. The causes were complex and intersecting, with threats varying by period and region. Direct persecution like shooting and intentional poisoning drove local extinctions in the late 19th and early 20th centuries, which is when griffon vultures vanished from Romania, and remain a danger even today in some places, although incidental poisoning—vultures feeding on carcasses laced with toxins to kill predators like wolves—is now more of an issue than intentional killing. Newer risks like collisions with electrical transmission lines and wind turbines have grown in importance, as has the risk from veterinary analgesics like diclofenac, which are harmless to livestock but deadly to vultures.

Vultures have made some impressive recoveries in western Europe, most notably Spain, which now holds more than 30,000 griffon vultures, more than one-third of the European population, but their conservation has lagged badly in the east and south of the continent. One of the most pervasive problems in Europe is a simple lack of food. Wild ungulate populations across many parts of Europe have been scant for much of the last century, which is why the vultures had long depended on domestic livestock, a win-win for the birds and for rural communities whose dead animals were efficiently tidied up. But when bovine spongiform encephalopathy, more commonly known as mad cow disease, spiked in Europe in the early 1990s, the European Union instituted draconian measures requiring farmers to bury or incinerate dead livestock of any sort.

Suddenly the table was bare, making for lean years for European vultures. The EU eventually relaxed sanitary regulations, allowing for the return of livestock carcasses as vulture food, but natural carrion would be preferable. That's one reason Rewilding Romania is focusing so much time and effort on bison, which besides being landscape engineers also represent, when they die, a lot of meat for scavengers like vultures. The group intends to return vultures to Romanian skies, and the Cerna River valley is key to those plans.

"We plan to bring griffon vultures back first, back to these cliffs," Seba told me as he maneuvered around another gaping, water-filled pothole. Rewilding Romania consulted with a vulture expert from Spain to assess the region with an eye for the best release sites, and the Cerna valley checked all the boxes—limited human settlement, and good potential nest sites on the cliff walls for griffons, which have responded well to such reintroduction efforts in other parts of Europe. In the meantime, until populations of bison and deer increase, supplemental food would be provided in so-called vulture restaurants, where toxin-free carcasses purchased from local farmers would be hauled to high, protected vantage points, another technique with a proven track record across Europe.

We drove for more than an hour before reaching Cerna-Sat, a few dozen scattered homes, farms, and fields a couple of miles below an immense impoundment on the Cerna River. Seba wanted to show me Cheile Corcoaiei, the Corcoaia Gorge, a narrow and twisting slot canyon along a small creek flowing out of the mountain nearby. As we carefully picked our way back along the smooth, sloped, and quite slippery rock (grateful for the old metal handrail, however rickety), he explained that the mythical figure Iovan Iorgavan, given supernatural strength by bathing in this spring and armed with a battle ax, was said to have fought a seven-headed dragon here, whose lashing tail created the tunnel-like gorge.

We saw no dragons, but there were wall lizards skittering away from us, and when we walked back out into the open I saw that the sky above us was churning with hundreds of swallows and swifts, including many alpine swifts, the largest species in Europe. They cleaved the air like small, white-bellied falcons—though when an actual falcon, an adult peregrine, flashed into view, the smaller birds scattered until the raptor had crossed out of sight once more.

For now, the silhouette of griffon vultures soaring among the cliffs of the Cerna River valley was something for the imagination. Before long I would be heading south to Bulgaria, to see a highly successful vulture restoration project that has already achieved what my Romanian hosts still hope to accomplish. But first I needed to travel east to the edge of Romania, to visit one of Europe's most important transnational bird refuges, one that has endured despite half a century of ham-fisted ecological blunders and is poised for a renaissance—a renaissance that even a raging war just beyond its margins had not been able to completely derail.

About a month earlier, as I was trying to get ready for my trip to eastern Europe, a story in the *Washington Post* caught my eye. It detailed the growing fears that the Zaporizhzhia nuclear power plant in Ukraine, occupied by Russian forces since the start of the war in February 2022 and already teetering on the edge of catastrophe, was in even greater danger of a nuclear meltdown following the destruction a month earlier of an enormous impoundment on Dnieper River that cooled the reactor.

This was not a subject of idle curiosity to me. After I completed my visit to the Southern Carpathians, I would be heading down the Danube River to its mouth at the Black Sea, where central Europe's mightiest river forms an almost incomprehensibly vast delta teeming with birds and other wildlife, and which rewilding proponents hope to make even richer biologically by restoring its natural hydrology. I would be staying in a lodge that normally caters to wildlife photographers on the west bank of one of the many river channels. Less than one-third of a mile away, across the water on the east bank, was the small fishing city of Vylkove, Ukraine.

Don't worry, I'd assured my wife, Amy, many times. Yes, there had been fighting in that part of the Ukraine during the earliest days of the war, but southwestern Ukraine had largely been quiet ever since.

On that rainy morning, I no longer felt quite so confident in my assessment. Google Earth showed me that the Zaporizhzhia plant was more than 300 miles to the northeast of where I would be. The winds are generally westerly in that part of the world; still, I made a quick online purchase, a couple weeks' supply of potassium iodide tablets, which block the thyroid gland from taking up radioactive iodine in the air, water, or food. No need to mention this to Amy, I thought; she was worried enough already.

Bidding farewell to Seba at the Timișoara airport, I flew to the Romanian capital, Bucharest, where a friend of his cousin's was picking me up and driving me east. Bobo—a nickname—was a towering but amiable young guy driving his father's car, with just enough English and a sense of humor that we were able to muddle through pleasant semi-conversation over the next four hours. We crossed the Danube at the village of Giurgeni, white storks nesting on utility poles for a couple of miles on either side of the river, which at this point flows almost due north before folding itself back to the east and south and splitting into multiple channels, some maintained for commercial shipping, that connect to the Black Sea.

Bobo dropped me off in Tulcea, one of Romania's important Danube River ports, a departure point for those, like me, traveling into the delta. I had reservations on one of the high-speed ferries that race up and down the Danube, stopping at the small river villages and towns along the channels. The boat was about forty feet long, a single roofed cabin with rows of double seats running its length. There wasn't a lot of room for luggage, and we all had plenty of it—weekend tourists; a family, exhausted and grumpy at what I took to be the end of a long and tiring trip; and a cluster of women coming back from a shopping trip to town with overflowing bags and baskets who glared at me as I squeezed in past them.

Once the pilot opened the throttle on the big engines we roared downriver at speed, and we left the industrial shoreline quickly behind. Below Tulcea, the Danube splits again, and we followed the Sulina Branch, which runs straightened and channelized through the heart of the delta. We buzzed past huge cargo ships moving up- and downriver, many of those outbound likely carrying Ukrainian grain that once would have gone out through Black Sea ports like Odesa, now closed by Russian attacks. Ukraine, nimbly shifting, had begun to move its exports to ports on its side of the Danube, which the Russians had not yet targeted. Soon the river banks were cloaked in heavy forest, with an occasional settlement or scattering of homes and small docks, into

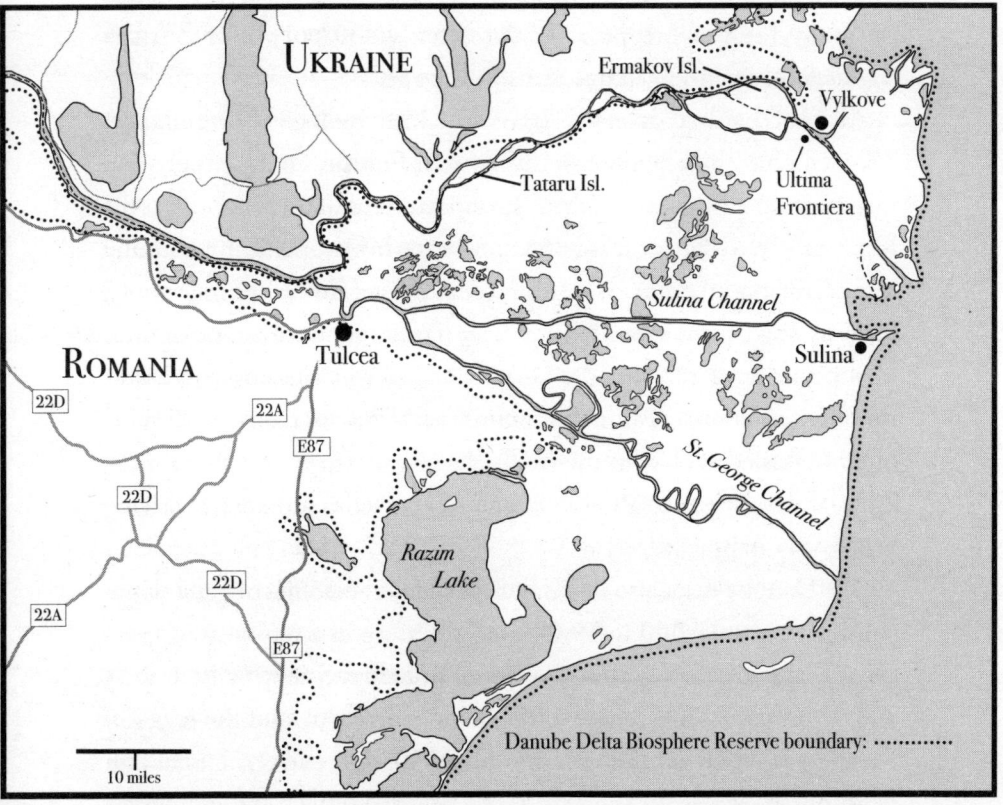

Encompassing parts of Romania, Moldova, and Ukraine, the Danube Delta Biosphere Reserve is one of Rewilding Europe's focal landscapes, despite the ongoing war in Ukraine.

which the ferry occasionally pulled to offload passengers. Great egrets and a few cormorants perched on dead snags, but it was impossible to see much from the cramped cabin.

The Danube delta lies mostly in Romania, with a bit in southern Moldova and extreme southwestern Ukraine; it is Europe's second-biggest delta after the Volga, and is the continent's largest and most biologically intact expanse of natural wetlands and reed beds, the latter said to be the most extensive in the world. Most is contained within the Danube Delta Transboundary Biosphere Reserve, a UNESCO World Heritage Site encompassing some 1.4 million acres (580,000 ha). Although a delta is defined most by its waterways and wetlands, the Danube's has a remarkable array of habitats; there are deep woodlands, sand dunes, seasonal mud flats, and, across the river in Ukraine, the grassy Tarutino Steppe, at 12,000 acres (4,800 ha.) one of the most significant remaining steppe areas in Europe.

All that habitat diversity translates into biological abundance. The delta has the highest fish diversity in Europe, continentally rare mammals like Eurasian wildcat, European mink, and otter, but most importantly to me, at least 365 species of birds, including globally important populations of wading species like storks, herons, egrets, bitterns, ibises, and spoonbills; greater flamingos, once a rare vagrant, now occur by the hundreds. Dozens of species of raptors are either nesting residents or seasonal migrants, including as many as 90 pairs of white-tailed eagles; immense flocks of waterfowl and shorebirds, especially during migration; and enough passerines to keep a visiting birder very happy indeed.

The Danube delta also holds Europe's largest colonies of great white pelicans, some 17,000 to 19,000 pairs nesting in a remote and inaccessible area that lies within the Roşca-Buhaiova Scientific Reserve, a strictly protected sub-refuge in the delta's north. Around the edges of these great white pelican colonies nest 350–400 pairs of Dalmatian pelicans, the largest of the world's 12 pelican species and among the heaviest flying birds of any sort, weighing up to nearly 30 pounds with wingspans of more than 11 feet. Their range, which once extended to Great Britain (hence the interest in reintroducing them there), contracted ever farther east, and by the 1940s they were extirpated from the lower Danube, only recolonizing it in the 1980s. Seeing a Dalmatian pelican was high on my hoped-for list, but because there was no access to the reserve where the birds nest, I knew my chances were poor.

Organizing the logistics for visiting the delta had proven complicated. The most obvious problem was the war; much of the most intensive habitat restoration work had been undertaken on the Ukrainian portion of the delta, but the Rewilding Ukraine staff had been evacuated, and while restoration work was continuing under the auspices of Ukrainian municipal partners, the area was off-limits to visitors like me. Fortunately, there was an alternative literally just across the river—a lodge called Ultima Frontiera. Run by an Italian ecotour company specializing in nature photography, it occupies a roughly 2,200-acre fishing concession of forest, wetland, and impoundments on the Romanian side of the Danube.

Normally, the lodge management brings in large groups of wildlife photographers for intense, week-long workshops, but none were planned for the time of my visit in midsummer. They were willing to host me despite that, and by further luck, my visit would coincide with a planning meeting that Rewilding Romania director Marina Drugă and some of her staff, including chief bison ranger Cătălin Josan, would be holding at the lodge, allowing me both to experience the delta and pick their collective brains about the restoration efforts there and in the Southern Carpathians.

I'd been disappointed that Cătălin wouldn't be in Armeniș during my time there, so I was especially pleased to find him waiting at the riverside with a pickup truck and two of his colleagues, operations officer Alexandra Stancu and enterprise officer Paula Bora. He proved to be a burly man with a luxuriant red beard and rather taciturn manner, while Alexandra and Paula were both far chattier. Cătălin said little on the hour-long drive along dusty sand tracks, focused as he was on which of the many unmarked turns and crossings we passed, often little more than two tire tracks in the sand, was the route to the lodge, though he did point out red-footed falcons, European rollers, and other birds along the way.

We passed through a few small villages, where many homes looked abandoned. Only 15,000 people live in the delta proper, making it one of the least populated parts of temperate Europe, with fewer and fewer each year as people leave for the city. Most of those who remain engage in grazing and farming, reed harvesting, and especially fishing.

Although people have lived in the Danube delta for tens of millennia, the history of large-scale ecosystem alteration is more recent. The Sulina channel of the river, the one along which I had traveled, was first deepened and straightened for maritime industry in the latter half of the 19th century. In the 1980s, the St. George branch was shortened from a meandering 67 miles to a channelized 40 miles. In both cases, these changes diverted water and sediment away from the delta wetlands, starving islands and marshes of replenishment while directing silt and pollution directly into the Black Sea, unfiltered by the great reed beds.

The other significant blow to the delta came in the mid-20th century from the enlargement and construction of canals slicing through the natural wetlands, of dikes that walled off seasonal floodwaters to create dry polders for farming, and of dams and sluices that drastically altered the original hydrology. Fish populations tumbled as their spawning areas were destroyed and their movements restricted, which in the 1950s prompted the government to embark on an all-out assault on waterbirds, ostensibly to protect declining fisheries; scientists estimate the delta's pelican population fell from around 1 million to about 300 pairs.

The fall of the Ceaușescu regime brought a focus on the delta for its ecological, not economic, value, however, and since 1990 the efforts there have been directed largely toward ecosystem restoration along the lower 620 miles of the Danube, a plan known as the Lower Danube Green Corridor. In the early 2000s, WWF laid out ambitious goals for restoring the delta, envisioning a time when some of the large, badly degraded islands on the Ukrainian portion of the delta, for example, could be brought back to health.

That started when the first dikes were removed on Tataru Island in 2003 and a more natural water flow restored; natural gallery forests thrived and the number of bird species using the island jumped by more than two-thirds, to 219. On much larger Ermakov Island, roughly 6,000 acres in size, an encircling dike that had completely blocked all natural flooding was breached in 2009 by WWF. In 2021, Rewilding Ukraine took out further sections of the dike to improve water flow, while introducing small herds of grazers like Konik horses, the small, semi-feral heritage breed from Poland often used in rewilding, as well as red and fallow deer. Elsewhere along the delta, work to restore several large and badly degraded lakes was moving ahead, to reconnect the severed water flow between the lakes and with the Danube itself, allowing migratory fish to move freely for the first time in years.

All this good news was contained in a press release from Rewilding Europe's main office in the Netherlands, promising additional work connecting damaged lakes on the Ukrainian side of the border that spring. It was dated February 2, 2022. Less than three weeks later, Russia launched its invasion.

Despite its proximity to Ukraine, the war was easy to forget at Ultima Frontiera, its main lodge and other buildings roofed with tightly packed, neatly trimmed reed thatch in a deliberate echo of the local building style. I was given just enough time to drop my gear in my room—the place echoed, so few of us were there—then I was introduced to the two guides on duty, a skinny, voluble 26-year-old Spaniard named Carlos Molina Camache, and a much quieter man named Marvin Iaynes, 38, who to my great surprise was from Guatemala. Marvin explained that he had, years before, guided the Italian owner of Ultima Frontiera to photograph resplendent quetzals in the cloud forests of Guatemala, and as a result had long been guiding seasonally in the Danube delta. I was their sole priority.

It became immediately clear that Carlos and Marvin had very different expectations than I for what I wanted from the visit, as we sat down to eat a quick dinner. Carlos opened a map of the lodge's concession, explaining that there were more than 30 photographic hides—and they were determined for me to squeeze in as many as possible in what they felt was a painfully short visit.

"Normally, photographers have a full week here! You only have three days," he said, the pain of this fact evident from his tone of voice. He proceeded to map out a schedule beginning the moment I finished my plate of spaghetti, continuing until far past midnight and commencing again in the predawn each of the following days, scouting for nocturnal animals by spotlight, jumping from blind to blind to photograph as much as they could show me. Yet he grew ever more confused as I tried to explain that, while I enjoyed photographing wildlife, that was not the reason I was staying at the lodge. I wanted to experience as much of the delta as I could, given the restrictions and access issues, but I also needed to spend time talking with Marina and others on her staff about Rewilding's work. I wasn't there to rack up a big shoot list, though I would be happy to photograph the place and its wildlife as opportunity allowed.

There was a silent pause from Carlos as he digested this unexpected information. I was clearly not the sort of client they were used to guiding, nor would this be the last hiccup before we eventually came to a meeting of the minds. I also (very sincerely) pleaded exhaustion after several days of travel, and excused myself for an early to-bed, promising to be a more energetic guest in the morning.

By arrangement, we met at 4:30 a.m. for a small breakfast of cheese, sliced meat, fruit, and juice; I likely cemented my reputation for eccentricity by passing up offered coffee, but took their advice to wrap a peanut butter and jelly sandwich in a napkin for later. Then we headed out in the dim first light, sunrise colors spreading in the east beneath advancing clouds, the previous day's heat and dust dampened and a heavy dew twinkling on every surface.

We drove dirt lanes that threaded between impoundments, past flocks of mute swans and great white pelicans, the latter skittish, rushing to noisy flight with wingbeats that sounded like someone smacking a carpet. I was delighted at the abundance of hoopoes, which seemed to appear around every corner; they are easily one of my favorite European birds—jay-sized, a faded burnt orange with wings psychedelically striped in black and white, and a crazy Mohawk of a crest that the hoopoe is forever flashing.

We arrived at what I was told was the white-tailed eagle and golden jackal hide, an elaborate structure built into the side of a sandy hill, with a glass front facing a wide open area punctuated by a number of artfully arranged stumps and tall dead snags. I had wondered what about this place made it so reliable for eagles and jackals in particular, and my growing suspicions were soon confirmed as Marvin and Carlos wired dead fish to the stumps and snags, carefully positioning them so the bait was hidden from view in the hide. While Marvin finished that job, Carlos began tossing large quantities of corn and other grain around on the ground. I groaned internally; we were going to have to have another uncomfortable conversation, but it was by then too late to protest much. Marvin waved and drove off in the truck, and Carlos joined me in the hide and set up his own camera and tripod.

The golden jackals were the first to show up. These coyote-sized canids are found from the eastern edge of the Mediterranean to southeast Asia, and are common in the delta, which has served as a springboard from which this adaptable carnivore has pushed across central and eastern Europe; some pioneering individuals have shown up as far north as the Netherlands and Lithuania. There was something to my eye slightly off about their proportions, probably because they have what for a canine seems a rather truncated afterthought of a tail, not the long, thick brush of a fox or wolf.

But like coyotes, they are nobody's fools, and those near the hide obviously knew what the presence and departure of a truck meant. Within a short while a family of three, including a half-grown cub, showed up. One of the adults made a few initial leaps up the side of the tallest snag before maintaining a grip and scrabbling to the top, where it wrenched away one of the whole fish intended for an eagle; Carlos muttered a curse under his breath. While that was going on, the scattered seed had attracted hordes of ravens, magpies, and hooded crows, which scuffled occasionally with the jackals for pieces of fish, earning tooth-baring charges from the canines.

"Carlos, I have to tell you that I don't agree with baiting wildlife for photographs," I said. "I would have said something if I'd realized that was your plan. What I'd really like is a chance to just spend some time in a hide overlooking some of the big wetlands, where there's the best chance to observe waterbirds and waders like pelicans and shorebirds. They don't have to be in close photographic range."

Meanwhile, a family of golden jackals made a careful, cautious approach through the surrounding brush, a peek-a-boo game that finally revealed five small kits with the parents. That's about the time that the first white-tailed eagle arrived, flushing the flocks of smaller birds and sending the jackal family back into hiding when it landed awkwardly on one of the high snags. The eagle was immense, the wings nearly eight feet wide; I will admit, seeing one at such close range was a riveting experience, whatever my feelings about using food to do so. This one was an adult, built along the same bulky lines as the somewhat smaller bald eagle, the body a dark, somewhat muddy brown, lightening to a blondish head with the massive yellow beak and powerful feet of the genus *Haliaeetus*. The all-white tail was short enough that it was largely hidden beneath the folded wings.

Although they are only now being reintroduced to England, white-tailed eagles have made a remarkable comeback in the past 50 years in mainland Europe, thanks to bans on persistent pesticides like DDT, strengthened legal protection, a more tolerant attitude overall toward raptors, and targeted reintroduction programs in Spain and France. Since 1970 the white-tailed eagle population has increased almost five-fold in Europe, to an estimated 25,000 birds, mostly in northern Europe and especially Norway, its neighbors, and the region around the Baltic Sea. In southeastern Europe there are fewer than 3,000 breeding pairs, mostly found along the Danube River and its estuary, particularly the Danube Delta.

Thanks to the jackals, there was little or nothing left for the eagle to eat, though it flew to the ground and plodded around in a spitting rain, looking for leftovers. The other corvids had returned, and spent most of their time harassing the big raptor. The eagle ignored them completely, unfazed and unhurried, except for one time when a magpie actually smacked the back of its head, the eagle spinning in impotent response as the magpie landed well out of range.

At length the eagle flew off, and Carlos texted to Marvin to come pick us up. They had a full morning laid out for me, none of it unfortunately including a chance to do some quiet wetland-watching. In fact, at the next stop they planned to use a recording—an intrusive technique called tape-playback—to lure a rare and elusive waterbird called a little crake into the open, which I put the brakes on in a hurry. Over lunch, I tried again to make Carlos and Marvin understand the kind of experience I was looking for—no more baiting, no more tape playback. I wanted to see as many of the habitats as the delta offered. I was as happy to watch with binoculars as to photograph with my camera. It was at this meal that I think they finally understood my goals, and from then on we got along famously.

I spent more time in a couple of hides, but we also explored the mature floodplain forests along the river, watching a black woodpecker dismantling a fallen log, an inky black bird only a bit smaller than a crow, with pale yellow eyes and a scarlet slash on its crown, whacking free great chunks of punky wood in search of insects. Another day we spent the afternoon far to the south of the lodge concession in an area of steppe and wetlands where cattle and horses were grazing in large, semi-feral herds and the land seemed bursting with thousands of waterbirds of dozens of species.

I also finally had a chance to spend time with Rewilding Romania director Marina Drugă. It turned out that she had conducted field work for her PhD here in the delta, studying the lovely whiskered terns, gray-bellied with a smear of white across each side of the face, that crowded the air over any of the marshes we passed, working in the deepest, normally closed sections of the reserve where even researchers are rarely allowed to venture. Where she went in those days, with local guides, there are no marked paths through the seemingly endless reedbeds; the only way in is to force the slim boat through by grabbing the sturdy stems that rise high overhead and heaving oneself forward, one lurch at a time.

We were sitting on safari benches in the back of one of the lodge's pickups as Carlos drove us around, a chance for me to learn more about Rewilding's plans for the delta. Marina had served as the bison project manager when she worked for WWF-Romania some years earlier. As previously noted, most of the work on the delta has been overseen by Rewilding Ukraine, with whose director, Mykhailo Nesterenko, I'd spoken some months prior to my trip, and whose wetland restoration officer, Robert Negru, I had been especially looking forward to meeting at the lodge. Unfortunately, just before my arrival Robert had suffered an injury serious enough to require a trip out of the delta to the hospital, and I was only able to catch up with him via video some weeks after my return to the United States.

As we rounded a bend, Carlos hit the brakes because the road was blocked by three hulking black water buffalo with heavily ridged, backwards-sweeping horns. I was face to face with perhaps the oddest and most surprising of the tools in the Danube Delta's rewilding kit, at least by my reckoning. Rewilding Europe often refers to water buffalo[*] as a European native, and this is strictly true, since there was a Pleistocene species, though judging from the sparse fossil record it became extinct in most of central and eastern Europe about 120,000 years ago. However, there were once hundreds of thousands of water buffalo in rural communities in Romania, of two local breeds dating

---

[*] Even though American bison are colloquially called buffalo, neither they nor European bison are closely related to true buffalo like Asian water buffalo or Cape buffalo of Africa.

back centuries, but which in the post-Communist era were largely replaced with more traditional dairy cattle, so much so that today there is concern for their survival.

Regardless of their local pedigree, the Rewilding staff in both Romania and Ukraine see water buffalo as another ecosystem engineer, and they make no apologies for using them. "Rewilding is using nature to heal nature," Marina told me as we jounced down the dirt roads of the reserve. "You can't restore exactly what we've destroyed, so what do we want? Do we want biodiversity? Ecological functioning? So we work with what we have. In the Southern Carpathians we use bison, here we are using water buffalo."

When I spoke with Robert Negru, the wetland restoration specialist whom I'd missed during my visit, he echoed Marina's comments. "The water buffalo basically has two ecological roles to play, one being that it eats up the weeds and vegetation, creating pathways through the water and swampy habitat for other vertebrates or fish or birds to use. They clear up some of the vegetation. This also [allows] light to penetrate through the thick vegetation, creating the conditions for proper photosynthesis so that also submerged water plants can also grow," he told me.

My last morning at Ultima Frontiera was finally the chance I'd been waiting for since my arrival. Marvin dropped me off at a hide perched at the edge of a large lagoon. My arrival caused a bit of a ruckus among the many black-headed gulls and a flock of young shelducks, but everything settled down and I at last had a chance to spend a morning doing nothing but being an observer. The camera lay by my side, and I took a few photographs, but I mostly just watched and listened. There was a confusing welter of shorebirds in their nondescript, non-breeding plumage, enough to make my American eyes swim; it was a good reminder of how it feels to be a beginner without 50 years of identification experience to fall back on. I was grateful for those that were easier to identify, like black-tailed godwits with their long legs and ice-pick bills, black-backed stilts whose legs were an even more extravagant expression of verticality, and a single spotted redshank, fresh from the Scandinavian Arctic and still in its arresting, all-black breeding plumage with crimson legs and bill.

A trio of mute swans flew low overhead, passing above me with loud, laboring wingbeats. The swans swung out of sight, but a single pelican, immense and white, followed them and glided to a landing, leaving a long slash across the surface of the water. More pelicans arrived until eight or nine of them were standing in shallow water, preening above their perfect reflections, as did flocks of waders. The more time I spent watching the shorebirds, which now numbered in the hundreds across the lagoon, the more confident I was with sorting them out—common greenshanks, green sandpipers and reeves (as female ruffs are known), marsh and wood sandpipers, some juvenile little stints in fresh plumage, and some species like big, curve-billed Eurasian curlews, black-and-white pied avocets, and more spotted redshanks that were blindingly obvious even to me.

Eventually I turned my attention back to the pelicans. Great white pelicans have a soft, creamy yellowish bloom to their necks and chests, matching the somewhat deeper color of their throat sacs, and these shone quietly in the low morning light. Looking carefully for the first time, though, I realized that one of them, the pelican that had first arrived and had kept somewhat to itself, was not only drabber and grayer, but noticeably larger. With a shock, it finally dawned on me that this was a lone Dalmatian pelican, the endangered bird I had assumed I would never have a chance to see—an immature individual, lacking the bright orange-red throat pouch of an adult, but with the gray legs, pale eye, and shaggy crest that differentiates the Dalmatian from the great white. I felt sheepish, knowing how close I'd come to missing this rarest of delta birds through simple oversight. It's like realizing the person sitting across from you at the airport gate is a celebrity, but you were too buried in your book to notice.

It was a peaceful morning after a disquieting night. Sometime after midnight, I wasn't sure when, I was awakened by a high, keening sound. The air conditioning unit that kept the room somewhat cool was noisy, but when I turned it off, I could hear more clearly—sirens, many of them, off in the distance. Sleep-blurred, it took me a few moments for the significance to sink in, but they were air-raid sirens sounding in Vylkove, less than a mile across the Danube in Ukraine.

I waited for a long while, unsure what to do. There was no place to go, really, no underground room in which to take shelter. I heard no hubbub from the Rewilding folks or lodge staff elsewhere in the building; when I looked out my door everything was dark and quiet. There were no explosions, and after a time the sirens ended. Eventually I fell fitfully back to sleep. The next morning, I learned that Russia had launched the first of what proved to be a long series of major missile attacks on ports along the Ukrainian side of the Danube, trying to stop the flow of grain on cargo ships like those we'd passed. None of the strikes was close to the delta; from the news reports, the nearest was some 50 or 60 miles from me, well upriver from Tulcea. I learned later that when there's a Russian air attack anywhere in Ukraine, the warning sirens sound in many parts of the country because no one knows where the missiles are heading.

Certainly, life along the Danube seemed relatively normal when, having left the lagoon and its pelicans, I loaded my gear into one of the trucks, and Marvin and Carlos drove me back to the Sulina channel, where the ferryboat would pick me up for the 90-minute ride back to Tulcea. A long string of cargo ships plowed the murky water toward the Black Sea as we waited, and the news feed on my phone had story after story about this latest twist in a war that had by that point already been going on for a year and a half.

It was a subject that came up after my return to the United States when I was talking with Robert Negru. Most of our conversation dealt with the mechanics of delta hydrology, the history of ecosystem degradation there, and efforts to repair the damage, but then the conversation turned to the war and its effects. Even he finds the paradox of the Romanian delta's peace and rich nature, and the omnipresence of the war just across the river, deeply disorienting.

"I keep coming and going from Ultima [Frontiera], because I live in Bucharest. So I come here for a month, two months doing field work.

When I'm here, I have to admit to you, after five days, I completely forget that there's a war 20 kilometers from where I am. You hear the sirens, but it's just like background noise. You have to detach yourself from it in an active, conscious way so that you don't live in this fear or with the constant pressure of the war every day."

I had the luxury of leaving it behind. The ferry, its engines roaring, raced back upriver, weaving past cargo ships that were putting to sea, and at last to Tulcea, where Bobo was waiting patiently for me near the landing. The next day I boarded a plane in Bucharest for the short flight to Bulgaria, where vultures were waiting.

Six

Rescuing the Unlovely

It's a very short flight, barely more than an hour, from Bucharest to Sofia, the capital of Bulgaria, which shares a border with Romania along the Danube River, but there's a bit of culture shock there for an English-speaker like me. Romanian is a Romance language based on Latin, expressed in a Roman alphabet, with just enough similarities with other European languages that I felt I could puzzle out written Romanian at least some of the time. Bulgarian, on the other hand, is a Slavic tongue expressed in the Cyrillic alphabet, which actually originated in what is now Bulgaria in the 9th century. I was eternally grateful that most important signs in Bulgaria used both Cyrillic and a Romanization transliteration.

Waiting for me at the Sofia airport was Stoycho Stoychev, conservation director for the Bulgarian Society for the Protection of Birds, who would be my host and guide for the next week as we explored the biologically diverse eastern Rhodope Mountains of southern Bulgaria, and as I learned more about the successful and expanding program BSPB and others have undertaken to restore several lost species of vultures to the country's skies.

Stoycho was an engaging companion as we drove southeast from Sofia, heading for his hometown of Haskovo where we would overnight before completing the drive to the mountains the following day. Forty-eight, slight and wiry with a close-shaved scalp, Stoycho grew up with his grandparents, who came from areas that are now in

Greece and Turkey; his paternal grandfather, a tailor and a beekeeper, read anything he could find about nature, and young Stoycho caught that bug early as well. "I was making lists of birds, trying to identify them," he said, but there were no field guides, just books with simple black-and-white drawings and dichotomous keys, the latter the kind of painfully dry, if-this/then-that scientific approach better suited to puzzling out tree leaves or mollusk shells than living, moving birds. "But there was no other way," he said. The only bird book he saw with color plates, from Russia, didn't include the southern Bulgarian species he was observing.

At 14, he encountered a teacher who shared his interest. "I met for the first time a person who knew more about birds than me. And he had a field guide. To me it was like seeing a bible—he became my hero," Stoycho said. A year or two later he had already decided to become an ornithologist, and entered a local academic ecology competition on the team for the Haskovo district; they won, and went on to the nationals in Sofia. By 18 he was hitchhiking to the Turkish border region to do bird-ringing (banding). That's also when he first saw a leaflet for the BSPB, which was founded in 1988 in what proved to be the final years of the Communist regime that collapsed completely in 1990.

Bulgarian politics were roiled for many years thereafter. During his studies at the University of Plovdiv, Stoycho was involved in street protests, but he also organized a local chapter of BSPB with fellow bird enthusiasts at school. He did field studies on eastern imperial eagles, finding previously unknown nests ("It was like an archaeologist to find a new tomb," he said). In the mid-1990s he got his first job, a position at BSPB made possible by funding from the Swiss government, which saw opportunities to foster conservation in rapidly changing eastern Europe. So did the Royal Society for the Protection of Birds in the United Kingdom, which Stoycho told me provided key underwriting for its Bulgarian counterpart starting in the early 1990s. In fact, he said, the RSPB provided a crucial hand longer than any other entity, only just wrapping up its support three years before my visit.

Soon Stoycho was organizing what he called Ornithology Olympiads, much like the competition he had won as a teenager. He and the 10 or so youth winners would spend a week in the mountains, swimming in the rivers, watching the few vultures that remained in the country, learning about birds. Those camps changed the lives of many of those youngsters, some of whom pursued careers in science, and a fair number of whom (as I would soon learn) work for BSPB today. "This is one of the things I am most proud of," he said.

These days, BSPB is one of several environmental NGOs working in the country. Rewilding has a Bulgarian affiliate, the Rewilding Rhodope Foundation, which collaborates with BSPB on vulture conservation, though its focus is more on large-mammal reintroductions similar to those undertaken by Rewilding Romania, including releases of European bison, Konik horses, red deer, and fallow deer. Stoycho was the part-time team leader of the foundation for four years, as well as serving as the BSPB's part-time conservation director, but when Rewilding decided it needed a full-time director he had to choose, and opted to remain with BSPB. His group has taken the lead on vulture restoration work in the Rhodopes, while other partner organizations—the Green Balkans Federation, the Fund for Wild Flora and Fauna, and the Birds of Prey Protection Society—work with vultures in other regions, such as in the Balkan Mountains farther north in Bulgaria.

It's hard to get people to care about vultures. Even though they are among the largest and most dramatic of all birds, they have obvious public relations problems, and though you wouldn't know it from their absence in most conservation appeals, scavenging birds as a group are among the most imperiled in the world. That apathy is one of a complex tangle of reasons why, across much of the globe, vulture populations have plummeted, in some cases catastrophically—and with that collapse have come serious consequences for humans.

The worst days for western European vultures, as I've mentioned earlier, came in the late 19th and first half of the 20th centuries, when targeted persecution decimated the continental population of Europe's four species. By the 1990s, however, ground zero for vulture conservation had shifted suddenly and alarmingly to the Indian subcontinent.

In the late 1980s ornithologists in South Asia, especially India, began to note the disappearance of formerly abundant white-rumped, long-billed vultures, and slender-billed vultures. It didn't matter if the birds were ranging the countryside or living within protected parks; they were found dead or dying, exhibiting a peculiar drooping-neck posture before succumbing to whatever it was. Over the course of the next decade millions of vultures died or disappeared in India, Pakistan, Nepal, or Bangladesh. Previously common species were soon all but extinct, their populations reduced by as much as 99 percent.

It wasn't until 2004 that the culprit was confirmed—diclofenac, one of a family of nonsteroidal anti-inflammatory drugs (NSAIDs), which veterinarians were urging farmers to use to treat aches and pains in their livestock, because a pain-free cow gives more milk. Coming off-patent in 1994, diclofenac was cheap and readily available—but it and several related NSAIDs were also astoundingly toxic to Old World vultures, with even small amounts causing renal failure and gout in the digestive system if the birds ate the carcass of an animal treated with the drugs.

Veterinary diclofenac, ketoprofen, and aceclofenac have been banned by several regional governments, but the damage was done. Where there had once been 40 million vultures in India alone, performing an essential role cleaning up carrion, shocked conservationists were gathering some of the relatively few survivors into protective custody, to form captive breeding flocks as a last-ditch hedge against complete annihilation. It remains the fastest collapse of any group of birds on earth, second only to the extinction of the passenger pigeon in terms of the sheer numbers of individuals lost.

There were serious consequences for human beings, too. Some of the damage was cultural, like the inability of members of the Parsi sect to perform traditional "sky burials," in which the dismembered dead are placed in high towers to be consumed by vultures. And in a country like India with half a billion cows, water buffalos, goats, and other livestock, the loss of carrion removal meant both greater disease transmission among people and exploding populations of rats and feral dogs, which suddenly had far more food.

Despite legal bans on the veterinary use of NSAIDs, two decades after the cause of the collapse was identified, illegal diclofenac use remains a serious problem in some areas. Conservationists, meanwhile, have applied an all-of-the-above approach to the crisis. Captive breeding centers were established, along with vulture restaurants that provided toxin-free carrion. Nepal pioneered the concept of "vulture safe zones," or VSZs, each with a diameter of about 125 miles representing a vulture's average foraging distance. Within each VSZ intensive work with local communities and veterinary pharmacies prevented NSAID use while community-operated vulture feeding stations, stocked with the carcasses of aging, diclofenac-free cattle, provided nontoxic food. By 2023, 76 of Nepal's 77 administrative districts had been declared diclofenac-free, while the safe zone concept had been adopted by other South Asian countries.

By the early 2010s, there was evidence that thanks to all that work, a corner had been turned in Nepal. Road surveys showed that the declines in white-rumped and slender-billed vultures had stopped by 2012 or 2013, and that by 2018, white-rumped vulture numbers had undergone what the scientists called a rapid increase, although only in comparison to the meager, post-crash population numbers of those two species. Still, the news was encouraging enough for conservationists in Nepal to decide to close its remaining vulture breeding center, which had produced 69 captive-reared birds, and release its remaining vultures to the wild.

Threats remain, however, and some, like electrocution on poorly designed electrical lines, and poisoning of carcasses to kill mammalian predators, seem to be increasing. Since the early 2000s, the situation has also become increasingly bad for vultures in Africa, where poisoning, sometimes intentional, sometimes not, is the biggest threat. Poachers, for example, often used poison to lace the carcasses of elephants they killed, so that swarms of vultures did not immediately tip off wardens, a practice known as sentinel poisoning. Elsewhere on the continent, carcasses treated with pesticides like carbofuran and aldicarb, set out to kill lions or hyenas, take a huge toll on vultures, while still other vultures have been targeted intentionally with poison for their body parts, like their dried heads, used in traditional belief-based systems, mostly as good luck charms. Seven of Africa's 10 vulture species are now listed as endangered or critically endangered, with populations having fallen by as much as 97 percent, especially in West Africa (where poisoning for traditional use is worst) and East Africa (where poisoning to kill predators is heaviest). Rüppell's vulture, the Cape vulture, and the white-backed vulture—the three members of the same genus, *Gyps*, that has been decimated in South Asia—have been especially hard-hit in Africa.

Poison is not the only threat. Food scarcity from the decline in big game populations, especially in West Africa; electrocution and collisions from the fast-growing electrical power grid, which hasn't been designed to keep large birds safe; lead ingestion from hunting ammunition; and general habitat loss, all have played a role in African vulture declines.

Conservationists have pushed back hard by training more than 2,500 rangers, law enforcement officers, and veterinarians to detect and prosecute wildlife poisoning. Sentinel poisoning has dropped off with a reduction in elephant and rhino poaching. African conservationists are also adopting the idea of vulture safe zones, but the threats are so complex and widespread, with the continent divided among 54 countries, that the zones must be correspondingly large and multinational in scope. Telemetry studies have shown that African *Gyps* vultures have some of the largest ranges of any nonmigratory land animal; each year, a single white-backed vulture may range over nearly 10,000 square miles, while a single Rüppell's vulture may use an astonishing 28,000 square miles. Such massive areas far eclipse the size of existing protected areas in Africa, and show the scope of the challenge facing these birds.

In fact, the only region of the world that's a clear bright spot for vultures is the Western Hemisphere, whose seven species are, with the exception of the critically endangered but steadily recovering California condor, and the even larger and declining Andean condor, doing fairly well. Part of that is hereditary. "Vulture" is a lifestyle description, not an evolutionary lineage. The New World vultures, which belong to the order Cathartidae, are off by themselves a bit on the raptorial family tree, quite distinct from their Old World counterparts, which belong to the great order Accipitridae, with hawks, eagles, and kites. The Old and New World branches sprang from different ancestors, but were shaped by the demands of a scavenging lifestyle into very similar forms, a process known as convergent evolution.* One happy accident of that difference in ancestry is a difference in their biochemistry. Based on the evidence so far, New World cathartid vultures do not appear to be susceptible to NSAID poisoning like the *Gyps* vultures of Eurasia and Africa; a turkey vulture from Arizona or Colombia can consume diclofenac at 100 times the level that would kill a white-rumped or slender-billed vulture, and not even burp.

The situation in Europe is also far more encouraging than in Asia or Africa. There are now between 70,000 and 90,000 griffon vultures in Europe, and their population growth in Spain seems to have been leveling off in the past decade or so, suggesting griffons may be reaching carrying capacity there. NSAIDs have been less of a danger in Europe, although the decision in 2013 by Spain to authorize the veterinary use of diclofenac alarmed conservationists, given that the country holds about 95 percent of Europe's vulture population, alarms that intensified in 2021 when diclofenac killed a fledgling cinereous vulture in

---

* Oddly, what we now think of as New World vultures appear to have first evolved in Europe about 50 million years ago, while there is evidence that so-called Old World vultures originated in the Western Hemisphere before spreading out beyond, and eventually disappearing from there. Similarly, hummingbirds, now restricted to the Americas, first appear in the fossil record in Germany. Evolution and geologic time like to shuffle the deck.

the nest in Catalonia. The bearded vulture, a bird of striking form and color that inhabits the highest mountain ranges from the Pyrenees to the Alps, Corsica, and Crete, continues a slow recovery thanks to reintroduction programs; in 2021, the reestablished population in the Alps fledged 44 chicks from 67 occupied territories.

In southern and eastern Europe, where vultures have been severely reduced in number, poison has been a consistent threat. Bulgaria's last bearded vulture was found poisoned in the 1970s, and the species has only been a rare vagrant ever since. The last cinereous vulture pair nested in the eastern Rhodopes, where we were headed, for a single year in 1993 and were never seen again. Egyptian vultures, once common village birds, had plummeted in number.

Griffon vultures were all but gone from Bulgaria when BSPB started, with just a handful of pairs remaining. The species had suffered what conservationists described as "catastrophic declines" throughout the Balkans from the 1950s through the 1970s because of widespread poisoning campaigns aimed at wolves, jackals, and feral dogs. Starting in 2010, griffon vultures from Spain were released in the Balkan Mountains as well as the Kresna Gorge in southwestern Bulgaria. By 2024 there were 138 pairs in the country, but while the overall population has increased in Bulgaria, Serbia, and Croatia, previously large populations in Greece and North Macedonia have collapsed, and griffon vultures remain absent from Romania as well as Bosnia-Herzegovina.

Poisoning, usually unintentional as farmers and hunters dose carcasses with highly toxic carbamate pesticides like carbofuran and methomyl to kill wolves, jackals, feral dogs, and other mammalian predators, remains one of the most serious problems for vultures in eastern and southern Europe. One of Stoycho's colleagues who joined us for dinner that evening in Haskovo, Nikolay Terziev, took what in Bulgaria was a groundbreaking approach to the problem eight years earlier when he traveled to Hungary to meet a young male German shepherd named Bars. Nikolay and Bars trained together for nearly two months so Bars could find poisoned bait and poisoned animals by scent, the first anti-poisoning canine unit in the country.

The name Bars, Nkolay told me, was a bit of word-play. *Aq Bars* is an ancient Bulgar and Central Asian god in the form of a snow leopard, one who can see through lies. "And of course, 'bars' can also mean a bar, in English," he said with a laugh.

Their first case came in the autumn of 2016. "We got a call from a guy who knows a guy who knows us," Nikolay said. It was in the southern Rhodopes, close to the Greek border, "a total mess. It was several hours of searching, and we found so many, maybe 15 or 16 poisoned animals—fox, hedgehogs, a wolf that the poisoner had buried."

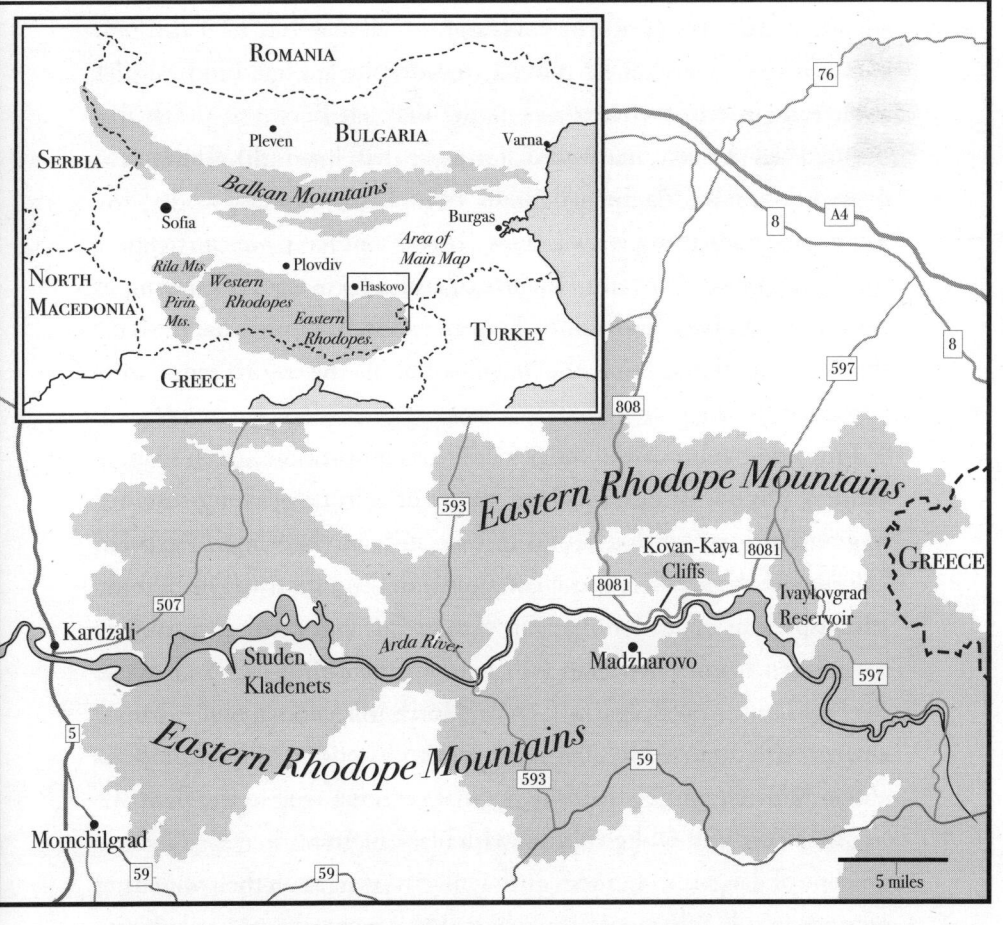

Thanks to reintroduction projects, once-vanished vultures are returning to the Eastern Rhodope Mountains of Bulgaria.

In the years since then, Nikolay and Bars have investigated more than 150 sites, uncovering evidence of several cases of poisoning and its victims, including griffon and Egyptian vultures. Despite these successes, there has never been a single conviction for poisoning wildlife, the blame for which Nikolay lays at the feet of the Bulgarian legal system, which he said doesn't take wildlife crimes seriously. That said, Bars has been a good ambassador for public awareness of the poisoning problem, awareness that Nikolay said is now much greater than it had been thanks to a lot of social media coverage.

I got to meet Bars the next morning, before we left Haskovo, when Nikolay brought him by the hotel. Bars was a handsome, darkly furred shepherd, russet behind the ears, and as Nikolay put him through some practice searches he moved well despite his age (and despite a bacterial infection three years earlier that left Bars near death and hospitalized at a veterinary clinic for more than a month). The lack of prosecutions hasn't dampened Nikolay's enthusiasm for the work. "The most important thing is awareness. This is a process, we can't expect results right away," he said. The use of anti-poison dogs is growing in Bulgaria, with two new trained Belgian Malinois joining handlers on the Bulgarian police force, the first anti-poison law enforcement units of the sort in the Balkans.

Protecting vultures and other wildlife is complex enough in a single country, but one of Europe's four species of vultures is a long-distance migrant, a situation that brings its own suite of challenges. Egyptian vultures are the smallest and most rapidly declining vulture in Europe, with especially acute problems in eastern Europe, where its numbers have fallen from more than 600 pairs in the 1980s to 50 or 60 in the four countries (Bulgaria, Greece, North Macedonia, and Albania) where it still occurred in 2015. The eastern Rhodope Mountains hold about 30 pairs, roughly half the population remaining in the Balkans.

These nearly all-white vultures with black flight feathers face a kaleidoscope of dangers in Europe, during migration, and on their wintering grounds in sub-Saharan Africa, where they congregate primarily in the semiarid Sahel region just south of the desert, Volen Arkumarev told me.

Volen, Stoycho, and I were about an hour from Haskovo, in the hills above one of the many small villages we'd passed through coming down from Sofia, with white stork nests, sometimes dozens of them in one town, all but enveloping the street lamps on which they had been built.

Once, Egyptian vultures were just as common as the storks in villages across the Rhodopes, essentially a backyard bird, helping to clean up offal and carrion. It was the focus of a lot of folklore and religious veneration. In Albania and Greece, its local name means "horse of the cuckoo," in the belief that Eurasian cuckoos ride them south to Africa. There's a Muslim tradition that these vultures were once brown, as the juveniles still are, but after one saved the Prophet Mohammed from an attacking golden eagle, it was blessed with white plumage and eternal life; older ethnic Turks call them *akbuba*, "white father," and hold them to be sacred in a sense.

Our attention now was on a distant cliff on which Volen had trained his spotting scope. Deep in a crevice up there was an Egyptian vulture nest, although I had to take this on faith as I failed to see any sign of it across the distance and through the hot, shimmering midafternoon air. But before long the male vulture flew in, carrying food in its mouth; it was the first Egyptian vulture I'd seen in the wild, and I suppose reading so many references to it being the smallest European vulture had given me the wrong mental image, because this was quite an impressive raptor, with wings spanning five feet or more, like those of a spotted eagle, "small" only in comparison to a truly enormous species like a bearded or cinereous vulture. It was also, apparently, quite aware of us despite the distance, for it avoided the nest and landed on a high rocky knob, watching us with what, through the scope, felt like a decidedly suspicious eye. I could see its bright yellow-orange facial skin, the only part of an Egyptian vulture's head that is naked, but the quarter-mile distance was too far to see what Volen told me was a unique identification feature on this and any Egyptian vulture, the black markings on its face.

"This one has a small black mark near the beak, the shape of a raindrop, and his female has a large black mark," he said.

Volen, tall, broad-shouldered, and bearded, has been working to restore the Balkan Peninsula's Egyptian vultures for years. Now 32 years old, he said he was a village kid interested in nature who took part in Stoycho's Ornithology Olympiad, and in 2005, at age 14, he began helping as a BSPB volunteer. All of that set him on a path that eventually led to a PhD and a job with the society, much of which revolves around Egyptian vulture conservation.

"It all started with Stoycho," Volen said, laughing.

"Yes, he's one of my kids," Stoycho replied with a grin, "and there are more of them you're going to meet."

Volen and a number of colleagues have spent years using telemetry and other techniques to figure out where the Balkans' Egyptian vultures go, and where the danger points lie along the way. It turns out there are many threats, some close to home, some far away. Poisoning has proven to be a very clear and immediate threat; of 43 dead adult Egyptian vultures found over 13 years in Bulgaria, Greece, and North Macedonia, 77 percent had died from poison. Many others died from electrocution on poorly designed electrical pylons, or by colliding with transmission lines. Those passing along the eastern edge of the Mediterranean, through countries like Jordan, were at risk of being shot by local hunters, and those that made it to African countries like Niger and Nigeria stood a good chance of being killed for their body parts. Even zealous nest-guarding and supplementary feeding in the Balkans proved insufficient to stem the continuing declines.

But information is power and provides a road map for recovery. Starting in 2017, armed with the knowledge about where the biggest threats lay, and with funding from the European Commission and others, a collaboration coordinated by BSPB involving 22 conservation or research organizations in 14 countries tackled all of these problems, with remarkable success. In addition to fielding poison-detecting canine units and publicizing the dangers of poison, which reduced the number of poisoning incidents in the Balkans by half between 2018 and 2022, they installed protective insulators on some 10,000 dangerous electrical pylons between eastern Europe and Saudi Arabia and

Ethiopia. Their efforts reduced illegal shooting in Jordan by almost a third, and working with thousands of people in West Africa—hunters, traditional healers who were encouraged to use herbal alternatives, school kids, local law enforcement officials—dramatically reduced the availability of vulture body parts in markets, including by 95 percent in Nigeria, once one of the worst centers for that trade. Volen said the healers themselves were open to the change, since they could see that vultures in general were declining. Overall, a 2023 review of the herculean efforts on behalf of this species found that the survival rate of juveniles increased almost 10 percent, and by 2024 the population had increased by 20 percent, a welcome reversal of fortune.

One key component of the multinational effort on behalf of Egyptian vultures is something Volen, BSPB, and their partners at Green Balkans, the Prague Zoo, and the European Association of Zoos and Aquaria have been doing since 2018, which is not a reintroduction but a "reinforcement" program, to bolster the fragile remaining Balkans population with captive-reared individuals from European zoos, and with wild chicks taken from nests, youngsters that hatched so late in the season they would otherwise stand little chance of surviving. Raised in isolation from humans over the subsequent winter, two months before their release the following summer, the cadre, usually half a dozen or so, are moved to what BSPB calls "Egyptian vulture school," a large aviary overlooking a vulture feeding site where they can observe wild griffon and Egyptian vultures while practicing flight skills.

Once released (and carrying GPS/GSM transmitters), they're monitored closely while they integrate into the local vulture community. As of 2024 five vultures from the reinforcement program had survived to enter the breeding population, including the first-ever pair in which both mates were alumni. In late summer that year, both of that pair's chicks were fitted with transmitters, marking the first time that an entire Egyptian vulture family from Bulgaria would be tracked on their migration.

Unfortunately, neither female chick survived the trip. One was shot by poachers on the Adrasan Peninsula of Turkey, while the other drowned attempting to cross the Mediterranean. Such drowning deaths, Volen said, were a previously unrecognized problem. While most of the vultures raised in the eastern Balkans or Rhodope Mountains tend to follow the edge of the Mediterranean and migrate south through countries like Turkey, Jordan, and Israel, those raised farther west, in Greece, Albania, and North Macedonia, tend to strike out straight across the Mediterranean itself—usually with fatal consequences. Like most vultures, the Egyptians depend on thermal air currents to provide lift when they fly; they are not built for sustained flapping flight. But open water rarely produces strong thermals, and of the 10 juveniles that tried to fly south directly across the Mediterranean, only one survived. Because Egyptian vultures originally migrated in large groups, Volen and others suspect that the lack of experienced adults in the population means the youngsters have no one to guide them around, rather than across, the deadly water. In this, the unlucky female from the nest we watched was unusual, since few fledglings from that far east try an overwater crossing.

Sadly, the one young vulture that had previously survived its Mediterranean crossing was later killed in Niger, Volen said. But its death wasn't entirely in vain. Thanks to its transmitter, which continued to function after it was killed, scientists were able to unravel the whole supply chain from hunter to middleman to traditional healer, helping to understand where and how vulture parts were making it to market, and giving them information to begin to curtail the practice.

Later, we visited the vulture school and its adjacent feeding station. There was not yet a fresh class of recruits in residence, but we saw some griffon vultures wheeling in the distance as we drove up, opened the gate, and entered the fenced-off hillside. "The boneyard," Stoycho said as we got out of the BSPB truck, and there was a whiff of decay in the air, although in the dry, ovenlike heat it was far from overpowering. Most of the remains scattered around the restaurant were either bare bones or desiccated, like the largely intact skeleton of a cow, its head still wrapped in mummified skin and hair. Overlooking the restaurant was a substantial observation hide built of rough stone with a concrete roof, green cloth curtains covering its small windows. Getting carcasses to feed the vultures was an increasing challenge, Stoycho said, because there are fewer and fewer farmers with livestock that BSPB can collect when it dies, saving the farmer the expense of disposal.

The next morning we drove to Madzharovo, a town along the Arda River which during the Communist period depended on nearby zinc and lead mines. The mines closed in 1997 after the Iron Curtain fell, bringing hard times, and Madzharovo itself, now home to fewer than 600 people, has a derelict feel to it, even with one nice new hotel in town, and a few immense murals on the sides of the otherwise forgettable 1970s apartment buildings. One mural, five stories high, depicted an Egyptian vulture looking down at an egg through whose translucent shell a human baby could be seen. It was eye-catching, but... puzzling. "I'm not really sure what the artist wanted to say," Stoycho admitted.

As run-down as Madzharovo itself may be, the town sits in a spectacular setting. The Arda, clear and fast-flowing, loops and twists through the caldera of an ancient volcano, with high, rusty-orange or gray cliffs on all sides breaking through the dry mountain forest, including Kovan-Kaya, "Beehive Cliff" in Turkish, which rears above an especially scenic horseshoe bend in the river, and where both griffon and Egyptian vultures nest. The cliff is named for the dozens of trapezoidal niches left by the ancient Thracians more than 2,000 years ago (to what exact purpose no one is quite certain), and it and the areas around it have been designated a natural landmark to protect the vultures. In fact, nature tourism is now the main economic driver in the region, and we would be staying at its epicenter, the BSPB's Nature Conservation Centre Eastern Rhodopes, aka the vulture center, perched above the Arda. In addition to serving as an educational hub for visitors to the region, it also has a restaurant and a small but very comfortable hotel where we would be rooming.

Stoycho and I had bid farewell to Volen the day before, but at the vulture center we met Ivaylo Angelov, who after some years as a freelance biologist had started working for BPSB again. Ivaylo, 42, who did his PhD on golden eagles, is a raptor guy, like a lot of the men (and so far as I could tell from the folks I met, it was all men) working on vulture conservation in Bulgaria.

The day was getting hot, even under the deep shade around the vulture center, so after we dropped our gear in our rooms we headed out before it grew much worse. Stoycho wanted to show me the next exciting step in vulture restoration in eastern Rhodopes, bringing back the cinereous vulture. We were on our way to the remote aviary where 13 young vultures from Spain, some raised in captivity, some rescued from the wild, were being prepared for their release in several months, when they would join 15 others that had been set free in 2022.

"Remote" was the operative word; it was a long, slow, jouncing ride on sometimes switchbacked dirt roads. This part of the Rhodopes is only a short distance from both the Greek and Turkish borders, so close, in fact, that my phone's international plan kept sending me, "Welcome to Turkey!" and "Welcome to Greece!" messages again and again as we zigzagged back and forth on rugged mountain roads. Verizon must have thought I was quite the gadabout. Others moved at a very different pace, like the weathered old male Greek tortoise, his shell worn smooth by the decades, which we lifted out of the middle of the road. Vehicles are not the only danger to tortoises; to my surprise, Ivaylo told me that his doctoral research showed they make up 65 percent of the diet of local golden eagles, which drop them from on high to crack them open to eat. I wished the old chap well and suggested he stay under cover.

At length we reached the huge and still new aviary, which had been funded by Rewilding Europe and built in collaboration with the Rewilding Rhodopes Foundation. Speaking in whispers, we slipped by a side door into an observation room, and I had my first close view of this largest of European vultures. The baker's dozen of them—nine males, four females—were dark umber, with massive beaks framed by pinkish skin around the nostrils and gape of the mouth, their heads covered in short, dense, brown feathers. Each vulture had a ruff of long, shaggy neck feathers that they could raise or lower like someone flipping up the collar of their coat against a cold breeze.

The Rhodopes Mountain reintroduction follows earlier, successful efforts by a different suite of partner NGOs starting in 2018 in the Balkan Mountains farther north, with more than 70 either Spanish- or captive-born cinereous vulture chicks released into the wild—the wild-bred birds from aviaries like this one, the captive-bred vultures from hack sites similar to those once used in North America to habituate falcons and eagles to the wild. By 2022, the 41 survivors had formed two distinct populations at opposite ends of the Balkan Mountains, each with three or four pairs that had already mated and begun breeding within two years, mostly on artificial nest platforms built high in trees. Now the idea was to replicate that success in the Rhodopes. (Despite the overall success in the Balkan Mountains, the times remain perilous for vultures. In March 2022, four cinereous vultures, including the first wild-fledged chick in 28 years, were killed in a single poisoning incident, which Nikolay Terziev and Bars investigated.)

Ivaylo opened a small door at the back of the cage and, wearing elbow-length red rubber gloves, started tossing in offal. Soon half the vultures were jockeying for food, moving in slow, hunched, exaggerated hops, wings drooping and heads held low as they tried to intimidate each other, tearing the food they snagged to shreds with those powerful bills. The vulture team has tracked hundreds of such interactions, noting the ever-changing dominance hierarchies through the alphanumeric codes on the birds' plastic leg bands—who's up, who's down, who's on the make. It was an oven inside the small, airless observation room, but the show was worth the discomfort.

And there is a hierarchy at a carcass, too, where each species plays a different role in breaking down and disposing of a large, dead animal, Stoycho explained. The griffon vultures, with their long and fuzz-covered neck and heads, reach far inside to feed on internal organs. Cinereous vultures like these focus on the skin and outer meat, hence their heavily feathered neck and lightly feathered heads, while Egyptian vultures, whose faces alone are bare, make do with the smaller bits. Once the carcass has been reduced to bone, the bearded vultures take over, dropping bigger bones to the rocks where they crack into pieces, or simply swallowing smaller bones whole and digesting them.

In this, bearded vultures are unique, the only vertebrates whose diet is primarily bone, and the older and more weathered the bone, the better. They are also beautiful birds—yes, a beautiful vulture. Almost as large as cinereous vultures, they have long, tapered wings. Adults are dark gunmetal gray-black on the back, while the undersides and chest are usually a rich rusty-orange, not from pigment inherent in the feathers, but because the vulture intentionally marks itself by wallowing breast-down in mineral soil of that color. The black tail is long and wedge-shaped, while the orange, fully feathered head and face has two long, black feathered "beards" that protrude down and forward on each side of the nostrils, and another below the beak.

In 2023, a seven-year, EU-funded project to reintroduce captive-bred bearded vultures to the Balkan Mountains was launched, this one led by Green Balkans with seven partner organizations. The 5.1-million-euro budget also covers additional releases of cinereous vultures in that Balkan range and in southwestern Bulgaria to create new breeding sites.

That evening back at the vulture center in Madzharovo, I joined Stoycho, Ivaylo, and Ivaylo's two kids as we worked our way downstream along the Arda River valley by vehicle, stopping occasionally to get out and, with binoculars and a spotting scope, scan the great coppery cliffs of Kovan-Kaya. Stoycho said there were 18 or 20 griffon vulture nests on the main cliff face; we could see a fledgling vulture sitting in one, hunched and quiet on its ledge, while an adult stood nearby on a rock splashed with whitewash droppings. Another nest was a double-decker, one above the other, each with two adults in attendance. The BSPB maintains a database of more than 460 known griffon nest locations in the country, of which about 120 are usually active in any given year, including four or five new sites added that year alone—a signal of continuing population recovery. But around us were signs of recent camping activity, and Ivaylo said there has been an increase in unregulated drone activity, which may explain (along with growing road noise and increasing use of the informal camping area along the river) why the griffon vultures at Kovan-Kaya seem to be shifting their nests higher up and farther back on the cliffs.

We drove the truck up into the hills on an ever-narrower track, then I followed my friends up a steeper slope on foot, scrambling hand-over-hand to the top of a high, rocky knob hundreds of feet above the river. It was a spectacular view, the setting sun bathing everything in rich, yellow-orange light, but it was also a little nerve-wracking, since we were jammed together onto a small, uneven perch without much elbow room, and were buffeted by powerful wind gusts that had me gripping the rocks and trying not to lose my hat or my balance. Looking behind us to the east, we realized there was a substantial wildfire burning near the big Ivaylovgrad Reservoir, one which, judging from its smoke column, must have stretched for miles. That summer was an especially awful one for fires in southern Europe, particularly Greece, where one blaze scorched more than 230,000 acres.

The next morning, my last full day in the Rhodopes, was overcast and breezy, a blessed change from the relentless heat and sun of the previous weeks there and in Romania. Stoycho, Ivaylo, and I drove through town, past the entrances to the old mines, and back to the river. There we met Dobromir Dobrev, 36, a muscular guy in a green BSPB tee-shirt, a short jawline beard, and his dark hair buzzed close on the sides and long on the crown, worn in a short ponytail. Dobri, as he's known, with his twin brother Vladimir are two more of Stoycho's "kids" from the Olympiad days, who had spent a week watching vultures around Madzharovo with him back in 2001, when they were in their early teens. As an undergrad, Dobri worked with Egyptian vultures but later completed a PhD on griffon ecology, while Vladimir's doctorate focused on Egyptian vultures. Both now work for BSPB on those respective species, with Dobri also working with cinereous vultures.

As the four of us scanned the sky above the narrow gorge, the pale silvery-green of the shoreline willows contrasting with the dark green of the oaks that covered the hills, we talked about Dobri's telemetry work with griffon vultures, and how out of 17 or 18 juveniles he's tagged, only two have survived to their second year. Poison put out for wolves and bears in the Balkan Mountains has been the biggest problem, but there's also been persecution when the juveniles (which, unlike the more sedentary adults, migrate to Africa for their first winter) have been killed in Sudan or Yemen. He's also concerned by the growing footprint of wind development in places like the edge of the Black Sea in northeastern Bulgaria, and the mountains on the Greek side of the country's southern border, not far from where we were. Turbines have proven dangerous for vultures elsewhere in Europe, and Dobri said he thinks the solution is to avoid core areas critical to the birds. "But I think we're going to have to make sacrifices elsewhere," he said.

That's when Ivaylo quietly pointed out a vulture trifecta overhead: a griffon, an Egyptian, and a hulking big cinereous vulture wheeling around together. It seemed a good omen, as I climbed into Dobri's truck while Stoycho and Ivaylo headed out to get something accomplished other than tour-guiding.

When Dobri started working with griffon vultures in 2010, there were only 47 pairs in the country, nesting on five or six cliffs. Today there are 120 pairs in 18 breeding clusters. "At that time [2010], we never imagined this would happen—there were so few then. But each year there are a few more, and a few more," he said. Supplemental feeding like that at the boneyard I'd visited, changes to electrical pylons to prevent electrocution, donations of electric fencing and shepherd dogs trained to protect sheep so farmers don't feel compelled to poison wolves and bears, even giving away hundreds of tee-shirts and hats with pro-vulture slogans, all have helped, Dobri told me.

"It's all about building trust, building responsibility. Once they trust you, they will support you," he said. Still, the vulture conservationists have to battle misinformation, like the rumor that the BSPB is releasing wolves to kill livestock so the vultures will have more to eat.

We spent the day driving through the countryside, with Dobri checking up on locations where recent telemetry results showed cinereous vultures had been hanging around, suggesting the possibility of a carcass there. Following up on one cluster of GPS points, we parked the truck and scrambled higher and higher up a steep, gravelly slope, past a haphazard series of dilapidated, tile-roofed stables, with cautious eyes on the gathering storm clouds, against which a short-tailed eagle was kiting, hanging motionless in the gusty wind, head down, scanning the earth for prey. Dobri kept looking at his phone, toggling back and forth between two maps, one with the telemetry data, one showing our location in ever-greater detail. "Just here," he said several times, looking in the brush for any sign of carrion that would have drawn in the vultures. Nothing. Cinereous vultures often feed on the remains of surprisingly small animals, Dobri said, so it's possible they ate all of whatever had attracted them here. Thunder was rumbling, and we were the highest objects on a fairly barren hill. Lightning flashed, much too close for comfort. "Let's go—*now!*" he said, and we skittered and slid downhill at a breakneck pace, loose rock rolling underfoot, making it back to the vehicle just as the rain sluiced down.

The storm passed quickly, and the sun was shining again when we arrived at Studen Kladenets Reserve, an enormous reservoir on the Arda River about 15 miles west of Madzharovo, where a small herd of European bison has been reintroduced by the Rewilding Rhodope Foundation, the first in the region since the Middle Ages. The land around this part of the reservoir is a huge hunting concession overseen by the Union of Bulgarian Hunters and Anglers, which Dobri said has also been helpful with vulture work; we ran into the local manager, who filled in Dobri on what vultures the fellow had been seeing. We stood on a high, windswept hill overlooking the impoundment, the electrical transmission lines that looped from tower to tower overhead spangled with fluttering, flickering reflectors to minimize collisions, while the pylons themselves had special insulators to prevent vulture electrocutions.

As we drove through the concession in and out of the hardwood forest and fields, we saw no bison but did flush plenty of fallow deer and a few, much larger red deer. The Rewilding Rhodopes Foundation has, with help from hunting associations and local communities, been stocking both species at several places in Bulgaria, including here at Studen Kladenets, releasing as many as 1,000 countrywide in the preceding decade. The idea is to provide more wild food for carnivores like wolves and eagles, and thus more carrion for scavengers like vultures. But I couldn't help but notice a very apparent browse line on many of the trees, the point below which hungry deer had stripped away much of the vegetation.

I later learned that the local impact I saw may have been exacerbated by intensive feeding and the provision of salt blocks by hunters, which concentrates the deer, but the question of deer abundance, and the potential for overabundance, was something that was rarely far from my mind while traveling both in the southern Carpathians and the Rhodopes. I understand the theory behind the Rewilding Europe philosophy, using large herbivores to maintain certain ecological functions and engineer various habitat conditions. But even leaving aside extreme examples, like those repeated starvation debacles at Oostvaardersplassen in the Netherlands, I've seen what happens when one of those ecosystem engineers runs out of control. I have lived my whole life among the hardwood forests of eastern North America, where arguably the single most pervasive, negative ecological pressure is overbrowsing by white-tailed deer, pressure that has radically altered the structure and composition of hundreds of millions of acres of forest with impacts on birds and pretty much everything else.

A persistent doubt, constantly niggling at the back of my mind when discussing rewilding plans involving large ungulates, was whether something similar would happen there, too. After all, the Rhodopes or Carpathians are not a fenced, carefully curated Knepp Estate, where managers can bring in sharpshooters with night vision scopes and cull exactly enough animals to keep the balance. Nor, I was assured in both Romania and Bulgaria, would that be necessary; I was told again and again that there are enough wolves, lynx, and bear to control the fallow, red, and roe deer (and, eventually, presumably the bison). In fact, when I tried to describe the hoofed and antlered apocalypse chewing away at American forests, I was chided that all we Americans needed was more wolves. Attempts to describe, say, the sprawling, horizon-spanning suburbs of the I-95 corridor, overrun with deer and with no place for large carnivores, received puzzled looks.

"We have wolves and bears right outside Sofia," Stoycho said, waving his hand when I broached the subject. "They eat the deer. You just need more wolves." But Sofia sits in what is still, despite its more than 1 million inhabitants, a largely agricultural valley, wrapped on three sides by mountains. There's nothing in eastern Europe like, say, the Washington, DC, metroplex, with nearly half a million households in Fairfax County, Virginia alone, and more than 1 million people jammed into thousands of cul-de-sac developments connected by thousands of miles of road, among which live deer at densities up to 100 per square mile, because suburbia is paradise for deer where the only predators roll on rubber tires.

The rewilding experiment is running, and the stakes are high. I hope the Bulgarian wolves stay hungry, and leave plenty of leftovers for the vultures, because after centuries of trouble the great birds deserve a break.

Seven

Guano-Bombed on Egg Rock

Squirt. *Whack!*
 Squirt. *Whack!*

The harsh *KEEER-yuuurr* of an angry common tern, close by my head, was the signal that another dive-bombing run was underway. As the tern flashed past me, I felt the splash of wet guano hitting my hat or back, followed instantly by the sharp crack of a pointed beak on the crown of my wide-brimmed hat. Fortunately, I'd followed veteran advice to armor up, with a piece of corrugated cardboard folded inside the hat to protect my scalp from jabs that can easily draw blood, over the hood of my by now well-soiled rain jacket.

The terns—many hundreds, swirling around us in righteous indignation—had every reason to attack. Seven of us were moving slowly through a dense breeding colony at the south end of Eastern Egg Rock, a treeless, seven-acre island off the midcoast of Maine, on which more than 1,500 common, Arctic, and roseate terns nest every year. They were joined by hordes of laughing gulls, whose manic cries are constant during the long June days, and continue through the short nights on the island, when the weird, tittering calls of Leach's storm-petrels, swallow-like seabirds that come and go from their nest burrows only under cover of darkness, add to the cacophony. Black guillemots the size of pigeons buzzed past over crashing surf, their stark white wing patches contrasting with their inky breeding plumage and carmine-colored feet (which, I knew from long familiarity, match the crimson linings of their mouths). A couple of duck-sized common murres in formal black and white evening wear, which like the guillemots are members of the alcid, or auk, family, rode the swells offshore, rare birds this far south that under other circumstances would have merited a lingering, thoughtful look.

Ironically, given the ceaseless summer racket of bird calls there, Eastern Egg Rock's most famous residents are also among its quietest. Atlantic puffins do vocalize; they growl, sounding a bit like a chain saw revving up, but that's not a call you usually hear as the puffins fly back from sea to loaf on the jumbled boulders that form this small island, less than 20 feet above sea level and five or six miles from land at the mouth of Muscongus Bay. Yet without the puffins, none of the other seabirds would be here. And without Stephen W. Kress, there would have been no puffins.

"Two eggs," Steve yelled, stepping past the common tern nest whose contents he'd just relayed to Theresa Rizza, that summer's Eastern Egg Rock island supervisor for National Audubon's Seabird Institute. She shouted the same thing back to confirm she'd heard and recorded the nest—shouting was the only way to be heard over the raucous birds. "Triangle," he yelled, referring to a nest with three eggs (a multisyllabic word like "triangle" carries more clearly through the cacophony of sound), and she echoed him at volume. Kress, 78 with a gray beard and a twinkling smile, wore a pair of yellow rainproof overalls and a tam o'shanter cap, while casually holding a long stick over his head. The terns were whacking the end of the stick, not his head, and I couldn't help but notice that he was somehow unmarked by guano. Meanwhile, and despite my own protective stick, I felt a double hit as two terns got me from opposite directions. "Triangle," he yelled, taking another careful step forward across an island he knows better than almost any other patch of land on the planet.

Eastern Egg Rock doesn't look like much, but it's hard to overstate the impact that the conservation work Steve Kress pioneered there in 1973, and which he dubbed Project Puffin, has had on the fate of endangered seabirds around the world. By succeeding in restoring an

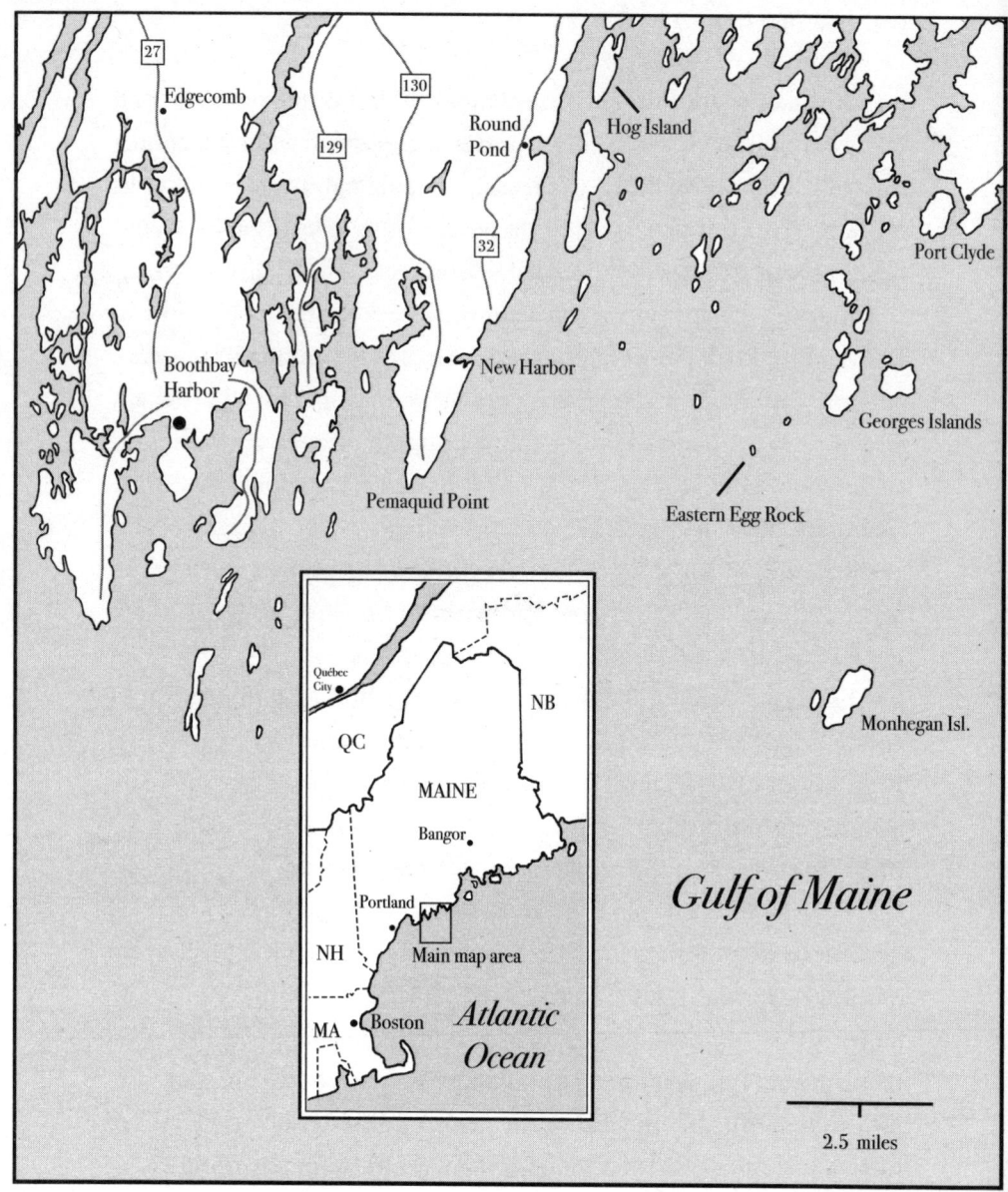

A tiny fleck in the Gulf of Maine, Eastern Egg Rock has an outsize importance in the history of seabird conservation, with global impacts.

Atlantic puffin colony wiped out a century earlier at the southern margin of the species' range, a goal that most experts considered unnecessary at best and foolhardy at worst, Kress showed that seabird colonies can be rebuilt to full ecological function in part by harnessing the social power of the birds themselves. I would see the globe-spanning results of that work on another island more than 5,000 miles away, but for now, I was joining Kress and the Eastern Egg Rock team for a couple of days as they conducted their annual tern census on an island that has become a symbol of successful and innovative bird conservation.

Rizza's four college-age colleagues—Arden Kelly, Harper Brown, Ke Coco Deng, and Camryn Zoeller—were also yelling egg counts, so on top of the noise of the birds, there was a hubbub of human voices as we walked slowly and gingerly in a line six abreast, Theresa trailing behind with her clipboard and pen, as we tried to find and tally each tern or laughing gull clutch. Next to each tern nest, which was just a shallow circle of grass on the gray-and-pink rock, we carefully laid a wooden tongue depressor, a temporary marker to show that the nest had been counted; after we completed our east-west sweeps through this sector, we would do the same north-south, picking up the tongue depressors and noting for Theresa any nests we'd missed on the first passes. We were counting only common tern nests; those of the Arctic and roseate terns, much less common on the island, had already been located and flagged by the interns: white flags for Arctics, pink for the roseates.

The five young women were staying on this isolated, exposed, storm-raked island all summer, arriving in May and not leaving until August after the terns and puffins had fledged their chicks and departed. In between they were leading a very spartan, extremely rustic life: no running water, sleeping in tents covered in plastic tarps to fend off the guano, using an outhouse, bombarded with poop from angry terns every time they stepped away from their small base camp (and often while moving around within it), rationing the fresh water that is delivered regularly in 20-liter plastic Jerry cans. They only wash themselves—and their dishes—when there is rainwater runoff collected in buckets. It hadn't rained for a while, so when Steve and I arrived for a couple of days to help, they apologized for any body odor. "Don't worry, you go nose-blind pretty quickly," Arden assured us.

Saltwater baths are available, obviously, but the surf can be dangerous and in early summer the water temperature is in the low 50s, tops, so warming up after a dip on a cool, foggy island poses a hypothermic problem. Normally the crew would have had a 12-foot-square wooden cabin, known as the Egg Rock Hilton, for more permanent shelter, but record-breaking storms the previous winter had battered the nearly 50-year-old structure and shifted it cockeyed off its foundations, so they were using two canvas wall tents on platforms for cooking, data entry, and equipment storage. I'd been advised that in the old seabird island tradition, visitors bring treats, so we'd brought a blueberry pie and brownies, and a cooler with two half-gallons of local ice cream. The ice cream was already soft by that first evening, and over the next two days became mousse, and then milkshakes, but there were no complaints. Like ourselves and our gear, their water, and the latest mailbag, the food came ashore in a small inflatable dingy that surged and fell with the swells as Arden manned the oars; we were strong-armed ashore and then picked our way carefully up through the rockweed and barnacles of the intertidal zone to dry land because there is no dock or wharf on the Egg Rock. Camryn had arrived with us, a South Dakotan who admitted on the 45-minute ride out to the island in Audubon's open motorboat that it was her first time on the ocean.

Steve and I set up our tents in an area of thick grass a short distance away from the derelict Hilton, scolded by gulls and terns nesting within a short pebble's toss, and with help from the island crew tied down tarps for poop protection. We may have done too efficient a job, as I found that getting out of my tent involved a game of limbo, trying to squeeze under the tightly staked edges of the mist-soaked tarp. I found Steve looking out into the gray evening.

"Penny for your thoughts?" I asked.

"Feeling like I've come home, a little," he said quietly.

Inside the cook tent, Theresa was making a group dinner as the others rested or entered data. These young biologists are employed by the National Audubon Society's Seabird Institute, under whose larger umbrella Project Puffin operates, and which manages seven nesting islands along the Maine coast, often in partnership with agencies like the US Fish and Wildlife Service or, as with Eastern Egg Rock, the

Maine Department of Inland Fisheries and Wildlife. Known as "puffineers," these young women were but the latest generation in an unbroken string of enthusiastic, idealistic, and deeply committed interns who have made a dream that Steve Kress had more than 50 years ago into a living, screaming, guano-bombing reality, and transformed seabird conservation around the world.

A little more than half a century ago, the scene on Eastern Egg would have been very different. There were no puffins, which despite nesting there and on neighboring Western Egg Rock in the 1870s had, just 20 years later, been extirpated by meat hunters. Terns had been slaughtered up and down the coast for the millinery trade, their feathers, wings, and sometimes whole stuffed bodies decorating women's hats, their eggs collected for food. Even gulls—yes, gulls—had been pushed to the brink of extinction in the East by the beginning of the 20th century; few people today realize that the first wardens hired to guard against feather hunters weren't posted to the great wading bird colonies of Florida, but rather to protect the last remaining common terns and herring gulls on the Atlantic coast, from Virginia to Maine, including both Egg Rock islands. Before the effort began in 1900, led by the American Ornithologists' Union with money raised by the noted painter (and ornithologist) Abbott Thayer, as many as 10,000 gulls were being shot each year in northern Maine for their wings and feathers, while tern eggs were routinely collected for eating—though to ensure that the eggs were fresh, collectors would methodically crush every nest, then come back a week or so later to gather up the newly laid replacements.

With the passage of federal laws in the early 20th century protecting wild birds and choking off market hunting in all its forms, gulls rebounded quickly—perhaps a little too well, flourishing in a world of open dumps, and fishing and lobster fleets that broadcast old bait and bycatch on the water. By the 1970s, both Egg Rock islands hosted robust colonies of herring and great black-backed gulls, the latter the biggest and arguably most predatory gull in the world. The two kinds of gulls essentially precluded any other seabirds, which would be quickly attacked and eaten if they tried to recolonize.

That Eastern Egg Rock is today a thriving, multispecies colony is testament to the power of a dream in the face of almost universal skepticism. That in itself would be an inspiring story, but the techniques that Steve Kress and his colleagues pioneered in the Gulf of Maine in the 1970s and '80s to bring Atlantic puffins back, like social attraction using decoys and sound lures; the translocation of chicks from healthy colonies to establish new ones; and predator exclusion or elimination, not only restored Egg Rock's lost seabirds, they have been instrumental in rescuing scores of other colonial seabird and waterbird species, from tiny storm-petrels to immense albatrosses, herons, and egrets to pelicans, all over the world. Those techniques have been adapted, expanded, and refined in ways Steve could hardly have imagined when he started, and have become so much a part of the language of bird restoration that some of today's conservationists may assume they've just always sort of been around, floating in the ether.

But like all good ideas, someone had to have the first light-bulb moment, and for Steve Kress it came in 1969, when he read a passage in a book that changed his life. Steve had grown up in the 1950s on the outskirts of Columbus, Ohio, a free-range childhood spent exploring locals parks with his best friend, collecting frogs and salamanders and lizards. Like me, Steve was a herp nut before he was a bird nut, though when adults in the local birding community took him under their wing, he quickly became enthralled with birds. (I've been lucky enough to count Steve as a friend for more than two decades, given our common link through Audubon's adult-oriented Hog Island Camp, not far from Eastern Egg Rock.)

It was at Hog Island, in fact, that Steve had his epiphany. In the summer of 1969 he was working as the camp's birdlife instructor, and in its extensive library he came across *Maine Birds*, a 1949 book by the ornithologist Ralph S. Palmer, who had compiled (along with Palmer's own observations) half a century's worth of notes dating to the 1890s by Arthur H. Norton, the curator of the Portland (Maine) Society of Natural History. Steve was riveted to read:

Western and Eastern Egg Rock in Muscongus Bay—Norton . . . reported that the Puffin bred on these rocks prior to 1860 and that there were "considerable numbers" still on both rocks in the late 1870s. He pointed out that they were much reduced by shooting in the early 1880s, leaving only five or six pairs on Western Egg Rock by 1885. He saw birds and an egg that had been taken there that year. During the next two years, the last birds disappeared from that place.

"Those six words, 'the Puffin bred on these rocks,' changed my life," Steve recounted in his book *Project Puffin: The Improbable Quest to Bring a Beloved Seabird Back to Egg Rock* (with Derrick Z. Jackson). Two years previously, he'd seen thousands of Atlantic puffins nesting at the extreme northern edge of the Gulf of Maine on Machias Seal Island, which while technically in US waters off Cutler, Maine, is claimed by Canada, which maintains a lighthouse—the source of a long-running territorial dispute between what until recently has been two otherwise collegial neighbors.* He knew that puffins also nested on Matinicus Rock, an isolated, bouldery, 32-acre pile nearly 20 miles off the Maine coast, which had been reduced to one pair by 1902 but had grown in numbers to a few hundred pairs by the 1970s. But there were many places in the Gulf of Maine, like the Egg Rock islands which had formed the southern limit of the puffins' historic western Atlantic range, to which the birds had never returned. That included Seal Island near Vinalhaven, which in the 19th century held the state's largest puffin colony before they were shot and netted out, and which was used as a bombing range by the US Navy in the 1950s and '60s.

---

* Nor is Machias Seal Island the only historical source of friction. It sits in the so-called gray zone, waters between Maine, Nova Scotia, and New Brunswick that are similarly claimed by both countries, and a point of serious dispute when it comes to valuable fisheries like lobstering.

The 65-acre island became a national wildlife refuge in 1972, making it safe for nesting seabirds, but the puffins were still absent.

Steve knew the Egg Rock islands well, as they were a routine field trip destination for Hog Island campers—but he knew them only as raucous gull colonies. He'd never imagined that puffins might once have nested there. But if they had once, why couldn't they do so again? After all, the cause of their extirpation, hunting for the pot, was no longer a threat.

With the unbridled optimism of a young man in his mid-20s, he decided to bring them back, even though no one had ever succeeded at such an undertaking. But this was the same time that raptor biologists were beginning to rear peregrine falcons in captivity and hack them back to the wild. There were no captive flocks of puffins, but Steve knew there were immense Atlantic puffin colonies to the north in Canada, which represented a potential source of wild chicks.

The plan, which developed over several years, called for moving 10- or 12-day-old puffin chicks from their nests and rearing them in artificial burrows in Maine until they fledged. Kress knew that by that age, the puffin parents no longer have to brood their single baby to keep it warm (he later found the chicks are self-regulating even earlier, at just three to five days old), yet are still nearly a month away from peeking outside the burrow at their surroundings. What's more, when young puffins do finally leave the burrow and fly to the ocean, they receive no further parental care and are completely independent. The expectation was that the young birds, looking around at Egg Rock and seeing it as home, would return there to breed themselves once they achieved maturity at four or five years of age.

Thus was born National Audubon's Project Puffin, though getting it off the ground was difficult. Steve found an early ally in William Drury, a noted seabird expert with the Massachusetts Audubon Society (the first modern Audubon society, and an independent organization not affiliated with National Audubon), whose guidance and advice helped him refine his plans. But he encountered stiff headwinds elsewhere—perhaps most surprisingly and painfully from Ralph Palmer, whose book had provided the spark of inspiration. Early on, Steve sent Palmer a letter outlining his idea and expecting quick support. "I was pleased to receive his response, mailed from nearby Tenant's Harbor. But I was shocked to read that he thought my idea was a stunt and a waste of time and that anyone who wanted to see puffins should go to Iceland," Kress would later recall.

Those who knew Palmer as a curmudgeon's curmudgeon might not have been as surprised as Steve was, but it wasn't the only pushback he experienced. Some critics pointed out that earlier attempts to move young albatrosses and shearwaters between islands in the Pacific had failed when the birds simply returned to their place of birth. Kress's initial request to the Canadian Wildlife Service, asking to collect eggs and chicks from Machias Seal Island, was rejected in 1972 by David Nettleship, the CWS's seabird expert in the Maritimes, who argued that puffins were losing ground at the southern edges of their existing range already; why try to take them even farther south when the species was clearly retreating north?

With Drury's help, Steve slowly began to win over the naysayers, including Nettleship. Eventually, a plan emerged with CWS backing that entailed bringing fluffy black pufflings (as the chicks are known) from the huge colonies on Great Island in Newfoundland's Witless Bay. Kress had meanwhile been experimenting with raising the young of black guillemots, whose populations had already recovered nicely along the Maine coast, rearing them in cardboard boxes on the porch of one of the staff cabins at Hog Island.* That did not go smoothly; he found that these half dozen guillie chicks lacked the natural waterproofing a seabird needs to swim; when Kress released the first one in the nearby cove, it sank without a trace and he was unable to rescue it. He realized that the best way to rear puffin babies would be under conditions that replicated natural burrows.

---

* That porch was later converted to a room for instructors, and I can attest that even decades later, there was still the faint, fishy whiff of seabirds on a warm, humid day.

One big question, which struck to the heart of why puffins had not naturally recolonized the Eastern and Western Egg, was what to do about the gulls that essentially owned the islands. Bringing pufflings to a gull-dominated place would simply result in fatter, better-fed gulls. Drury was the one who pointed out that the high gull population along the Maine coast was the result of human interference, in the form of subsidized food from open trash dumps and waste from lobstering and especially from the industrial-scale offshore fishery then dominated by foreign vessels. In the 70 years since the feather trade had ended, and bolstered by all the human-provided largesse, gull numbers had exploded all along the New England coast. Humans, Drury felt, needed to "interfere" proactively in ways that balanced the ledger for other, more sensitive species.

That meant, before the first significant translocation of 50 pufflings could begin in 1974 (a year after Kress and his team released five chicks on an experimental basis), that the gulls had to go, and there was no easy way to do it. A federal animal control officer named Frank Gramlich took charge of the deeply unpleasant chore of destroying gull nests and leaving pieces of bread slathered with margarine and an avicide known as DCR-1339, which would poison the great black-backed gulls that ate it, but not any other animals that scavenged the carcasses, like one of Maine's then-rare bald eagles. In subsequent years, the presence of biologists on the island, along with more direct control like selective shooting, would keep the gulls from returning. But Steve knew he needed a more permanent and environmentally sound solution, though at first that alternative seemed elusive.

It's hard to adequately summarize the years of challenges that Project Puffin had to overcome to return puffins as a breeding species to Eastern Egg Rock; it's an object lesson in the triumph of pure, cussed stubbornness over repeated adversity. When it became clear that trying to raise pufflings in a building wouldn't work, Kress tried building rock "burrows" on the shore of Hog Island, again with guillemot chicks as stand-ins; hungry raccoons got every one, as well as one puffin chick. Moving the operation to Eastern Egg, where there were no mammalian predators (the reason seabirds use such islands, after all), that first experimental cohort of five puffin chicks in 1973 were placed in nests made of rocks and concrete, but while these chicks survived, the fake nests didn't even make it through their first winter, during which storm waves battered them to almost nothing; when we took a break from conducting our tern census, Steve showed us the last bits of cement still clinging to the granite ledge above the high-tide line that marked where those experimental nests had been.

Pivoting again, they next tried making faux burrows out of long, rectangular ceramic chimney liner sections, but these proved much too hot for the chicks, even when covered in thick layers of sod, and became badly fouled by excrement and condensation as the season went on, despite frequent cleaning. The team tried digging burrows where there was enough soil on the rocky island, but these flooded every time it rained. It took several years, but the puffineers finally hit on a solution, one that mimicked the deeply dug burrows from which the puffin chicks had been taken in Newfoundland—"puffin condos" made of thick sod laid on *top* of the existing soil, and thus above runoff water, with a series of long entrance tunnels, each with a 90-degree turn into a nest chamber. A protective layer of wire, wooden lathe and then another thick layer of sod on top provided clean, natural and well-insulated housing for the increasing number of pufflings making the trip from Newfoundland every summer (in the first years traveling by personal jet flown by Intel founder Bob Noyce, a Hog Island neighbor and an early supporter).

By the mid-1970s, Kress and his team were moving roughly 100 young puffins to Egg Rock annually, banding them all before they fledged, while growing increasingly concerned that they'd seen no sign of any returning birds from the earlier summers. David Nettleship, the Canadian Wildlife Service biologist, also seemed less and less enthusiastic about the prospects for success, and by 1977, Project Puffin appeared to be on the verge of losing its supply of baby puffins.

And even if the puffins came back, would they stay? Puffins are drawn to a colony by, well, the colony itself—the noise and commotion and presence of others of their species. How do you replicate that from scratch?

The answer was what has come to be known as social attraction, perhaps the single biggest contribution that Project Puffin had made to seabird conservation—the use of decoys to create the impression of large flocks, and (in later years) an audiolure broadcasting endless loop recordings of the sounds of an active colony. Clever devices known as mirror boxes, narrow upright glass triangles scattered among the decoys which reflect back any puffin or tern peering at them, work just like a small mirror in a parakeet's cage to fool the visitor into thinking it sees another real bird, and add still more to the sense of a hustling, lively colony. The inspiration, ironically, had come from a photograph Kress had seen in *National Geographic* of a puffin hunter netting the birds at a nesting colony, while using dead puffins propped up around him as impromptu decoys.

In the summer of 1977, with everything on the line, the Project Puffin team deployed floating puffin decoys anchored in the water, and standing decoys fixed to the rocks. On June 12 of that summer, Kress spotted a puffin flying into Egg Rock and landing not far from the boat he was in. Stunned and excited, he and his companions could tell by its bill markings that the bird was two years old, and they were eventually able to see that it was banded. One of the Egg Rock babies had come home.

Chick translocations continued for 12 years. The puffineers struggled with persistent problems with great black-backed gulls before Kress realized he could recruit another ally in the battle to keep the big, predatory birds at bay: terns. Healthy puffin colonies like Machias Seal Island and Matinicus Rock were often also healthy tern colonies, and Kress had already experienced the wrath of angry terns defending their nests when he visited Machias Seal years earlier, plucking a tall sprig of angelica and waving it over his head to give them a higher target than his scalp. If they could encourage enough terns to nest on Eastern Egg Rock as well, it would be a conservation two-fer. Terns had themselves declined significantly in the Gulf of Maine since the early 20th century, and a new colony could help reverse that trend. He suspected correctly that the fierce birds might provide the necessary umbrella of protection for the puffins, driving away gulls, eagles, and other hunters. It also explains what has become Steve's signature head-gear, that tam o'shanter cap with a knobby yarn ball on top. He did not choose it to make a fashion statement; with precision aim, the terns invariably wallop the cap's yarn ball, leaving his crown unscathed.

However, the biologists couldn't translocate tern chicks as they were doing with puffins. The nesting ecology of terns is entirely different, with both parents bringing a constant supply of small fish to up to three chicks in an open nest, and providing care weeks after fledging. But terns, like puffins, can be lured to an island by the illusion of an active colony, so a new phase of social attraction began, again using decoys and recorded audio of nonaggressive tern calls.

The tern project started in 1978, and the effect was immediate; common and Arctic terns gathered in numbers that very summer, chasing away what few gulls still approached. In 1980, with the addition of more decoys and all-day audioluring, 80 pairs of common and Arctic terns began to nest. Although most of the decoys were reasonably realistic, they didn't really have to be. One of the guaranteed laughs during the program Steve gives about the history of Project Puffin is a slide showing an absurdly basic tern decoy, one long, gray-painted block of unshaped wood for the body, a smaller triangular one with a black cap and red beak for the head. But it worked, because in the picture, a real common tern is displaying to the decoy; in another, a male tern is shown offering a decoy a courtship gift of fish.

Roseate terns, whose Northeast population is federally endangered, joined the colony in 1981, and by 1982 the decoys and recordings were no longer needed—the more than 400 pairs of actual terns provided all the social attraction required. Today, the most abundant species by far remains the common terns, roughly 1,500 pairs in a typical year, but the island also hosts 50 or so pairs of Arctic terns, the world's greatest migrant bird in terms of the return flight it makes each year to and from its nesting grounds. The Project Puffin biologists call them "arties," from the four-letter bird-banding code, ARTE, for ARctic TErn. Those that have in recent summers been tagged with small geolocators on Egg Rock have flown as much as 61,000 miles between nesting seasons, some of them wintering as far away as the southern Indian Ocean before returning.

By contrast, recent tracking data show that the common terns in the Gulf of Maine winter along the Atlantic coast of South America from Venezuela to Argentina. There are also on Egg Rock roughly 70 pairs of nesting roseate terns, affectionately known as "rosies," named for the delicate wash of pale pink they show on their undersides in spring, something nearly impossible to see except in the hand. In flight, rosies appear almost angelically white, with long, flowing tail streamers that twist and dance magically in the wind. After leaving the breeding grounds, the northeastern population that breeds in Nova Scotia and New England stages up in late July and August on the coast of Massachusetts before migrating to their wintering grounds off the eastern coast of Brazil.

With a pugnacious air force patrolling the skies, and interns staffing the island, the risk of predation on Egg Rock fell to manageable levels, with only the occasional culling of a few too-relentless gulls now required.* More and more returning puffins, marked by recognizable leg bands, showed up each year as later cohorts of the translocated birds

---

* Gulls are not the only predators of concern. One year a female river otter and her kit made it to Eastern Egg Rock and began killing puffins in their burrows; both had to be removed. Some of the tern-nesting islands that Audubon manages, like Outer Green and Stratton islands along the southern Maine coast, are close enough to the mainland that great horned owls can be an issue, as are black-crowned night-herons, either of which can cause abandonment of the entire colony. The owls can be trapped and removed, but the night-herons are themselves a state-listed species, so if a night-heron can't be hazed off, island managers are forced to make tough decisions in consultation with Maine's wildlife agency: Is it better to lose one state-listed threatened heron or an entire breeding season for thousands of seabirds, including federally endangered roseate terns? In 2024, a single heron in a single night ate two-thirds of the chicks in Stratton Island's colony of least terns, before it was killed with state permission. There are no easy answers.

matured. That quieted some of the skeptics, while others still groused that no puffins had yet nested, even though many of the earliest releases should have reached sexual maturity several years earlier. The summer of 1980 finally found puffins billing and courting, exploring below the boulders and even carrying grass to perhaps make rudimentary nests. But the clincher came on July 4, 1980, when a puffin carrying fish in its beak landed on Egg Rock and disappeared down into the rocks—incontrovertible proof that the first Maine-born puffling in a century was down there somewhere, since adult puffins only carry fish when they are feeding their chicks.

In all, Project Puffin brought 954 puffin chicks from Newfoundland to Eastern Egg Rock, of which 940—an astonishing 98.5 percent—successfully fledged. Having proven the model on Egg Rock, Kress and his colleagues expanded the playing field. Richard Podolsky, one of the original puffineers, used social attraction and artificial burrows like those made for the pufflings to lure Leach's storm-petrels to a number of Muscongus Bay islands like nearby Old Hump Ledge. In subsequent years, Kress's team again transferred the techniques from Egg Rock to reestablish a puffin colony on Seal Island, to which Newfoundland chicks were brought from 1984 to 1989. By 1992 puffins were nesting on Seal, which (like Mantincus Rock) today holds hundreds of pairs, along with all three tern species, black guillemots, common eiders, the largest colony of state-endangered great cormorants, as well as Leach's storm-petrels and another puffin relative, the dapper alcid known as the razorbill.

In all, by 2024 there were roughly 1,500 pairs of Atlantic puffins on Maine islands restored or protected by National Audubon and its partners. Puffins colonized Petit Manan on the Downeast coast on their own nickel, after gulls were removed to support a return of nesting terns. A small number of especially gutsy puffins have even colonized another island, Great Duck, entirely without backup and despite the presence of great black-backed gulls. In addition to raising seabirds, the Audubon-managed islands also raise young conservationists. Over the years, more than 800 fledgling scientists have spent their summers on those lonely outposts, many of them going on to careers in seabird restoration all over the world—in many respects, at least as important a contribution to seabird conservation as the on-island work itself.

My time on Egg Rock wasn't all spent being pasted by guano from enraged terns. That morning, Steve and I had walked oh-so-carefully out one of the paths from camp, stepping past tern eggs laid in the middle of the trail; in places, the island paths are lined with the brick-orange fragments of those long-ago chimney tile puffin burrows, repurposed in the old rural Maine tradition of never throwing out anything that remains remotely useful. We sat together in largely contemplative silence in one of the gray-painted observation blinds that stud the island, from which the puffineer interns take three-hour shifts monitoring the colony. As we walked up, several dozen puffins flushed from their loafing ledge, as such gathering places are known, but they soon returned; one pair rubbed their orange, yellow, and blue bills together in courtship.

The island sat in a hole of dim, overcast sunshine in a world of fog, out of which, mid-morning, appeared the *Harbor Princess*, a tour boat out of Boothbay Harbor to the west, one of several commercial boats that bring tourists out to circle the island and see the puffins. (Both it and the Hardy Boat, operating out of New Harbor, are staffed with National Audubon outreach specialists in the summer who provide expert narration and commentary.) By one estimate, such trips share the birds of Eastern Egg Rock with tens of thousands of Maine visitors a year, a not-insignificant contribution to the state's Vacationland economy. "When we started here, we didn't have an outhouse, and the routine was to urinate below the tideline," Steve told me as we watched the boat. "Once the word spread about the puffins, and all the tourists and tour boats started showing up, that had to stop."

The rocks around us were splotched with plate-sized patches of bright red paint, on which were painted in white the numbers of nearby puffin burrows, so the researchers could keep track of which burrows had active puffin nests; one marked 305 was visible nearby, a testament to how many puffins now nest on Egg Rock, though obviously not all burrows are used each summer. In a few weeks, once eggs had hatched and the parents were bringing food, the island team would conduct as thorough a count as possible. Still later, as the chicks reached full size, the biologists would spend long, uncomfortable days "grubbing"—squeezing themselves down into impossibly narrow, claustrophobic openings in the rocks, trying to reach, remove, band, measure, and weigh as many pufflings as possible before returning them to their nests.

The puffin count on Eastern Egg seems to have plateaued in recent years at around 175 pairs, although it is extremely difficult to accurately census a bird that nests below ground. "I've come to the conclusion that the nest count isn't really important," Steve said as we watched a female common eider, whose down-lined nest was probably hidden in the vegetation just below the blind, trying to decide if we were enough of a threat to keep her off her eggs; in the end we passed muster and she vanished among the angelica stems. "What's important is chick health, their weight at fledging, but the problem at Egg is that not a lot of the chicks are accessible. The rocks are too deep to reach a lot of them."

The story that chick health tells is a cautionary one. The Gulf of Maine has set and broken sea surface temperatures records again and again in the past two decades. Puffins, like all alcids, "fly" underwater with their wings, and while they are capable of reaching depths of more than 200 feet when pursuing fish, most foraging dives are less than half that. Warmer waters can force the schooling species they prefer to feed their chicks, like Atlantic herring and white hake, down deep in search of cooler temperatures, too deep for the puffins to reach.

Some years, like 2012, those species disappear almost completely from the prey puffin adults bring back, replaced by fish like American butterfish, a deep-bodied species that, while nutritious, is often too large and too wide for the youngest puffins to swallow whole, as they must. That same year, 2012, Project Puffin and National Audubon installed a video camera for the first time in a puffin burrow on Seal Island, broadcasting the life of a puffling dubbed Petey. It was a short life; Petey's parents brought little except butterfish, which he tried, and tried, and tried to swallow, but without success. Puffin Petey starved to death on camera, surrounded by inedible prey, while people all over the world watched. (No, the scientists did not interfere; feeding the baby down in its inaccessible burrow was simply impractical, and it was perhaps a grim but instructive lesson to a shocked world that climate change has consequences, even for darling little pufflings.)

Still, the news isn't all negative. Ocean heat waves like those in 2012, 2013, and 2016 caused a significant collapse of puffin nest success, but in more recent years two fish previously unknown in puffin diets, haddock and Acadian redfish, have helped to bolster the food supply, making up for fewer herring. Haddock and Acadian redfish, both of which had been badly overfished in earlier decades, have been recovering thanks to better management. And because puffins can live for more than 30 years (one of the original Newfoundland transplants to Seal Island was still there in 2024, at age 35), their biology is designed to withstand an off-season once in a while. After all, they need only replace themselves and their mate during the course of that long lifespan in order for the population to remain stable.

The question is, what happens if those off-years eventually become the norm? Average sea surface temperatures in the Gulf of Maine set a new record in 2021, and 2022 missed beating it by only a whisker. The summer of 2024 was well above average, but ranked seventh warmest of the 42 years since satellite temperature data became available. The Gulf of Maine Research Institute, which issues annual "warming updates," noted that the gulf is warming faster than 97 percent of the world's oceans. There has also been concern that as atmospheric CO_2 levels rise, so will the acidity of the gulf's water, threatening, for example, to literally dissolve the carbonate shells of mollusks like mussels and clams. New research suggests the pH of the Gulf of Maine has held surprisingly steady for the past century, even creeping up a bit in the past 40 years, but the researchers who documented this ascribed it to the intrusion of highly alkaline water from the Gulf Stream entering and buffering the Gulf of Maine's growing acidity. "Once ocean circulation-driven buffering effects reach their limit, seawater pH decline may occur swiftly. This would profoundly harm shellfisheries and the broader Gulf of Maine ecosystem," they warned.

As these changes progress, will suitable alternative prey species always be available as traditional forage fish like Atlantic herring fade? How will puffins and terns and other seabirds adapt?

We have some clues. Atlantic puffins have an immense range that stretches far from the Gulf of Maine—across the north Atlantic from eastern Canada and western Greenland to Iceland, the United Kingdom, northern Norway (particularly Spitsbergen in the Svalbard archipelago), and Russia; there are even small colonies in northern France along the English Channel. The global population has been estimated at between 12 million and 14 million individuals, with an estimated 7.4 million in northern and Arctic Europe.

Which sounds like a lot, but for two facts. One, the past decades have seen serious trouble in many of the puffin's biggest strongholds. In 2023, experts concluded that Iceland, which has long held the world's largest puffin colonies, has experienced a 70 percent decline since 1995, far worse than previous estimates. The primary reason seems to be that their prey species, especially sand lance, have moved north or offshore in response to warming waters, causing year after year of nesting failure at the big southern Icelandic colonies. Overfishing is also a culprit. On the other hand, some of the northern Icelandic puffins have done fairly well where water temperatures still favor their prey. But Iceland also continues to allow a puffin hunt both for private consumption and public sale, killing more than 3 million between 1997 and 2021, a level scientists contend is far from sustainable. "Generally speaking, hunting declining populations is not a good philosophy," the study's author said with deadpan understatement, calling the practice "a peculiar exemption from common sense."

In the United Kingdom, puffin numbers increased by more than a third from about 1970 to 2000, before reversing course in the early

2000s and declining at some of the biggest colonies like the Isle of May in Scotland, which lost more than 30 percent of its puffins in the 2000s, and the Farne Islands off Northumberland in England, where the number of puffin pairs fell from more than 55,000 in 2003 to fewer than 37,000 in 2008. A comprehensive, seven-year-long survey of Great Britain's seabird colonies, completed in 2021, found an overall 24 percent decrease in puffins over the previous 20 years. The good news is that some of those populations have since recovered to a significant extent. Puffins on the Isle of May in 2024, for example, were up by about one-third since 2017, occupying 52,000 burrows on the island. Avian influenza, which in the early 2020s devastated some UK colonial seabirds like northern gannets, seems to have largely spared Atlantic puffins. But issues remain. In February 2023, hundreds of emaciated puffins washed up on the Atlantic shores of northern Spain and Portugal, including many that had been ringed in Scotland; this echoed similar "wrecks" of starving puffins that have occurred on the New England coast in winters like 2012–13, caused by a lack of food for them at sea, which in turn is likely tied to overfishing and sea temperature changes.

The second caveat is that, as noted, puffins are exceptionally long-lived. This allows the species to weather a few lost breeding seasons, but if there is little or no reproduction for an extended period, as has been happening in southern Iceland, a senescent population may appear to be stable for many years before suddenly and catastrophically collapsing as a large proportion of adults begin to die of old age with no young replacements entering the population. For all these reasons, Atlantic puffins are listed as globally vulnerable on the IUCN's Red List of imperiled birds, but as endangered on the European Red List, and they are similarly red-listed in the United Kingdom. (The state of Maine lists its population as threatened.)

My visit to Egg Rock coincided with the very first puffin hatchings of 2024; as we sat and watched and took photos, a puffin flew into the loafing ledge with its beak full of fish and plunged immediately down among the rocks at burrow number 82. Steve missed it, and grilled me about what kind of fish the adult was carrying: Hake? Herring? Sand lance? What did I estimate their length to be, in relation to the beak? A good puffineer would have been able to answer those questions, but I only had the briefest impression of flashing silvery bodies.

It was at that time too early to know how 2024 would turn out. At the end of the season, the Gulf of Maine Seabird Working Group, an international, multipartner effort organized by the state of Maine, convened for its annual wrap-up meeting on Hog Island. Presenters in person and via Zoom reported on the breeding summer's results at colonies stretching the length of the gulf, from North Brother Island in Nova Scotia to Monomoy Island and several small tern colonies in Buzzards Bay in southeastern Massachusetts.

Audubon teams on the seven islands they manage, including several like Jenny and Pond islands on the southwestern Maine coast that host terns but no puffins, reported good tern chick weights and high fledging rates, perhaps thanks to the fact that the birds began nesting earlier than usual, when sea temperatures were still cooler. Seal Island saw 672 active puffin burrows, a new post-restoration record. Numbers of Atlantic herring, the gold standard for prey species, being delivered to puffin chicks were down, while haddock were up, but the birds seemed to compensate for this somewhat less nutritious primary food by making more, and more frequent, prey deliveries. Terns at a number of colonies throughout the Gulf of Maine switched to small crustaceans called euphausiids, better known as krill, in quantities not seen in the past—as much as half the prey brought to chicks at Seal Island. Unlike 2023, when midsummer storms drenched and killed many of the young terns, fledging rates were very high, thanks to the weather. "Flower gardeners like a wet summer, but tern gardeners, we prefer a dry summer like the one we had," Steve Kress joked a few days later.

I'm not really sure why, but sitting in the blind with Steve Kress that day on Egg Rock, watching the comings and goings of all the birds in this island ecosystem he willed into existence, there was one question

I kept returning to, but just couldn't quite bring myself to ask. Maybe I was worried that I would spoil the mood, which is a lousy excuse for not confronting reality. But: What happens next?

While 2024 was a good year for its seabirds, the Gulf of Maine isn't getting any colder. Increasingly intense summer rainstorms that flush billions of gallons of murky runoff from the land into the gulf make the seawater more turbid, diminishing sunlight needed by phytoplankton, themselves the food for a foundational species of zooplankton, a copepod called *Calanus finmarchicus*, which occurs in incalculable numbers and underpins many of the region's marine food chains, including those upon which the puffins depend. There are plenty of examples of how climate change is worsening the outlook for puffins in many parts of their range. Maybe it was a bad idea, as David Nettleship suggested back in the 1970s, to fight that tide by bringing puffins back to their southernmost outpost. Maybe I didn't ask because I didn't want to bum myself out; maybe I didn't want to bum out Steve.

So that question came some weeks later, after Steve was back home in Ithaca, New York. How optimistic are you about the future, I asked? How much comfort should we take from the ways the puffins have sometimes been able to shift to alternate prey like redfish and haddock? What keeps you up at night, and what helps you keep plugging away?

His answer, sent back by email, was characteristically thoughtful, and I'll summarize it as best I can while trying to preserve its nuance and complexity.

"I am hopeful that the restored seabird communities will continue to thrive in the Gulf of Maine, because these are very resilient species," he wrote. "The threats from climate change are real and will test their ability to adapt to sometimes less than ideal conditions, but we have seen adaptability by both chicks and adults. In most parts of the puffin's range, there are relatively few species of forage fish, so when something happens to these keystone species the puffins can suffer spectacularly. In midcoast Maine, while puffins are at the edge of their range—usually not optimal—the Maine coast puffins have a wide diversity of possible forage fish." Besides haddock and Acadian redfish,

Steve mentioned sand lance, which boom and bust in importance in the puffin's diet, and two other warm-water species, rough scad and Atlantic saury, that also appear in the gulf. Counterintuitively, the way the Gulf of Maine is warming, with sharp demarcations between colder and warmer areas of water, may actually be increasing the diversity of prey available to seabirds like terns and puffins, Steve said.

The Maine puffins also have another advantage, he said, because the colonies are relatively small, so they require less food and demand less competition for what's there. "I think of parent puffins like fishing boats heading out each day to look for the catch of the day." He's impressed by the variety of prey they bring back, the way they can increase the number of feedings each day if the food they're catching isn't of the highest quality, as was the case that year. Adult puffins can delay their migration away from the colony by up to three weeks, if they need to continue to feed a lagging chick—"but," he said, "they seem to have a 'wisdom' about when these costs are too great (abandoning the nesting cycle or not even starting it). So far this extra effort does not seem to increase adult mortality in the year following a poor fishing year," something known as a carryover effect, which is a serious issue for many migratory birds that experience a difficult winter.

Thanks to tracking data, scientists now know that Egg Rock's puffins, and those from the other Maine islands, winter on the edge of the Gulf of Maine, meaning they're not far from their breeding grounds. That gives them the opportunity to begin to nest earlier than in the past, and while he said the Seabird Institute researchers who now carry the old Project Puffin torch have not seen a consistent trend toward earlier nesting, when the puffins do start early, while the waters are colder, they are more successful, fledging heavier chicks that enjoy a head start when they go to sea.

With new knowledge comes new insight. A good example are those Atlantic butterfish, too big and wide for Petey the doomed puffling to eat. They've been seen as a negative force for puffins, but recent DNA barcoding of puffin poop, conducted by a young Oregon State University master's student named William Kennerly to identify the species the adult puffins have eaten, shows that butterfish are actually an important part of their diet, something that wasn't known because the adults don't carry their own food back to land, but swallow it at sea. "It's the very young chicks, confronted with too large of a butterfish, that have a problem," Steve said. "Fascinating, too, that some of the older chicks will peck off bits of butterfish and eventually swallow them—actually a nutritious meal." So butterfish, far from being a fresh evil, may be part of the path to a stable future.

"It's too easy to oversimplify these narrative stories," Steve concluded. "I see a very complex response to climate change and the seabirds are so far doing okay, or better, in the face of the heat waves and tests of their resilience. They are long lived, highly productive birds and they do not need to be successful every year. As long as the adults survive, there will be another year."

Wish I'd asked when we were sitting on Egg Rock.

In 1986, with the puffin colony on Eastern Egg Rock growing every year, Steve Kress ran into Ralph Palmer, by then in his early seventies, whose book had sparked the whole project some 17 years earlier, and whose initial rejection when Kress had first approached him for support had stung. So had Palmer's hectoring complaints about the "ballyhoo" around puffins, which he had voiced both to Steve's boss at National Audubon and to a high-ranking official at the Canadian Wildlife Service, trying to get the project shut down. Both Kress and Palmer were at Hog Island, marking the Audubon camp's 50th anniversary, and Steve couldn't help but wonder if the success of his bold idea might have changed the older man's feelings about it.

"I asked Ralph if he'd been following the progress of Project Puffin, and said that the puffins were doing well," Steve said. "All he said was, 'I hope they continue to flourish—because puffins taste very good.'"

Ralph Palmer may never have become a convert, but a lot of other people who saw what Steve Kress accomplished in Maine needed no convincing to try the same thing with other rare seabirds. Today, the

Seabird Restoration Database, maintained by Pacific Rim Conservation, a Hawaiian NGO, in partnership with a consortium that includes National Audubon, the Nature Conservancy, and the New Zealand Department of Conservation, has documented more than 850 seabird restoration efforts at 550 sites worldwide, involving 138 species of threatened or imperiled seabirds, all of which can trace at least some of their inspiration back to Eastern Egg Rock. Even the conservation decoys that make social attraction possible have, in a sense, migrated back to the Maine coast. For years, those that Project Puffin and other restoration projects used were produced by Mad River Decoys in Vermont, an offshoot of the Mad River Canoe company, founded by Jim and Nancy Henry; the Henrys had realized the same process that produced their molded canoe bodies could create durable, easily painted polyethylene replicas of terns, puffins, albatrosses, and other birds, and they had worked tirelessly to produce them. Preparing to retire, in 2016 they gave Mad River Decoys to Audubon's Seabird Institute, which now manufactures the decoys in a barn just across the channel from Hog Island.

Of course, nesting islands like Eastern Egg Rock only support puffins for a few short months; the rest of the year the birds simply vanish out to sea, their whereabouts long a mystery that was finally solved when Maine puffins were fitted with tiny geolocators that recorded and stored tracking data. The critical wintering site for them turned out to be a huge area of ocean along and off the edge of continental shelf scored by immense submarine canyons and punctuated by submerged, extinct volcanic mountains, some of which rise more than 13,000 feet above the abyssal sea floor, about 130 miles southeast of Cape Cod. Cold, nutrient-laden waters upwell here, creating a rich web of life, from fragile, deep-sea corals to rare beaked whales, sharks, billfish, sea turtles, and dozens of seabird species. In 2016, President Obama declared almost 5,000 square miles of this region the Northeast Canyons and Seamounts Marine National Monument, the first of its kind in the Atlantic, restricting most commercial fishing within its boundaries. The designation withstood first a legal challenge from the fishing industry, then a regulatory whipsaw when the first Trump administration removed the fishing ban in 2020, only to have the Biden administration restore it in 2021. In May 2025, the second Trump administration announced that commercial fishing within the entire monument would resume.

In 2019, Steve Kress retired as vice president for bird conservation of the National Audubon Society, though he remains informally involved in seabird work, and in 2024 received a lifetime achievement award from his peers in the Pacific Seabird Group, a professional association that formed at roughly the same time Project Puffin was getting off the ground. The ripples from that little island in the Gulf of Maine have gone even farther than a migrating Arctic tern. In order to see how the legacy of Project Puffin continues to help seabirds, half a century on, I need to head to another island half a world away, far out into the Pacific.

Eight

Islands of Sanctuary

There were a couple of reasons why the island of Kauaʻi, the oldest and most northerly of the major Hawaiian Islands, seemed like an ideal location to see how the seeds planted on Eastern Egg Rock have flourished elsewhere. It was the first place where Steve Kress's social attraction techniques were tried away from Maine, and some of the most ambitious seabird restoration work in the United States is going on there. And I would be less than honest if I did not admit that, when planning the trip during the miserable dreg-ends of a New England winter that had featured a whole series of pummeling storms and long power outages, the idea of a little getaway to paradise sounded awfully appealing.

The fact that I'd convinced Amy to join me was icing on the cake. What's more, I had another old Hog Island acquaintance, Hob Osterlund, the founder of the Kauaʻi Albatross Network who (like Steve Kress) was more than happy to connect us with many of the movers and shakers of seabird restoration there. I did note with mild concern as the trip approached that the weather forecast for Kauaʻi looked rather wet, even by the standards of an island that holds the US record for the most rainfall in 24 hours (49.5 inches that fell in 2018 at Waipā Garden). But Kauaʻi is famous for its rain forests, and you can't have rain forests without rain. Right?

What followed was not the welcome to paradise we expected.

The last 45 minutes of our plane's approach to the Lihu'e airport was a turbulent martini-shaker of a ride, and when we landed we could see, just as darkness was falling, that the rain was torrential, Noahic. We were soaked in the seconds it took us to throw our gear into the trunk of our rental car, then we tried to pick our way through the lighting flashes and stygian darkness to our lodging for the week. Shortly after we pulled onto the road, both of our cell phones began blasting ear-splitting emergency alert tones, followed by texts warning of "potentially life-threatening flash flooding" and advising against any unnecessary travel, "unless you are fleeing an area subject to flooding or under an evacuation order." Variations on those warnings came blaring throughout the night as we tried to sleep, with no way of knowing whether the place we were renting was, in fact, in an area subject to flooding.

By the next morning, the rain had stopped but the wind was still howling; we were staying on the east side of Kaua'i, where the surf was brown and ragged in the wake of the storm. Red-footed boobies played on the gusts, slicing just over the crashing waves as they flew down the beach by the dozens. By late morning the clouds were tearing apart as we explored north along Kaua'i's eastern side, the rivers flowing down from the high, jagged, deeply eroded peaks of the interior mountains swollen and muddy. For the next several days the same cyclonic system kept wobbling back over the island with punishing floods before finally being pushed southeast.

Kaua'i, which at 550 square miles is about half the size of Rhode Island, was formed some 5.1 million years ago when it sat over the tectonic hotspot that today fuels active volcanic eruptions on the big island of Hawai'i, the youngest of the chain 300 miles to the southeast. In the millions of years since then, the crustal plate on which the archipelago sits has crept northwest, carrying Kaua'i along with it, leaving the source of lava behind. The island's ancient volcanic bones have been sculpted ever since by rain and wind into weird and fantastical shapes—needlelike spires, buttresses, and vertiginous cliffs, all cloaked in forest nourished by what, under normal circumstances, are gentle, trade-wind-generated rains, giving it the nickname the Garden Island.

Fewer than 75,000 people live on Kauaʻi permanently, but something like 1.2 million tourists come each year—almost all of them, like the residents, sticking to the narrow rim of lowland along the north, east, and south of the island. Much of the rest of Kauaʻi is roadless and inaccessible to any but the most determined and prepared hikers. That includes the heart of the justly famous Nā Pali Coast on the island's northwest, named for the cliffs (*nā pali* in Hawaiian) that rise 4,000 feet from the ocean in less than half a mile, and which, except for a few overlook points and a rugged, 11-mile hiking trail, can only be seen from a boat or a flight-seeing trip.

The tourists that come to Kauaʻi will see a lot of birds, but virtually none of them are native to the island. Walk around the condos and resorts in a place like Kapaʻa, where we were staying, and the two most obvious species are the common myna, a popular cage bird from southern Asia related to starlings which has been introduced in tropical locations around the world, and feral chickens—what seems like millions of feral chickens. There are two species of cardinals (northern cardinals, the one most Americans are familiar with, and red-crested cardinals from South America); rose-ringed parakeets native to equatorial Africa and South Asia; warbling (also known as Japanese) white-eyes, small greenish birds with prominent ivory eye-rings; and tiny zebra doves and larger spotted doves, both again Asian in origin, among many others.

Except for a few species like the boobies and magnificent frigatebirds that are common along the beaches, it's entirely possible for a tourist on Kaua'i to never see a native Hawaiian bird during their visit, and never realize what they have missed. This is tragically ironic because Hawai'i is, with New Zealand, one of the world's two great cradles of avian evolution, where speciation ran wild. This was especially true for the Hawaiian honeycreepers, a remarkably diverse branch of a family of finches. Genetic research suggests they descended from Asian rosefinches, which some 5 million to 6 million years ago made it across the north Pacific to the earliest islands, Ni'ihau and Kaua'i, which had by then emerged from the sea. From there the honeycreepers spread throughout the Hawaiian chain, evolving into more than 50 known species, and exhibiting a bewildering range of bill shapes and behaviors to exploit an equally wide range of empty ecological niches, from species with heavy, finch-like bills for cracking seeds to others with extraordinarily long, deeply curved beaks for probing flowers, and fringed tongues for drinking nectar.

No one really knows how many Hawaiian bird species existed before Polynesians discovered the island chain in the 13th century,* but human arrival, and that of their commensal mammals like pigs and Polynesian rats, had a devastating effect. Roughly half the species of birds known from subfossil remains to have been on the islands at first contact became extinct prior to European arrival, including

---

* The generally accepted chronology of Polynesian colonization of Hawai'i has shifted significantly over the years. Archaeologists initially believed the first big, sea-faring outrigger canoes may have carried settlers there as early as the 1st century CE, though radiocarbon dating in the 1990s pushed the dates back to 600–950 CE. More recent, higher-quality dating of a large number of sites indicates a human arrival time in the Hawai'ian Islands of 1219–66 CE, part of a single great expansion of Polynesians north to Hawai'i, east to Rapa Nui (Easter Island), and south to New Zealand.

flightless ibises, a unique genus of day-hunting "stilt-owls" that (based on pellets recovered from lava tubes and sand dunes) preyed on birds, and large flightless waterfowl that have been dubbed by paleontologists *moa-nalo*, "lost fowl," the largest of which likely weighed more than 16 pounds.

As bad as the first extinction wave was, since European and American contact about half of what bird species still remained have also vanished, many of them due to introduced mosquitoes that carry two diseases, avian pox and avian malaria, to which the native birds had no resistance. In all, at least 77 species of Hawaiian birds have become extinct since humans arrived, representing 15 percent of all bird extinctions worldwide in the past 700 years—the greatest proportion of avian extinctions on the planet. More continue to wink

Kaua'i is the oldest and most northwesterly of the main Hawaiian Islands, and the first place away from Maine where social attraction techniques were used with endangered seabirds.

out, despite strenuous conservation efforts. The Kauaʻi ʻōʻō, the last of seven species of these large, slender, black birds with yellow wing tufts, was down to a single pair in 1981; after the female disappeared that May, the male continued to build nests and call plaintively for a mate that would never appear until he, too, vanished in 1987. The poʻouli, a honeycreeper restricted to the island of Oʻahu, became extinct only in 2004 when the last known individual died in captivity.

In all, of the 23 species of landbirds native to Kauaʻi, only nine remain, and four of them are either threatened or critically endangered; the population of one bird, the Kauaʻi creeper or ʻakikiki, had by the time of our visit fallen in mere months from five down to a single individual in the wild. A small captive population provides a slim buffer against immediate extinction, although the catastrophic 2023 fires on Maui came within a hair's breadth of destroying the Maui Bird Conservation Center, where the ʻakikiki and many other imperiled native birds are housed. Meanwhile the single wild ʻakikiki, like the other Kauaʻi forest birds, is squeezed into the relatively few high-elevation refugia where mosquitoes and their diseases do not yet occur, in places like the Alakaʻi Swamp, a montane wilderness preserve, and Kawaikini Peak on the central massif of the inactive Waiʻaleʻale volcano which formed the island, the highest point on Kauaʻi at more than 5,200 feet above sea level.

So far as is known, only one Hawaiian seabird, the lesser Hawaiian petrel, a species described only from subfossil remains found in archaeological sites, was lost to extinction, but many of those that remain are in rough shape, if not in so precarious a situation as the forest birds. While avian malaria doesn't pose the same threat to seabirds as it does to Hawaiian forest birds, some seabirds like albatrosses do suffer from avian poxvirus, which causes lesions and sometimes blindness. By far the bigger problem, however, is some of the other animals that humans have brought with them, especially introduced predators like rats, pigs, cats, dogs, and mongooses, along with modern infrastructure like artificial lights and utility lines. Restoring the seabirds is an uphill fight, and for some people, as much a calling as a job. Once the storms finally cleared, we drove south to meet one of those on the front lines of Hawaiian seabird conservation.

André Raine may have been predestined to work with seabirds. Born and raised in Bermuda, he has the most sterling of pedigrees, having been mentored by David Wingate, the acclaimed conservationist who, in 1951, rediscovered the cahow, or Bermuda petrel, which had been thought extinct since the 1620s and which, even today, numbers only about 164 pairs nesting on a few protected, rat-free islands off Bermuda. As a young man Raine spent long nights watching over soon-to-fledge cahow chicks to keep them safe.

Despite that foundation in endangered seabirds, he veered away for the first part of his career, earning a wildlife biology degree as an undergrad in Canada, then a master's and PhD in England, the latter focusing on twites, small finches that breed on the moors of the northern British Isles and Scandinavia. He worked in Zambia for a couple of years doing biodiversity surveys, then the Peruvian Amazon. Eventually he joined BirdLife Malta as their conservation manager, battling rampant illegal bird killing on that Mediterranean island nation while producing its first breeding bird atlas. (By small-world coincidence, I later discovered that Raine had worked closely with Steve Downing, the former wildlife policeman and RSPB hen harrier guardian whom I'd met in northern England. They connected when Raine was doing his doctoral work, and Downing spent years with Raine trying to stem the slaughter of birds in Malta.)

Seabirds pulled Raine back in the end. On Malta, he and his wife, Helen, who is also a respected conservation biologist, worked with the rare Yelkouan shearwater, but after four years on Malta they opted for a change, and in 2011 moved to Kauaʻi, working for the Kauaʻi Endangered Seabird Recovery Project, a joint state-academic program, until 2020. That's when they established Archipelago Research and Conservation (ARC) with André as science director and Helen as executive director. They and their staff of 16 now handle challenges not just in

Hawai'i but throughout the Pacific, such as a new three-year project in American Samoa that in 2023 discovered the first nesting Tahiti petrels seen there in more than 40 years.

Raine, 49, is tall and lanky, with close-cropped hair and a tattoo of seabirds and flowing waves on his left forearm. We met him at the ARC office in Hanapepe, on the upper floors above a coffee shop, before jumping in his truck and heading into the mountains. As we drove up the endlessly looping, endlessly climbing road that winds through Waimea Canyon and Kōke'e State Parks in western Kaua'i, Raine explained that in addition to being the last refuge for the island's rarest forest songbirds, the mountains are also the beleaguered stronghold for endangered seabirds like the Newell's shearwater, known as 'a'o in Hawaiian, and the Hawaiian petrel, or 'ua'u. These two species nest in burrows they dig beneath the sheltering roots of native ferns and trees like ōhi'a, whose red, filamentous starburst flowers we began to see more and more frequently as we reached the tops of the 4,000-foot-high peaks.

Both birds are relatively small and superficially similar, with a wingspan of less than three feet for the shearwater, whose adult plumage is a snappy black above and crisp white below. The Hawaiian petrel is a bit bigger, with a smooth, grayish-colored back, black crown and wings, and white face. Both belong to the order Procellariiformes, or tubenoses, which encompass petrels, shearwaters, albatrosses, and the diminutive storm-petrels, and all of which are profoundly pelagic, coming to land only briefly each year to rear their single chick. The shearwaters plunge-dive for their prey, primarily fish and squid, often looking for places where hunting packs of tuna have pushed the schools of smaller fish toward the surface. The shearwaters tend to stay within a few hundred miles of the colony when foraging. The petrels are surface hunters, using their extraordinary aerial skills to snatch flying fish, squid, and other marine prey from the water, and may travel more than 6,000 miles from Kaua'i to Alaska and back again on a single hunting expedition.

Both species were also all but given up for extinct in the early 20th century, the assumed victims of massive habitat loss and predation. In fact, the 'a'o, Newell's shearwater (then considered a subspecies of the Manx shearwater), was written off entirely after about 1900 until a few were spotted off Kaua'i in 1947. Small colonies of both birds exist on other major Hawaiian islands, but it's impossible to overstate the importance of Kaua'i for these two birds; roughly 90 percent of the world's 'a'o, and about one-third of its 'ua'u, breed in these mountains.

Kaua'i's mountain forests are also assumed to be breeding habitat for a population of a third seabird, the band-rumped storm-petrel, chocolately brown with slender wings and not much bigger than a small thrush, weighing just two ounces. Only four active nests have ever been documented anywhere in the state, all on the slopes of the Mauna Loa volcano on the island of Hawai'i. Reports of their distinctive nocturnal calls, and the capture of birds with brood patches—areas of bare breast skin that help warm eggs—suggest they breed on at least a couple of other islands like Maui; not surprisingly, the storm-petrel, like the 'a'o and 'ua'u, is listed as federally endangered.

These three exceedingly rare tubenoses face a number of hazards, but among the biggest is simply being eaten when they come to earth. Kaua'i, like the island of Lana'i farther east in the archipelago, is fortunate that it has no mongooses, ferociously predatory, weasel-like mammals that were introduced to all the other major islands with devastating results for native birds, which they ate instead of rats as intended. However, there are a number of other pernicious exotic predators on the island, including unleashed dogs, three species of rats (Norway, black, and Polynesian), and feral pigs descended from the diminutive Polynesian pigs the first Hawaiians brought with them, which later crossed with much larger European hogs that white settlers brought. And perhaps worst of all, there are a lot of cats on Kaua'i; no one knows exactly how many, but the estimates for feral cats are well north of 20,000, which Raine considers a serious underestimate, with a large but unknown number of pet cats also allowed to roam at will.

Altogether, these alien predators form a cadre of catastrophe for the island's native birds. Sadly, it doesn't stop there. Those shearwaters and petrels that avoid being eaten have also suffered from the electrification of the island. Fledging from their nest burrows at night and disoriented by artificial lights, shearwater chicks wind up on the ground, from which they are physically unable to lift off (their nests are on high cliffs, providing the necessary jump-off space). If not rescued, many fall victim to predators or vehicles, or starve. And adults of both the shearwaters and petrels, which come and go to their nests under the protective cover of darkness, collide with utility lines, especially those strung along roads in the interior mountains.

The result has been a disaster for both species. "They've had massive declines between 1993 and 2013," Raine told me. "[Using] annual radar surveys, we had a 94 percent decline of the 'a'o and a 78 percent decline of the 'ua'u. So they've just been tanking, which is obviously really concerning when this is one of the last places for these birds. There's a whole bunch of threats, but the main ones are cats and powerline collisions because the birds have to transit from the coast up into the mountains to their breeding colonies—every night if it's the 'a'o, and every three nights with the 'ua'u."

Steve Kress knew he had to eliminate or exclude predatory gulls from Eastern Egg Rock to bring back puffins; in Kaua'i, as in a number of places in Hawai'i, the predators lack wings, so exclusion fences have become a primary defense. We parked at a lookout point where a lot of tourists were unhappy that the mist was blocking any view of the dramatic Kalalau Valley of the Nā Pali Coast below. Raine quietly led us around the end of a barrier near the lookout and down a steep, muddy trail that followed the perimeter of an anti-ungulate fence designed primarily to keep out pigs, goats, exotic black-tailed deer, and other larger mammals. The mesh, which was wire to about waist height (including a wide skirt at ground level to prevent anything from digging under it), then plastic mesh eight feet high, wasn't designed to completely exclude smaller mammals like cats and rats.

Inside this fence, though, in a number of select locations on the high hills and cliff escarpments, were far more secure fences designed to keep out anything without wings, enclosing social attraction sites—

islands of sanctuary. These fences use marine-gauge steel mesh fine enough to bar even young mice, topped with outward-curved caps so nothing can climb over, and with wide skirts of buried mesh to prevent an animal from digging under. Inside, these oases are seeded with artificial burrows, and every night the hills echo with the recorded sounds of active tubenose colonies. They're even trying decoys, though the target birds spend no more time above ground than they can help, diving immediately into their burrows when they return from the sea.

Even so, Raine told us that such protection requires constant vigilance. "The average time from a breach in the fence, like a hole or a fallen tree, to a rat getting in is eight hours. Just eight hours. They're relentless," he said. Once there's a breach, conservationists have to assume that rats or cats got inside, and so the painstaking hunt for them must start all over.

Given the storms, floods, and winds we'd been experiencing on Kaua'i since our arrival, Raine was worried that there might be damage along some of the fences, and he was dispatching crews to the sites that ARC is responsible to check. It isn't easy; the best seabird nesting sites are the most remote, many of them only accessible by helicopter. One team had been waiting three days for the weather in the mountains to clear enough to drop them off, and Raine said they would arrive ready to be self-sufficient for days on end in the cold, wet conditions if they couldn't be picked up again because of weather. (The later news was good; a section of fence damaged by a fallen tree was quickly repaired, with no evidence of cat or rat incursions.)

We hiked steeply downhill, careful on the muddy trail and (speaking for Amy and me) very cognizant of the precipitous drop-off just an arm's length away. It was unnerving enough in the hypothetical, with the valley completely shielded by clouds and mist, but when that began to lift and part, allowing us to see several thousand feet almost straight down from our feet, the effect was dizzying. "Oh, there's a tropicbird," Raine said, and it took me a second to realize he meant the barely visible speck of white moving far, far below in the gulf of air among densely forested green cliffs.

For all the necessary labor and worry, though, seabird restoration has made some significant gains on Kauaʻi as some of the worst dangers have begun to be mitigated. We'd already noticed thousands of curious, dangly objects hanging from utility wires along many of the lowland roads and some of those climbing into the mountains. These, Raine explained, are visual flight diverters, designed to allow adult petrels and shearwaters commuting at night to and from their nest burrows to see the wires and avoid fatal collisions—thus averting mass mortality among the breeding adults, which from a conservation perspective are the most valuable individuals in the population. The local electrical provider, Kauaʻi Island Utility Cooperative (KIUC), is installing tens of thousands of such diverters.

KIUC was not doing this entirely from the goodness of its corporate heart. The diverter installations are just one facet of a sprawling, 50-year agreement the utility was close to finalizing after a long and acrimonious dispute with the US Fish and Wildlife Service. In 2010, KIUC pleaded guilty to two counts of a 19-count federal indictment charging it with violating the Endangered Species Act and Migratory Bird Treaty Act (MBTA) by knowingly allowing Newell's shearwaters, the ʻaʻo, to be killed by its electrical lines. Such federal charges against a corporation, especially under the terms of the MBTA, are exceedingly rare, and in this case the indictment came only after years of what the US Department of Justice essentially characterized as foot-dragging by the utility when it came to minimizing the danger to the shearwaters by shielding streetlights and taking other steps to limit collisions with transmission lines.

Under natural conditions, the brightest glow a fledgling shearwater would see, leaving its nest burrow for the first time, would be from moon- or starlight off the ocean, directing them to the safety of the sea. Instead, they often wind up crashing into street lamps, buildings, or high school football fields, since football season coincides with the fledgling peak from September through December. In 2010, the Justice Department found the county, too, in violation of the MBTA for failing for five years to retrofit stadium lights at its parks. Night games were banned, to the fury of football-loving residents. During that tense period, "Buck the Firds" tee-shirts were common, and even some ardent conservationists worried that the action, while warranted, may have made more enemies for native seabirds than the ban had helped them, since games played in the blistering heat of day were a potential health hazard to the young athletes. (Some games were allowed on nights when the moon was full or nearly so, when the risk of confusing chicks with artificial light was reduced. Once the county finally shielded its stadium lights, night games were allowed to resume in 2017.)

In 2023, the electric utility submitted a draft habitat conservation plan (HCP) that outlined the many steps adopted to prevent future seabird deaths, in return for a permit that allows a limited degree of "take," the legal term for the death or injury of a protected species. The plan runs to more than 370 pages, and covers more than just endangered seabirds; the utility's actions that impact endangered native waterbirds like endemic and federally endangered Hawaiian stilt, Hawaiian duck, Hawaiian coot, Hawaiian common gallinule, the nēnē, the federally threatened Hawaiian goose, and green sea turtle are also covered.

Part of the HCP requires ongoing funding for Save Our Shearwaters, an effort started in 1979 by the state of Hawai'i to rescue and rehabilitate downed shearwater and petrel chicks during the fledgling "fallout" season. In years past, more than 2,000 Newell's shearwater fledglings had been gathered in a single season, rehabilitated, and released, though the population has shrunken so badly that the annual total is now 200 or fewer. SOS has grown into the only licensed wildlife rehabilitation facility on Kaua'i, handling native birds and the Hawaiian hoary bat, the state's only native land mammal. SOS even provides "aid stations," where Good Samaritans can place a chick that they've found in small, protective compartments, then call a toll-free line to report the deposit.

Still, the hurdles are significant. Most of Kaua'i's petrels and shearwaters don't nest in fenced-in colonies, and remain at the mercy of introduced predators, especially cats. Like all the seabird conservationists I met on Kaua'i, Raine finds cat predation especially frustrating because so many of the cats are either unsupervised pets or feral cats that are fed out of what he sees as a misguided sense of kindness.

"There's nothing worse than going up to a colony where you've been following this pair [of birds] for 10 years—and they can live for 30, 40 years—and one of them has been torn up, and there's bits and pieces of it lying outside the burrow, and then you walk around the corner, there's another one, and then you walk around the next corner and there's another one. The cat advocates always say you can't put one species above another. But as I keep saying to them, that's literally what you're doing. These are invasive predators that you're feeding in the wild that are eating every single other native species," he said.

Raine ticked off a litany of other dangers and threats to the nesting colonies, like invasive plants such as ginger and Australian tree-fern, that create such dense root mats that seabirds can't burrow through them. "And then if they survive all that, when the chicks fledge, they fly out from the darkness of the mountains and are attracted like moths by the lights of the cities. They circle around until they're exhausted, end up on the ground where they're either run over by cars, eaten by invasive predators, or just starve to death because once they're on the ground it's almost impossible for them to get back up again. And then couple all that with the changes at sea, with things like bycatch, overfishing, marine pollution like plastics, the looming threat of climate change. You can see why these guys are not doing well," he said.

It sounded excruciatingly depressing. "How do you get out of bed every morning?" I asked.

"Well, because with all of that in mind, and with this massive population crash that's been ongoing, the work that we're involved in to monitor and help guide management actions in the colonies is having amazing results," Raine said. "The 'a'o and the 'ua'u respond really well to management in the mountains. If the birds aren't being killed by predators, then they fledge their chicks, you get more and more birds come back not being eaten. So after a couple of years of management, you see this really pronounced impact of the work you're doing."

Raine said that ARC monitors about 1,900 nest burrows on 10 management sites in the mountains, using observation, camera traps, and autonomous recording units (ARUs) that measure the nocturnal call rates of the birds coming and going from the managed colonies. "In our management sites, which we've now been running for 11 or 12 years in collaboration with predator control teams run by Hallux Ecosystem Restoration and National Botanical Gardens, we've seen massive increases in reproductive success rates," he said. "We have 10 [ARUs] per site, and we have seen a huge annual increase in call rates. And call rates, as we've discovered, are directly related to the number of burrows on the ground. So the colonies are all increasing. That's how I get out of bed, because I can see there is a very clear difference, and it's all down to the removal of predators in the mountains or eradication of them inside social attraction sites."

He also expects a major, further boost from the changes that the electrical utility has been implementing, removing the most dangerous, top wire known as the static line from the entire grid and installing the diverters in the areas where collisions have been such a long-standing problem. "So that's having a massive, massive impact by decreasing the number of birds that hit power lines. We're currently at a 41 percent reduction on strike numbers from 2021, but we reckon it's going to be 60, 70 percent reduction. So you have fewer birds dying on power lines, you have fewer birds dying in the mountains, so the fate of these birds is changing very much for the better," Raine told me.

I guess I could get out of bed every morning with a spring in my step for that, too.

Predator-proof fences are expensive, costing nearly $1 million a mile depending on the location and design, and there are ongoing maintenance and eventual replacement costs. Imagine how much more effective it would be to get rid of the invading mammals entirely.

On a populated landmass the size of Kauaʻi that isn't yet practical, but when the island is smaller, it can be possible to remove the threat, often with dramatic results. All over the world, conservationists have been taking the fight to the introduced animals that overwhelmed seabird nesting islands and turned what had been vital colonies numbering in the millions to almost nothing. Remove the introduced predators, though, and those colonies can rebound, sometimes with the assistance of translocation and social attraction techniques. But as Project Puffin found with its initial and ongoing battle against gulls, eradicating predators is never a pretty process, and often a gruesome one.

Globally, mammals remain the biggest threat, and New Zealand—which, like Hawaiʻi lacked any native land mammals except for bats and possessed an extraordinary avifauna, and like Hawaiʻi has lost a huge proportion of its native birds to extinction—has been the primary incubator of techniques for tackling mammalian eradication. The need on New Zealand is urgent; in all, 80 percent of the country's native bird species are classified as threatened or at-risk, with introduced mammals estimated to kill 68,000 native New Zealand birds *each night*. Starting in the 1960s with a few tiny offshore islands, and constantly expanding in scope and breadth, New Zealanders have perfected the means of removing invasive mammals, mostly using the aerial distribution of enormous quantities of rodenticides over every nook and cranny of larger and larger islands, but also employing traps, shooting, and even biological warfare where feasible. It is laborious, unpleasant work, but the results can be spectacular, as when 49-square-mile Macquarie Island, lying between Tasmania and Antarctica, was cleared over the course of years of European rabbits, black rats, house mice, and feral cats, these last of which were killing an estimated 60,000 seabirds annually. Declared pest-free in 2014, Macquarie is now home to 3.5 million seabirds of 13 species. Island size has become less and less of an obstacle. In 2018, all 1,300 square miles of South Georgia Island, between the Falkland Islands and Antarctica, was declared free of the rats and mice that had been decimating its native wildlife.

Still, eradication becomes exponentially more difficult as the size of the area increases, if only because it makes the possibility of missing a rat or two, which is all it takes for failure, more likely. But there's ambitious, and then there's audacious. In 2016, then-New Zealand prime minister John Key announced a goal of completely eliminating some of the most destructive bird-killing invasives—rats, mustelids (stoats, weasels, and ferrets), and opossums—from all of its offshore islands by 2030, and from the entire country by 2050. Many people scoffed, or balked at the price tag, an estimated $3 billion NZ per year. The challenges remain enormous, but the progress on Predator Free 2050, as the effort is known, has been surprising. By 2023, the New Zealand Department of Conservation estimated it had significantly or completely cleared predators from some 1.7 million hectares, about 6,500 square miles, which did not include enormous additional expanses of land being tackled by private individuals and nongovernmental partners. At last count, about two-thirds of New Zealand's nearly 500 uninhabited islands have also been cleared.

Massive, community-sponsored trapping campaigns have so reduced pest numbers in the capital, Wellington, that native birds absent for generations—kākās (parrots with a brilliant splash of red or orange on their underwings), purply-green native pigeons called kererūs, Australasian honeyeaters called tūis with outsize personalities that were once down to nine or 10 pairs in the entire city—have surged back in such numbers, residents say, that they have to keep the doors closed in the morning if they want to sleep in, because otherwise the birdsong wakes them. Even brown kiwis have been reintroduced to one newly stoat-free Wellington suburb, where they immediately began raising chicks.

Island pest eradications in the United States have mostly been restricted to Alaska, where in the 1700s and 1800s dozens of islands in the Aleutian chain were seeded with red or Arctic foxes, creating in effect insular fur farms to which Russian and American hunters could periodically return. The results for birdlife, including seabirds, waterfowl, and migratory shorebirds, were predictably awful. After most of the Aleutians became part of what is now Alaska Maritime National Wildlife Refuge, the federal government in 1949 started a systematic campaign of fox removal, using poisoned baits at first, then switching to dedicated teams of trappers and sharpshooters. By 2017, more than 40 Aleutian islands had been cleared of foxes, including Attu, the farthest west and the first island on which foxes had been released in the 18th century, and from which they were removed in 2003. The once-endangered Aleutian cackling geese, down to fewer than 800 birds in 1967, numbered 238,000 in 2022. "If you go to Attu now, the valleys are deafening with the noises of Aleutian cackling geese," an Alaskan Maritime NWR biologist said.

Besides the elimination of large herbivores like sheep and goats, there have been relatively few island eradications in Hawai'i. The most recent, and one I was anxious to see for myself, was Lehua Islet, which lies about 19 miles west of Kaua'i. Lehua is a collapsed, crescent-shaped caldera of volcanic tuff a little less than 300 acres in size, owned by the Coast Guard but managed as a state seabird sanctuary. Pollen samples show that the island once supported native (and now critically endangered) loulu palm trees, but no longer. European rabbits that were present by at least 1856 ate away the vegetation, leaving it a rather barren and bleak place, while Polynesian rats attacked and killed nesting seabirds like Bulwer's petrels and wedge-tailed shearwaters, and devoured any seeds or fruits the island's plants managed to produce.

The rabbits were the first to go, eliminated in 2005 and 2006 by an intensive hunting operation. The rats proved to be a tougher nut to crack. In January 2009 the US Fish and Wildlife Service, Hawai'i Department of Land and Natural Resources, and USDA Wildlife Services used aircraft to spread almost two tons of the anticoagulant rodenticide diphacinone over the island, choosing that time of year because rat populations were at their lowest in winter, as were the number of migratory birds on the island. It didn't work, at least initially. Either the first attempt missed one or more of Lehua's rats, or the animals reinvaded the island, so the partners tried again in 2017. This time, monitoring and surveys showed no sign of the animals, and Lehua was declared rat-free in 2021.

It didn't take long for the islet's seabirds to respond. André Raine has been part of the team monitoring Lehua's recovery, as vegetation fills in the once-denuded landscape, providing increasing cover and nesting sites for birds like black noddys, brown and red-footed boobies, Laysan and black-footed albatrosses. When we were together in the mountains he enthusiastically described it to us—not only Lehua's great birdlife but the amazing snorkeling in the caldera among monk seals, manta rays, and sharks. That was especially welcome news because the only way to experience Lehua, which is closed to any landings, is to sign up for an all-day cruise and snorkeling trip, which on the advice of several other local seabird experts we had already booked for the following morning.

The weather, alas, had other plans. Seas too rough for the crossing from Kauaʻi, even in a large catamaran, forced a cancellation of the first date we booked, and when we tried again two days later we were informed that the conditions were again too bad to go to Lehua; we could accept a refund, or join the crew as they attempted to take us up the Nā Pali Coast and possibly all the way around the island in a circumnavigation.

Figuring a day on the water is better than a day on land, we opted for the cruise. But the boat had barely rounded the southwestern corner of Kauaʻi, with Niʻihau hazy in the distance, when the crashing swells had half the participants leaning over the rail or watching the horizon with the deathly intensity of the badly seasick. Wedge-tailed shearwaters flashed past us as the crew put out lunch for those able to eat, and reversed course to try to find a sheltered cove on the eastern side where those who wanted to swim in the storm-muddied water could do so.

As the catamaran swung around, a huge white bird with impossibly long, slender wings swept into view, sidling up on the gusting southwest winds—a Laysan albatross, one of the species benefitting from Lehua's newly rat-free state, and a bird that took it upon itself to reclaim its prehistoric place on Kauaʻi.

Albatrosses include the world's largest flying birds, and are increasingly among the most endangered of any sort. There is a lot of disagreement over the taxonomy of their family, the Diomedeidae; anywhere from 13 to 24 species have been recognized by various authorities, with 22 a generally accepted compromise among all the complexity. While albatrosses are believed to have evolved in the Southern Hemisphere, where most still occur, three species do inhabit the north Pacific. The largest, once the most abundant and now rarest of these, is the short-tailed albatross, which barely escaped extinction in the early 1900s at the hands of both Japanese feather hunters and a volcanic eruption on their main nesting island, Torishima. The other two northern species are smaller: the black-footed albatross, a chocolate-colored bird with a six-and-a-half-foot wingspan, and the white-and-black Laysan albatross, which makes up for its even slighter stature by today being by far the most abundant of the three.

As many as 546,000 pairs of albatrosses, the vast majority of them Laysans, nest on Midway Atoll, a national wildlife refuge and national memorial almost 1,200 miles from Kaua'i in the Northwestern Hawaiian Islands. If you're of a certain age, the phrase "gooney bird" may ring a bell where "Laysan albatross" does not, because these are the sweetly naive birds that caused headaches for military aviation during the years from World War II through the Cold War when the US Navy maintained an airfield on Midway, before leaving the small cluster of islands entirely to the birds. Midway's been called the mother ship of albatrosses, but it's a ship with a bad leak; sea-level rise may completely inundate this low-lying complex of coral reefs and two sandy islands before the end of the century, and storm surges and tsunamis have already caused great destruction to nesting albatrosses there.

There are other islands, of course, high enough to stay above the waves, but most do not have albatrosses, at least any more. The only evidence that Laysan albatrosses—known by the Hawaiian name *mōlī*—ever occurred on Kaua'i are subfossil bone remains, suggesting that if they nested there, they vanished sometime after Polynesians arrived in the 13th century. But starting in the 1940s, and sporadically through the 1960s, albatrosses tried to recolonize the island, their attempts to raise chicks (always just one per pair) consistently thwarted by dog attacks. It wasn't until 1979 that the first mōlī chick successfully fledged from Kaua'i.

The ripples from Steve Kress's pioneering work with puffins reached Kaua'i early. In 1982–83, Richard Podolsky, who in 1978 was among the first of the Eastern Egg Rock puffineers, was working on his PhD at the University of Michigan, where he wanted to expand on the work he'd done in Maine using social attraction with Leach's storm-petrels. Podolsky eventually set up nearly 100 mōlī decoys and an elaborate system of 12 audio speakers to replicate the sights and sounds of an albatross colony at three places on Kīlauea Point National Wildlife Refuge. Success came quickly, because the site was primed with albatrosses already in the skies and waters around western Kaua'i.

Even more remarkably, mōlī began nesting on their own among private homes in the toney and albatross-proud community of Princeville, the only place in the world where albatrosses choose to breed in close proximity to people. Amy and I spent a morning in Princeville with albatross protectors like local resident Cathy Granholm, who has been tracking their nesting success for 25 years, and retired USFWS biologist Mike Mitchell, astounded by the sight of these huge seabirds feeding their big, ridiculously cute, fluffy brown chicks and ignoring humans weeding the flowerbeds just yards away. The defenseless babies are left alone for long stretches while their parents make hunting forays that average 7,800 miles to and from the Bering Sea, so community volunteers like Mitchell and Granholm zealously guard them from the constant threat of cats and off-leash dogs, including an aggressive feral cat-trapping operation. If it evades cats and other dangers, including long-line fishing that kills an estimated 160,000–320,000 seabirds (many of them albatrosses) each year, an albatross chick may live for—well, we don't really know for how long. The oldest known wild bird of any species is a Laysan albatross, a female called Wisdom, banded as a breeding adult (so at least five years old) in 1956, and thus at least 74 years old when her newest chick hatched in January 2025. In truth, she may be considerably older than that.*

Obviously, keeping nesting birds shielded entirely from predators is the best option. On our last day in Kaua'i we drove back north, turning off before Princeville to Kīlauea Point NWR, where Rich Podolsky had first tried social attraction with albatrosses more than 40 years ago, and where the mōlī still nest by the hundreds. The refuge had just set a new benchmark for seabird protection, a more than two-mile-long fence designed to keep out everything down to the size of a baby mouse. Built of more than 1,800 heavy wooden posts and marine-gauge steel mesh more than six feet high, it is the biggest pest exclusion fence in the United States, completed in October 2023 and protecting 168 of the refuge's 203 acres.

Our guides were Jen Waipa, the visitor services manager for the refuge, and three young field technicians with the Hawai'i-based NGO Pacific Rim Conservation, which has been working with seabirds in the region for decades. The team leader was Dylan Blanchard, 30, who had jettisoned a budding career in finance to work with endangered birds, including seabirds, on the Indian Ocean island of Mauritius, before coming to PRC several years previously. With him were Dave Hanna, burly and bearded, who spent 10 years working with seabirds and shorebirds on Maui, and Crys Moosman from Idaho, who had

---

* Because seawater is hard on metal leg bands, Wisdom has been rebanded several times, but her first band was placed on her leg by Chandler S. Robbins, an iconic ornithologist with the US Geological Survey. Among Chan's many other accomplishments was creating the North American Breeding Bird Survey in the 1960s, and he wrote one of the most influential mid-20th century field guides to birds, which was my entry to birding as a kid. Chan was a wonderfully gentle, deeply wise person. He died in 2017 at 98, active and insightful right to the end, and while the American bird world misses him, Wisdom remains a very direct, living connection to everything he meant to ornithology. And she means the world to those who guard her home on Midway.

come to PRC a few months earlier after doing seabird work in Iceland. We jammed ourselves into one of the trucks, passed through a locked gate, and entered the refuge.

The fence had come just in time, Blanchard told us; the previous nesting season, before it was complete, pigs had destroyed 70 Laysan albatross nests on the refuge. Although the newly finished enclosure may be predator-proof, its construction had inevitably trapped within it plenty of mammals that were already present on the landscape, including pigs and cats, which were slowly being eliminated. "There's one, maybe two cats left, but we're fighting a war with the pigs," Blanchard said as we bumped up the dirt road deeper into the refuge. Hunters search for them at night, using spotlights and 12-gauge shotguns loaded with buckshot, and had killed 35 or so, including the pigs that appear to have been the main culprits attacking the mōlī nests. "At this point, I think there's a good handful left," he said, but they were proving elusive.

Here and there we passed Laysan albatrosses tending large chicks, many of them sitting in the shade of *Casuarina* trees, the exotic Australian "pine" that is common on Kaua'i. Before long we reached the refuge's inner sanctum, the Nihokū Ecosystem Restoration Project, a seven-acre fenced oasis created in 2012 to provide a predator-free island of safety before the main refuge fence had been built. We opened a chest-high half-gate in the inner fence, climbing up and over and into the restored habitat within. To my untrained, mainland eye, the view was gorgeous—the land sloped steeply down, a strong sea breeze blowing in our faces as albatrosses and red-footed boobies flew by and humpback whales periodically breached in the distance—but what I couldn't immediately appreciate was that through a lot of hard work, invasive exotic plants like Christmasberry tree (a species known as Brazilian peppertree in places like Florida that it has also invaded) had been removed, replaced by carefully nurtured native species like *hala*, a *Pandanus* screw-palm, and *naio*, or false sandalwood. "It's labor-intensive," Waipa explained, "clearing out the exotics, growing the natives, installing drip irrigation, but it pays off."

Here, PRC, the USFWS, and its partners, notably the Kauaʻi Endangered Seabird Recovery Project (KESRP) at the Pacific Cooperative Studies Unit of the University of Hawaiʻi at Mānoa, in association with the state Division of Forestry and Wildlife, launched a project that was part rescue mission, part long-term restoration effort. Much as Steve Kress had moved pufflings from Newfoundland to Maine to start a new colony in a protected site, between 2015 and 2020 ʻuaʻu (Newell's shearwater) and ʻaʻo (Hawaiian petrel) chicks were pulled from at-risk burrows in the mountains a month or so before fledging, placed in artificial nests in Nihokū, and fed each day until they flew to the sea. In all, 106 petrels and 86 shearwaters fledged, a 98 percent success rate. (At the time, André Raine from Archipelago Research and Conservation was working for KESRP, and was one of those removing chicks from risky burrows in the mountains for relocation.)

Waipa explained that Nihokū was ideal for the birds; its high slope and nearby cliffs were perfect for takeoffs and landings, and there was no light pollution at night to disorient fledglings nor any electrical lines along the wild Nā Pali Coast for them to hit. It's also thousands of feet above sea level, so ocean rises are not a concern. Now the site is peppered with artificial burrows to save the birds the several years of work it usually takes them to dig their own nest tunnels, and a solar-powered social attraction sound system that broadcasts the nighttime sounds of a busy colony.

It has paid off already, even though many of the transplanted birds are only now reaching maturity, a process that takes four or five years. We followed Blanchard down the slope, moving quietly and carefully after he put a finger to his lips and crouched next to a square wooden box that rose from a mound of dirt, with a black corrugated plastic pipe poking out of the front and a heavy sandbag on top. When he lifted the lid and I peeked inside, I saw a male Hawaiian petrel sitting quietly on the earthen floor of the artificial burrow. It was the size of a small duck, its face white, its crown black with a streak of white nail polish on its head where the PRC team had marked it for identification, its back feathers scalloped in pewter-gray deepening to charcoal on the folded wings and tail. This bird had only just returned to the colony, and with luck would soon have a mate, and a chick. The previous season, four pairs of translocated petrels nested, fledging two chicks, while one of the transplanted shearwaters mated with an unbanded female that had been attracted by the sound system, although she did not lay an egg. (By October 2024, the site had fledged its first-ever wild-born Newell's shearwater, the critically endangered 'ua'u, the offspring of a translocated male and a socially attracted female.)

There are even more ambitious attempts to find safe refuge for seabirds in a changing world. From 2017 to 2021, PRC moved black-footed albatross chicks from Midway and Tern Island to fenced enclosures on high, windy cliffs at James Campbell National Wildlife Refuge on O'ahu to create a new colony there. They joined Laysan albatrosses moved to the refuge from the missile range at Barking Sands in western Kaua'i, where they create a hazard. Working with the Mexican organization Grupo de Ecología y Conservación de Ilas, PRC began transplanting black-footed albatross eggs and chicks completely across the Pacific to Guadalupe Island off the Baja Peninsula, one of several Mexican islands that Laysan albatrosses (which raise the transplants) had already colonized on their own since the 1980s, nesting high above the rising sea.

Nihokū's seven acres might not seem like much, but if there's one thing colonial seabirds like, its company. Lindsay Young, the director of PRC, who has since moved to the National Geographic Society, estimated that this small inholding alone could easily accommodate more than 100,000 nesting petrels, shearwaters, storm-petrels, albatrosses, and other seabirds—a density very much in keeping with the busiest nesting islands in the Pacific. With a vastly larger area of the refuge now enclosed, from which all predators will eventually be excluded, the sky is the limit.

"Nihokū could serve as a translocation site for a lot of the birds of the Northwestern Hawaiian Islands that are losing out to sea level rise," Waipa said. "That would really only work with seabirds—they're so malleable, so easy to work with." And you never know what's going to show up on its own. Nihokū has been visited several times by Kermadec petrels, a species that nests (above ground, not in burrows) primarily in the subtropical south Pacific. There's no evidence yet that they are breeding at Kīlauea Point. "But it's remarkable that the only place in the Northern Hemisphere that they chose is a protected site with social attraction," Blanchard added.

To this point, the discussion had been a standard-issue, Western-style conversation about science, seabird ecology, and population dynamics. But Waipa, who is Native Hawaiian, said the refuge also recognizes the spiritual and cultural importance of the work they're doing. "Seabirds were traditionally held in very high esteem by Native Hawaiians—they were seen as closest to the gods," she said. The refuge has worked with local elders on the restoration work, including a traditional blessing of the newly completed perimeter fence.

We carefully slipped the lid back on top of the petrel's nest box, then made our way back up the hill and through the half-gate to the trucks, where we gathered. That's when Dave Hanna noticed a mōlī chick sitting in the shade of a *Casuarina* tree a few yards away. As we squatted in a half-circle around it, the bird sat up very straight, its webbed feet sticking out in front of its pleasantly round belly. No one said much, just quietly enjoying the presence of this endearingly goofy, toddler-sized bird.

"You know, it really gets to me sometimes," Dylan Blanchard said quietly, "knowing that if this chick survives the next few years, it's probably going to outlive me, maybe by a lot."

I have to admit that hit me pretty hard, and not only because I have far fewer decades left than Dylan. There is nothing fleeting about the life of an albatross, nothing ephemeral about the literally millions of miles it will fly in its long, long life. If that fluffy babe survives—if it avoids hungry tiger sharks on its maiden flight, if it steers clear of longline boats and plastic junk, if it becomes the new and perhaps even more venerable Wisdom of a later generation of mōlī—what will the world be like?

It would be easy to think grimly about Midway disappearing under the waves, taking the mother ship of mōlī with it, but on that hillside with the whales leaping and this fluffy chick looking at us with guileless eyes, I instead imagined Kīlauea Point as it could be in a few decades, Nihokū jammed to the gills with hundreds of thousands of birds, their multitudes spilling over into hundreds of thousands more in the entirety of the now-fenced refuge, one of many havens around the world safe from teeth and claws, high above a rising sea—an ark to carry the sacred seabirds of Hawai'i into the future, and just one more blossoming expression of an idea born on the cold waters of Maine long before.

Nine

Tastes Like Chicken

I am not a beach person.

Well, let me qualify that; I am not a *summer* beach person. I love the winter beach: elemental, raked by cold winds that make the sand hiss and shiver across the surface of the dunes, stripped of its human crowds and restored to its wild owners. Especially restored to the birds, be they loons and scoters rolling among the gray, foam-topped breakers, sanderlings on frantic feet following the swash of the waves, gannets plunging for prey far offshore like javelins hurled down by angry gods, horned larks with their bleached, straw-yellow throats skittering among dune grasses whose tips, as they spin in the breeze, carve circular tracks in the sand. Or, in the best of winters, a snowy owl down from the Arctic that sits quietly all day in the sheltered lee of a driftwood tangle, safe from the gaze of passing eagles, only to come alive at dusk, eyeing with growing intensity the duck that for the past hour mistook the owl's lassitude for disinterest, and is about to pay for that misjudgment.

Spare me summer beaches, though, with their traffic jams and hordes of people. Which is why I had to wonder why I was doing this to myself as I crept along with day-before-the-Fourth-of-July traffic trying to cross the Sagamore Bridge to Cape Cod in Massachusetts. But if I wanted to understand how, against huge odds, a tiny shorebird that all but vanished from New England—from North America—had been brought back from the brink, this was the ideal time to head for the shore. Along with everybody else.

There are few groups of birds in deeper trouble, worldwide, than shorebirds. Among the world's greatest migrants, they are uniquely at risk by virtue of the extraordinary journeys many must make every year, which include the longest nonstop migration of any non-seabird, the 8,100-mile, trans-Pacific flight of the bar-tailed godwit from Alaska to New Zealand and Australia. Other species travel even greater distances, if not all in one fell swoop: Hudsonian godwits flying 9,000 miles one way from the Pacific coast of southern South America to Hudson Bay or Alaska; red knots doing the same from southern Argentina to the Canadian Arctic. Such journeys happen everywhere there are shorebirds, along flyways that connect places as far-flung as Svalbard and West Africa, or the Russian Arctic and the Yukon with Australasia or Oceania.

To accomplish these astounding flights, the birds need the right habitat with abundant food at critical way-stations known as stopover sites, where they can rest and refuel. One of the most important is the Yellow Sea, between China and the Korean Peninsula, whose expansive mudflats support an estimated 11 million to 13 million migrant shorebirds a year, the nexus of what is known as the East Asia–Australasian Flyway (EAAF). But over the decades, as much as 70 percent of those mudflats were destroyed, walled off from the sea and buried under millions of tons of sediment to create dry land for industry and housing. In 2018, China dramatically slowed, but did not entirely halt, coastal destruction on its shore, which came just in the nick of time for species like the spoon-billed sandpiper, numbering only about 400 adults and one of the rarest birds of any sort in the world. But dozens of other species of shorebirds using the EAAF, like Eastern curlews, great knots, the Asian subspecies of red knots, curlew sandpipers, and those Alaskan bar-tailed godwits, had already suffered grievous losses over the preceding decades of "reclamation" and had seen large declines in their populations.

The situation hasn't been much better in North America. Market and sport hunting of shorebirds ended in the early 20th century[*] with, perhaps surprisingly given the carnage, only one species lost to extinction, the Eskimo curlew. That bird somehow lingered until at least the 1960s, when the last photograph (in Texas) and specimen (from Barbados, a notorious shorebird-hunting hotspot) were obtained. There have been scattered sight records in the years since, but in the absence of photographs, these later reports, which have continued as recently as 2008, have been considered hypothetical at best. If the Eskimo curlew is gone, it joins another relative, the slender-billed curlew, which was declared extinct in 2024, only the third European bird species to fall into extinction within historical times. It was a bird so rare for so long that save for one naturalist's records from southwestern Siberia in the 1910s and '20s, its breeding grounds were never discovered.

The most recent assessment of shorebird numbers in North America, an analysis looking at population trends from 1980 to 2019 for 28 species, found all but two in steep decline, with more than half of the species studied having lost more than half their population in that time: Black-bellied plovers and buff-breasted sandpipers, down by as much as 60 percent. American golden-plovers, ruddy turnstones, stilt sandpipers, and lesser yellowlegs, by as much as 70 percent. Hudsonian godwits and red knots, down by more than 90 percent in that period. Worse, the rate of decline appears to be accelerating, falling faster in the last three shorebird generation periods than the three before. The steepest losses have been along the Atlantic coast, a major flyway for waders moving between their primarily Arctic breeding grounds and wintering areas in the Caribbean and South America. In late 2024, the International Union for the Conservation of Nature, which maintains the global Red List of threatened and endangered species, downgraded the conservation status of 14 species of North American shorebirds,

---

[*] With two exceptions: Wilson's snipe and American woodcock are still legal gamebirds.

including many like killdeer and least sandpiper that have always been considered of the lowest conservation concern, because of continuing declines with unknown causes.

The potential reasons are legion, however. By their very nature—by their very name—shorebirds need coastlines, beaches, mudflats, marshes, wetlands, and other sensitive habitats that humans have altered and destroyed, or have overrun, as we do each summer with our warm-weather love of sand and sun. Rising ocean levels are inundating coastal wetlands that, blocked by inland development, have no place to go and thus drown. Horseshoe crabs, on whose eggs northbound shorebirds once feasted on the Delaware Bay, have been overharvested for fishing bait, and had their blue, copper-based blood drained for the pharmaceutical industry. Shorebird hunting along their migration routes continues at unsustainable levels in parts of the Caribbean and South America; this appears to be a particular issue for several species including lesser yellowlegs.

Climate change is also scrambling the seasons in the far North where most shorebirds nest, and there is the question of competition. Scientists have noted that the easternmost breeding population of the semipalmated sandpiper, still one of the most abundant of the Western Hemisphere's shorebirds but a species whose numbers have fallen nearly 70 percent since 1980, has declined more steeply than westerly populations; it is not a coincidence that the eastern group's range overlaps with that of the fast-burgeoning colonies of greater snow geese, which have eaten much of the coastal wetland vegetation among which the sandpipers nested.

Yet for all this bad news, there is a bright spot—two, in fact. Two species of shorebirds that have made remarkable comebacks that prove it's possible to reverse those depressing trends. Which is why I was heading to the beach.

The piping plover is among the smallest of the North American plovers, a group that includes the ubiquitous killdeer, and long-distance migrants like the black-bellied plover and the American and Pacific golden-plovers, which may travel as far south as central Argentina for the former, or to Hawai'i, the Philippines, the Solomon Islands, and Australia in the case of the latter.

Piping plovers make no such hemispheric journeys. The muted color of dry sand, with a white belly, yellow legs, and (in summer) a yellow, black-tipped bill, a piping plover is barely seven inches long and weighs not quite two ounces. A ring of black feathers encircles the neck, completely in the male, partially in the female, and fades to gray come winter. The name comes from its call, which the early 19th century ornithologist Alexander Wilson described as "a single plaintive note occasionally repeated." They nest on beaches along the Atlantic coast, on sandy shorelines along the Great Lakes, and on sandbars along inland rivers like the Missouri that flow through the northern Great Plains and Canadian prairies. In winter, all move to the coast, the Great Plains population mostly to the Gulf of Mexico in Texas, those from the Great Lakes migrating to the Southeast, primarily to beaches in Georgia and Florida. Some of the Great Lakes birds travel to the Bahamas, which is where the majority of the Atlantic coastal population spends the winter.

Piping plovers have been a species on the edge for a long time. Probably never very abundant, they suffered (as did most birds) during the unregulated market hunting period, then bounced back to a degree in the early decades of the 20th century once that practice was banned. They received a further boost, ironically, from the Great Hurricane of 1938, which cleared a lot of the southern New England coast of shoreline development and scoured its dunes of dense vegetation, creating the early successional conditions the plovers prefer, making their nest scrapes where there are scattered clumps of beach grass and laying four (almost always four) freckled eggs that match the sand and shell bits around them. By the end of World War II, piping plover numbers had rebounded significantly from their earlier trough.

Their fortunes took a reversal after 1945, however, when the

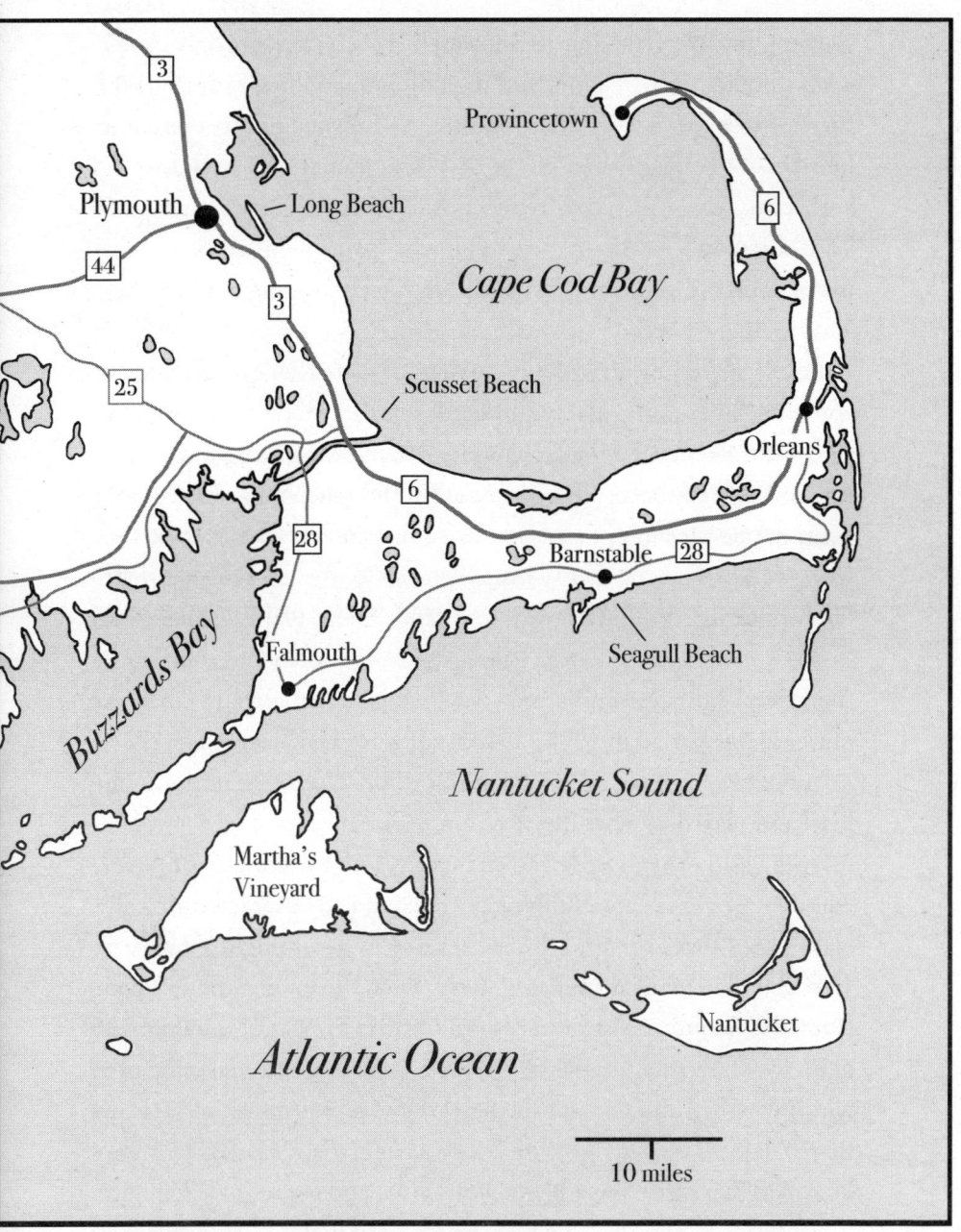

The beaches of Cape Cod, Massachusetts, are among the most important nesting sites for federally threatened piping plovers, where—not without a great deal of early controversy—people have learned to share the shore with birds.

growing middle class and its increased leisure time brought Americans flooding to the shore, and directly into conflict with this bird. Increasingly, the plovers found themselves crowded out by ever-larger numbers of humans who saw such places merely as a backdrop for barbecues, fireworks, kite-flying, Frisbee-throwing, swimming, off-leash dogs, and, on many beaches in the eastern United States, free use of oversand vehicles (OSVs) under whose tires many plover eggs and chicks perished.

Piping plovers have two things going for them. For one, they are an appealing bird, plump and bright-eyed, and the babies are simply adorable, little mottled fluffballs a couple of inches long and mostly head, perched high on toothpick legs. Secondly, and much more importantly, they became a federally listed species, so that cute factor was backed up with some serious regulatory muscle. In 1986, the US Fish and Wildlife Service listed the Atlantic and inland (Great Plains) populations as threatened, and the Great Lakes population as endangered, under the federal Endangered Species Act. (Canada had already listed the plover as threatened in 1978, downgrading it to endangered in 1985).

Suddenly, whether they wanted to or not, a lot of Americans who lived and played in what they had not realized was piping plover habitat were told things needed to change. Which meant a lot of people who'd never even heard of piping plovers suddenly decided they really, really hated that little bird, no matter how sweet it might look.

When the 1986 federal listing took effect, there were just 790 pairs along the Atlantic coast from eastern Canada to North Carolina, 135 of them—fully one-quarter of the US population—in Massachusetts, which was then and remains the heart of the piping plover story. More than half of those pairs were on the beaches of Cape Cod or on what's known as the South Shore below Boston, around towns like Plymouth. These beaches, any one of which might be crowded with as many as a thousand vehicles on a summer weekend, became ground zero for the ensuing plover wars, pitting angry residents and local politicians against conservation groups like the Massachusetts Audubon Society, and state and federal agencies, primarily on the issue of OSV use.

In 1990, a resident of the Cape Cod community of Orleans, site of a lot of OSV activity, asked the town conservation commission to determine whether the beach vehicle access violated the state's wetlands protection act, the first such state law in the country and one of the strongest. The commission's vote ended in a tie, but the state Department of Environmental Protection and its Division of Fisheries and Wildlife ultimately ruled that beginning in 1991 Orleans—and soon thereafter, towns up and down the Massachusetts coast—were required to restrict OSVs in such a way as to protect piping plover nests and chicks during the spring and early summer breeding season.

By 1993, the state had drafted guidelines for managing recreation use, primarily OSVs, when the unfledged chicks of piping plovers and least terns (another state-listed, beach-nesting species that was being killed routinely by OSVs) were present. The guidelines called for plover nests to be found and monitored at least twice a day, at dawn and dusk. Until the eggs hatched, vehicle traffic could be permitted to pass the nest site, but once the chicks hatched, vehicles were banned within 100 yards on either side of the area the young plovers were using, which would stretch from the ocean waterline, across the dunes and on to the bay waters on the back side of the peninsula. If the chicks moved, so did the restricted area, a mobile zone of theoretical safety. Restrictions could be enforced prior to hatching if the state determined that the traffic was causing too many dangerously deep ruts, or damaging the wrack, the washed-up seaweed and other tide-tossed debris full of invertebrates, in which the birds fed.

The results for plovers from even the initial vehicle restrictions were immediate, with the number of pairs on affected beaches doubling from 1991 to 1992. The public backlash was also instantaneous, and fierce. The notion that the God-given right to drive on the beach was being impinged by a bird few people had heard of set off a firestorm of protest. Tee-shirts and bumper stickers that read *Piping Plovers Taste Like Chicken* became common.

There were few places in Massachusetts where the fighting over plovers was hotter than in Plymouth. The flash point was Plymouth Long

Beach, a nearly three-mile-long spit that brackets Plymouth Harbor of Mayflower fame, and for which the town annually issued more than 2,000 OSV permits. Under a 1992 agreement, parts of the beach were open to OSV traffic, parts were closed, and parts were monitored and partially fenced off (well, "symbolically" fenced, marked with do-not-enter signs and string designed to keep walkers and vehicles out) when plovers were nesting there.

There were years of increasing acrimony between Plymouth officials and federal and state wildlife personnel. Hundreds of angry residents packed town council meetings to lambaste efforts to protect the plovers and least terns on Long Beach. The natural resource officer, having been hanged in effigy at the beach, was fired for trying to follow the town's own plover management plan. Then in 1998 the US Fish and Wildlife Service sued the town of Plymouth in federal court and won an injunction ordering Plymouth to abide by a series of measures designed, in the judge's view, to balance plover protection with beach access.

In 1986, the same year that piping plovers were federally listed, Mass Audubon established its Coastal Waterbirds Program, hiring people to act as monitors, patrolling beaches, maintaining symbolic fencing, chatting up beachgoers about the plovers, cautioning them that they needed to keep their dogs on leashes and to stay out of posted areas. Especially in the early days it required equal measures of diplomacy and a willingness to withstand a lot of scorn and abuse. One of those who signed up in 1995 was a 19-year-old college junior from Plymouth named Amy Bourque. Many years later, she would be my wife, but that summer, she became a target.

"I was pretty naive," she said, recalling that summer. "I knew that it was going to be controversial, but I wasn't expecting as much of the outrage as there was." Twice a week, sometimes alone, sometimes with one of the other monitors, she had to walk the almost three miles out to the far tip of Long Beach, which the town had closed to OSVs. People threw beer cans and F-bombs at her. She learned not to wear her Mass Audubon vest or binoculars until she reached the parts of the beach closed to traffic.

It wasn't all hurled profanity. "The birds were unbelievable," Amy said. She helped the team banding tern chicks at the point, recording data, breathing in the guano smell of a seabird colony. "I can smell it like it was yesterday." And it was a transformative experience. She realized she didn't want to be a field biologist collecting data, but instead focus her career on figuring out how to change people's attitudes toward conservation.

Having gotten her feet wet in bird conservation through the coastal waterbird program 30 years ago, and having in recent years come back to work for Mass Audubon, Amy herself supervised the waterbird program for a time. Those three decades have made an enormous difference for piping plovers. Thanks to careful management and herculean effort by Mass Audubon and its many partners, backed by growing public acceptance, the plover population in Massachusetts alone was almost 1,200 pairs in 2024, a 500 percent increase from the 1980s and yet another annual record in a long string of them. Massachusetts remains the core of the plover's northeastern range, holding more than half of the Atlantic coastal population. And while there can still be anger about the beach restrictions, especially when plovers move into a new area, Amy said the waterbird team mostly encounters acceptance.

"Are there still people out there that would love to throw cans or yell at us as bird lovers or tell us that piping plovers taste like chicken? Sure. But for the number of people who say something negative, there are three times as many who say, 'Isn't it amazing to see a piping plover?'"

When I'd reached out to Lyra Brennan, who directs Mass Audubon's coastal waterbird program today, she suggested I visit two beaches: Scussett Beach State Reservation, which sits in the town of Sagamore where the Cape Cod Canal empties into Cape Cod Bay, and Seagull Beach in Yarmouth, about halfway out to the "elbow" of the cape where the peninsula bends sharply to the north like a flexed arm.

I arrived at Scusset at eight o'clock in the morning, among the first vehicles to line up in the bright, muggy sunshine. I looked around for anyone who might be a biologist, but no one else was packing binoculars and a day pack like me. A park employee came out and raised the American flag for the morning, and I asked if he knew where the plover monitors might be.

"I don't know, they come in their own vehicles so I can't tell if they're here. But when are we gonna be able to take vehicles back on the beach? Yesterday we had a lost child, and it's impossible to do that on foot with 2,500 people on the beach," he said. I explained that I didn't work for Mass Audubon, and promised I'd ask the staff to find him. "Okay, tell them to ask for Bruce. We want to help the birds, but. . . . " He let the thought dangle, unfinished.

Moments later I encountered Grace Mulvey, whose small team of three cycles between Scusset and seven other beaches in the Sagamore-Wareham area of the coast. Twenty-nine years old, Grace taught high school science for three years before opting for a career change, and was in her first season as a field technician. Knowing my wife's history, I was expecting to hear similar stories of conflict, but I found her to be incredibly upbeat and positive.

"It's been a pleasant surprise, there's been very few complaints," she said. "But we've also been very lucky that we haven't had to fence off much of the beach, and the pair have been staying mostly on the less busy part. The DCR [state Department of Conservation and Recreation] staff have been fantastic, and the lifeguards have been great to work with—they're awesome kids."

We headed to the far end of the beach, away from the crowd that was already forming near the dune crossover from the parking lot. We finally encountered the plover pair near the jetty that brackets the northeast corner of the Cape Cod Canal's mouth. Two half-grown chicks, still downy but growing into their comically large legs and feet, were with the female; a short while later we saw the male, his markings more distinct and intense, who had the third chick. There had been four eggs in the original clutch, but the fourth baby disappeared its very first night.

"Oh good," Grace said when she spotted the third and final chick at the edge of the dune grass. "Every morning, I feel a little knot in my stomach come undone when I see them all. I've tried to prepare myself for those sadder moments when they come, but nature does as it does."

That's about when a fish crow, which had been hanging around the crowded middle of the beach where the junk-food pickings are ripest, flew down the sand toward us. Actually, what tipped us off was the melodic but distinctly angry calls of the male plover, which launched himself into flight and went straight at the crow, dogging its movements with ringing alarm cries.

"This male is the toughest one I've ever seen," she said. "I've seen him grab the tail feathers of crows and gulls." Despite the male's close-quarters harassment, this crow landed at the edge of the dune grass and walked slowly along, occasionally stopping to peck up some unidentifiable item, but nothing as large as a plover chick. We had no idea where the baby had vanished to; the second an adult gives a warning call, the chicks hunker down and freeze, trusting to their terrific camouflage.

The male plover shadowed the crow as the big, black bird moved methodically along the edge of the dune, disappearing from sight for long moments. Eventually it took off and flew back to the land of lost potato chips, the male plover harrying it with more loud cries as it departed. The male quickly returned, and the missing chick emerged from wherever it had been hiding. The relief on Grace's face was obvious. A few weeks earlier on a different beach, she'd seen a crow grab a chick by the neck. "I was about 30 meters away, and I don't think I've ever moved so fast," she said, rushing the crow and forcing it to drop the baby, which scrambled away, apparently unharmed.

The other issue Grace had occasionally run into were dog-walkers. Dogs, even on leashes, are banned on this particular beach after April 1, but not everyone gets the message, and plover guardians will tell you that they sometimes encounter more than a small sense of entitlement from dog owners who bristle at the notion that *their* dog needs to be restrained. But plovers and terns are exquisitely sensitive to the presence of dogs, since to them the pets are no different from coyotes, foxes, raccoons, and other mammalian predators that pose such a serious threat to their eggs and chicks—and an off-leash dog can be just as deadly and destructive as a wild animal.

In fact, dogs have been the more recent equivalent of OSV access in terms of a flash point involving plovers and people. The matter came to a head a few years ago in Maine, a state with relatively few sand beaches, all primarily along its southern coast, and thus perhaps with more focused attention to what the presence of piping plovers means for visitors. In July 2013, an unleashed dog killed a piping plover fledgling on a beach in Scarborough, a town that had ignored a series of letters from the USFWS in previous years advising it to change its beach dog rules or face possible legal action. After the chick's death, the agency threatened the town with a $12,000 fine, the maximum provided by law. The town revised its regulations, and the next summer hired a part-time plover patroller. Among those especially unhappy with the new regulations were some local hotel owners, who had for years been advertising Scarborough's beaches as particularly dog-friendly.

In the years since, though, Scarborough's dog-restricted beaches have become especially productive for piping plovers. Overall, Maine's 143 successful plover pairs fledged an impressive 237 chicks in 2024, even though historic nor'easter storms the previous winter had severely damaged many of the nesting beaches. As in Massachusetts, a wide cadre of people, including beach monitors, interns, and volunteers organized by Maine Audubon, state, federal, and town personnel, and others provide the human buffer between nesting beach birds and visitors.

Things may have cooled off on the Massachusetts coast since the late 1990s, but piping plovers have remained a point of serious contention elsewhere, particularly at Cape Hatteras National Seashore on the Outer Banks of North Carolina, near the southern edge of the bird's breeding range. There, surf-fishing—and the opportunity to drive at will on the beach—have been deeply ingrained activities since the national seashore opened in the 1950s, and something whose impact on plovers, black skimmers, least terns, and endangered sea turtles the National Park Service seemed to be in no hurry to address in the following decades as visitation steadily increased.

The agency dragged its feet for years on establishing ORV rules, and when it finally did so it became ensnared in further years of litigation between conservation groups, which thought the rules were too lenient, and pro-beach-driving organizations that wanted them loosened or removed. Finally, a 2007 federal lawsuit brought by Audubon North Carolina, Defenders of Wildlife, and the Southern Environmental Law Center resulted, in 2012, in the current regulations, which restrict beach driving, but only to an extent. Vehicles are permitted on the majority of the national seashore's 67 miles of beach—28 miles open year-round, 13 miles open seasonally, and just 26 completely closed to vehicles. The NPS also implemented predator control and buffer zones around plover nesting areas.

Piping plover numbers, which at one point in the early 2000s had fallen to just a couple of pairs in the entire, more than 24,000-acre seashore, have increased but continue to struggle both at Cape Hatteras and farther south along the Outer Banks at Cape Lookout National Seashore, which is accessible only by boat and ferry. Vehicles are permitted on some of Cape Lookout's beaches, but visitation is dramatically less intense, something like 400,000 visitors a year at Cape Lookout versus more than 2 million at Cape Hatteras, which has a road down the middle of it. Yet even at Cape Lookout, which holds about 80 percent of North Carolina's breeding population, the rare shorebirds have a hard time bringing their chicks to fledging. In 2024, the 27 pairs of piping plovers nesting on Cape Lookout laid 116 eggs, but fledged a grand total of two chicks, just 3 percent. The reason? At least part of it, a national park biologist told me, was predation by growing colonies of gull-billed terns, which snatch up the young chicks.

Grace Mulvey and I walked back north along Scusset Beach, tagging behind the plover male and his baby. I needed to move on, because I'd arranged to meet someone else from Mass Audubon's waterbird program at a beach farther out on the Cape proper, and the traffic was building quickly. I reminded Grace she needed to find Bruce the reservation staff guy, and joined the slow-motion queue to cross the Sagamore Bridge across the canal, buoyed by happy thoughts of bird-friendly beachgoers.

An hour later I arrived at Seagull Beach in Yarmouth, where my optimism received a sharp reality check after I met Elizabeth Kaufmann, 25, the team leader for that part of the coast. "Sorry," she said, after we had a little confusion about where to meet, "we've been having a lot of problems with people dragging their beach carts through the symbolic fencing near the entrance and knocking it down." There was more tension than perhaps was usual at Seagull that year, in part because with nine pairs of plovers and three or four pairs of least terns, more of the beach than usual was marked off with strands of twine that form the "fences," and partly because winter storms and erosion had significantly whittled away at what beach there was, so that in some places only a few dozen yards lay between the symbolic fencing and the water.

One large closed area was just east of one of the main beach entrances; this was where the terns were nesting, delicate birds half the size of the common terns that had bombarded me on Eastern Egg Rock, with bright yellow beaks, white foreheads, and high, squeaky-toy calls.

"We try to be here every day, because this is one of our highest-use sites, and it has a lot of birds. But no one was here yesterday, which is why all the fencing is awry," she told me as we walked along its edge, scanning for plovers and their families. The fencing, which also keeps people from climbing through the fragile dunes, provides a physical respite to the birds from the summer crowds, but these are *shore*birds; they need access to the water's edge, because that's where their food is found. Unlike the least terns, which carry food back to their nestlings, all the adult plovers can do is lead their brood to good hunting places.

As the beach fills up with people and towels and sun shelters and sand castles and umbrellas, finding a path from the safety of the fence to the edge of the sea and back becomes a greater and greater challenge. Elizabeth said that, on average, the plovers take their young to the water about every half hour, but threading the needle during a holiday crush can become almost impossible.

Ask anyone who works with wild animals and they'll tell you: the real challenge is usually people management, and beaches tend to bring out unfortunate behavior in some folks. While Elizabeth said she's not encountered aggression, she's certainly felt uncomfortable many times, for example when dealing with drunk college-age men happily relieving themselves over the fence into the plover areas, or chasing errant frisbees or empty beer cans into the closed area where a single misstep might crush a clutch of camouflaged eggs or chicks.

That said, the people we ran into while I was with her were friendly. One man has had a summer home at the west end of the beach for decades; she'd had to chide him earlier in the season (as he reminded her) for bringing his dog to the beach, but he told me he was grateful for the plovers because their presence had prevented the town some years ago from creating a huge new parking lot that would have come right up to the edge of the houses. Another beachgoer asked her about a plover pair that had lost their first two nests to high tide overwash; Elizabeth was able to assure her that the pair had nested for a third time, well up in the dune grasses and above the tideline.

The coastal erosion and sea level rise are obviously a problem for the birds as well as recreationalists. Earlier in the summer, Elizabeth was checking on a pair at Seagull that had nested as far back on the beach as they could, beneath an eroded overhang of sand that storm waves had hollowed out. At first, she was puzzled because she couldn't seem to find the nest, before realizing that the entire bank had collapsed on it. Although she wasn't sure she was really supposed to do so, she began frantically digging where she thought it had been, and uncovered the female.

"She was barely breathing, her eyes were closed, she was just taking a big breath every minute or so. But after an hour and a half she seemed to recover. She only lost one egg that was crushed under her when the sand fell, and after I dug her out the male started incubating the others right away. They incubated a week longer than usual, but all three eggs were viable and hatched," she said. "It's funny, I saved her life but that female just *hates* me."

"Well, she probably associates you with a really traumatic experience," I said. "She was barely conscious when you dug her out. She may not realize you saved her and didn't actually cause all of her problems."

The past 30 years have been a clear win for piping plovers on the New England coast, especially in Massachusetts, as their numbers climb and their range expands each summer to new beaches. Which is, of course, also a challenge, because with that expansion comes the potential for an ever-growing impact on human activity. If people only see their access to the ocean being whittled away year after year, whatever good will that's accrued for the birds may start eroding.

But with a growing, more stable population comes the chance to provide a greater degree of latitude between people and plovers in some situations, as Lyra Brennan explained to me. The mechanism that allows for that compromise between recreation and conservation is known as a habitat conservation plan, or HCP, which may sound familiar because it's the approach used on Kaua'i to manage threats to endangered seabirds from artificial lights and electrical transmission lines.

"Because there's so many birds in Massachusetts, the state got a federal permit that allows exposure to 'take' "—meaning the potential loss of birds or eggs—"for piping plovers. Only a certain percentage of them can be exposed to activities that might create take, and any given year, there's maybe eight landowners or beach managers who get a certificate of inclusion and have a take limit," she said. "The goal is to try to allow for recreational use of these beaches that otherwise would not be possible without the HCP. It means that you might be able to deter plovers from nesting in a vehicle path if it's an OSV site, or it means that maybe your fencing can be smaller, or that you can rake the beach" and remove some of the wrack among which the plovers feed.

In return for being cut some regulatory slack, those entities that participate are expected to provide, either directly or by covering expenses, mitigation that benefits an average of 2.5 plover pairs for every pair impacted by their actions. Brennan said that can include law enforcement, outreach, or habitat management, but it most often comes down to predator control—live-trapping and euthanasia, or night-time spotlighting and shooting mammalian predators like coyotes, although the control is meant to target only those individuals known to be killing plovers or terns, not every fox or raccoon attracted by human leftovers.

The HCP, Brennan said, is "a way for us to release the pressure. There are more birds, and we have to keep in mind the economic impact of that for towns, and also allow folks to engage in recreational activities to try to avoid a backlash effect." Working productively with stakeholders like the Massachusetts Beach Buggy Association has also been critical, Brennan said.

"Because the last thing you want to do is make enemies for the birds," I said.

"Exactly. We don't want biodiversity to become the scapegoat."

Still, there are times and places when finding that balance becomes extraordinarily difficult, as happened in South Boston a few years ago.

"Southie" was a historically working-class, predominantly Irish American Boston neighborhood that's undergone a lot of gentrification and diversification in recent decades. It's also a neighborhood with almost no beachfront, except for that beyond the 1930s-era L Street Bathhouse, which closed (along with its quarter-mile-long beach) in 2020 for a $31.2 million renovation. By the time it reopened in 2023 as the Curley Community Center, four pairs of piping plovers had taken up residence.

"There was a lot of fear because plovers showed up, they did well [in previous years], so more of them come back to the same site. The number of plovers is increasing, you've got this brand new center and everyone was really worried about beach access," Brennan said. So she and her team went into outreach overdrive, talking to the mayor, to state senators, giving programs at the South Boston Library, to anyone who would listen. In 2024, the beach at the Curley Center opened to visitors—and three of the four plover pairs fledged chicks. "This year speaks for itself," Brennan told me later that summer. "We implemented the habitat conservation plan at the site, the birds are successful, people are using the beach." Urban sites, she said, give an opportunity to engage with new and often very different populations than the ones conservation groups usually interact with. "There are thousands and thousands of people that could fall in love with the birds, and we want them to see that this is still a wild place," Brennan said.

To be clear, piping plovers are not on quite the same roll everywhere that they are in the Northeast. Their numbers are not only still meager at the southern end of their breeding range in North Carolina; in Atlantic Canada, scientists counted 190 plover pairs, which despite some excellent fledging rates, especially in New Brunswick, was far below the 310-pair goal for that region.

The federally endangered Great Lakes population hit a new record in 2024 for the third straight year, 81 pairs fledging 124 chicks, along with 17 additional chicks that were raised by hand in zoos after the eggs from which they hatched were rescued from abandoned nests, a technique currently only being used with the Great Lakes population. There, in addition to the usual hazards piping plovers face, they're also confronting more and more nesting merlins, those bird-hunting falcons that have colonized far south of the boreal forest in recent decades. The merlin threat has been viewed seriously enough that the Smithsonian Migratory Bird Center was contracted to do a study to see if trapping and relocating merlins was a feasible alternative to shooting those that hunted near piping plover territories. Sadly, the initial results suggested that trapping was neither effective nor practical.

After the season was over, I checked back with Lyra Brennan to see how the plovers I'd watched had fared. The Scusset Beach pair, including that fiercely defensive male, managed to fledge two chicks, and 16 chicks fledged from nine pairs at Seagull. Unfortunately, none of the least tern chicks at Seagull Beach survived; twice that summer, hungry coyotes swept through the colony, eating all of them.

In the case of piping plovers, it was pretty obvious back in the 1980s what the biggest problem was: human disturbance on the nesting beaches. But for another shorebird that is making an impressive recovery, the American oystercatcher, part of the solution was figuring out what was causing the decline in the first place. Once that was done, the other part of the solution was a business plan.

"Oystercatcher" is one of those bird names that doesn't make a lot of sense, since a bivalve doesn't require much catching. "Oyster-stabber," or "oyster-hammerer," would be more appropriate, because these large, noisy, black-and-white shorebirds use their table-knife-shaped, bright red or orange bills to either slip inside an open clam, mussel, or (yes, especially in winter) oyster shell, then neatly slice the adductor muscle that holds the shell closed—or, if it's not quite fast enough to do that, to slam its beak against the portion of the shell that protects the muscle, achieving the same end.

American oystercatchers are found all along the Gulf of Mexico and up the Atlantic coast of North America. (There is also a population on the coast of Mexico north to Baja, beyond which it is replaced by the black oystercatcher.) They may once have nested as far north as Labrador, but by the start of the 20th century oystercatchers occurred regularly no farther north than Virginia. There is nothing subtle or retiring about oystercatchers—they are big, boldly colored, and weigh a pound and a half, and even though they were not especially tasty (one 1867 guide to the culinary merits of hundreds of kinds of wild game said "the flesh is dark-colored, and quite strong and unpalatable") they were nonetheless shot along with almost anything else that flew.*

With legal protection oystercatchers began a slow recovery from their nadir, recolonizing lost ground farther and farther north—Maryland by 1939, New Jersey in the years after World War II, New

---

* The same guide said of the piping plover, or "beach bird," that "In the months of September and October it gets very fat, and its flesh is excellent."

York in the 1950s, the coast of southern New England in the 1970s and '80s. The first pair in well more than a century to nest in Maine was found in 1997.

But even as oystercatchers expanded back north, their population was hollowing out elsewhere, increasingly crowded off beaches. In 2017, 60.2 million Americans, or more than 18 percent of the country's population, lived in counties along the Atlantic and Gulf of Mexico coasts, so American oystercatchers have been caught in the same habitat squeeze as piping plovers and least terns. But because they are not a federally listed species like the plovers, there have been fewer resources available, and less leverage to change conditions on the ground, where oystercatcher numbers kept sagging. Looking again to Cape Hatteras National Seashore in North Carolina, the oystercatcher population there fell by more than half over a nine-year period ending in 2008, even though the habitat had not changed; what had changed was the level and intensity of human use, and the knock-on effects of things like increased populations of wild predators such as raccoons, skunks, and foxes that thrive around campgrounds and parks, as well as free-running cats and off-leash dogs.

Overall, by 2008 the oystercatcher population on the Atlantic and Gulf coasts had dropped to 11,000 individuals and was still falling. Without action, conservationists expected a further decline of at least 12 percent in the following decade. It's not that no one was trying to turn things around for oystercatchers, but the efforts had been scattershot and disorganized, and initially it was unclear which of the many pressures facing this species were driving it down. But a scientific working group established in 2001 had been marshalling research that eventually showed the two biggest problems were nest loss to increasingly common beach predators, and disturbance by humans on the shore. There were ways to counter both issues up and down the coastline, but it would take organization and resources.

In 2008, the oystercatcher working group created a business plan for the American Oystercatcher Recovery Initiative, to be implemented by a sprawling collaboration of 40 or more state and federal agencies, refuges, organizations, and institutions, and funded by the National Fish and Wildlife Foundation (NFWF) to the tune of $500,000 a year over 10 years. Its goal was deceptively modest: increase oystercatcher productivity by an average of about half a chick per pair, per year. That doesn't sound like a lot, but the working group's models suggested that even such a minor boost would be enough to halt the regional decline and propel the oystercatchers back into the black, making the business plan's goal of a range-wide, 30 percent increase in that decade-long span possible.

Managing predation and beach disturbance were major parts of the plan, but there were a number of other, equally important aspects. Tracing the seasonal movements of oystercatcher populations, and documenting the survival rates of oystercatchers at different parts of their life cycle, were critical to filling in serious gaps in science's understanding of the species. To that end, oystercatchers have been marked with field-readable leg bands that biologists—or anyone with a pair of binoculars or a spotting scope—can easily see and report. Habitat modification and restoration improved conditions for oystercatchers along the coast. Other elements were more under-the-hood, like coordinated sharing of information, real-time evaluation of what was and was not working, and adaptive approaches based on emerging data.

It worked. Comprehensive aerial surveys of the oystercatchers' wintering range along the mid-Atlantic and southeastern coasts showed that oystercatcher numbers, rather than falling 12 percent in the subsequent decade, rose instead by 23 percent. While that wasn't quite the 30 percent goal the plan had set for itself, it was only the start, and by 2023 the oystercatcher population was up 45 percent over the previous 15 years, to nearly 15,000 birds tallied on winter surveys. In Massachusetts, which oystercatchers only recolonized in 1969, all the work on behalf of plovers and terns has paid off for them as well, with an estimated 250 pairs in the state in 2024. Compared with the dire outlook for most shorebirds, the oystercatcher initiative has been a huge win.

In 2015, building on the early success of the oystercatcher model, a second business plan called the Atlantic Flyway Shorebird Initiative was developed by the USFWS in coordination with NFWF and its partners. It proposed a 10-year, $90 million budget, but that money would be used to try to recover 15 species instead of one, and the federal appropriation to NFWF proved to be a small fraction of what was needed.

To see what serious support for shorebird conservation looks like, we need to look to Asia. In 2021, the Asia Development Bank, along with BirdLife International and a global collaboration of 40 governmental and nongovernmental entities called the East Asian–Australasian Flyway Partnership, pledged to secure at least $3 *billion* over the following 10 years for wetlands conservation in that enormous and enormously important migratory system, on which more than 50 million birds of more than 200 species depend—shorebirds, waterfowl, herons, egrets, pelicans, cranes, storks, and many more—as well as the nearly 200 million people in communities along the flyway who often depend on those wetlands for shellfish and finfish, protection from rising sea levels and storm surges, and other ecological services. Investing in shorebirds means investing in ourselves through healthy coastal ecosystems. We just seem too shortsighted as a society, as a species, to grasp this simple fact.

As with so many aspects of bird conservation, we actually know much of what we need to do to move the needle for many species of shorebirds. Piping plovers and oystercatchers don't have to be the exceptions; the lessons they provide show how they can become the rule. If we had the political gumption to make the kind of flyway-wide commitment the Asia Development Bank and its partners are making in the EAAF—or the kind of investments Americans made for waterfowl restoration starting with the North American Wetlands Conservation Act—we could certainly begin to address the shared problems that face both shorebirds and the huge slice of the country's population that lives in coastal zones at increasing risk from storms and flooding. It's a matter of will. We just need to find some, before the Eskimo curlew and slender-billed curlew have more company in limbo.

I have always been equally fascinated and heartbroken by the story of the Eskimo curlew, which may be why I have always been especially moved by the sight of whimbrels, one of the three remaining species of curlews in North America and the one that most powerfully evokes those lost "prairie pigeon" flocks. Some whimbrels nest on the same barren-grounds tundra of the Northwest Territories where the Eskimo curlews once did, and while they do not go as far as Argentina, they are epic travelers in their own right, flying from the northeast coast of North America far out over the western Atlantic to the northern coast of South America, fearless of tropical storms and hurricanes, sometimes flying straight into their most ferocious winds. They show extraordinary fidelity to the places where they winter, and to their migratory stopover sites, showing up every spring across a lifetime that may span as much as 20 years on exactly the same few square yards of the same small tidal creek on the Eastern Shore of Virginia to hunt for fiddler crabs each May.

Springtime migration counts at places like coastal Virginia have allowed conservationists to trace just how far whimbrels have fallen. In 1915, one experienced shorebird hunter estimated the spring flight through South Carolina at hundreds of thousands of whimbrels. But those multitudes eroded steadily through the 20th century, especially after about 1970. Between 1994 and 2009 their population fell by a further half, and fresh surveys in 2020 showed no relief, leaving only about 40,000 using the eastern flyway. (There is a western population of the same subspecies, which migrates down the Pacific coast as far as Chile. Whimbrels are also found across Eurasia.)

Whimbrels are one of those 15 species of shorebirds that the Atlantic Flyway Shorebird Initiative was designed to help, though some of the whys of its decline remained murky—at least until 2011. That year satellite tagging revealed not only the whimbrels' habit of migrating through and around tropical cyclones, but their dependence on the islands of the Lesser Antilles as a resting site under such conditions—and the fact that shorebird hunting remained a popular pastime there, condemning many of them to death. The world's media, having breathlessly followed the journey of two whimbrels, nicknamed Machi and

Goshen, which had flown through Tropical Storm Maria and Hurricane Irene respectively, were shocked when both fell to shotgun blasts on the French-controlled island of Guadeloupe that autumn.

Nor, as it turned out, was Guadeloupe alone. At the time the two whimbrels were killed, an estimated 30,000 shorebirds a year were being shot on Barbados, the former British colony where the last known Eskimo curlew died in 1963, and shorebird shooting on Martinique, another French overseas region, was essentially unregulated. Spurred by the recognition of the extent of shorebird shooting in Latin America and the Caribbean, conservationists looked more closely and found that the numbers being killed may more than explain the long-term declines in species like whimbrels, buff-breasted sandpipers, and lesser yellowlegs. Although shorebird hunting for sport seemed to be on the wane on Barbados, killing for subsistence and for sale appears to be rising in places like Suriname in South America, where the annual toll for all species may exceed 180,000 birds.

In the years since, there has been progress. On Barbados, half the "shooting swamps" maintained to attract shorebirds for gunning have closed since 2010, and two or three that stopped hunting still maintain critically scarce shorebird habitat by cutting vegetation and pumping water, though only one, known as Woodbourne, is a formal sanctuary with support funding. On Guadeloupe and Martinique, bag limits have been reduced and some species like Hudsonian godwits, whimbrels, and red knots are on no-shooting lists (though how often these regulations, promulgated in Paris, are observed, and to what extent hunters bother to identify species, is unclear). A moratorium on shooting lesser yellowlegs has gone into effect, a significant step for this fast-declining species for which hunting may be the single biggest threat, but how long it will remain in place is anyone's guess.

In the meantime, even though we may not deserve it, the birds themselves occasionally deliver a gift so precious you can easily call it a miracle.

At dusk a few years ago I waited in the gathering twilight on a low, flat, sandy island at the mouth of the North Edisto River on the coast of South Carolina. It was May, the peak of the northbound shorebird migration, and the beach was lively with semipalmated plovers and least sandpipers, with black skimmers and gulls, and with the songs of marsh wrens from the stands of cordgrass. But I was waiting for something bigger, something few people had witnessed in more than a century.

I heard them before I saw them, the birds the old shorebird gunners called "seven-whistlers": whimbrels. By the dozens, then by the hundreds, then by the thousands, they poured toward me and rushed on, their high, ringing, seven-syllable cries all around me, their long, powerful, tapered wings that had carried them from the mouth of the Orinoco or the Amazon rowing against the sea breeze. The last of the sun disappeared into gray clouds, and they kept coming; in full dark they still streamed in, perhaps as many as 20,000 of them jamming onto a slender teardrop of sand yet farther out in the bay, where they would, in densely packed flocks, pass this night of the full moon, when the tides rise their highest and there are few other places they can rest beyond the reach of land-bound dangers.

Compared with hundreds of thousands of whimbrels in 1915, this may seem like a pittance, but in an age when abundance is the rarest thing, Deveaux Bank, where I stood, holds what today is the single greatest gathering of whimbrels known on the planet. It is as close as I will ever come to imagining what the great Eskimo curlew flocks were once like. Fully half of the Atlantic flyway whimbrel population, and one-quarter of all the whimbrels that nest in North America, spend a month or so on this part of the coast, which holds some of the most expansive and well-protected tidal wetlands in the United States, 350,000 acres of which comprises the ACE (Ashepoo, Combahee, and Edisto) Basin, teeming with the crabs and other marsh invertebrates the whimbrels need to fuel their flight back to the subarctic.

And once, watching those birds each aggressively defending its own a small patch of cordgrass marsh against other whimbrels, biologists assumed that all that tidal marsh was enough. When the sun went down and whimbrels flew off, the scientists went home, wrote up their data, and maybe felt good knowing that the bounty of the ACE Basin was underpinning this global migration. But what no one knew, for years, was that those whimbrels, for all the abundance of food by day, were critically short of one equally important thing—a safe place to spend the night. So tens of thousands of them made the long commute, hidden from human eyes by the falling darkness, back to Deveaux Bank, this rarest of sanctuaries. Flying as much as 30 miles twice each day, the whimbrels may burn 20 percent of their energy on this commute even before they start to migrate north at the end of May. Biologists talk about the importance of understanding an organism's full annual cycle, the knowledge gaps in which can lurk dangers we don't recognize and thus do not address. This was a case of not understanding the full daily cycle, and overlooking an equally vital but largely unmet need.

There are only two other such nighttime communal whimbrel roosts known in the Southeast, and neither holds more than 2,000 birds. But how hard would it be to create more such roosts, strategically placed near prime foraging habitat so the birds needn't waste so much energy on long back-and-forths? There has been talk about using dredge spoils, which already can be repurposed as nesting islands for waterbirds like terns and pelicans, to make whimbrel roosts that would allow the birds to spread out and more efficiently bank up the fertility of the ACE Basin as calorie-rich fat beneath their skin, allowing them a greater margin of safety on their northward migration.

Can sparking full recovery for some shorebirds be as simple as instituting reasonable bag limits in the Caribbean and building more nighttime roosts? No, probably not, but they would be solid first steps—and who would have thought that simple fixes like reducing nest predation and disturbance would have turned around oystercatcher fortunes so quickly and dramatically? Remember, all that took was a slight increase of half a chick per pair, per year, in annual productivity to start the oystercatchers on the road to rebound. Simply reducing hunting mortality in the Caribbean and South America could have equally profound and immediate effects. And there is now a working group initiative focused on whimbrels, one that closely follows the successful oystercatcher model, to build the kind of demographic model that guided oystercatcher recovery.

Full darkness was at hand, there on Deveaux Bank. In the last vestiges of twilight, a flock of a few dozen whimbrels appeared right in front of me, at head height, only yards away. Without thinking—and not from any defensive instinct, really for no reason I can now imagine—I threw my left hand high into the air, fingers wide, just as they barreled around and past me in a great rush.

And I felt . . . something. Perhaps the brush of primary feathers on my fingertips. Maybe just a gust of the sea wind. Maybe a little of the urgency that carries tens of thousands of birds on slender wings from Venezuela to the Arctic and back, and on this night to a newborn spit of sand on the South Carolina coast.

Whatever it was, I stood, breathing hard, my arm still raised like a benediction, as the night swallowed them.

Ten

Prairie Ghosts

Russell Davis was *not* happy.

It was late spring in 2001, in the middle of calving season at his family's Wineinger-Davis Ranch on the shortgrass prairie of southeastern Colorado, and he was constantly patrolling the grasslands looking for newborns. When he noticed sunlight glinting off a pickup truck in the distance he didn't pay much attention, assuming it was a neighbor who liked to hunt prairie dogs, which was fine with him. Ranchers don't like prairie dogs.

But when he realized the truck was a Toyota, and that the person standing near it was a young woman wearing shorts, a floppy hat, and a pair of binoculars, he was both confused and angry. Ranchers can be hospitable, but trespassing is beyond the pale.

Before he could even ask this unexpected young woman why she was on his ranch, though, she said, "Mr. Davis, they're *everywhere*."

"Well, I thought to myself yes, we're standing here in the middle of a prairie dog town, and yes, there are prairie dogs everywhere," Davis recalled. "And she says, 'No, not the prairie dogs. You have mountain plovers everywhere here.' That kind of caught me off-guard. We're 80 miles from the Rocky Mountains, so whatever this mountain thing is, it's lost."

He learned that this young bio-tech was part of a regional survey for mountain plovers, one of the rarest birds in western North America. The name, as he already suspected, is a misnomer; "prairie plover" would be better, because it's a shorebird that has utterly forsaken the water at every point in its life cycle, preferring bare dirt against which its brown plumage vanishes as if by magic.

Mountain plovers nest on the shortgrass prairie, the immense ecosystem that exists in the rain shadow of the Rockies—the westernmost and most arid of North America's great grasslands, where 10 or 11 inches of rain counts as a wet year. Although nearly half the shortgrass prairie has been destroyed or converted to agriculture, it has actually fared better than its more easterly counterparts.

Mountain plovers nest from New Mexico to Montana (nudging, just barely, across the Canadian border), although they once ranged farther east into Nebraska, Kansas, and Oklahoma, so plentiful that 19th-century market hunters sometimes killed hundreds in a day. In winter they retreat to dry plains, harvested alfalfa and grass fields, and similarly parched, sun-baked habitat from southern California to south Texas and northern Mexico.

The young woman also told Davis—and this was perhaps the worst news a rancher could hear—that the plovers were being considered for listing under the Endangered Species Act (ESA). One of the few things most ranchers hate more than prairie dogs is federal restrictions on their land, and the ESA is near the top of the list. She tried to explain that she was working with researchers at Colorado State University to find and monitor the plovers, that she'd been searching southeastern Colorado for two months with little success. Could she leave the name of their lead researcher with him?

But Russell Davis had heard enough. "I said, I don't want to hear anymore. You need to go," he told her.

It was not an auspicious start to a journey that, as Davis, 74, now describes it, has transformed his life, turning him into a vocal advocate for ways to ranch in partnership with bird conservation. It meant he became a pariah to many in his very conservative rural community, labeled a prairie-dog lover in the pages of the local newspaper. Some of his neighbors have come around, so much so that they open their homes every spring to host birdwatchers from around the world for a unique plover-watching festival. Some likely never will. But when I heard about the intertwined stories of the Wineinger-Davis Ranch and its relationship with the mountain plover, I knew I wanted to see for myself.

Along with shorebirds, grassland birds are among the most imperiled avian cohorts in the world, because grasslands are both exceptionally easy to transform into something else, like cornfields or tract housing, and because to the average eye they lack the kind of landscape majesty that prompts people to want to protect, say, dramatic mountains or scenic coastlines. As a result, only 11 percent of the midwestern tallgrass prairie, and less than one-quarter of the mixed-grass prairie farther west, is left, most of that in badly degraded, highly fragmented condition. On the other hand, fully 54 percent of the shortgrass prairie, about 72,000 square miles, remains today, half of it intact—but only one-half of 1 percent is in some form of significant conservation protection. That means that much of the future of the shortgrass prairie and its birds lies in the hands of private landowners. People like Russell Davis.

Not everyone sees it this way, but I'm one of those who finds a prairie landscape viscerally exciting, the sweep of sky and wind-tattered clouds above a western grassland, the 360-degree horizon and breathtaking changes in the weather that will rarely show up on a colorful travel poster. It can come on you suddenly. As I drove east on Route 96 from Pueblo, I passed through the definition of sleepy country, small towns like Boone and Olney Springs that punctuate the course of the Arkansas River. But at Ordway I turned off and headed due north, quickly leaving behind the farmland and rising into the much drier, emptier land beyond, where the pale yellow-green of shortgrass prairie rimmed the horizon beneath a deep blue sky and ragged white clouds. Horned larks flushed from the edges of the road; I saw pronghorn here and there, rusty brown against the sere grass, and in a muddy pasture pond with a few cows standing hock-deep there were half a dozen avocets and a smattering of ducks—gadwall, teal, a few mallards.

What I didn't see were many people; I passed exactly one pickup truck over the next 30 miles, and a few blink-and-you-miss-it farmsteads and ranches. I blinked and missed my turn, too, having to make a U-turn back to a gravel road running east, past a marble slab engraved with the Wineinger-Davis Ranch name. I pulled into the low ranch house sheltered by a grove of cottonwoods visible for miles in the open country.

Russell Davis's family has owned the ranch since 1937, when his grandfather bought the first of what today is more than 13,000 acres, in two roughly equal parcels about 10 miles apart. It's a cow-calf operation, from which Russell is now partially retired, splitting his time

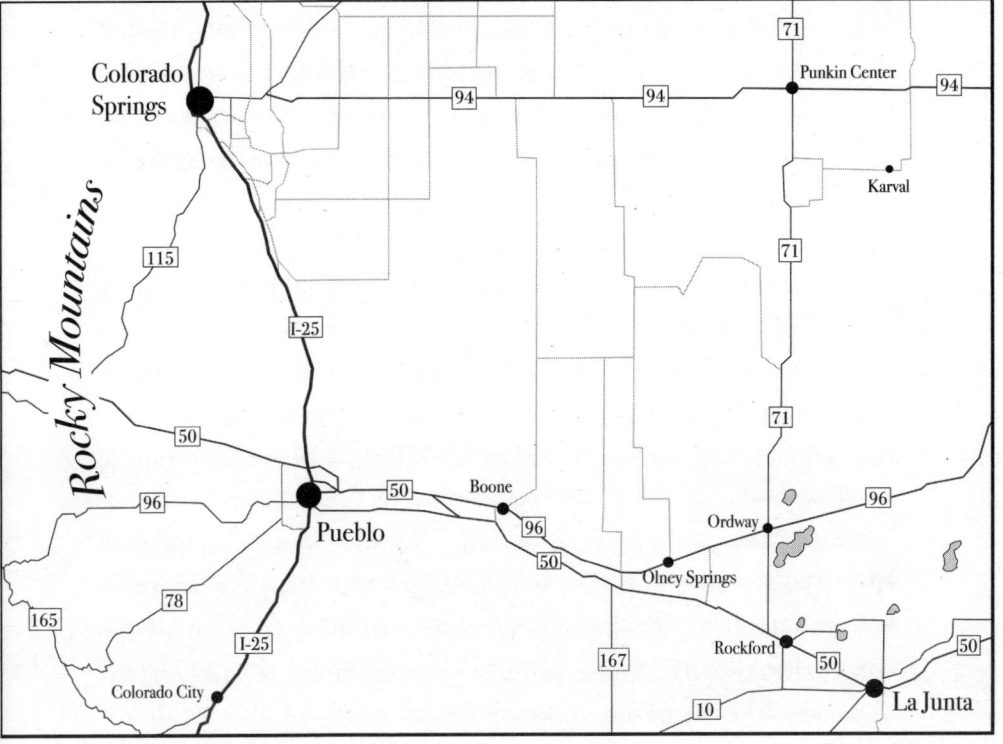

The plains of southeastern Colorado, in the rain shadow of the Rocky Mountains.

between the ranch and Texas, where he and his wife can be close to their son and his family, and where he was during my visit. Responsibility for the North Ranch, which I was visiting, has passed to a fourth generation, Russell's nephew John Davis, a tall, soft-spoken man with a short beard and weathered ball cap.

I was more than usually grateful for John's time, because two weeks earlier enormous floods had ripped out miles of fence and left piles of debris everywhere, and the cleanup from it was still underway. But as we headed out into the North Ranch block, my general impression was of vigorous, luxuriant grassland spilling to the horizon in every direction. Even with floods, the abundant rain this region had experienced in 2022 and 2023 was a welcome change from many years of extreme drought, which had brought the ranch to the edge of financial ruin—but which also set the stage for the embrace of the birds that initially gave Russell Davis such heartburn.

In the wake of that confrontation in the prairie dog town, Russell heard from one of his neighbors, who belatedly told Davis that he'd invited the scientists onto his own land to look for plovers. Then he told Russell about a workshop, to be hosted by a third rancher and presented by the Rocky Mountain Bird Observatory (now the Bird Conservancy of the Rockies), one of the groups studying mountain plovers in the area, along with the Colorado Division of Wildlife. Dr. Victoria Dreitz, a post-doc at Colorado State University who was the lead researcher on the study, would be there. Would Russell join them? It took some persuading—including from Russell's then-16-year-old son, who was ultimately tempted by the offer of a free lunch—but he finally agreed.

What Davis didn't know is that the workshop was being planned largely for his benefit, since the Wineinger-Davis Ranch appeared to hold the mother lode of mountain plovers in the area, the most the conservationists had found in three years of combing southeastern Colorado. The day of the workshop Russell was so gun-shy he almost bolted as soon as he stepped out of his truck, but he stayed—and learned a great deal about mountain plovers and the kind of landscape they need. The kind of landscape the Wineinger-Davis Ranch, without ever meaning to, was providing.

At the end of the workshop, Ken Morgan, the private lands manager for Colorado Division of Wildlife said, "Russell, there's a reason the birds are at your ranch, and we need to figure out why. We need to figure out what it is that you're doing that the birds are there."

In truth, Russell and his family had plenty else on their minds. Just a few years earlier, in October 1997, a monster blizzard had hit Colorado, dumping up to three feet of snow with 60 mph winds and wind chills of –40°F. The ranch lost half its cows and all of its calves. Now 2001 was shaping up to be a drought year, though he and his neighbors had no way of knowing that it was just the start of a punishing, multiyear run of profoundly dry weather. Between 2001 and 2004, a total of just two inches of rain would fall, and one-quarter of the ranch's grass would die. To keep their cattle alive, Russell and his family would have to buy hay, not just for the winter as they sometimes did, but to feed year-round, 500 tons annually at $350 a ton. The debt would grow so great, it would seem the only way to clear it would be to sell the North Ranch parcel and try to hold on to the South Ranch.

That's where the plovers eventually came to the rescue. Morgan broached the idea of a conservation easement—a legal agreement under which the Davis family would permanently forgo development rights to the land and agree to manage the ranch in ways that maintained plover habitat. Since the birds were already there in surprising numbers, they were being asked to simply keep doing what they were already doing; in fact, one aspect of the agreement was that regardless of who owned the ranch in the future, it had to remain a cow-calf operation. In return, the family would receive a significant payment for giving up those development rights, perhaps enough to clear much of the debt hanging over them.

There was a catch, and to a rancher it was a big one. By "plover habitat," the state meant prairie dogs and their towns.

"There is a very close association between large prairie dog colonies and high densities of nesting mountain plovers," Brandt Ryder told me. The chief conservation scientist for the Bird Conservancy of the Rockies, Ryder plays a key role in the organization's stewardship program, working with landowners from Montana to New Mexico to help them make a profit while managing their land in ways that benefit birds. In the case of mountain plovers, that can mean some uncomfortable tolerance for prairie dogs.

"Prairie dogs do a really good job of clearing the vegetation and keeping the ground relatively bare. And that's what mountain plovers love. They love either very, very short grass or, even more, bare soil," Ryder told me. They'll nest in plowed fields, but prairie dog towns are perfect.

It didn't seem so perfect to Russell Davis. To qualify for the state easement, the ranch had to agree to permanently maintain at least 500 acres of prairie dogs on the property. Worse, the agreement required a sign-off from the county board of commissioners, which Russell, who describes himself in those days as a "staunch, conservative Republican" in an area with mostly like-minded folks, did not realize.

"The county commissioners only heard one thing, and that was 'Russell was protecting 500 acres of prairie dog habitat.' This whole plover discussion thing went completely over their heads," he told me. The local newspaper's headline summed it up: WINEINGER-DAVIS RANCH PROTECTING PRAIRIE DOGS.

John pulled his truck to a stop beside the prairie dogs in question, a large town in a wide, fenced-off pasture, inside which dozens of pale brown rodents watched us in alarm, craning their necks as they stood on their hind legs and barking in agitation. Ranchers generally despise prairie dogs for eating the grass that would otherwise fatten cows and calves, and this town had wide areas of exposed earth. The plovers also have an attraction for a graceful native bunchgrass called blue grama, especially as foraging habitat once their chicks hatch, and as we drove deeper into the ranch I saw blue grama in abundance in all directions, each clump festooned with flaglike seed heads that flickered in the wind, lending a mesmerizing shimmer to the prairie, like flowing water lapping the legs of the cattle we passed.

But what made it hard to concentrate on what John was telling me was the astonishing number of birds. We must have flushed hundreds of horned larks during our hours-long tour of the ranch, each one robber-masked with a black chest band. Male lark buntings—unusually beefy sparrows, inky black with bold white wing markings—leapt into the air repeatedly all around us on short, exuberant song flights, singing wonderfully complex medleys. A dozen or more were usually lofting up at any given moment; it was like riding through fields of fluffy jack-in-the-boxes.

Back in 2003, that prairie dog headline in the local paper landed with a predictable thud. "People quit calling me, quit talking to me," Russell said. "In the springtime when we'd have brandings, they quit inviting me to come." That was an extraordinary snub in ranch country, where neighbors help neighbors. And it wasn't just the community. Russell's brothers, and his father who lived on the South Ranch unit, were deeply suspicious of the conservation easement. His neighbors were telling him it was only a matter of time until the government owned the ranch outright. It was a period of great isolation.

The bird that sparked all of this ranch-country turmoil is unassuming to an extraordinary (and sophisticated) degree, but so is its habitat. The shortgrass prairie is a land that looks simple but evolved with dynamic natural forces—wind-driven grassfires set by lightning or Indigenous inhabitants, immense bison herds, drought and heat waves, blizzards or flash floods. Against the brown earth, the pale brown plover seems to vanish, especially when it hunkers tight to the ground as when a raptor flies over, so that even its betraying shadow disappears and it merges with the soil—hence one old name, "prairie ghost."

Like most wild birds, they were once considered fair game. A buffalo hunter in Kansas bragged of killing as many as 200 in an hour. One ornithologist, writing in 1916, said the approved method in southern California was to drive a horse and buggy into a flock, which would swirl up into the air and land, tightly packed together and huddled against the ground not far away, trusting to their camouflage. That might work on a falcon, but a market gunner would "ground sluice" the flock with one barrel from his shotgun, then fire the second barrel when the surviving plovers took flight. "My informant stated that he once killed 65 birds with two shots, and this method very rarely netted less than 30." (The same informant, immune to irony, also noted that "they don't seem to be as plentiful as they were 25 years ago.")

Today, there may be fewer than 20,000 mountain plovers remaining, a population decline of 81 percent since 1968, and about half of those breed on the plains of eastern Colorado. Even there, the birds are increasingly scarce. In the 1970s, an estimated 7,000 nested on the Pawnee National Grasslands of Weld County, Colorado; by the early 2000s, fewer than 80 remained. The plover was proposed for the federal threatened species list in 1999, in part because in the absence of prairie dog towns, they tend to gravitate to plowed agricultural fields on private land, which seems an obviously dangerous place to lay one's eggs.

That listing proposal was initially withdrawn by the US Fish and Wildlife Service in 2003, reinstated by court order after a lawsuit, and finally withdrawn entirely in 2011 during the first Obama administration, with the agency arguing that "threats to the species as identified in the proposed rule are not as significant as earlier believed, and current available data do not indicate that the threats to the species and its habitat are likely to endanger the species in the foreseeable future throughout all or a significant portion of its range." One reason for the change was Vicky Dreitz's research, showing that the plovers actually nest at least as successfully in plowed fields as in native prairie.

It was not easy, but Russell Davis got the county's approval for the conservation easement on the ranch, prairie dogs and all. It took one-on-one conversations with the commissioners, folks he knew well but who now looked askance at him. It took another long, excruciating public meeting with several of his angry neighbors in attendance. It took conversations with the local reporter who'd splashed the prairie dog headline in the paper, explaining *why* he was going to protect some prairie dogs, only on certain parts of the ranch.

To change attitudes in his own family, though, took something more personal, a long and difficult conversation over dinner as his youngest brother Steve grilled Vicky Dreitz, who hadn't expected to run into a buzzsaw of deep suspicion that evening. She stressed that far from wanting to force the family to change its practices, she wanted to understand what they were already doing that made the ranch such a productive place for the birds, and a model for others. In the end, the birds themselves did the trick, when she took Steve's kids out to help her band an adult plover at its nest. By the next morning, Steve told Russell he'd had a change of heart. "Boy, talk about relief for me. That was probably the biggest hurdle for my family," Russell said.

Prairie dogs are only part of the mountain plover equation. Southeastern Colorado's arid environment naturally promotes the kind of patchy, scruffy shortgrass vegetation that the plovers prefer, land that can look worn-out and beaten down to someone who doesn't realize that prairie grass roots may reach 14 feet deep in the soil, storing energy to allow the plants to wait out dry years and explode into new life when the rain and snow returns.

The easement was finalized in 2004; while the payment didn't clear the debt, it covered about half of it and made it feasible to keep both ranches. And a few cracks began to appear in the social ice. Russell was surprised to find himself invited to a meeting of a newly formed community alliance in the hamlet of Karval, about half an hour north of the ranch. There's not much to Karval, population 39; a few churches and post office; no gas station, no cafe, no hotel. That year the school had 32 students from kindergarten to 12th grade, and not a lot of options to keep kids around once they graduated.

For months the alliance kicked around ideas for community revitalization, at a time when Russell was more and more involved in talking up wildlife conservation with landowners around the state. He was coming to realize that a lot of people like birds, and are willing to pay to see them. Against his wife's advice—was he certain he wanted to kick that hornets' nest again? —he suggested Karval start a bird-watching weekend devoted to the infamous mountain plover.

"You could hear a pin drop in that room, just deafening silence," he said. Where were visitors supposed to stay, someone asked, since there is no hotel? Another deep breath, and Russell suggested local families could put them up in their own homes. The local women's group could provide meals, and they'd run birding field trips to area ranches to look for the infamous mountain plover.

To his shock they agreed, and thus was born the Karval Mountain Plover Festival, undoubtedly the most unusual birding event of its kind in the country. Unlike, say, the Biggest Week in American Birding, a 10-day event in northwestern Ohio that attracts an estimated 90,000 participants every year, Russell said the Karval organizers were hoping for seven attendees their first year in 2008; they got 14. It's grown every year since—there were 44 festival-goers in 2023—but the format has remained the same. Attendees are welcomed into ranch homes, paying their hosts directly for the stay. They're fed ranch meals, including a big dinner Saturday with some nature-themed entertainment. And of course they come for the birds themselves.

It's been a wonderful cross-pollination between ranchers and birders from places like Denver and Colorado Springs, folks who might have viewed each other with skepticism at best or open hostility at worst. It's hard not to see someone's viewpoint when you're sharing a meal with them or staying in their home, though. The discussions have opened unexpected lines of communication, even when the subjects are touchy ones.

It was pretty obvious I needed to return to Lincoln County in the spring.

There's a growing body of research that shows how important prairie dogs are for the health of prairies, and for maintaining the diversity of the birds that use them, but not every bird benefits from the colonial rodents. Different species of grassland birds use different habitats and microclimates up and down the Great Plains, with prairie dog towns being just one component of a vast mosaic that plays out at a continental scale. Saving the mixed- and shortgrass prairies also requires a continental-sized approach.

Perhaps the most ambitious attempt to grapple with the enormous challenges posed by grassland conservation is the Central Grasslands Roadmap Initiative, which is nothing less than an effort to protect and restore more than 700 million acres of native prairie across southern Canada, the western United States, and northern Mexico. Spurred by the loss of some 50 million acres of grassland in the past decade, more than 200 private, NGO, tribal or First Nations, and agency partners, with BCR serving as its founding "backbone" organization, have developed a collaborative framework to identify problems and guide the search for solutions, using sophisticated digital tools, immense datasets, and remote sensing technology to identify core areas for protection and at-risk regions that need urgent conservation protection and restoration.

The obstacles aren't getting any less daunting. The World Wildlife Fund produces an annual report assessing grassland losses to "plowprint," the amount of formerly intact native grassland plowed up for grain and other row crops. In 2021, that amounted to 1.6 million acres lost in the United States and Canada, an area equal in size to Delaware. By WWF's estimation, 32 million acres have been converted to agriculture since the organization began tracking the issue in 2012.

Keeping grassland in grassland is important, but the devil is in the management details, and most ranchers have not had the kind of road to Damascus experience that Russell Davis did. Still, there are a growing number of programs designed to encourage ranching approaches that both generate a profit for producers, while creating habitat for the greatest possible diversity of wildlife. The National Audubon Society has its Conservation Ranching program, which by 2023 had certified 114 bird-friendly ranches covering 3 million acres in 14 states, with each ranch developing habitat management protocols in conjunction with Audubon biologists. The Bird Conservancy of the Rockies doesn't certify properties, but it employs dozens of biologists, foresters, and other staff working in 13 field offices in six states, collaborating with ranchers.

When I asked BCR's Brandt Ryder who might give me another perspective on ranching in harmony with birds, he thought for a minute. "Well, there's Grady," he said.

"Thank God for pocket gophers," Grady Grissom told me with what appeared to be a perfectly straight face.

Still, I had to wonder if he was pulling my leg, given how ranchers usually feel about gophers—that is, only slightly more charitably than they do toward prairie dogs. The chunky, hamster-sized burrowing rodents create elaborate networks of tunnels as they dig for tubers, roots, and plant shoots. The fan-shaped mounds of dirt they pile at the entrances to their tunnels are utterly ubiquitous across the West, and (along with their hungrily herbivorous diet) a reason for the pervasive hatred; a rock-hard gopher mound can do a number on farm machinery that hits it.

But to Grady, the busy little diggers are an ally in his quest to create as much shortgrass prairie diversity as possible on the 14,000 acres that compose the Rancho Largo Cattle Company, which he and his wife founded with two partners in 1996 in southeastern Colorado. In fact, what sparked this particular expression of enthusiasm was, as far as I could see, just an unusually colorful splash of wildflowers the size of a small table. But that was the point, he explained.

"The gophers create openings in the blue grama, which can be a monoculture otherwise. They turn up the soil, aerate it, bring seeds to the top, create this little hotspot of successional sequence. They're doing that everywhere, all the time," he said. From the microscale, like a gopher mound, to the impact of grazing across thousands of acres, shepherding the land back to its richest and most robust condition

Stoycho Stoychev, left, and Ivaylo Angelov scan the cliffs of Kovan-Kaya for nesting griffon vultures. (© SCOTT WEIDENSAUL)

Three Atlantic puffins loaf on a boulder on Eastern Egg Rock, to which their species was returned in the late 1970s. The techniques pioneered there have been used to restore nearly 140 species of imperiled seabirds around the world. (© SCOTT WEIDENSAUL)

In the crew tent on Eastern Egg Rock, Steve Kress discusses the day's work with island supervisor Theresa Rizza, right, as Camryn Zoeller, Ke Coco Deng, and Arden Kelly listen. (© SCOTT WEIDENSAUL)

Sheltered between a few of Eastern Egg Rock's many boulders, the camouflaged eggs of a roseate tern await the return of the incubating female. (© SCOTT WEIDENSAUL)

A Laysan albatross and its chick rest in a front yard in Princeville on Kauaʻi, perhaps the only place in the world where albatrosses of any species choose to nest among human habitation. (© SCOTT WEIDENSAUL)

André Rain has been trying to save endangered seabirds since his childhood in Bermuda, and now works in the high, wet forests of Kauaʻi, where exclusion fences create islands of sanctuary in a predator-filled world. (© SCOTT WEIDENSAUL)

A fenced sanctum inside a fenced sanctum, the Nihokū Ecosystem Restoration Project at Kīlauea Point is just seven acres of restored native habitat, but could eventually host more than 100,000 nesting shearwaters, petrels, storm-petrels, and albatrosses. (© SCOTT WEIDENSAUL)

(*Above*) Its head marked with a dab of nail polish for identification, a male ʻaʻo, or endangered Hawaiian petrel, waits inside an artificial nest burrow at Nihokū. (© SCOTT WEIDENSAUL)

(*Left*) On a crowded beach the day before the Fourth of July, Elizabeth Kaufmann of the Massachusetts Audubon Society scans a closed area where piping plovers and least terns are nesting. (© SCOTT WEIDENSAUL)

(*Above*) A piping plover chick, already growing into its outsize legs and feet, rests with one of its parents on a Massachusetts beach. (© SHAWN CAREY)

(*Right*) Thanks to research that identified its main threats, and a business plan to implement addressing them, the population of American oystercatchers on the Atlantic and Gulf of Mexico coasts has increased 45 percent in the past 15 years. (© SHAWN CAREY)

Russell Davis was initially upset to learn that rare mountain plovers were nesting on his family's ranch in southeastern Colorado, but the birds set him on a journey to embrace working the land in ways that also benefit wildlife. (© SCOTT WEIDENSAUL)

A thunderstorm sweeps across the Colorado plains near Karval. Though bruised, there are still more than 72,000 square miles of shortgrass prairie in North America, home to scores of species of grassland birds, most found nowhere else. (© SCOTT WEIDENSAUL)

Second-largest grouse in the world and the iconic symbol of the sagebrush sea, greater sage-grouse have been in steep and steady decline, along with their habitat, since the market-hunting days more than a century ago. (© SCOTT WEIDENSAUL)

Before Grady Grissom shifted to a style of ranching that emphasized biodiversity, the ranch he and his partners own, Rancho Largo, almost went under. Now it's an exemplar of shortgrass prairie health and grassland bird abundance. (© SCOTT WEIDENSAUL)

Sagebrush, blue-gray in the morning light, rolls to the horizon in southwestern Idaho, with the Silver City Range capped in snow and cloud in the distance. (© SCOTT WEIDENSAUL)

(*Left*) A sharp line marks the edge of a conifer removal area on the BOSH Project in Idaho. There are pros and cons in pushing back the "green glacier" of encroaching conifers, especially if not done in a way that takes ecological nuance into account. (© SCOTT WEIDENSAUL)

(*Right*) The soaring walls of *Tthegéré Nué*, known as Redcliff Island in English, dwarf a fishing boat on Great Slave Lake in Thaidene Nëné Indigenous Protected and Conserved Area in the Northwest Territories. (© SCOTT WEIDENSAUL)

Every year, some 3 billion to 5 billion birds of more than 300 species breed in the Canadian boreal forest. (© SCOTT WEIDENSAUL)

Pete Enzoe, angry musk ox left behind, pauses at *Tthe Káljka Tué* (Stark Lake) in Thaidene Nëné. (© SCOTT WEIDENSAUL)

is Grady Grissom's defining passion—along with raising premium grass-fed beef, most of it sold direct to consumers at premium prices.

Grady is all about grassland diversity, and the two days I spent with him on Rancho Largo felt like a compressed graduate course in short-grass steppe ecology, as I tried to keep up with the flow of unfamiliar Latin names, grass identifications, and rotational grazing concepts. "When we first came here, this was mostly all blue grama, maybe three or four species of perennial cool-season grasses altogether—once they're grazed out they don't come back quickly. There are 13 species now—western wheatgrass, blue grama, needle-and-thread, some winterfat—winterfat's that shrub over there," he said, pointing as the pickup rocked slowly across the uneven ground. "Green needle, I found that for the first time in 2006. By 2012 it was in most draws on the ranch, today it's everywhere. I never saw mushrooms before 2008, now they're everywhere, too, another indication of changes in the soil ecosystem."

Before we met I had, as one can't help but do, built a mental image of Grady Grissom, based mostly on what I knew of his background: Princeton undergrad who took a graduate degree in geology at Stanford, whose wife Lynda had retired from a career as a chemist in the pharmaceutical industry. They went into the ranching business with capital from Grady's California-born Princeton roommate, Rob Lovelace, by then a hugely successful investment manager, and Rob's wife Alicia. ("Largo" is a sort-of anagram of their initials, plus an O.) A brief phone call a couple of weeks earlier with Grady hadn't changed the slightly patrician, Ivy League picture I'd created in my head.

Rancho Largo lay off Colorado Route 10 about 70 miles southwest of the Wineinger-Davis Ranch:. This was noticeably rougher, drier country than that up by the Davis place, more jumbled, creased with deep canyons, more cholla cactus raising their angled, needled arms and pink-purple flowers above the prairie grass and clumps of yucca. Turning off the road onto a gravel lane, where a nice pronghorn buck stood like a marker of a different sort, I eventually reached the main ranch on the crest of a hill, corrals and stock pens below. As I drove up, a guy perching on one knee on the back of a four-wheeler zoomed over to meet me.

Grady Grissom in the flesh proved to be 60 years old, lean almost to the point of gaunt and weathered to the point of desiccation, wearing an aging work shirt that had once been white but now bore dozens of blotches and grease marks, its right sleeve torn halfway free at the elbow, but still in better shape than his stained blue jeans. He wore a straw hat and a huge grin through a couple days' worth of stubble, with a few flecks of tobacco dip showing in his teeth.

"Hey, welcome to Rancho Largo," he said, squeezing my hand. "Gimme a few minutes. Those two heifers"—he pointed to two cows backed into a corner of the fence beside the driveway turnaround—"got free and they're scared. I may need to saddle a horse to get 'em back in the corral."

Over the next two days I learned that, his academic pedigree notwithstanding, Grady had grown up summering on his grandparents' ranches in western Kansas and northeastern Colorado, and had worked his way through Stanford shoeing horses. He jokes that the ranch is the result of sweat equity—Grady's sweat, his buddy Rob's equity. But its success has also been the result of a decades-long education in working with the land in ways that produce healthy grass, fat cattle, and as I saw everywhere I looked, an abundance of prairie birds. It's a process that's resulted in Rancho Largo being singled out for a number of prestigious honors, including the Sand County Foundation's 2017 Leopold Conservation Award recognizing "extraordinary achievement in voluntary conservation by agricultural landowners." (The Wineinger-Davis Ranch has also been a recipient.)

I dropped my gear in a freshly stuccoed, 1930s-era adobe house where he and Lynda had generously offered to put me up. "We'll make some dinner later, but first I want to show you the canyon," he said when he pulled up in a dusty truck. We thumped and bumped half a mile to the east, parked and walked a short distance to where the land fell away hundreds of feet into a deep ravine—Averson Canyon, whose layered walls glowed a warm orange-brown in the late-day sun.

"That's Dakota sandstone," Grady said, settling himself beneath the shade of a juniper, legs outstretched toward the canyon; he fished a tin of tobacco from his pocket and took a dip. "The Dakota formation is Cretaceous, famous for its dinosaur tracks, they're all through this rock. Averson Canyon here connects to South Canyon down that way, and the springs in them flow to the Apishapa River." Bighorn sheep, elk, and mule deer use the canyon as a throughway.

The air was still and largely quiet; I heard the whiny *pee-eer* calls of a Say's phoebe, and a gush of music from a western meadowlark back in the flatter land behind us. Far away, already hunting insects above the gash of the canyon, a common nighthawk's fluttering flight was just visible. We sat and chatted about his journey toward a more ecologically sophisticated approach to grazing after nearly going broke trying to ranch, and his partnership with the Bird Conservancy of the Rockies, which dates back almost 20 years.

For all Grady's boyhood experience with ranching—in fact, perhaps because of his early experience and ingrained, utilitarian views on how cattle ranching should be done—Rancho Largo almost went belly-up in its first years, and not only because the first winter brought an epic blizzard and five feet of snow, the same one that almost ruined Russell Davis's family. "This isn't a generational ranch. We didn't inherit the place from anyone, we bought it. And in the late '90s, I was having a hard time making this piece of land pay a mortgage and a salary," he said, looking out over the canyon. He tried to increase stocking rates, the number of cattle per acre, hoping to break even only to see the quality of the range slide even further, pushing the operation deeper into the red.

He was already reassessing his approach, wondering if there was a way to work more closely with the land, when in 2000 he met Ted Toombs, who at the time was the prairie partners coordinator for what is now BCR. The group was interested in working with private landowners to improve bird habitat. Before long, Grady was sharing dinner with Toombs and his director Tammy VerCauteren, who at that ambush workshop had helped bring Russell Davis to a new way of looking at his plovers. It was the start of Grady's own journey to a more sustainable, profitable and, though not the main goal, birdy future for the ranch.

Grady stood up and dusted off his jeans. "Pretty special place, isn't it?" he asked, looking back at Averson Canyon one last time. "Our daughter Brooke used to bring her high school friends out here. Now she's named her daughter Averson."

"If I'd have thought about it, I would have thawed out some steaks, but I just made a couple of burgers," Grady said as he, Lynda, and I sat down at a table with the main house's great room at our back, thick beams and log walls rising around us. Maybe they were "just burgers," served hot from the grill with vegetables and salad but no roll or dressing besides some coarse salt, but they were hands down the best ground beef I've ever eaten, from one of Rancho Largo's Corriente-Longhorn-Wagyu crosses that had spent two years feeding on nothing but prairie grass, and had never seen the inside of a barn or a feedlot, summer or winter. I could only imagine what one of the steaks tasted like, but I didn't feel I was missing anything.

Outside, thunder rumbled and the wind began to whip as a storm swept through, cooling the air but bringing no rain, to Grady's disappointment. Even in a wet year, an arid-land rancher rarely spurns any precipitation. The breeze moved through the windows I opened in the adobe, and sleep came quickly.

I was up with the first bit of light, a little before 5 a.m., awakened by the *peeeents* of common nighthawks, half a dozen of them flying loops and swoops around the building hawking bugs. A blue grosbeak's loud warble was the first real birdsong of the morning, followed quickly by the fast-rolling flute notes of a western meadowlark, one of many singing before long. Half an hour later, as I wandered up one of the dirt tracks to higher ground, I was surprised by the level of song, given that it was early July and getting late in the nesting season for so much carrying on. House finches, green-tailed and brown towhees, and ladder-backed woodpeckers called, and as the first pink hit the undersides of the clouds—it was a cooler, more overcast day—mockingbirds and western kingbirds popped up from their night roosts and took up position on the tops of junipers. Lark sparrows with their rusty-red war paint perched on barbed wire, and horned larks scurried ahead of me, flitting just a short distance before landing again and again as I walked on, as though refusing to believe I was really coming all that way.

Over dinner the previous night, Grady had expanded on his approach to managing the land. "My goals are all about plant diversity," he said. To accomplish that, he tries to mimic the kind of grazing dynamic the shortgrass ecosystem evolved with under the teeth and hooves of bison—short, intense grazing followed by long fallow periods of rest. Natural disturbance like pocket gophers or (within what he considers reason) prairie dogs add to the mosaic effect. When they bought the former A-Bar Ranch to create Rancho Largo, the property was fenced into nine pastures; Grady quickly divided it into 36, with cattle grazing each section for a typical period of about 10 to 14 days. Recovery periods have grown over the years to roughly 450 days, though in a drought he may let a pasture rest for two or more years. He has plans to further divide some pastures, hitting them very hard for a matter of a few hours and then giving them a long recovery period—much as a herd of thousands of bison would have hammered a piece of prairie flat, then vanished a few hours later, not to return for years.

Brandt Ryder at BCR had stressed to me that for grassland birds, habitat variety is crucial. The shortgrass prairie may look monotonous to the untrained eye, but in its natural state it is a complex of microhabitats.

"That's the pivotal piece for grassland birds. They're not all created equal, and they all have subtly different habitat requirements," he said. Mountain plovers and thick-billed longspurs love sparse grass and a lot of bare earth. Chestnut-collared longspurs like their grass a bit lusher and longer, a mix of short species like blue grama along with taller grasses. Lark buntings like those I saw with John Davis prefer tall grasses mixed with a few shrubs for perching; western meadowlarks are more Goldilocks in their tastes, looking for prairie that's neither too barren nor too high, and with some singing perches.

"The structure of the grass is going to be the important thing," Ryder explained. "If at the end of the day we care about [bird] diversity and abundance, then we're going to have to manage the landscape to create a mosaic of habitats."

That's exactly the approach Grady Grissom has embraced at Rancho Largo, and was excited to share with me. After breakfast we jumped back into the truck and headed southwest across the ranch, into higher ground. The double summits of the Spanish Peaks, more than 13,000 feet high and sacred to the Ute and the Comanche, rose in the distance, but the closer horizon was pegged with dozens of tall, white wind turbines, the leasing fees from which help keep the ranch profitable. We spooked small herds of pronghorn does and fawns, and a seemingly endless number of grassland birds—almost none of which, I was surprised to realize, could Grady identify.

"No, I'm not a birdwatcher," he said with a laugh. "But even given my lack of knowledge, there's no doubt in my mind that our bird population is more dense, and more diverse, than when we started the ranch. Same with insect diversity, mushroom diversity, just a huge change in biodiversity in general. That's what I want. I want to manage an ecosystem, not just move meat." He stopped deworming his cattle, concerned that feeding them insecticides was making his herd "drop poison in the manure" and killing the dung beetles that normally recycle old cow pies and nourish the soil.

We drove past two playa lakes that were his first step into bird-friendly management, restored with BCR's help and federal funding. They were dry at this time of the year, but in some wet years like 2010 the long-billed curlews stay through the summer to nest, and in autumn flocks of migrating sandhill cranes, bugling and trumpeting to the sky, drop in to rest. Rancho Largo is an official stop on the Colorado Birding Trail, with a nominal access fee.

None of his neighbors have jumped as fully and enthusiastically into a diversity-based approach as Grady, but he said some are moving toward rotational grazing. "There's a ranch to the east that's pretty progressive—the father managed a big Texas ranch that was already interested in the ecology of grazing," he said.

This is when the conversation turned to pocket gophers, and the benefits of disturbance and succession in a shortgrass ecosystem. Given his enthusiasm for gophers, and knowing how prairie dogs had soured relations between Russell Davis and his neighbors, I was curious if Grady Grissom was similarly open-minded about the colonial rodents. I found that even he has his limits, and will control them when the topsoil begins to blow away. But they have a role to play.

"Being a geologist, I love processes and time scales. Gopher disturbance lasts a few months. Prairie dog disturbance lasts for years." He echoed something Vicky Dreitz had told me. "Grasslands are very resilient," Grady said. "It's hard to hurt them in one year, it takes three or four years and even then they usually recover quickly." But do the wrong thing long enough, and even the most resilient grassland will buckle. He'd come pretty close in his first years at Rancho Largo, but when he changed course, working in concert with shortgrass ecology instead of against it, the land and its birdlife rebounded beautifully.

Still, it's challenging country. "If you brought a Nebraska cow here and asked her to make a living on 11 inches of rain, she can't. She's too big to be efficient, she partitions too much energy into milk, and so won't get pregnant again," he said. Instead of the typical Hereford-Angus cross, Grady's cows are small and compact, a mix based on longhorns and Corrientes descended from colonial Spanish cattle, with a bit of Japanese Wagyu and a little Belted Galloway. They are hardy even in snowstorms, eat almost anything, and don't need babysitting during calving.

Later, Grady wanted to check some plots he'd marked with flagging to monitor its succession. "Over here's one of the old homesteads," he said, gesturing to a few low, slumped rock walls that I would have overlooked had he not pointed them out. They were remains from the final wave of attempted settlement in the first decades of the 20th century.

"What were they trying to raise here?" I asked.

"Dryland wheat, beans. I don't know what they were thinking—it's three miles to the nearest spring, down past the house. And three miles to nearest rocks. Someone carried all of these up here," he said, kicking at a few while shaking his head. "They were set up for failure, suckered by the Homestead Act. What made sense in Nebraska damned sure didn't in southeastern Colorado." Starving and broke, the homesteaders soon moved on, letting the land remain prairie, albeit bruised by the decades of utilitarian grazing that followed. Grady Grissom is trying to bring it all the way back to health.

Behind us, a meadowlark let loose with another blast of melody.

April may be a gentle time in many parts of the United States, but it's still the edge of winter in parts of the Great Plains, as I found out when I flew back to Colorado, nine months after my first visit to the Wineinger-Davis Ranch, to attend the Karval Mountain Plover Festival.

Russell Davis had invited me to stay with the family on the ranch. Also joining us was Seth Gallagher, who works for the National Fish and Wildlife Foundation, the independent nonprofit chartered by Congress in 1984 to fund conservation at a large scale. In 2023 alone, that meant almost 800 projects that, along with matching support for grants, totaled $1.7 billion. NFWF (everyone calls it "Niff-Whiff") is by far the largest conservation grant funder in the United States, supported by private philanthropy as well as money drawn from court settlements, fines, and legal disbursements. Gallagher had worked for Bird Conservancy of the Rockies for years before moving to NFWF, and knew both Grady Grissom and the Davis family well.

The festival meals and indoor events took place in the Karval Community Building, a 1930s-era Civilian Conservation Corps barracks later used as a dance hall before being moved to Karval. Proving that the birding world is a small one, among the 56 people that gathered for the opening dinner and ice cream social I was stunned to find my old friend Greg Butcher and his wife. Among the many bird-conservation hats Greg has worn was as director of bird conservation for National Audubon, and he retired as the migratory species coordinator for the US Forest Service's international programs. Neither of us had a clue the other would be there.

After dinner, Russell, Seth, and I stayed up late talking in the sitting room of the bunkhouse, Russell telling stories about the years he ran the ranch, the difficulty of navigating conservation with neighbors and family on his plover-sparked journey, all of which happened at the same time he and his wife lost their adult daughter to cystic fibrosis while weathering their financial nightmare. It gave me a deeper view of the tough but illuminating road this quiet man has traveled since 2001.

"You can stick your head in the sand, put a chain across your cattle guard and say, 'Stay out,' or you can embrace it," Russell said. "Did you see what's parked out front? I used to drive a Ford, now I drive a Toyota. I used to be hard-right, now I'm moderate. I know that compromise is essential."

The next morning we were up well before dawn, lightning flashing off to the west over the Front Range. I rode with Seth Gallagher and his college-age son Will; besides the lightning, the horizon to the northwest showed long strings of slow-flashing red lights. "Those are wind turbines," Seth said. "Development's closing in from that direction, and the plowprint is coming from the other." The shortgrass is caught in a squeeze.

After breakfast at the community building, we piled into the Karval Alliance's refurbished school bus, which had a large STOPS FOR MOUNTAIN PLOVERS sign on the rear door and John Davis at the wheel, and headed out through town. As we passed the local school, guide and enthusiastic civic booster Katie Zipperer explained that the district covers more than 400 families in the region, but there were just 30 kids currently enrolled, six of them in preschool. The graduating class that year was a single girl. "Doesn't take too much to make valedictorian," she joked.

The plan was to do some birding near town, then head over to the Wineinger-Davis Ranch, but the weather closed in; we were soon pulled over and sitting out a hailstorm, the racket of the ice hitting the metal roof of the bus so loud it was sometimes hard to talk over the noise. Russell called John to warn him there was three inches of hail on the ground at the ranch and the roads would be impassable for a while. We diverted to a prairie dog colony not far away, where burrowing owls flew from perch to perch, bobbing their bodies up and down each time they landed—one reason old-timers often called these odd, subterranean-nesting raptors "howdy owls," since it looks as though the owls are dipping their heads in greeting.

We also had our first view of a distant mountain plover, my first ever—a BVD, in birder parlance, "better view desired." Even through the spotting scopes, it was tough getting a fix on the bird, partly because of distance and our wind-teared eyes, partly because the plover really did seem like a ghost, blending so well with the background that the moment it froze it would all but vanish from sight, brown against wind-swept brown. Fortunately, there would be more and closer views of other plovers in the hours ahead, but for those who like me were straining for their first, life-bird glimpse, it was a little frustrating. Still, in typical birder fashion, no one wanted to leave until the last person who wanted to find the plover had done so, with patient help and chattering teeth.

Even when we eventually tried to see the Wineinger-Davis Ranch, the bus was fishtailing so badly on the sloppy dirt roads that we diverted back to the firmer gravel county lanes, finding plenty more birds as we did—a great horned owl guarding three fluffy chicks, and Swainson's hawks newly returned from the grasslands of Argentina refurbishing their own bulky stick nests. We found more mountain plovers, near enough to the road this time to really drink in their subtle beauty. Up close, their pale brown plumage is warmed by hints of rust at the shoulders and upper chest, the black cap like a tiny beret cocked forward on the head, the alert black eye accentuated by a dark line to the base of the short, thin beak. Definitely a better view.

Fairness dictates that I tell you that the afternoon field trip, to the Karval Reservoir a couple of miles southeast of town, is where the bus finally got mired up to one axle in mud, and eventually had to be pulled out with heavy machinery. The cavalry was called in, a convoy of vehicles dispatched from Karval to get us, a typical rural America, everyone-pitch-in response. We spent some time birding around the impoundment, watching ducks and grebes on the lake, some early shorebirds along its margins, songbirds in the thickets, and tree and rough-winged swallows scouring the chilly, gusty air for any insect able to stay aloft. Then most of us walked the mile or so back to the main road, where our biggest concern was not mucking up the insides of the nice, clean cars that arrived to ferry us back to the community building. "No, don't worry about it, it's just mud," the woman behind the wheel assured us as several of us jammed into her back seat, painfully aware of the condition of our boots. "They have cookies and coffee waiting back in town," she said.

Dinner always has an extra savor after a cold day outside, and that evening we piled our plates high and settled in to listen to Casey Weissburg, a CSU doctoral candidate studying the local plovers, who had shown up at the previous year's festival not knowing a soul, but was now all but part of the community. Mountain plovers, she told the crowd jammed into the small hall, like disturbance regimes—grazing, fire, tilling, and (say it softly) prairie dogs. They also hedge their bets in a unique way by literally not putting all their eggs in one basket. Each pair, Weissburg explained, makes two nest scrapes; after the female lays three eggs in each one, both adults incubate their own set of eggs independently. If they lose a clutch, the pair quickly renests and lays two more sets of eggs. Chick survival and growth rates are at the heart of the field work she's doing for her PhD, and she had photographs of crazy-cute little plover chick fluffballs which, like their parents, are incredibly well camouflaged.

She also emphasized Colorado's importance for the mountain plover. The global population is estimated at about 18,000 birds, which represents a 70 percent decline since 1970, though Weissburg said there hasn't been a really rigorous attempt to assess the range-wide population in years. About 11,000 of those estimated 18,000 plovers nest in Colorado, she said, and virtually the entire world population passes through the grassland plains of eastern Colorado every year.

Riding back to the ranch with the Gallaghers, I asked Seth about how ranchers like Grady and Russell fit into the overall picture of grassland conservation, since they're still very much a minority.

"Russell and Grady, I've known them for 20 years now, and those are the two sort of ranchers and ranching communities where I cut my teeth as a conservationist. Folks who don't spend a lot of time thinking about this work, they feel like there's some formula, some template. People want it to be very cut and dried—here, follow this plan and then magical things will happen. But it's way more complicated than that. Every ranch is different; every rancher's motivation is different. It's super complex across the landscape," Gallagher said.

Certification initiatives like Audubon's Conservation Ranching program have come in for criticism in some quarters not so much because they don't produce results on participating properties (though depending on the program, these are still early days and it's hard to tell how big an impact they're having) but because they represent such an infinitesimally small slice of the ranching industry as a whole. One hundred fourteen ranches, even totaling 3 million acres as the Audubon program did by 2023, is a drop in the bucket, compared with the hundreds of millions of acres devoted to beef and dairy cattle.

I spoke with several people who are to varying degrees skeptical of bird-friendly ranch certifications but were not comfortable going on the record about it, primarily because they work in the field and need to maintain cordial relations. Nor did they necessarily feel the ranch-by-ranch work isn't valuable nor the positive results valid, at least not at a local level. They just don't see a way to easily scale it up sufficiently to make a continental difference, and some of them worry that unless certification programs are promoted with a degree of nuance they see lacking thus far—drawing attention to praiseworthy actions by some ranchers while also holding the larger industry to account for management that damages grassland ecosystems—the effect is to greenwash beef production overall and leave the public with the idea that cattle as a whole are not a problem.

Of course, there is one large grazing ungulate that evolved on the Great Plains in concert with the grasses and birds and everything else—the American bison. Thanks to their evolutionary history, bison offer some significant advantages over cattle; they are heat- and drought-tolerant and tend to move constantly when feeding, choosing to eat more grasses and fewer forbs and woody plants than cattle do. When it gets hot, bison move to high, windy ridgelines and wallow in dust, while cattle tend to congregate in wetter lowlands and in water, badly degrading riparian areas unless fenced out. Bison shrug off winter conditions that would leave most cattle dead for the spring scavengers.

In 2018 and 2019, scientists from the Smithsonian Conservation Biology Institute and the Smithsonian Migratory Bird Center, and one of Vicky Dreitz's graduate students from the University of Montana, where she now teaches, compared grassland bird abundance and diversity across almost 277,000 acres of bison and cattle pasture in north central and northeastern Montana, a region Vicky and her colleagues had previously identified as having the greatest diversity of grassland- and sagebrush-obligate birds in North America. They looked at land on which the cattle were rotationally grazed from March through November, and compared it with that on which bison moved freely year-round. They concluded that when cattle are managed well, the differences in bird diversity and abundance between cows and bison may not be as important as other variables like stocking rates, the kind of soil, precipitation patterns, and topography. "Managed well" is the key, however.

Cattle are still the norm in the West, but that's changing rapidly in Indian country. One of the bison pastures included in the Smithsonian study was a 25,000-acre tract on the Fort Belknap Indian Reservation, where bison have been grazed for more than 30 years. Many tribal nations are moving to replace cattle with bison, or to bring in bison for the first time since they were extirpated, most often for cultural and economic reasons but with ecological benefits as well. The InterTribal Buffalo Council, founded in 1991, now has more than 80 member tribal nations managing more than 25,000 bison in 22 states. In 2024, an important new partnership, the Tribal Buffalo Lifeways Collaboration, was announced between the IBC, Native Americans in Philanthropy, the Nature Conservancy, and the World Wildlife Fund to greatly expand tribal bison restoration.

While the Gradys and the Russells are still rare, their numbers are growing. Russell has developed a national standing as an officer of Partnerscapes, a landowner-driven nonprofit focused on collaborative, voluntary conservation on working lands, and there is a growing emphasis on land health in many quarters of the West. Some weeks after the Karval festival, I caught up with Seth Gallagher to pick his brain further about the challenges and opportunities for conservation on the Great Plains, and when I asked about examples of ranch communities doing it right, he rattled off a long list.

"In Phillips County, Montana, there's a group called the Ranchers Stewardship Alliance," Gallagher said. "Their primary threats are generational turnover of the ranches, keeping generations on the land and economically viable. The board is made up of landowners and their conservation community, [including] the state game and fish agency, the US Fish and Wildlife Service, NRCS [Natural Resources Conservation Service], and then a number of nonprofits, World Wildlife Fund, the Nature Conservancy, Pheasants Forever, are all present in that landscape. And they have this really unique conservation committee made up of experts so when they get grant money from NFWF, they triage what the most important projects are. They've been hugely successful because they are a landowner-led organization."

He was just getting started, mentioning similar coalitions, alliances, and associations in Wyoming, North and South Dakota, Kansas, and Oklahoma, among other states. These are not explicitly bird-conservation groups, obviously, and not all of their actions and investments are tuned to creating a better world for grassland birds.

The Ranchers Stewardship Alliance, for example, has been fairly vocal in its opposition to American Prairie, the huge rewilding project in Montana, seeing it as a threat to traditional ranching. But to Gallagher, this growing shift toward a more holistic approach to grassland management is in the main a positive, given that in many places the threats these lands face would eliminate the habitat entirely, either through development or tilled farming.

"Cattle production isn't perfect, but for a working landscape in an area where you have to support families and communities, it's by a very significant margin the most compatible land use when we talk about biodiversity being a goal," he said. "If you look at where all the species that we currently care about are, it's in these last remaining grass-based economies where ranching is the driver."

Sunday was the last day of the Karval festival, and an inconveniently early flight home from Denver meant I was going to have to miss the morning field trip. But I was able to enjoy one more good ranch breakfast at the community building, and had a chance to say goodbye to new friends with whom I had bonded over muddy boots and stuck vehicles. I'd like to say I saw one last mountain plover as I headed out of town, but the prairie ghosts, true to their name, were nowhere to be seen.

Saving the grassland birds of the Great Plains means working across millions of acres to protect habitat that hasn't yet been destroyed. For another iconic bird of the American West, however, one that looks and acts a bit like a loose floozy when the mating urge comes on, salvation may paradoxically come at least in part from the roar of a chain saw, applied across immense swaths of some of the emptiest land in the Lower 48.

Eleven

Good for the Bird

They call it a sea, and—especially to someone like me, who has spent his life swaddled by the deep forests and abbreviated horizons of the Appalachian Mountains—there is definitely something oceanic about the size and emptiness of the sagebrush country of the American West.

I was on the border of southeastern Oregon and southwestern Idaho, in one of the most remote and lightly settled corners of the Lower 48. From my high vantage point, I looked east and south across a brown landscape on which I had to peer hard to see any sign of humanity beyond the faint squiggle of a dirt road miles away. It was easy to imagine the hills and basins that spread in every direction as waves, frozen and cloaked in sparse vegetation; a sagebrush sea indeed.

Across the West, from central Washington to the eastern edge of California, through the Great Basin, the intermountain region and the western extent of the Great Plains from Montana and western North Dakota, south to Arizona and New Mexico, the sagebrush steppe (as it is also known) encompasses some 175 million acres across 13 states, as well as a wee bit of two Canadian provinces, making it the largest contiguous terrestrial ecosystem in the United States. It is also, despite that, little known to most Americans except as a movie backdrop.

The anchors of this biome are several drought-tolerant species of sagebrush, which are not true sage at all but shrubs of the genus *Artemesia,* famous for their silvery-green foliage and aromatic scent; smell it once, and it will forever conjure that world of pale blue skies, wheeling raptors, and treeless horizons. Sagebrush thrives in the hot, dry summers and cold, somewhat wetter winters that characterize this part of the world, where other woody plants struggle.

To view the sagebrush sea as I was, the land still chilled and winter-brown, the fingerprints of humans seemingly faint, is to allow yourself to believe it is as it has always been. But I knew the sagebrush expanse, for all its immensity, is a profoundly altered habitat, facing an onslaught of threats that reinforce one another—invasive grasses that fuel destructive fires, which wipe out the sagebrush while favoring the grasses, which in turn creates perfect conditions for even greater conflagrations. Industry and development chew away at its integrity. Generations of poor range management and overgrazing have left ecological scars. One recent assessment found that what the researchers called "core sagebrush areas," where the habitat is essentially intact, had declined from about 54 million acres in 2001 to a little more than 33 million acres in 2020—still a lot of land, but a loss of a little more than a million acres a year.

Not surprisingly, all this conversion and degradation has had an impact on the thousands of species of plants and animals that depend on the sagebrush sea. These are organisms most people have never heard of: Plants like Wasatch desertparsley and Torrey's four-nerve-daisy. Great Basin spadefoot toads, sagebrush lizards, and pygmy rabbits that weigh barely a pound and could nestle comfortably in a person's palm. Birds like sage thrashers, green-tailed towhees, Brewer's sparrow, and sage sparrows. Sagebrush voles and Wyoming pocket gophers.

But there is one sagebrush native that a lot of people *have* heard of, a spectacular bird whose declining fortunes have for years driven most of the efforts to forestall the further loss of the sagebrush steppe biome. It's a bird that has sparked ferocious debate and legal battles, playing out over decades while the bird itself has grown scarcer and scarcer. But it is also a bird on whose behalf a new model of conservation in the sagebrush sea has more recently taken shape. I had come to this corner of the West where Idaho, Oregon, and Nevada meet, because here there is an attempt to match the breathtaking scope of the problem with an almost equally breathtaking scale of response. Not everyone is convinced, but it may represent the only realistic hope for the greater sage-grouse, and all the less famous species that share its world.

A male greater sage-grouse is a porker, weighing up to seven pounds and measuring 30 inches from beak to tail, the largest grouse in North America and second only to the male western capercaillie of Eurasia, which weighs twice as much and is the heaviest grouse in the world. Both sexes are a lovely mottled gray-brown that blends seamlessly with the sagebrush, the female wholly so. The male has a black belly, a broad, white collar that extends down the chest in a deep vee, and a long tail of sharply pointed feathers. A small, fleshy comb of yellow skin sits above each of his eyes.

Sagebrush utterly defines a sage-grouse's world. From autumn through spring green-up, its diet is almost entirely the buds and leaves of the sagebrush, especially big sagebrush, *A. tridentata*, one of the three dominant species of the steppe. Summertime brings a wider mix of greenery like wildflowers and other tender forbs, especially for the nesting females, and a lot of protein-rich insects for growing chicks.

Given their size, sage-grouse are arresting birds under any circumstances, but the most dramatic thing about them is their mating displays, which occur on central courtship arenas known as leks, where the males gather and the females can pick and choose. Many species of grouse perform highly ritualized dances on leks, like the fast-stomping, whirling pirouette of a male sharp-tailed grouse, or the "booming" dances of greater and lesser prairie-chickens.

The display of the greater sage-grouse eclipses them all, if only because the birds themselves are so much larger and more imposing—and because they can gather in remarkable numbers, with 30, 50, or even 100 males crammed into a single lek spanning hundreds of square yards. The show begins at daybreak, often early enough in spring that snow still covers the ground. The male sage-grouse gulps as much as a gallon of air, forcing it into two esophageal sacs that lie hidden beneath its white neck ruff, which expands into a thick vest. Rearing back, the bird partially opens his wings and fans his tail, which forms a circle of narrow spikes. Long, specialized feathers known as filoplumes, which look like stiff hairs, encircle the back of his head. The male draws his wings across the feathers of his ruff, making a swishing sound, then shakes his body forward, exposing the two greenish-yellow air sacs while making an explosive, rather liquid "plopping" sound that carries for miles on a still morning.

You must see this to fully appreciate it; I encourage you to lay this book aside for a moment and do a quick internet video search. The effect, as you will see, is that of a well-endowed matron wearing yellow mascara and an extravagant white feather boa, and showing an absolutely scandalous amount of décolletage. Multiply that by dozens and dozens of males, all shaking and plopping and swishing, and you'll understand why witnessing greater sage-grouse on the lek is a bucket-list experience for many birders and naturalists.*

Greater sage-grouse once ranged as far south as Arizona and New Mexico, east to Nebraska, Kansas, and Oklahoma, and north across much of central Oregon and Washington into the southern edge of the Canadian prairies. Lewis and Clark were the first to provide a written account of what they called the "Heath cock or cock of the plains," a bird William Clark said was "the Size of a Small turkey, of the pheasant kind."

Meriwether Lewis described the "great abundance" of sage-grouse their party encountered, and modern estimates suggest there may have been as many as 2 million sage-grouse. Early Euro-American accounts

---

* In the 1990s, scientists realized that the tiny population of sage-grouse that inhabit southwestern Colorado and southeastern Utah, numbering fewer than 5,000 birds, were physically, behaviorally, and genetically distinct. In 2000, they were formally described as a new species, the Gunnison sage-grouse, which was quickly listed as threatened under the federal Endangered Species Act.

of their numbers can beggar belief, as one report from George Bird Grinnell, founder of the first Audubon Society, makes clear. In October 1888 he was in a valley known as Bates Hole, just south of what's now Casper, Wyoming. Sage-grouse were a constant presence, and his observations give a hint of how abundant these grouse were: "The number of Grouse which flew over the camp reminded me of the old-time flights of Passenger Pigeons that I used to see as a boy. . . . I have no means whatever of estimating the number of birds which I saw, but there must have been thousands of them."

Both their numbers and their range have contracted significantly since Grinnell's time. Initially, the biggest threat was unregulated hunting, but worse were the attacks directed not against the sage-grouse, but against its habitat. The final decades of the 19th century and the start of the 20th saw massive overgrazing by sheep and cattle across most of the West, and the steady degradation of the range. Cattle don't eat sagebrush, so ranchers often saw it as a competitor to grass, and cut, burned, or sprayed it with herbicides. What replaced it was a real nightmare, an invasive Eurasian exotic known as cheatgrass.

Unlike the native perennial bunchgrasses like bluebunch wheatgrass, Indian ricegrass, and needle-and-thread, which set down deep roots and live for years, cheat is an annual, dying back completely in winter and sprouting come spring from trillions of seeds. As it dies off, it becomes explosively flammable, and a spark—from a dry lightning strike, a braking train, an overheated vehicle pulled off along a road—can set off a wildfire of an intensity the sagebrush lands had rarely seen.

It's only gotten worse. For one thing, there are other invasive plants like Russian thistle, colloquially known as tumbleweed, and another monster of an annual grass called medusahead, named for its multi-branched seed heads, which like cheatgrass was introduced accidentally in hay and straw. All three make the lands they infest dramatically more prone to bigger and hotter fires, and they are able to quickly colonize burned areas to reinforce the cycle.

Fires were always a natural part of the sagebrush sea, though these were, for the most part, fairly small and rather low intensity blazes, kept in check by the scattered nature of the bunchgrasses and posing far less of a risk to established sagebrush. Big, stand-clearing fires were probably rather rare. The fires today, pumped up by annual grasses and to at least some extent by climate change, are growing bigger, hotter, and more destructive. The region where I was standing has seen some enormous burns, like the 2015 Soda Fire, which encompassed 283,000 acres across Idaho and Oregon. I could easily see the fire's path across the landscape; where it had burned, the ground was pale yellow with the thatch of old cheatgrass and medusahead, while the unburned areas were gray-green with healthy sagebrush.

Annual grasses are invading exotics, but they are only half the botanical assault on the sagebrush sea. The other threat comes from a cohort of natives, whose fortunes changed when white settlers initially altered the natural rhythm of fire on the shrub-steppes. Conifers, including pinyon pine but most notably western juniper in the part of the Intermountain West where I stood, were originally kept in check by those periodic, small-scale fires, which burned away their seedlings and restricted the trees to higher, rockier, less fire-friendly terrain, or created mosaics where sagebrush and forest mixed and mingled. Once freed from regular fires, though, the conifers began to spread—slowly, almost surreptitiously, creeping outward at so incremental a pace that most people didn't really notice, year on year, decade on decade, how profoundly the land had changed.

The striking degree of that change is starkly evident when you compare historical photos to those from today, like pictures taken at research reference sites scattered across the West. In a faded photo from 1969, a guy with a high-and-tight crewcut stands in front of a hillside of sagebrush, holding a clipboard on which the coordinates and other data are written. A dozen or so small, dark junipers, none more than waist high, fleck the hill. By 1977, the trees in the reference photo are bigger, and there are twice as many. By 1989 the hill is half woods, and by 2005, you can't see the sagebrush except along the dirt road — it's a juniper woodland. By accessing images back to the late 19th or early 20th centuries, researchers realized this tide of trees, dubbed a "green glacier," has been creeping inexorably for a very long time. By one estimate, since 1860 the percentage of sagebrush area occupied by trees has increased by as much as 625 percent, and today, only one-third of what had been treeless sagebrush steppe remains so.

Trees crowd out not just the sagebrush but also the native bunch grasses and forbs that provide food for grouse and other sagebrush biome species. They also pull so much water from the soil that what had been perennial streams eventually run dry. But junipers ruin the land for sage-grouse long before such levels are reached; biologists have found that when the tree cover within a kilometer or so of a lek reaches just 4 percent—a little as one juniper per acre—the grouse will move out and abandon that site. Other researchers have found even lower thresholds, just 1.5 percent, and that it holds as well for nesting females. That 1969 photo with the crewcut biologist? That land likely already had lost its sage-grouse. Trees are perches for raptors like golden eagles that eat adult grouse, and nest predators like ravens that take eggs and chicks; something deep in a sage-grouse distrusts a tree. Conifers have generally started high and been moving lower and lower into sagebrush, while annual grasses are moving steadily upslope.

Worried land managers call it "the big squeeze," and it's a problem beyond sagebrush country. Similar green glaciers of red cedar are crowding out grasslands in Nebraska's Sand Hills; in other formerly treeless landscapes across North America, the advancing army may be made up of Douglas fir, while in the Southwest it's often mesquite, a nonconifer. The characters vary but in each case, grass- or shrublands are vanishing beneath their spreading shade.

Sage-grouse have been feeling these cumulative pressures for a long, long time, and I've only mentioned a few of the problems facing them. For example, sage-grouse have proven to be highly susceptible to West Nile virus, which first appeared in North America in 1999 and is spread by mosquitoes. While a serious human health issue, West Nile has been even more of a disaster for many wild birds, with greater sage-grouse taking an especially bad hit.

Although sage-grouse undergo natural boom-and-bust cycles that make it hard to say, year to year and place to place, exactly how they are faring, the long-term trend for the past century has been fairly clear and disheartening. In 2021, the US Geological Survey put the decline in sage-grouse since the late 1960s at more than 80 percent, with a 37 percent drop just since 2003; they now occupy only a little more than half their historic range. Conservationists have been trying to reverse that trend for a long time, without much success; that same USGS assessment found the only sage-grouse populations that were stable or increasing were in parts of Wyoming and Montana. Not surprisingly, that's the region with some of the healthiest remaining sagebrush and the fewest insults to it.

Many of the problems facing sage-grouse lie somewhere between difficult and impossible to address. Residential and industrial development, and resource extraction like mining, and oil and gas drilling, which have fragmented many parts of the species' range, aren't going away. Now renewable energy development in the form of wind farms and solar arrays is moving into sagebrush country as well. Poor livestock management continues to damage the range in many areas, intensifying issues like annual grass invasions. Those issues demand policy-level changes. Invasive annual grasses can be treated with specialized herbicides that prevent germination, but the work is expensive, requires repeated treatments, and introduces toxic chemicals to the landscape. Megafires can be contained, but that means creating an extensive network of hundreds of miles of fuel breaks, where otherwise healthy sagebrush is mowed to create wide gaps.

On the other hand, cutting down trees is pretty straightforward. What would happen if crews were simply unleashed to chop down, pile up, and burn every juniper that's encroached on what had been open sagebrush? What if they started doing so in the highest-quality sagebrush habitat remaining, working out from the intact core to remove the first tendrils of invading conifers, then were increasingly aggressive, removing older and more established stands on the periphery to turn forests into open range again?

First, defend the core. Then, grow the core. Then, find ways to mitigate the harm. And what if this were done at a scale large enough to actually match that of the problem it seeks to solve? Would it finally turn the dial for sage-grouse? And how large is large enough?

How about 617,000 acres? Would that work?

I was in southwestern Idaho to find out. Among my goals was to avoid being almost knocked out by a sage-grouse. Again.

This was not my first time chasing these birds around Idaho. On a magazine assignment more than 25 years ago, I'd come to spend time with a state wildlife biologist named Jack Connelly, who had been studying sage-grouse for two decades and was one of the acknowledged experts on the species.

What followed was one of the more hallucinogenic experiences I've ever had in the guise of serious ornithology. It was past midnight when Connelly, a research tech named Thalia, and I grabbed landing nets of the size used for giant salmon, and followed another tech named Nathan, who was loaded down with a radio receiver connected to headphones, a hand-held directional antenna, and a car battery in his backpack wired to a powerful spotlight. Oh, and a boom box over one shoulder, because these were still the days of boom boxes. Nathan dialed in the frequency of a radio transmitter on a female sage-grouse somewhere out in the high desert darkness, punched a button on the boom box, and the night was filled with the high-decibel sounds of U2 playing "Helter Skelter." As Connelly had explained to me earlier, the music would hide the sounds of our approach and cause the grouse and its flockmates to hunker down in place; once Nathan had fixed a grouse in the light, blinding it, one of us would slip in from the side and drop a net over it.

This was a great plan, but the execution was tricky. We couldn't use headlamps ourselves because they would backlight Nathan and spook the birds, so we had to stumble blindly over loose lava rock and cactus (and hopefully no angry rattlesnakes) for many miles. Over the course of five or six hours we experienced a number of false starts and flushed flocks before we finally got lucky. Nathan's beam settled on a hen grouse; Connelly expertly netted her. Thalia got the next one, then it was my turn, a big male. I was far less polished, but I got the net over him, though in the process I slammed my hand hard on a prickly pear cactus at the same time that another male, leaping into flight and gaining speed fast, came out of the dark and walloped me on the side of the head—a seven-pound projectile with some serious momentum. The bird went one way, my eyeglasses went another, and the stars I saw weren't only in the sky.

Sage-grouse are the big, sexy stars of the sagebrush, and while I would argue that the 350 or more species that share the steppe habitat deserve the same care and concerted action, the reason sage-grouse get the limelight isn't just their size and remarkable courtship displays—it's the fact that they have come very close to being listed as a federally threatened or endangered species, and that's not something that many landowners, ranchers, or politicians in sagebrush country welcome. Fear of a federal listing has been a powerful motivating force when it comes to sage-grouse conservation.

An estimated 64 percent of sage-grouse habitat is on public land, but an ESA listing would also impact activities like mining, ranching, and wind development on private land, much of it wetter lowlands and riparian areas where the sage-grouse hens nest and raise their chicks. The announcement in 2010 that the USFWS would consider listing the bird sparked panic across the West—but also an unprecedented level of cooperation. If industry, landowners, NGOs, cattle producers, states, and federal agencies could agree on sweeping actions, across enough of the grouse's range, and show enough progress toward reversing the decline, then perhaps a listing could be averted.

In September 2015, then-Secretary of the Interior Sally Jewell announced that the USFWS had decided not to list the grouse, mostly because just that sort of hugely ambitious cooperative agreement had been reached, one that would conserve 35 million acres of federally owned grouse habitat in 10 states, and take a variety of actions to reduce threats on 90 percent of the bird's range. It directed the Bureau of Land Management (BLM) and US Forest Service, which manage most of the federal land holding sage-grouse, to put greater emphasis in their land-use plans on protecting the birds. It highlighted state-level management frameworks, and partnerships with private landowners and ranchers, to conserve and restore habitat. A more holistic approach to fighting rangeland fires would be implemented, and energy development would be steered away from sensitive sage-grouse habitat.

At least, that was the idea. With the 2016 presidential election and arrival of the first Trump administration in January 2017, a lot of what had been folded into the plan went by the wayside. Regulations restricting oil and gas drilling near courtship leks were relaxed, oil and gas leases on millions of acres of what was supposed to be protected grouse habitat were auctioned off, and plans to bar mining on millions more acres were jettisoned. A USFWS status review—basically a rigorous, science-based health check on the state of the sage-grouse population, which under the 2015 agreement was to happen in 2020—was likewise scuttled.

While some of the Trump administration's plans were blocked by the courts, the impetus generated by the 2015 agreement stalled, and sage-grouse numbers continued to fall. The 2020 election brought another change in administration and yet another change in the federal attitude toward sage-grouse, this one veering sharply toward conservation. Four years later, a second Trump administration was in the wings, one that would prove even more immediately and aggressively hostile to anything that smacked of environmental protection.

These pendulum swings, from one administration to the next and back, have been head-spinning. But there's been one effort in sagebrush country that's been quietly plugging along for more than 15 years, through liberal and conservative agendas in Washington, DC, driven by a simple mantra: "What's good for the bird is good for the herd."

I first heard that phrase in July 2021, when I, like most of the world, was still ensnared in some form of Covid-19 lockdown. I was listening to the third of the Road to Recovery Initiative (R2R) virtual workshops started by the team that had authored the 2019, 3-billion-birds-gone *Science* paper. This three-day event focused on developing the process for advancing bird recovery, and it was also the first time I heard the term "co-production," which I have to admit initially mystified me, since none of the speakers or panelists really defined it. I eventually came to realize it meant up-front collaboration between scientists and those whose lives will be impacted by their science, or who will use the results of their research. And it was also the first time at a bird conservation conference that I heard much discussion about social science—the study of how, for instance, to get people who might not care that much about birds to take actions that advance conservation. Another way of putting it might be finding common ground.

The morning of the second day was devoted to species recovery stories, most of which I was familiar with, but what caught my eye was the third talk of the morning: "Recovery Story: Greater Sage-grouse." Huh? Since when had the sage-grouse, which for decades had been a depressing example of relentless loss, recovered?

The speaker was Tim Griffiths, with the USDA's Natural Resources Conservation Service (NRCS), one of the smaller and, outside of ag country, lesser-known federal agencies. Griffiths was the western lead for NRCS's Working Lands for Wildlife program, which facilitates conservation on private property. In 2010, just as the USFWS announced the possibility of a sage-grouse listing, NRCS launched what it called the Sage-Grouse Initiative (SGI), an attempt to get ranchers and landowners to embrace voluntary changes in how they manage their land to benefit the birds. The most effective approach, NRCS argued, was also the least complicated: removing conifers from encroached areas.

The results that Griffiths outlined certainly sounded impressive. He pointed to work in the portion of the Warner Mountains that poke up from northern California into south central Oregon, where juniper removal resulted in a respectable 12 percent increase in sage-grouse numbers, with the grouse quickly moving into newly tree-free areas.

And it wasn't just grouse, he said; cleared areas saw large increases in the populations of a suite of sage-dependent songbirds. Seasonal streams, free from the thirsty roots of junipers, held water for weeks later in the summer, and that meant as much as 60 percent more forage for cattle.

"What's good for the bird is good for the herd," Griffiths said. "That's our motto." Ranchers might like sage-grouse well enough, but cattle production is a business of dollars and cents and thin margins, and anything that increases forage by such eye-opening amounts is going to get attention. Griffiths told the conference that SGI had enrolled 2,300 ranches covering 8.5 million acres.

But, he said, there was a broader lesson to be learned. The big mistake in sage-grouse conservation, he argued, was "spending a lot of time focusing on microhabitat-scale issues instead of, from Day One, focusing on what were clearly the big drivers of habitat loss and fragmentation," like conifer encroachment. "None of that led to any actionable conservation outcomes."

Don't treat all threats as equal, Griffiths told participants. NRCS took aim at the encroaching conifers, the biggest threat they could identify and against which action was practical. "That's when the magic started happening," he said.

It was the most improbably optimistic take on the sage-grouse situation I had ever heard, so I eventually got Tim Griffiths on the phone.

SGI eventually morphed into the larger Working Lands for Wildlife program at NRCS, working with dozens of species across an array of American ecosystems, but sage-grouse were the seed. Until 2010, Griffiths said, a lot of the focus on sage-grouse conservation was aimed at policy and regulation, and in a sense, an ESA listing would have been the neutron bomb, affecting every aspect of land use within the sage-grouse's range. Sage-grouse policy was already highly polarizing, with entrenched interests on either side, and a lot of private landowners were deeply suspicious of anything that smacked of the government telling them what to do.

"NRCS doesn't do policy, but we can do conservation," Griffiths told me. "We deliberately stayed away from policy, never talked policy, just conservation action focusing on the big drivers [of sage-grouse decline]. If you're going to implement enough conservation at a large enough scale you need a large, diverse army, and if you take a policy position you're going to alienate people. So that's our bright line, and we never cross it," he said.

In the SGI's early years, with the threat of an ESA listing vivid, the initiative enjoyed strong support across sagebrush country. Some skeptics said the only reason was fear of a federal listing. "Well, Fish and Wildlife decided not to list, and the participation has only grown since then," Griffiths said—up 32 percent in 2023 over just the year before.

"That's because we demonstrated actions, not words. It's relationships built on trust," he said. Part of the reason for SGI's success, Griffiths told me, was that NRCS was using insights from social science to craft the way the agency approached and worked with landowners, and because they took a co-production approach, collaborating with cattle producers in ways that benefit not just the grouse but the people using the same land.

There are still major problems facing sage-grouse. Cutting junipers and pinyons is a matter of sheer brute force, applied to the landscape with chain saws and drip torches. Cheatgrass, medusahead, and other annual grasses are a more stubborn challenge, and one that can actually increase in the immediate wake of conifer clearing. Griffiths said there were some new chemicals coming into use, preemergent herbicides very specific to annual grasses like cheat and medusahead that leave native perennial bunchgrasses alone, but they're expensive to apply, and it takes years of reapplication to completely deplete the seed bank in the soil.

Still, agencies have been getting increasingly ambitious in their approach to conifer removal and sagebrush protection, working at an ever-increasing scale in ever-broader partnerships. The philosophy has three parts. One: Defend the core. Identify the very best remaining sagebrush habitat, places with little or no conifer and annual grass intrusion, and prevent that intrusion from happening in the first place. Two: Grow the core. Attack peripheral areas that have manageable levels of invasion, and eliminate the trees and the grasses, pushing the boundaries of the high-quality core outward. Three: Mitigate impacts. Find ways to restore badly degraded habitats like wet meadows and riparian areas, rich in insects and tender greenery like wildflowers that are critical to sage-grouse and other shrub-steppe species at various points in their life cycle.

Where would be the best places to see that three-pronged approach in action? I asked Griffiths, and several other people involved with sage-grouse conservation. One place kept coming up again and again, something known as the BOSH Project. I was going back to Idaho.

This time, Connor White promised to show me sage-grouse without fear of physical assault.

Thirty-two years old and rail thin, White works for the nonprofit Pheasants Forever as coordinator for a sagebrush restoration undertaking of unprecedent scope—the Bruneau-Owyhee Sage-grouse Habitat, or BOSH, Project, a collaboration involving federal and state agencies, NGOs, and private landowners, meant to roll back the tide of junipers, get wildfires that promote annual grasses under control while reintroducing controlled burns to the ecosystem, and thus create landscape-level benefits for sage-grouse and other sage-dependent species. It represents the largest attempt at sagebrush restoration ever undertaken.

The BOSH Project area is huge, 1.67 million acres in all, with about one-third of that, 617,000 acres, slated for active treatment, primarily through boots-on-the-ground, square mile by square mile removal of conifers. That sounds like a lot of land, but this part of the West simply swallows acreage like that. Owyhee County, Idaho, within which the BOSH Project lies, covers more than 7,600 square miles—just 200 square miles smaller than the entire state of Massachusetts, though it's still only the second-largest county in the state. (For the record, Idaho County is almost 8,500 square miles, only a smidge smaller than New Jersey.) Owyhee County has just 12,000 residents, and the county seat, Murphy, has a population of 96.

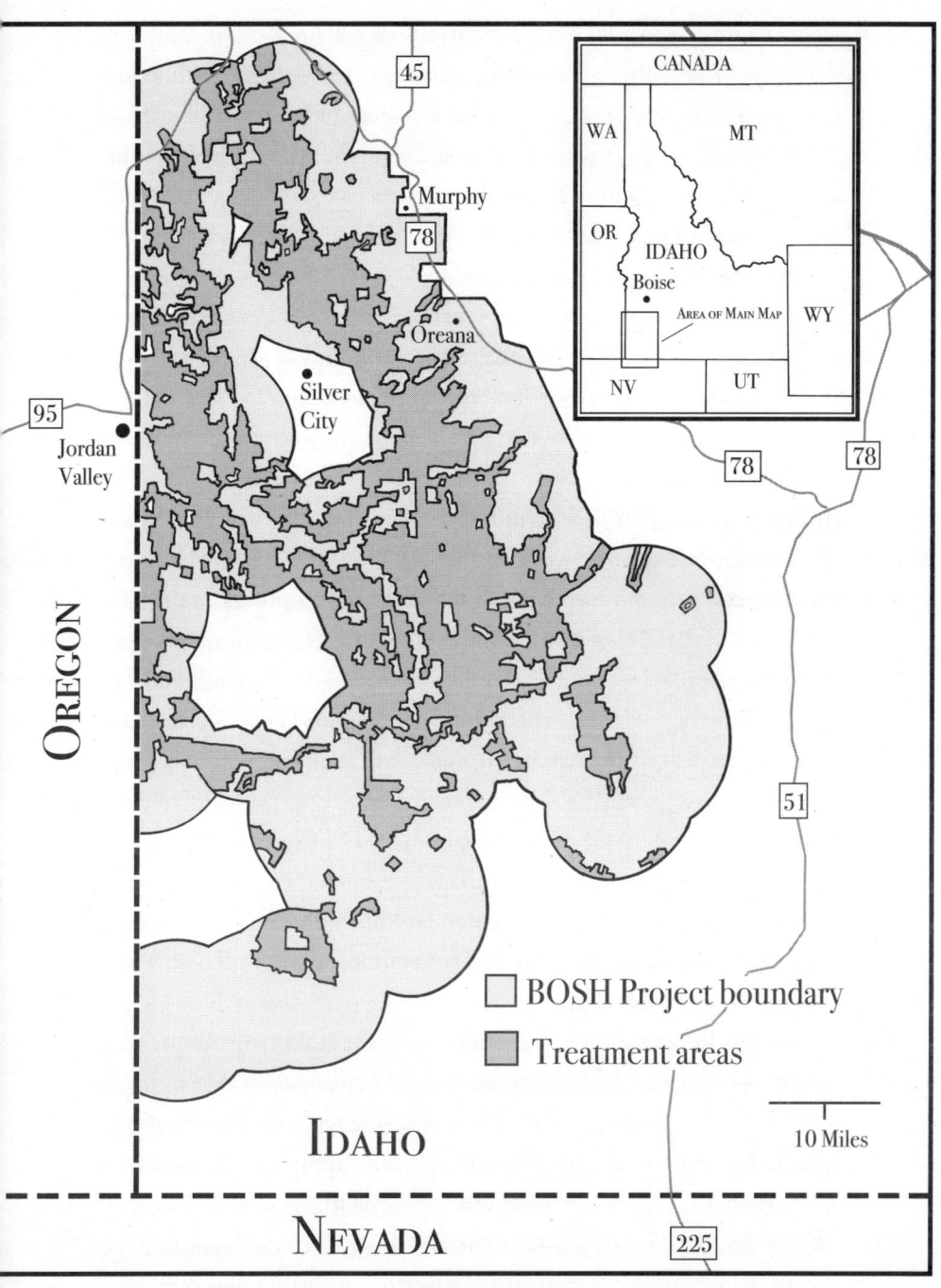

The entirety of the Bruneau-Owyhee Sage-grouse Habitat (BOSH) Project encompasses 1.6 million acres, on which 617,000 acres are being actively treated to remove encroaching conifers.

It can be spectacular country; anywhere else in the United States, almost anywhere else in the *world*, the deep and twisting, 60-mile-long canyon of the Bruneau River, a whitewater tributary of the Snake and a federally designated Wild and Scenic River, would be a marquee tourist attraction. Instead, there is just one BLM scenic overlook off a badly marked back road, from which you can peer across the quarter-mile-wide canyon and down along its 800-foot-deep walls of volcanic rhyolite and basalt, walls marked with countless petroglyphs, pictographs, and other evidence of the long and continuing habitation of the Shoshone and Northern Paiute peoples. And the Bruneau Canyon is just one of many dramatic canyons and gorges bisecting the Owyhee Plateau in Idaho and Oregon.

The Bruneau-Owyhee region also holds some of the largest and most intact remaining sagebrush habitat in this part of the country, the kind of core that the defend-grow-mitigate approach is designed to protect. A 2022 framework designed to guide the restoration of the overall sagebrush biome, prepared by the Western Association of Fish and Wildlife Agencies and the US Fish and Wildlife Service, classified just 13.6 percent of the remaining sagebrush steppe as "core sagebrush areas," the most pristine habitat—but that seemingly small percentage nonetheless totals some 33.4 million acres. The expert panel devising the framework classified another 34.4 percent, or 84.3 million acres, as "growth opportunity areas," which face more threats and challenges than core sagebrush but should benefit from restoration, the grow-the-core part of the equation.

That's a lot of land, and working at such scale will take a lot of money. The annual budget for the BOSH Project alone is roughly $2 million, White told me. While acknowledging the scale of conservation required to address the problems facing the sagebrush ecosystem, the 2022 framework's authors noted the obvious analogy—the billions of dollars invested, and millions of wetland acres restored, through the North American Waterfowl Management Plan, which has been spectacularly successful in the face of similarly daunting challenges. "The NAWMP highlights the value of establishing a broad partnership and producing a framework with a landscape-scale vision that can unify stakeholders and help to focus complex ecological issues into clear, well-aligned goals and actions to work toward reversing declines in ecological integrity," is the drily bureaucratic way they put it.

All this was going through my head as I rode shotgun in a BLM pickup truck being driven through the predawn darkness by Lance Okeson, the supervisory fire management specialist in his agency's Boise District. Okeson grew up in Burns, Oregon, and went to Oregon State to study range ecology, following in his dad's footsteps to become a second-generation BLM employee who was nearing retirement. He's a bear of a guy with a beard and a "Grave Before Shave" sticker on his jumbo coffee mug, a loud laugh, and a habit of agreeing with something you say with an emphatic "Right on!," which is a phrase I had not heard in a very long time.

I'd flown into Boise, the state capital, because that's where the federal offices are located. But the BOSH site is a long way from Boise, so that morning four of us had set off a couple of hours before daybreak, aiming to arrive at dawn for what we all hoped would be a good show—male sage-grouse displaying on their leks. White was riding in the back seat, along with Jason Pyron, the local lead for the USFWS's Partners for Fish and Wildlife program, which provides technical advice, funding, and support for landowners, tribal governments, NGOs, and others who want to implement conservation programs. The habitat restoration work on the BOSH Project includes federal agencies; state agencies like Idaho's Department of Fish and Game and Department of Lands; and private nonprofits like Pheasants Forever and the Rocky Mountain Elk Foundation. Funding comes from BLM, NFWF, federal Pittman-Robertson Act funds (which in turn come from a national excise tax on sporting arms and ammunition) funneled through the Idaho Department of Fish and Game, and even some of the $1.4 billion included for ecosystem restoration in the 2021 federal Bipartisan Infrastructure Law.

Since the BOSH Project's inception in 2019, more than 140,000 acres have been treated, including more than 50,000 acres in 2024, exceeding the annual goal of 30,000–40,000 acres. Even that scale reflects a strategic approach to conifer removal. The target areas are all within 10 kilometers (6.2 miles) of 70 sage-grouse leks, on ground with less than 20 percent tree cover and more than 15 percent sagebrush. The cutting takes place in late summer, after the birds have reared their chicks. Even so, it will take 10 or 15 years to complete the job.

Fire is at once the shaper, menace, and possible salvation of functioning sagebrush steppe. Like almost all Western ecosystems, the steppe evolved with fire, at appropriately low intensity, modest scale, and extended "return rates," the term for how frequently a particular area burns. In its original state, sagebrush would have burned anywhere from once every 60–80 years to perhaps as infrequently as every 200. The paucity of fuel would have kept the fires relatively cool, as fires go, scorching the sagebrush but not annihilating it, refreshing the ground for wildflowers and other forbs, while killing off any juniper or pinyon seedlings that had taken hold.

With the intrusion of annual grasses like cheat and medusahead, and the shift from open range to dense conifer, the fuel load exploded, even as fires were being suppressed as a matter of national Smokey Bear policy. As a result, those fires that do occur have grown exponentially in size and ferocity. "One reason that you have 600,000-acre fires, or 1.2 million-acre fires, is because we took fire out of the system for a hundred years," Pyron said.

We drove almost two hours through the darkness, a waning gibbous moon high and slightly smudged by a thin smear of clouds. When we crossed the Snake River at Grandview, a low serpent of fog mirrored its course, hanging just above the treetops. From there we turned off the paved road near the little hamlet of Oreana. The light was coming up now as we moved higher into the hills, flushing horned larks from the dirt road, and a few bands of mule deer bounding away with their peculiar, bouncing-ball gait known as stotting or pronking. The Silver City Range, a branch of the Owyhee Mountains, rose piebald with snowfields far to our west, with Quicksilver Mountain, just a shade over 8,000 feet, completely white, its peak tucked shyly into a single lenticular cloud. A few small herds of pronghorn, russet against the gray-green sagebrush, moved against a far hillside.

White was watching our progress on his phone's mapping app, slowing Okeson as we neared the red pin that marked the lek's coordinates. Our visit wasn't just for my benefit, but part of an annual survey of known lekking sites, an important tool for monitoring sage-grouse populations and trends. We were on a high, broad ridge, looking toward the rapidly lightening east. As soon as we pulled over we saw one cock grouse standing erect, his ruff starkly white against the dark ground. Scanning carefully, we quickly spotted two more males in the sage, then a fourth; rarely were all visible at the same time, appearing and disappearing in the shin-high sagebrush. Earlier in the week a state biologist had counted 15 males here, but this appeared to be a slow morning, though with time more and more arrived until 10 or so were strutting and displaying.

Sage-grouse tend to choose wide, open, often high locations for their leks, with low, scattered sage, the better for the males to show off for females. Still, the leks need to be fairly close to good nesting habitat, so that once the hens have mated, they don't need to travel far to raise their chicks. Once established, sage-grouse leks can last for—well, no one really knows for how long, but Pyron said you can sometimes find arrowheads on the leks, suggesting that the Northern Paiute, Shoshone, and other Indigenous people were hunting the big birds on those same spots long before American settlers showed up.

We were far enough away that our presence had no discernible effect on the grouse, which kept posturing and calling, loud *swishes* like drawing a bristle brush against a hard surface as they brushed their wings against their white neck ruffs, then made three *coo* calls and two explosive *Plops!* Males battle, sometimes violently, when they feel territorial lines within the lek have been crossed. The hens watch everything and make their choices accordingly. Just one or two males perform up to 86 percent of copulations on a lek, regardless of how many others are displaying. There is nothing long-term about the pairing; it's a wham-bam-thank-you-ma'am interaction lasting a few seconds, and repeated with a different female as often as every few minutes. Hopeless romantics should avoid sage-grouse leks.

The females slip off to a nest site they likely selected earlier, usually less than three miles from the lek, each one creating a shallow nest bowl lined with grasses and feathers from her breast, hidden beneath dense, tall sagebrush, where she incubates six to nine eggs. Once the chicks hatch—fluffy, eyes open, able to run and feed themselves from the get-go—the hen moves them to areas where they will find an abundance of insects like grasshoppers and succulent forbs like clover, salsify, and dandelion. The best place for a new brood is often one with a mosaic of sagebrush, wet creekside meadows, maybe some irrigated alfalfa or cropland.

There's the physical landscape an animal inhabits, and the political one. The 2015 USFWS decision not to list the sage-grouse under the ESA was based on the BLM excluding large-scale development from many areas within sagebrush country. After the court challenges to the looser Trump-era regulations, the Biden administration took a different tack, and just a week or two before my visit in early 2024, a new draft plan had been released for public comment by BLM, one covering 121 million acres in 10 states. The agency's preferred alternative was by no means the most restrictive of the bunch, but even that seems unlikely to survive a second Trump administration. Because the conifer removal has buy-in from ranchers, it may stand a better chance of continued federal support.

By late morning we'd driven through Murphy, the county seat, and turned back into the Reynolds Creek valley to meet Jerry Hoagland, a rancher and Owyhee County commissioner. The previous autumn, BLM had worked with Hoagland to conduct a prescribed burn on 2,500 acres that included a sizeable chunk of his land. If I had any preconceptions about how a rural Idaho rancher and elected Republican official would feel about issues like climate change, Hoagland quickly disabused me of them. The 90-square-mile Reynolds Creek watershed is among the oldest experimental watersheds in the country, established in 1960 by the USDA's Agricultural Research Service, where an extensive network of sensors and monitors has for decades tracked changes in temperature, precipitation, and stream flow. Hoagland noted that data from the valley were among the first to document the effects of climate change, and as we discussed conifer removal, something Hoagland started undertaking on his own in 2010, he wondered aloud whether higher atmospheric CO_2 concentrations might be "pumping up" juniper growth.

While Hoagland is an enthusiastic partner with USFWS and BLM, Owyhee County wasn't always friendly terrain for federal agencies. "When I came to US Fish and Wildlife, I was told to work on sage-grouse, but I was not to work in Owyhee County. It was a no-go area for federal employees," Pyron said as we talked with Hoagland, pausing to watch a small flock of sandhill cranes land in a nearby pasture. "The amount of distrust was incredible."

But with time that changed, in part, Hoagland said, because unlike a lot of federal and NGO staff who cycle through the rural West, parachuting into a post for a few years and then gone, people like Okeson, Pyron, and White have stayed put and built relationships. As the junipers have come out, the water has come back—spring seeps and springs that had been dry for decades that began to flow again.

Hoagland was one of several ranchers I met during my time in Owyhee County who have come around to support the BOSH Project. Sometimes that's as simple as marking the top strand of barbed wire fences with white plastic tabs hung every few feet. Fences are deadly to sage-grouse, which fly, low and fast, toward their leks before daybreak. One study in Idaho found an average of more than one fatal strike per mile of fence, mostly near leks, though the researchers admitted that was a very conservative estimate because dead birds are easy to miss and their carcasses are quickly scavenged. More and more ranchers are hanging these plastic markers, just cheap, three-inch-wide pieces of vinyl home siding trim and not unlike the visual deflectors on utility wires in Kaua'i that deter seabird collisions.

Even more promising in the long run may be "virtual fencing," GPS-enabled collars on livestock that produce a mild shock if the animal crosses a boundary the rancher has delineated on a computer. Given that "fencelines" can be changed or redrawn with a few clicks of a mouse, and that physical fencing now costs as much as $15,000 per mile to purchase and install, more and more cattle producers are at least giving virtual fencing a careful look.

The following morning we headed to Sheep Creek, a long tributary of the Bruneau River in an expanse of high desert only 10 or 15 miles north of the Nevada border, to check a different and significantly larger lek; we counted up to 33 males at any one time, but with birds constantly shifting in and out of sight behind hillocks and depressions in the land, we figured that there were at least 50 displaying in all. Four or five hen grouse flew in, precipitating even more frenzied courtship activity, and an even-louder chorus of gurgles and pops and swishes as the cock grouse reared and shook. Every so often, one of them would cross some to-us invisible line, and two males would leap into the air, feet lashing, sparring with each other.

Later, Okeson led the way back along a series of what might charitably be called roads, and then along even rougher old fuel breaks, until the ground simply fell away at the edge of the Bruneau Canyon. We were nowhere near the scenic overlook; the world was silent, empty, the sky dull under lowering clouds, the brown and gray walls of the canyon stepped and terraced down to the narrow thread of river flowing far below.

"We have to work horizon to horizon, and across generations. We manage landscapes, not postage stamps," Okeson said, as if the view across the canyon didn't make that point for him. Even the BOSH Project is still relatively small beans when stacked against the 17 million acres of sagebrush habitat in Idaho alone. Is it possible to scale it up further? "Absolutely," Jason Pyron said. "The question is, how big is big enough? We have to remember, people spent 150 years degrading this habitat. They punched the Oregon Trail through the middle of it, ran cattle with no real management for decades. You won't just get it done in 10 years."

So, what has the science shown? Does conifer removal actually work? The study that first caught my attention, one that Tim Griffiths mentioned in his Road to Recovery talk, had been conducted by Andrew C. Olsen, who at the time was a doctoral candidate at Oregon State University and now works for the Intermountain West Joint Venture in Montana, where his job is to translate conservation science into conservation action with landowners and partners. Between 2010 and 2017, roughly 34,000 acres of conifers were removed from a 98,000-acre treatment area that became his PhD study site. Using lek counts, radio telemetry, and other techniques, Olsen tracked the populations, survival rates, and movements of sage-grouse there, comparing their fate to those on an adjacent 74,000-acre control site that had remained untouched.

Olsen confirmed that overall, sage-grouse populations in the treated area rose about 12 percent, and that the grouse gravitated quickly to the newly cleared areas (other researchers had already shown that removing evergreens prompts a rapid flush of perennial grasses and forbs, which are attractive to sage-grouse). He told me he found increased survival at pretty much all stages of the sage-grouse's life cycle, from eggs in the nest to juveniles to yearlings to adults, as well as a steadily increasing use of conifer-removal areas by the birds in each of the five years after an area was cleared.

Of course, sage-grouse are not the only birds—not the only animals—in the sagebrush steppe. Another study in the same area found that the number of vesper sparrows in the treatment area increased by 38 percent, Brewer's sparrows by 55 percent, while green-tailed towhee numbers jumped 81 percent. But there was also a clear loser—the gray flycatcher, a species whose population has been increasing across the West along with the pinyons and juniper trees it prefers. On the cut areas, gray flycatcher numbers declined by 78 percent.

Seeing a decrease in the population of gray flycatchers is perhaps less worrisome than it might at first seem, because it's a species that has shown large population increases in recent years—up more than 22 percent range-wide since 2012, according to eBird status and trend data, and up more than 50 percent in that period in southern Idaho. But not every conifer-associated bird has fared as well, and some ornithologists have been eyeing the attack on the green glacier with concern that it may exacerbate problems facing one of the fastest and most mysteriously declining birds in North America, the pinyon jay.

Few birds have been as well named. Roughly the size of the better-known blue jays of the East and Steller's jays of the Western mountains, steely blue-gray and crestless, pinyon jays have co-evolved with the pinyon (or piñon) pine, a complex of half a dozen or more southwestern and Great Basin tree species that freely hybridize. Pinyon pine is an uninspiring-looking tree, small in stature, scraggly in posture, rarely more than 15 or 20 feet tall. But inside the tree's knobby cones you'll find fat, tasty pine nuts, a nutritionally and culturally vital food source for Indigenous tribes in the region, and as central to a pinyon jay's world as sagebrush is to a sage-grouse's.

A pinyon jay pries free the nuts, holding as many as 50 of the large seeds in its expandable esophageal pouch, then ferrying them for miles to traditional storage areas where the nuts are cached below ground. Pinyon jays, which are also intensely social, living in highly stable family clans, have evolved an extraordinary spatial memory, using landmarks and triangulation to remember the locations of hundreds of such seasonal caches, returning and retrieving them months later, even under deep snow. (Of course, jays die and their caches go unrecovered, thus ensuring the next generation of pinyon pines.)

Given the expanding footprint of pinyon-juniper woods in the West, you'd expect this to be salad days for the pinyon jay. Instead it has, in the words of the *Birds of the World* account for this species, experienced "steeper and more sustained population declines than any other songbird associated with pinyon–juniper woodlands." By one estimate, pinyon jays have lost about 84 percent of their population in the past 50 years, declining at an annual rate of more than 3 percent as measured by Breeding Bird Survey data.

Oddly, no one is quite sure why pinyon jays are in such rough shape. They certainly took it on the chin during Nevada's silver-mining boom in the mid- to late 19th century, when half a million acres of pinyon pine forest were cut for mine timbers and fuel for ore smelters, and again in the 1950s and early '60s, when 3 million acres of pinyon woodland in Nevada were destroyed by "chaining"—which, much as it sounds, means dragging heavy metal chains between bulldozers to rip out vast swaths of trees to create cattle pasture.

Still, if pinyon forest cover is increasing in the West, why haven't pinyon jays shown the same population increases as birds like gray flycatchers? There are a welter of possible explanations. One is that more pinyon pines doesn't necessarily equate to more productive pinyons; as pines crowd the landscape, a process known as in-fill, the competition between trees may leave them starved for resources and less able to produce an abundance of cones. Climate change seems to be playing a role, especially in the Southwest.

John Boone, the research director for the Great Basin Bird Observatory based in Reno, Nevada, is a member of the national Pinyon Jay Working Group that is trying to get to the root of the bird's problems and reverse its declines. Boone told me that while questions of climate change and in-fill may be at work, he and other experts are coalescing around evidence that the problem lies as well in the age structure of the pinyon-juniper forests of the West.

"The most productive trees are not the oldest, most mature trees," he said. Instead, pinyon pines reach their peak productivity in middle age, which means from about age 20 to about 50 or 60 years old. Beyond that their cone production drops as they get older. Once, Boone said, the pinyon pine forests would have been fairly dynamic, with a lot of disturbance and a mix of age classes hodge-podged across the landscape. Today, though, the stands are far more uniform, and older. "In other words, they're starting to age out," he said.

And this is where the kind of habitat conversion that is being trumpeted as salvation for sagebrush-obligate species like sage-grouse throws another wrench into the works. Boone's research has shown that pinyon jays spend a lot of their time in lower elevation areas where the conifer forests meet the sagebrush sea—an ecotone, where two ecosystems blend. With the emergence of the paradigm that conifer encroachment is bad and conifer removal is good, "far and away the easiest places to do that are lower elevation, relatively young stands that can be removed with relatively little effort. And what that has tended to do is to leave recovered shrub land remaining down low, denser woodland at a higher elevation, and this very unnatural, sharp border between the two," Boone told me.

To be clear, pinyon jays don't occur in the part of southwestern Idaho where the BOSH Project is taking place, so the conifer-clearance work there is having no impact on the species. But those kinds of sharp-edge boundaries between restored (from a sage-grouse perspective) shrub-steppe and pinyon-juniper forest were what I'd been seeing, and they are definitely occurring in places where pinyon jays do exist.

Boone stressed that it's possible to have what's necessary for both birds, jays and grouse, two species he's studied himself. After all, they coexisted in the Great Basin and Intermountain West for hundreds of thousands of years.

"The good news is that I believe there are almost certainly ways for vegetation management to reasonably accommodate the needs of both sage-grouse and pinyon jays," he said. The bad news is that accommodating both means rethinking the approach at a project design level, and making sure that the folks on the ground, running machinery or toting a chain saw, understand the necessary nuances.

In reporting this subject, I also spoke with people who did not want to talk on the record, much as some of the critics of ranch certifications did not. One point that came up repeatedly was concern that conifer clearance, while a legitimately helpful tool for sage-grouse conservation, was also an example of tackling an easy issue while dodging much more politically sensitive options, like making a sage-grouse ESA listing or pushing back against the most sacred of sacred cows in the West, the impact that grazing has on sagebrush habitat.

One person who was willing to go on the record saying that cutting conifers and spraying cheatgrass isn't enough was Andy J. Boyce, a research ecologist with the Smithsonian Migratory Bird Center based in north central Montana. (Boyce was one of the scientists whose work comparing grassland bird diversity between cattle- and bison-grazed land I mentioned in the previous chapter.) When I asked him about the largely voluntary steps landowners have taken through NRCS's Sage-Grouse Initiative and other conifer-removal efforts like the BOSH Project came up, he took a measured, if contrarian, stance.

"I see value to that, but I think the [sage-grouse] populations are telling us that's not enough," Boyce said. "Conifer removal is great in the right circumstances because it increases the amount of grass for cattle forage on ranching operations. So it's very palatable for ranching operators, good for the bird, we know it's good for sage-grouse. I don't think that's debatable. But there's the whole pinyon jay issue, so we have to be very, very careful that we're not applying that to areas where it's not appropriate or it's just going to rob Peter to pay Paul."

Meanwhile, Boyce pointed out, the one part of the greater sage-grouse's range where the population is stable or increasing is up where he works, on the grasslands and shrub-steppe of north central Montana. Why is that, I asked?

"Well, for one, the pressure for conversion of land in that area for human habitation and extractive industry is very low. There's no oil there. There's no natural gas, and there's very few people. There's very little pressure for conversion. The second big thing is substantially less invasion here by cheatgrass and related invasive annuals. So all of those major pressures are dramatically less in north central Montana," he replied.

I had one more day in Idaho before it was time to head home. After another predawn departure, Connor White and I headed to Jordan

Valley, a small community on the Oregon side of the border, then crossed back into Idaho into a part of the BOSH Project where a lot of the most recent work had been done.

Unlike some of the places I'd seen earlier, the evidence for the conifer clearance was still pretty raw, including big piles of dead juniper weathering and drying before it was time to burn. A lot of this landscape had been densely thicketed with conifers, White was explaining, when he went quiet, slowed, and pointed to our right. Perched on a rock a hundred yards or so off the road, with a dramatic sweep of high-desert scenery beyond, was a single male sage-grouse, all by himself, plopping and swishing to beat the band.

"Is this a known lek?" I asked.

"No, this was all juniper until we cut it last year," White said. We sat and watched the grouse for quite some time, almost feeling that such a performance demanded an audience, if only a human one.

A few hours later, on our way back out, White spotted a rancher he'd gotten to know, a fellow named Kenny—I never did catch his last name—whose spread was a long, long way from the paved road. They traded pleasantries, then White mentioned the single male grouse we'd seen.

"Yeah, my wife's been seeing six or seven of 'em there," Kenny replied. "Used to be a lek there when I was a kid, we'd see it going to school every day, but it disappeared years ago. Never knew why." Kenny is a grandfather now, so his schoolkid days were a long time ago. All the juniper stumps around that reborn lek make the reason for its disappearance pretty obvious. Now that it's open sagebrush again, the birds are back. Maybe it's a coincidence, maybe it's that generational memory that keeps these birds tethered to their leks across the years and even centuries.

Will the BOSH Project be big enough? Will all the money and effort there turn the dial for sage-grouse and all the other species that depend on this beleaguered ecosystem? Or are the skeptics right, and the money should be diverted to other approaches, backed by the muscle of a federal ESA listing? Watching that one male, throwing himself into the business of mating on a landscape reshaped, made me wonder. It was just one bird, of course, and in science, a sample size of one doesn't tell you a lot. But that male's devotion to the task, and to that place, made me suspect we shouldn't underestimate the tenacity of that bird. Or of any bird.

Twelve

Land of the Ancestors

Pete Enzoe stopped abruptly, holding up his hand and peering ahead into the dense tangle of scrubby black spruce, stunted birch, and soggy sphagnum moss through which we had been threading our way. Just out of sight ahead, something very big was thrashing the brush, but I couldn't see anything. A guttural, rumbling roar, a staccato growl so low-pitched I felt it almost as much as I heard it, came from the same direction.

"Musk ox. He's not happy we're here. And dangerous, if we get too close," Pete said.

"How close is *too* close?" I asked.

"Oh, this close," Pete said, breaking into a smile. "Maybe we'll go that way instead," he said, laughing and flicking his head in a different direction as the roar and the thrashing seemed to grow louder.

I didn't need much convincing. I'd encountered musk oxen in Alaska and knew these shaggy Ice Age survivors, with their flowing coats of long hair and curved horns that meet in the middle of the head like a helmet, could be aggressive when pushed. This irritable bull, though, was in the middle of Thaidene Nëné Indigenous Protected and Conserved Area in Canada's Northwest Territories—an exquisite gem of tundra, muskeg bog, conifer forest, and stunning cliffs hundreds of feet high that run for miles, all surrounding Great Slave Lake, the deepest lake in North America and the tenth largest freshwater body, by area, on the planet. It is a land of moose and black bears in the forests, grizzly bears and caribou on the open tundra, and musk oxen, which have colonized the region in recent decades, moving back and forth between both.

At 6.5 million acres, Thaidene Nëné (pronounced *thy-DEN-ay nen-ay*, meaning "land of the ancestors" in Dënesųłiné Yati) is huge—twice the size of Yellowstone, Yosemite, and Grand Canyon national parks combined. About half of it is designated as a national park reserve; the remainder is divided between a territorial protected area and a wildlife conservation area, all of it separated from the 20,000-square-mile Thelon Wildlife Sanctuary by a relatively short gap. Yet despite its size, Thaidene Nëné is only a blip in the immensity that is the North American boreal forest, which sprawls across 1.5 billion acres from Newfoundland to Alaska, most of it in Canada. This—not the Amazon, not the Congo—is the world's largest and most intact old-growth

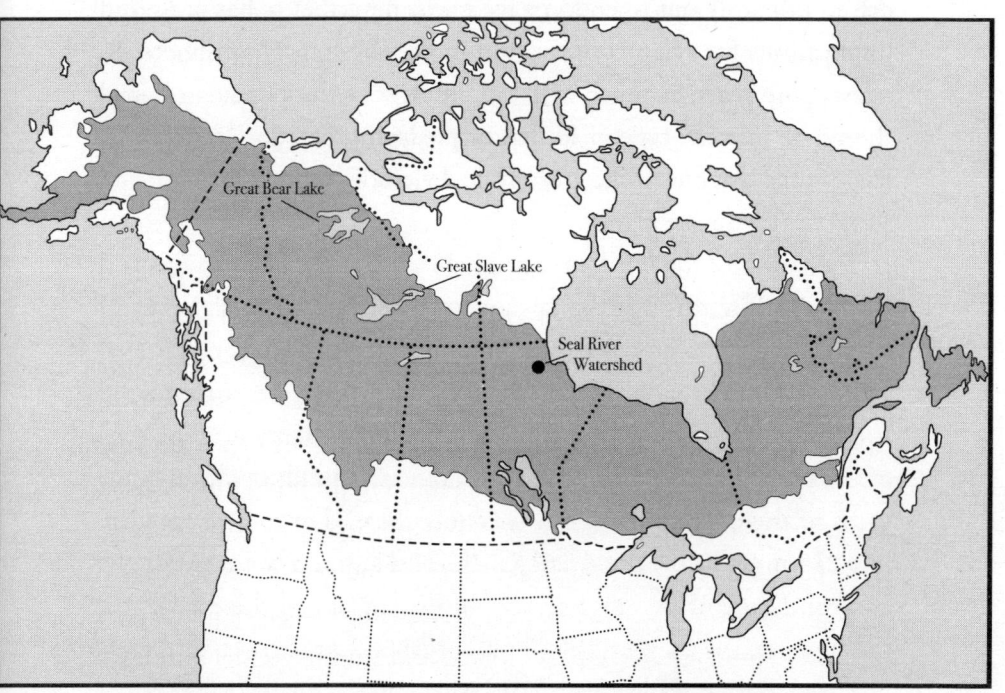

The North American boreal forest stretches from Newfoundland to Alaska, covering more than 1.5 billion acres, making it the largest intact forest on the planet.

forest, arguably the world's biggest and healthiest terrestrial ecosystem of any sort (although it also holds more than one-quarter of the planet's wetlands, so it is also one of the largest aquatic ecosystems anywhere). The North American boreal is also one of the most important expanses of bird habitat in the Northern Hemisphere, which is why conservationists have been lobbying for its protection for decades.

Now, though, a new wave of protection is sweeping across the Canadian boreal forest, building on what was already one of the most ambitious conservation initiatives in the world. After centuries of repression, the people who have lived in the boreal for 10,000 or more years are asserting their right to protect and shepherd their own land in their traditional ways—and they are doing so across hundreds of thousands of square miles, at a breathtaking scale commensurate with the boreal landscape but unmatched almost anywhere else on earth. In many respects, Thaidene Nëné helped kindle this revolution, which if not driven primarily out of concern for birds, nevertheless has profound implications for avian conservation in the Western Hemisphere. In a few more years, as much as 1 billion acres of the Canadian boreal should be in some type of formal or pledged protection, much of it Indigenous-led, one of the greatest dual victories for conservation and social justice on the planet.

The growls of the musk ox faded behind us as my companions and I followed Pete through the taiga woods. We flushed small flocks of redpolls and white-crowned sparrows; ruby-crowned kinglets scattered scolding notes at us as we passed, and a few times we encountered spruce grouse, sooty gray and brown, the famously tame "fool hen" of the North that paid us little heed even as we walked within a few yards of them. Even though it was only the end of August we were just 275 miles below the Arctic Circle, and autumn was asserting its control. Many of the migrant songbirds that nested there earlier in the summer, the warblers, swallows, thrushes, and vireos, had already departed, but waterbirds were everywhere on the vast lake—flocks of scaup, scoters, and other diving ducks, Pacific loons whose silvery gray heads and napes echoed the white frost that covered the land every morning before sunrise. Ospreys hunted whitefish and grayling in the outflow of rushing rivers, while young peregrine falcons, the crowns of their heads the burnished gold that marked them as belonging to the Arctic-nesting subspecies, chased ducks or harassed bald eagles.

Sixty years old, with a bristly gray-white beard and salt-and-pepper mustache, Pete had over the previous couple of days proven himself the ideal guide, quiet, wryly funny, and deeply knowledgeable. He is Dene, and grew up on the lands surrounding the East Arm of Great Slave Lake* near the community of Łutsël K'é, whose people had a long and antagonistic history with the idea of a national park on their ancestral lands. They'd seen how other Canadian parks and preserves, like Wood Buffalo National Park which straddles the Northwest Territories–Alberta border, and especially the Thelon Wildlife Sanctuary, had excluded Indigenous residents from terrain they had used since time immemorial, fining and jailing anyone who tried to exercise what should have been treaty-protected rights to hunt and fish.

When a national park on the East Arm was first proposed in 1969, it met a wall of opposition from the First Nations people of the region, and elected Chief Pierre Catholique refused consent. When the idea emerged again in 1982, and government officials flew to Snowdrift (as Łutsël K'é was then known) to sell the plan to the community, Chief Joe Lockhart met them at the landing strip and demanded, "Pack your maps and go." They did.

But with the growing risk of extractive industries like diamond and base metal mining, and the staking of extensive mineral claims in the region, Indigenous communities like the Łutsël K'é Dené First Nation

---

* The name "Great Slave Lake" stems from the historic term "Slavey," applied to the Dene people living around the lake. "Slavey" is an exonym, a derogatory term they never used themselves but rather was used by Cree to the south who at one time raided and occasionally captured them. English and French colonizers adopted the term from their Cree allies. Not surprisingly, there is a growing sense among the Dene living along it that the lake's name should be changed, but which of several Indigenous names—*Tu Nedhé* in Dënesųłiné Yati, for example, or *Tucho* in Dehcho Dene—should be chosen is unclear.

(LKDFN) realized their best chance of preserving their land, spiritually important sites, and their millennia-old culture of hunting, fishing, trapping, and foraging lay in brokering unprecedented agreements with the same federal and territorial governments that had for so long usurped Native lands and rights. It required almost two decades, but by 2019 those agreements were in place, and Thaidene Nëné became a reality. It, in turn, has helped spark a movement across Canada, with dozens of other First Nations communities asserting sovereignty over their traditional lands through similar Indigenous Protected and Conserved Areas (IPCAs). While the Canadian government only formally recognizes a few IPCAs, including Thaidene Nëné, some Indigenous communities are not waiting for federal blessing; many are declaring them based on their own, inherent legal authority as the original stewards of the land.

Even though this wasn't my first trip to the Northwest Territories, it remains hard for me to wrap my head around the scale and, espe-

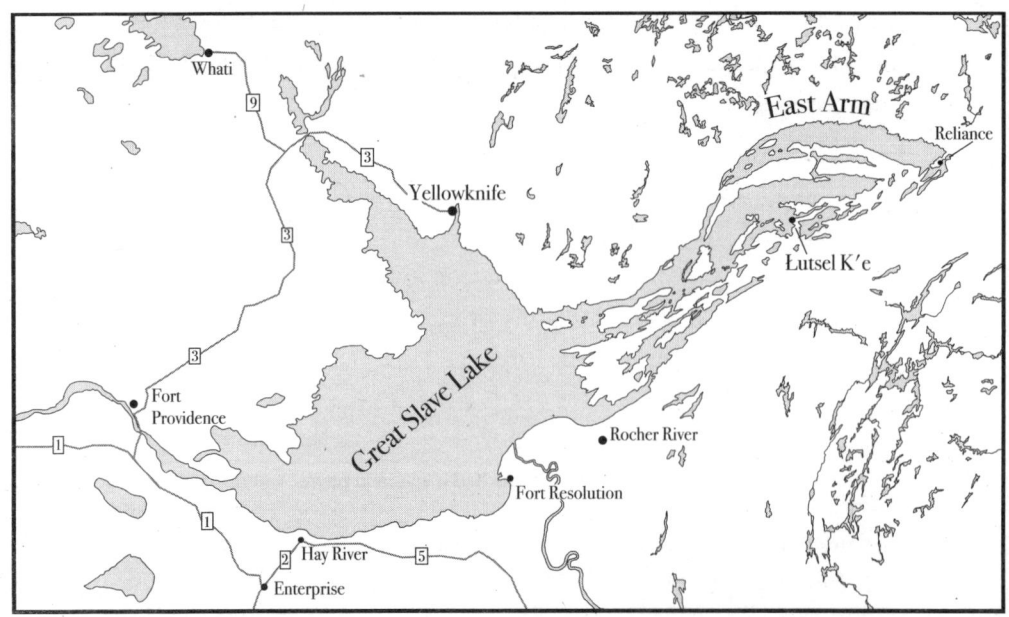

Indigenous communities on the East Arm of Great Slave Lake resisted the idea of a national park for generations, until they realized it was their best hope of protecting their land and culture.

cially from an American perspective, the sheer emptiness of the land. The NWT, as it's often shorthanded, is some 442,000 square miles with just 40,000 or so people, meaning it's fully two-thirds the size of Alaska but with just 5 percent of Alaska's population, fully half of those folks living in the territorial capital of Yellowknife.

Only 350 people live year-round in Łutsël K'é, at the mouth of the nearby Snowdrift River, Dene people who still follow a seasonal round of movement across the tundra and forest—hunting caribou in the autumn, trapping for fur through the winter, and fishing once the ice leaves the lake in summer. The village sits at the end of a long peninsula jutting west into Great Slave Lake, near a historic seasonal fishing location; in fact, *łutsël k'é* means "place of the little fish," referring to ciscoes, a small species of native whitefish traditionally speared there.

I was joining a group of staff and board members from two organizations that had been at the forefront of the fight for the boreal forest for decades. One was the Pew Charitable Trust's International Boreal Conservation Campaign (IBCC), which grew out of a recognition in the late 1990s that the Canadian boreal forest represented one of the best opportunities in the world to do old-growth forest conservation at a globally significant scale. Pew partnered with Ducks Unlimited and Ducks Unlimited Canada, as well as Canadian bird conservation organizations and the National Audubon Society, setting a goal to protect at least 50 percent of the remaining intact boreal, with managed and sustainable development in the remainder. This evolved into a roadmap for action called the Canadian Boreal Conservation Framework (CBCF), envisioning a network of immense, interconnected protected areas, designated through a cooperative process involving First Nations communities, government ministries, conservation groups, and representatives of extractive industries.

Another crucial collaborator in the CBCF was the Boreal Songbird Initiative, a US-based NGO that started in 2002 as a project within Ducks Unlimited, and became an independent nonprofit in its own right in 2004, focused on educating North Americans about the importance of the great northern forest to birds. That importance is almost impossible to overstate. More than 300 species, which by the end of the summer breeding season number an estimated 3 billion to 5 billion individuals, call the boreal zone home. For one-third of those species, the boreal forest's mix of conifers and hardwoods, tundra, bog, and millions of glacier-dug lakes and ponds is their primary habitat—birds like Tennessee and Connecticut warblers, 97 percent and 91 percent of whose global population, respectively, nest in the boreal. So do 93 percent of all red-necked grebes, 84 percent of black scoters, 94 percent of lesser yellowlegs, 86 percent of Philadelphia vireos, 73 percent of Swainson's thrushes, and 85 percent of North America's white-winged crossbills.

The IBCC and other outside groups may have provided some of the initial impetus for landscape-sized conservation. But in the end, protection of the Land of the Ancestors was driven entirely by the people who have lived there for millennia.

I'd visited the NWT once before, in 2008 at the invitation of Jeff Wells, a Maine-based biologist whom I'd known for years, and who was then BSI's senior scientist. I and a couple of other bird writers joined Jeff to learn more about the CBCF, which was at that point five years old and making good strides toward its goals. Over the course of a week, as we traveled from Yellowknife north to the Sahtú Dene community of Délı̨nę on Great Bear Lake, less than 100 miles below the Arctic Circle, and then still farther north along the lower Mackenzie River, I grappled for the first time with the enormity of the land and its importance for birds.

Nor was I the only one. My old friend and legendary birder Pete Dunne, the former director of the Cape May Bird Observatory, spent the 90-minute flight to Délı̨nę trying to grasp what he was seeing below. "It was like we were flying a survey transect," he said of the 350-mile journey over innumerable wetlands and ponds. "Figure even if it was only one pair of loons for every two or three lakes, that's a lot of loons," he said. "Plus, how many blackpoll warbler territories did we cross? Two thousand? Ten thousand? Twenty thousand? That's just one species of warbler. It's mind-blowing."

So was the birdlife we saw at Délı̨nę, as we prowled the edges of the immense lake the next morning; it was early August but we were grateful for our coats and gloves in the cold. The shoreline shrubs and thickets, purple with masses of blooming fireweed, were frantic with small birds, mostly yellow-rumped warblers ("butterbutts," as birders call them), redpolls, American tree sparrows, and white-crowned sparrows, feeding after a night of migration. A gull-like parasitic jaeger—the word is German for "hunter," a perfect name for this group of burly, aggressive, superlative predators and pirates—chased a lesser yellowlegs off the lake and literally between Pete's legs, flaring up just a few yards short with what I can only describe as a seriously malevolent glare.

The Canadian boreal forest is the font from which much of North America's avian riches flow. Now I was back in the NWT again, also tagging along on a BSI trip, though unfortunately without Jeff, now vice president of boreal conservation for the National Audubon Society. He was supposed to have come with his son, but to their great disappointment, they had tested positive for Covid-19 just before departure and had wisely remained behind.

Even without Jeff, our group of about a dozen included people who had been in the trenches of conservation in the North for decades. Steve Kallick, now in charge of international conservation for the Resources Legacy Fund, was the founding director of the IBCC. Steve is an expert in conservation policy and law who cut his teeth as an environmental attorney working in Alaska on issues like preserving the coastal rain forest, and who later worked on conservation campaigns from the Australian Outback to Chilean Patagonia.

Also in the group was Maggie Wente, a member of Serpent River First Nation in Ontario and a renowned attorney specializing in Indigenous affairs, along with Fritz Reid, a BSI emeritus board member who in a few months' time would retire after a storied career as director of boreal and Arctic conservation for Ducks Unlimited, where he was a crucial cog in Northlands conservation efforts like Thaidene Nëné. In addition to Lane Nothman, who had been the managing director of BSI for a decade, we were joined by several staff including IBCC communications director Emily Cousins and BSI/IBCC coordinator Jen Cerulli.

Access to Łutsël K'é, the only permanent community on the immense East Arm of Great Slave Lake, is the daily shuttle flight in a four-engine turboprop. Only moments after takeoff, Yellowknife and its surroundings dropped away, replaced by a seemingly endless expanse of subarctic landscape on which I could see almost no sign of human occupation for the next 45 minutes until we landed on the gravel strip near the community. A chilly wind was whipping as we deplaned and gathered our gear, piling into big motorboats and zipping around a spit of land to Frontier Lodge, a previously white-owned fishing camp now managed by the community where we would be staying.

Although we were all interested in birds, the lodge specializes in fishing, for which Great Slave Lake is renowned, especially its justifiably famous trophy lake trout, which can reach weights of 40 pounds or more. One wall of the dining room held a white board on which the heaviest lake trout of the season were being tallied, fish ranging up to 27 pounds. It didn't take much convincing for most of us to pay for a five-day NWT fishing license, and after a quick lunch we headed out two-by-two with guides in a flotilla of boats.

By luck, Steve Kallick and I were paired up with Pete Enzoe as our guide. It was a sparkling clear day, an almost cobalt-blue sky layered with popcorn clouds, the waters of the huge lake calm and reflective. Pete opened the throttle, and we raced west at speed for half an hour, grateful for a couple of layers of fleece and Gore-tex against the wind chill despite the bright sun, only peeling off our jackets when Pete throttled back the outboard and had us begin trolling slowly, our fishing rods trailing wobbling metal spoons some distance behind the boat. The fish started to hit almost immediately, and Steve soon hoisted from the water a 30-inch-long, 20-pound lake trout, held it for a quick photo, then released it. Except for a couple of much smaller trout kept each day for a group shore lunch, the fishing at the lodge is strictly catch-and-release, a necessity in these cold subarctic waters where fish growth is painfully slow; the largest of Great Slave's lake trout could easily be a century or more old, too precious to kill for a trophy. No sooner had Steve's fish slid back down into the dark water than I had a slam on my rod, and an equally nice laker was fighting me to the surface, its dark green body mottled with paler dots and speckles, its pectoral fins flashing orange. Pete netted it and slipped the barbless hook from its mouth, remarking that it was "another little one."

Frankly, it was hard to keep our minds on the fishing, because the scenery was, in the original sense of the word, awesome. We motored along *Tthegéré Nué,* known in English as Redcliff Island, one of Thaidene Nëné's iconic landscapes, a 15-mile-long lancehead whose nearly 600-foot-high, brick-orange cliffs plunge without preamble into the cold, deep waters; the boat that Fritz and a buddy were in, trolling ahead of us, provided breathtaking scale, appearing as a speck beneath the looming wall. Later, we pulled the boats into a quiet cove, where stands of fireweed growing from the lichen-covered rock were starting to go to seed. One of the other boats had encountered a black bear along the lakeshore; several others had seen small herds of musk oxen. It was a chance for people who had spent decades trying to save boreal landscapes to savor one of the finest.

But this trip was also a swan song for the International Boreal Conservation Campaign. After more than 20 years of fighting to protect the Canadian boreal, the IBCC was dissolving—not because the battle was won, but because there were better hands in which to place the torch. The Indigenous Leadership Initiative, which in 2013 became the first Native-led conservation organization in Canada, was helped into existence with funding and guidance from Pew, the IBCC, DU, and others. By the time of our visit to Thaidene Nëné in 2022, the ILI was preparing to assume primary responsibility for pushing ahead with the overall boreal campaign, including aiding in the creation of new IPCAs, moving from a partner in a largely white-led movement to its rightful leader. In 2023, it absorbed into itself many of the staff, programming aspects, and funding streams that had flowed for years through the Pew Charitable Trusts and IBCC. Maggie Wente, who was with our group, would serve as the ILI board's chair.

It was the next and perhaps most fitting step in the long and increasingly successful fight to permanently protect not just the boreal landscape, but the cultures that evolved with it and which have stewarded it for millennia. And not only the boreal. Across Canada, from the deep spruce woods of Manitoba to the Arctic, and from the temperate rain forests of the British Columbian coast to the shores of the Atlantic, Indigenous communities are increasingly taking control of their ancestral lands. The concept of IPCAs took a major step forward thanks to a seminal 2018 report, *We Rise Together*, by the Indigenous Circle of Experts (ICE), charged with helping Canada meet its obligations for land protection under global biodiversity goals. As envisioned by the circle, IPCAs are "lands and waters where Indigenous governments have the primary role in protecting and conserving ecosystems through Indigenous laws, governance and knowledge systems."

IPCAs vary in terms of governance and management. Some are established based solely on local Indigenous authority, while others, like Thaidene Nëné in the NWT and Gwaii Haana National Park Reserve on Haida Gwaii in British Columbia, have been established jointly between government agencies and Indigenous nations. Regardless of the underlying structure, IPCAs are all Indigenous-led, focused on long-term conservation and speaking directly to empowering Indigenous communities.

IPCAs are also an increasingly global phenomenon, because conservationists have, much too late, recognized that something like 80 percent of the planet's remaining biodiversity is on lands controlled by Indigenous communities, and that biological richness on Indigenous-managed lands in places like Australia, Brazil, and Canada equals or exceeds that on governmentally designated protected areas. IPCAs, or designations similar to them, are formalizing Indigenous protection from Latin America to Southeast Asia. In Australia, whose Indigenous communities began asserting local control beginning in the 1990s, there were by 2025 more than 90 Indigenous Protected Areas covering more than 400,000 square miles of land. Nor is the idea of Indigenous-led conservation an entirely new one in the Western Hemisphere, although the scope and pace at which progress is occurring is definitely novel. In 1995, the Indigenous Izoceño-Guaraní people of southern Bolivia were instrumental in creating, and continue to partner in managing, the 13,000-square-mile Kaa-Iya del Gran Chaco National Park, and in 2002, the Inga people of Caquetá in southwestern Colombia succeeded in establishing the 187,000-acre Alto Fragua Indi Wasi National Park.

It had been an exciting introduction to Thaidene Nëné. Evening found us back at the lodge, well fed and, even if no one had posted a record lake trout on the whiteboard, looking forward to the days to come. We watched the sunset from the edge of the bay, gathered around a crackling fire that warmed our hands and shins in the sharp breeze, with pairs of loons and big flights of ducks crisscrossing the lake as the orange sky deepened and eventually dimmed.

Fishing was fun, and next morning each two-person boat quickly landed the pair of smallish trout that would provide our lunches, but we were all anxious to see more of the land. Because Frontier Lodge is first and foremost an angling destination, the guides, too, seemed happy to have a break in the routine that kept them in their boats day after day, so we all motored up Portage Bay where a traditional canoe-carry route crosses a narrow isthmus to Stark Lake. Pete led us overland through spruce and poplar forest, following what at times was a barely discernible trail, and at others just plain bushwhacking. That's where we encountered the hidden, grumbling musk ox, which we successfully skirted without further complications. We found ourselves fighting squishy, sphagnum soil and ankle-grabbing shrubs and roots, but before long we popped out into the open along Stark Lake, *Tthe Káljka Tué* in Dene. The shoreline was shingled with slabs of flat, red, shalely rock, some of which someone had stacked to form an inuksuk, one of the human-like figures traditionally built by more northerly peoples like the Inuit as landscape markers and guideposts.

By the time we hiked back to the boats, the guides who had stayed behind had built a fire, laid a bed of spruce boughs beside it, and were filleting the lake trout, cutting the deep orange-red flesh into sizeable chunks. These went into a heavy cast-iron skillet full of sizzling hot oil, while another was full to overflowing with onions and potatoes. Cans of baked beans bubbled around the edges of the fire. As the fish were done, the pieces were transferred to the spruce boughs to cool, and soon we were piling trout, beans, and taters on rugged old plastic trays, and tucking in with the kind of appetite that comes from fresh air and good food in a beautiful setting.

Another sunset, another crackling fire, and a shake on the shoulder that woke me at one o'clock in the morning. I stumbled outside in the cold dark and found that the sky, too, was on fire—one of the most vivid auroras I've ever seen was dancing and shimmering overhead. We were so far north that the brightest curtains of green, red, and white light were actually high in the southern sky.

Although the Dene had battled against the idea of a national park for years, by the 1990s, diamond mining had begun north of Łutsël K'é, and mineral claims were being staked across traditional Dene territory. In 2000, then-Chief Felix Lockhart approached Canada about a park reserve that would allow the continued traditional uses of the land.

One of the thorniest issues facing both the community and the government—indeed, facing anyone trying to pursue land conservation in much of Canada—is that of land ownership. In a nutshell, much of the land in question is considered by the Canadian government to be Crown land under government control, while the Indigenous communities, hearkening back to treaties signed at the turn of the 20th century, firmly believe it is theirs.

That fundamental disagreement stood in the way of progress for many years, until those on both sides made a remarkably simple decision, Steve Kallick told me. Many agreements, including that for Thaidene Nëné, sidestep the issue. "They just agree to disagree about that. They don't fight about who owns the land, they just agree on how it's going to be managed under Indigenous leadership—and if they do that, it almost doesn't matter who owns it," Steve said. This was a tactic borrowed from fights over land sovereignty between the government and First Nations on Haida Gwaii in British Columbia many years ago, he said, and one that is being adopted across Canada as IPCAs are established.

The man who actually led the Indigenous negotiations over establishing Thaidene Nëné confirmed Steve's interpretation. "That's a hundred percent accurate," Steven Nitah told me. The first line of the agreement says the Dene claim jurisdiction. The second line says the government claims jurisdiction. "The third line is, we agree to disagree on the top first two, but we agree that the area of interest is important enough for all of us that we're going to manage it together," he said.

Nitah, who served in the Northwest Territories Legislative Assembly in the early 2000s and was elected chief of Łutsël K'é in 2008, became the lead negotiator for the community during the long process of hammering out the agreements that led to Thaidene Nëné National Park Reserve. He grew up living a very traditional lifestyle; his mother was just 18 when he was born in 1967 in Yellowknife, and rather than halt her education, her parents took in and formally adopted the boy, who was carried by dogsled from the capital to the community then known as Snowdrift. He grew up on the land, not knowing English until kindergarten, living with and learning from his grandparents and other elders who had avoided the cultural assimilation and abuse of the government residential schools, retaining their traditional knowledge.

"We were living the old ways, following the seasons," he told me. "Fall was when you start to prepare for the winter trapping season for fur-bearing animals like marten, lynx, mink, wolverines. So you're going south or east into the boreal in mid-October, and come back [to the community] for a brief period for Christmas and back out there until pretty much March. And then you move closer to the Great Slave Lake for the spring beaver and muskrat trapping season, and then go back to the community to the south when the ice is melting. And then early July, as the ice is starting to recede from the shorelines, we started making our way east on Great Slave Lake and into the tundra to harvest some caribou to bring back to the community until mid- to late August. And then we do some fishing and [foraging] and then repeat the process."

When I said that sounded like a wonderful life, Nitah agreed—to a point. "Well, it was, in retrospect, back then," he said, laughing. "But that's a pretty lonely upbringing. A lot of times I was the only kid in camp."

Leaders in Snowdrift/Łutsël K'é had learned a number of cautionary lessons from the experiences of Indigenous nations elsewhere in Canada when national parks and other formally protected areas were declared, Nitah explained—not just Wood Buffalo National Park and Thelon Game Sanctuary, where Indigenous groups were banned in the 1920s, but Pacific Rim National Park on Vancouver Island, British Columbia, which in the 1970s and '80s took control away from the Nuu-chah-nulth First Nation. Łutsël K'é remained adamantly opposed to an East Arm National Park for generations.

"So what changed the community's willingness to accept some sort of government designation on the land?" I asked.

"Well, in 1982 Canada created its own constitution and broke away from England officially, and as part of that process, they recognized Aboriginal and treaty rights within Section 35 of the Constitution," Nitah said. The language that begins Section 35 seems unambiguous: "The existing aboriginal and treaty rights of the aboriginal peoples of Canada are hereby recognized and affirmed." But it took almost two decades of Supreme Court of Canada cases to make the ramifications of that section clear, and provide enough comfort for the Łutsël K'é Dene First Nation to move ahead.

First, they needed a counterpart. "When we started, we didn't know we were going to partner with Parks Canada. We researched best practices globally and in Canada, and really talked about why it is that we wanted to create a protected area. What do we want to do there? The size of the area also informed the need for legislation that's respected by industry. We wanted to create a conservation economy, and we wanted hard and strong protection. So for that reason, Parks Canada, the national parks agency, became an attractive partner."

"Even though Canada had taken the position that the treaties nullified any jurisdiction we had on our lands, we didn't believe that. Our position is that we agreed to share the lands, share the responsibility and management of the lands and everything on it, and share the benefits," he said.

As immense as Thaidene Nëné is, it was originally meant to be significantly larger. As initially mapped out, it resembled a person lying with outstretched arms and legs, its head toward the northeast not far from the Thelon Game Sanctuary boundary. As negotiations progressed, the government of the Northwest Territories pushed back hard against including the two "arms," the one to the northeast believed to hold diamonds, the one to the southwest rich in base metals. There were also conflicts with other Indigenous groups, notably the North Slave Métis Alliance, which was not part of the establishing agreement and asserts traditional claims to land in the north of Thaidene Nëné, protesting that the park reserve infringes on their rights to use the land.*

With time, these two areas and a bit of a third were amputated, bringing the total area of the Thaidene Nëné Indigenous Protected Area from roughly 8.3 million acres to 6.5 million acres. Within that vast area are lands with three formal designations: the 3.4-million-acre national park reserve, which is managed by the signatory Indigenous communities: the LKDFN, the Northwest Territory Métis Nation,

---

* The Métis are, with First Nations and the Inuit, one of three formally recognized Indigenous groups in Canada. They trace their ancestry back to the 18th-century fur trade and the intermarriage of European (primarily British and French) and Indigenous (primarily Cree) peoples.

Deninu Kųę First Nation, and Yellowknives Dene First Nation, in partnership with Parks Canada; a 2.2-million-acre territorial protected area managed by those communities in collaboration with the NWT government; and the northernmost portion closest to Thelon Game Sanctuary, covering about 77,000 acres, which is a wildlife conservation area managed under Northwest Territories regulations.

In the end, Łutsël K'é held a plebiscite in 2019 asking whether the agreement should be ratified. All community residents, about 1,000 people including those then living outside the village, could participate. It passed with 89 percent in favor. Once the agreement was ratified, with a signing ceremony in Łutsël K'é on Aug. 21, 2019, attended by representatives of the Canadian and territorial governments, the work of implementing the vision for the protected area began.*

"We started with our value systems and our knowledge systems," Steven Nitah said. "We tried to incorporate the different ecosystems within Thaidene Nëné, our relationship with the different keystone species and what their needs were, represented in our defined areas. The wildlife conservation area is very unique to the sense that the language in the establishment [agreement] speaks to how the caribou will tell us if that conservation area is needed. So along with Western science and traditional knowledge, we give voice to caribou."

"What have the caribou been telling you?" I asked.

"The caribou have been telling us they need that space," Nitah said. "And now that it's established, any type of research that's going to be done in Thaidene Nëné will be approached from indigenous science *and* Western science perspectives. So we'll be asking questions, along with questions that'll be asked from the Western perspective. It's really working to align knowledge systems and understandings, which to me is what the original treaty relationship was supposed to have generated."

The all-Indigenous group that oversees the park reserve is called

---

* The formal agreement with the Yellowknives Dene First Nation was signed in 2020.

Thaidene Nëné xá dá yáłti — "Those Who Speak for Thaidene Nëné." Nitah was at pains to make two points to me. One is that all the members, who are drawn from the First Nations and Metís groups whose ancestral lands encompassed the park, agree to set aside their personal loyalties and represent, not the communities that selected them, but the land. And they will do so under what Nitah likes to call not a land use or management plan, but a relationship plan.

"We're not going to be managing Thaidene Nëné. We manage the people who are maintaining the relationship or experiencing a relationship with Thaidene Nëné. We recognize that we don't have the power to manage Thaidene Nëné to a point at scale. What we could do is manage ourselves and manage others' interests in it," he said. Relationship plans are becoming more the norm for IPCAs in the Canadian boreal forest.

During our time on Great Slave Lake, we met some of the folks directly involved in navigating those relationships. One afternoon we boated around to Łutsël K'é, arriving as Chase and Rupert, two of the then-five members of Ni Hat'ni Dene, "Watchers of the Land," the fulltime Indigenous Land Guardians, pulled up to the launch towing the guardians' patrol boat, emblazoned with the community logo, a stylized eagle plucking a fish from the water. The Ni Hat'ni Dene, established in 2008, handle a wide array of tasks—interacting with visitors, monitoring water quality and fish populations in the summer, conducting caribou surveys and collecting hunting data in winter, using generations of traditional knowledge of living on the land. There is also a youth guardian program designed to share those skills with fresh generations.

At the park reserve office we met Iris Catholique, who is the manager—her official title, relationship plan or not—of Thaidene Nëné, a position she's held since 2019, although she had become involved years earlier in the long effort to protect the region. Iris radiated a sense of barely contained, slightly distracted energy, which seemed understandable as she rattled off a litany of recent and impending projects she and her staff were shepherding, including organizing a three-week excursion out on the land for the Ni Hat'ni Dene guardians. She cued up a PowerPoint as our group crowded around a conference table and reviewed the history of proposals for a park on the East Arm, as well as one of the most critical aspects of the establishment process, the creation of the $30 million (Canadian) Thaidene Nëné Trust Fund, half of which came from the LKDFN and its supporters, and half from the government of Canada. With interest and investments, the trust fund covers the roughly $1 million annual operating budget of the reserve, including the Ni Hat'ni Dene guardians.

Steven Nitah served as a member of the Indigenous Council of Experts that produced the 2018 *We Rise Together* report that was so influential in the drive for Indigenous-led land conservation. "So Thaidene Nëné has its hands all over that report and the subsequent Indigenous Protected and Conserved Areas that have been declared across the country. Now there's over a hundred today," he said.

Those IPCAs vary greatly in the landscapes they protect, the Indigenous communities at their hearts, and their approaches to establishment, but most share one commonality—they are vast. Edéhzhíe Protected Area northwest of Great Slave Lake, established as an IPCA in 2018 by the Dehcho First Nation and designated a National Wildlife Area in 2022 by the NWT government, encompasses more than 3.5 million acres. The Ts'udé Niliné Tueyata Indigenous protected area near Fort Good Hope in the northern Northwest Territories covers 2.4 million acres, and was established in 2019 under an agreement between five First Nations and Métis governments and that of the NWT under its Protected Areas Act. Together with Thaidene Nëné, these three IPCAs make up an area larger than the country of Costa Rica, but another five candidate areas in the Northwest Territories are waiting in the wings, potential IPCAs totaling nearly 5.8 million acres that are in some stage of negotiation between the NWT territorial government and the Indigenous nations who have traditionally used them.

That's just the Northwest Territories. On what is now Cape Breton Island in Nova Scotia, the Mi'kmaw (L'nu) have been working for years to protect culturally sacred locations on a 12,000-acre proposed

IPCA. In the northeastern Yukon, four First Nations agreed in 2019 to co-lead with the territorial government a 2019 land use plan for the 26,000-square-mile Teetł'it Gwinjik (Peel River) watershed that straddles the Arctic Circle. In 2024, the First Nation of Nacho Nyak Dun and the Gwich'in Tribal Council, Parks Canada, and the government of the Yukon agreed to work on a feasibility study to examine the possibility of designating about 1,110 square miles of the First Nations' territory in the watershed as a new national park.

In northern British Columbia the Kaska Dena—whose traditional territory encompassed 92,000 square miles across British Columbia, the southern Yukon, and parts of the western Northwest Territories—are working through the Dena Kayeh Institute to establish Dene K'éh Kusān, an IPCA protecting the last completely pristine, intact wilderness in the province, a 9.8-million-acre area the size of Switzerland with no roads, power lines, mines, or other development. Dene K'éh Kusān, which evocatively means "It will always be there," covers parts of five ecosystems, contains 10 watersheds within the Mackenzie River basin, and holds some of the only remaining healthy woodland caribou herds in British Columbia, as well as serving as nesting grounds or migratory habitat for multitudes of northern birds. It would link more than a dozen provincial protected areas, as well as close a key gap in the Yellowstone to Yukon (Y2Y) conservation initiative.

In 2023, the governments of Canada and British Columbia signed a tripartite agreement with the First Nations Leadership Council recognizing Indigenous leadership in stewarding ecosystems in British Columbia, which calls for the protection of 3.2 million acres of high-priority old-growth forest, the restoration of at least 345,000 acres of wildlife habitat, and work to specifically restore populations of northern spotted owls and imperiled boreal caribou herds. The federal government pledged at least $500 million (Canadian) over the life of the agreement, matching a commitment from the government of British Columbia.

Still, some of the most exciting progress continues to be made in the Northwest Territories. In 2024, after a process guided by the ILI, an agreement was signed between 22 Indigenous governments in the NWT, the governments of Canada and the Northwest Territories, the Pew Charitable Trusts, and a variety of donors including Ducks Unlimited, establishing "NWT Our Land for the Future"—what's known as a project finance for permanence (PFP) initiative. PFPs are new and innovative funding mechanisms that seek to overcome one of the most stubborn problems in conservation, how to pay for ongoing protection and stewardship of the land. In the case of Thaidene Nëné, the trust fund assembled when the IPCA was created provides that cushion, but NWT Our Land Our Future expands that model at a territorial scale with an initial investment of $375 million Canadian (approximately $270 million US) provided by the signatories to the agreement. NWT Our Land Our Future represents one of the largest PFPs in the world both in terms of the land area it will cover—as much as 146,000 square miles—and the magnitude of the Indigenous conservation leadership it signifies.

Piece by piece, IPCA by IPCA, it adds up. By 2023, close to 1 billion acres of the Canadian boreal forest had been ratified or pledged under some form of conservation: 429 million acres in formal protection or sustainable development areas; 175 million acres pledged to future protected areas; 273 million acres pledged to future sustainable development zones; and 103 million acres pledged to Indigenous-led land use in Manitoba alone.

That's a billion acres that won't be viewed only through the lens of extractive resources to be mined or cut or drilled, or at the other extreme treated as some artificial concept of wilderness that tries to wipe away its long human connection. Instead, a billion acres as a living landscape guarded by the people who know it best, at a time when climate change and record wildfires, like those in 2023 that forced the entire city of Yellowknife to evacuate, are altering age-old rhythms.

Wildfires are only the most recent trauma that those fighting to create new Indigenous Protected and Conserved Areas have battled. In Manitoba several First Nations groups, including two communities that had to overcome an appalling history of past abuses at the hands of the Canadian and provincial governments, are now asserting their right to protect their ancestral land, a pristine watershed the size of Nova Scotia that includes the last undammed river in the province, and fully reclaim the sovereignty that had once been stripped from them.

"This looks just like home!"

Lianna Anderson, with a big smile on her face, was standing on a boardwalk that juts out into a boggy wetland and small pond in Hidden Valley Nature Center in Jefferson, Maine, almost 1,600 miles from her home in northern Manitoba. But she was right; the habitat around the bog—tamaracks and scraggly black spruces like trees from a Dr. Seuss book, mats of sphagnum moss out of which grew lovely grass-pink orchids and a variety of boreal shrubs like leatherleaf, Labrador tea, and sheep laurel, all in bloom—was much the same as one can find hundreds of miles to the north in the heart of the Canadian boreal zone.

Lianna is a Land Guardian from the O-Pipon-Na-Piwin Cree Nation, one of four First Nations whose traditional territories include parts of the 200-mile-long watershed of the Seal River, which itself encompasses some 12 million acres stretching from deep, clear inland lakes to the salty tidal waters of Hudson Bay near Churchill. Only a single permanent community of about 400 people, Tadoule Lake, exists within the entirety of the watershed, which is also the traditional territory for the Sayisi Dene First Nation, Northlands Denesuline First Nation, and Barren Lands First Nation. The four nations have banded together as the Seal River Watershed Alliance, and are close to creating one of the biggest and most important IPCAs in Canada, one that will be almost twice the size of Thaidene Nëné.

It had been a stressful trip for Lianna and the other Land Guardians who were spending a week at the Hog Island Audubon Camp in Maine, arranged by Jeff Wells, their visit by luck overlapping an adult field ornithology session I was directing. Not long after Lianna and fellow guardians Chaz Collier and Darryn Yassie arrived in June

2023, Lianna received word that wildfires were burning toward her community, South Indian Lake. I can only imagine how hard it must have been to be away at such a time, trying to focus on learning more about bird research that they could carry back to their homeland as they work to integrate Western science with traditional knowledge, while conversely—as at that day at the Hidden Valley bog—generously sharing with our group their deep knowledge about the plants and animals of the boreal ecosystem.

Seal River's importance transcends its mere size, or its largely unspoiled condition, or even its extraordinary ecological richness. There is a human component to the drive to make Seal River one of the biggest Indigenous protected areas that hearkens back to very dark days, and some of the worst effects of colonization. Both the O-Pipon-Na-Piwin Cree and the Sayisi Dene suffered in different but devastating ways. The stories of those histories are not pleasant.

For the O-Pipon-Na-Piwin Cree, the damage came in the 1970s when their lives were upended by the massive replumbing of northern

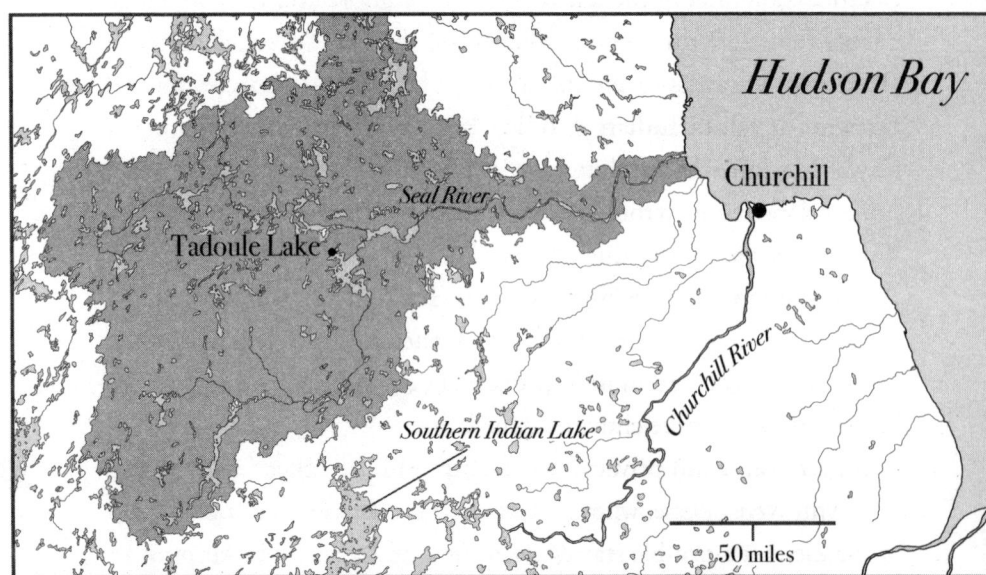

The pristine Seal River watershed in Manitoba covers 12 million acres, an area the size of Nova Scotia, with just one permanent settlement at Tadoule Lake.

Manitoba's rivers for hydroelectric power. Manitoba Hydro pushed through the Churchill River Diversion (CRD), damming the outflow of Southern Indian Lake, about 500 miles north of Winnipeg, creating a huge impoundment that would flood more than 320 square miles of land, then send almost all of the Churchill River's water through a newly blasted channel to the Nelson River to boost electrical production at five generating stations there.

Manitoba Hydro paid no mind, nor conducted any research, into either the enormous ecological consequences of its scheme, nor the equally serious social impact on the roughly 800-person Cree community of South Indian Lake whose lands would be inundated. When the CRD was completed in 1976, the level of Southern Indian Lake rose by nearly 10 feet and the northern half became stagnant and muddy, destroying one of the most productive commercial whitefish fisheries in the North, one that had provided the Cree with an average household income nearly 10 times the norm for Canadian Indigenous communities at the time.

None of this carried any weight for those far away who saw only electrical potential in the North Woods. "The communities of native people that exist throughout Manitoba—and this is equally true of all parts of Canada—have no future.... [T]he flooding of the settlements at South Indian Lake has done nothing more than move forward in time the breakup of this community and way of life," the project consultants wrote in an especially heartless 1967 letter to the development authority director.

Before the CRD was finished, the community was moved across the lake to its eastern shore, after which the original village structures were burned. The Cree found themselves assigned suburban-style tract homes unsuited to the climate, on suburban-style roads affording little of the seclusion and privacy they had once enjoyed.

For the Sayisi Dene, whose name for themselves translates as "people of the east," the trouble started with their traditional caribou hunt in the autumn of 1955. Canadian Wildlife Service biologists, witnessing the eons-old practice of men and boys from the community of Duck

Lake spearing migrating caribou at a traditional crossing site, then stashing the carcasses along the shore where they would freeze for the winter—and convinced that "waste" by the Dene was the reason caribou numbers had been falling for several years—prompted the government the following year to round up the entire community with only several hours' notice, load them into a huge amphibious plane, and dump them on a barren, wind-blown beach outside the port town of Churchill on the shores of Hudson Bay 135 miles away.

Winter was only weeks off and they had nothing but tents for shelter. It was the beginning of an 18-year nightmare that would see fully one-third of those relocated to Churchill die from disease, racist violence, alcoholism, fires, or accidents. The Sayisi Dene were later shoehorned into scantily insulated, prefab plywood cabins erected cheek-by-jowl in what was known by the military designation Camp-10. There was no water, no sewerage except slop buckets, no privacy, no access to the land or a way to support themselves. Even worse, Camp-10 sat next to a Catholic cemetery, which was a particular horror because the Dene traditionally stayed very far from burial grounds to avoid *e'thzil*, night spirits, the ghosts of those who could not pass into the afterlife and which were believed to cause illness.*

People whose lives had been shaped by seasonal preparations for hunting, fishing, and foraging that had always sustained them found themselves with nothing to do, and scant government support. They scrounged at the town dump for scraps of food or items they could barter, like copper wire they could melt down and sell. Alcoholism became a near-universal scourge. Sexual assault was common; many girls and women were gang-raped, some repeatedly. After 10 increasingly miserable years, the Dene were moved again but once more shamefully shortchanged, either by malice or negligence. The new site was boggy muskeg that never dried out, and what new homes were

---

* *Night Spirits*, the 1997 book written by survivor Ila Bussidor with Canadian Broadcasting Corporation journalist Üstün Bilgen-Reinart, offers the best, and harrowing, account of the Sayisi Dene's years in Churchill.

built (besides those shanties moved from Camp-10) were once again prefabricated models wholly unsuited to subarctic conditions, with no septic connections, and uninsulated doors and large picture windows that did nothing to keep out the subarctic cold.

Eventually they'd had enough. In the fall of 1969, a small group of Sayisi Dene, led by 50-year-old Ronnie John Bussidor, who had continued to hunt and trap with his family at North River some 20 miles across the bay, decided to reestablish their traditional lives. Bussidor led the party up the South Knife River, hunting geese and moose along the way, then overland to North Knife Lake, arriving in November of that year.

By the winter of 1971–72, 20 Dene were living at North Knife, but the site wasn't suitable for a permanent village; there were too few caribou or fish. After more prospecting, they settled on Tadoule Lake, *Ts'eouli* in Dene, on the South Seal River, deep in the forest, with plenty of fish. This time, when the government plane landed full of Dene in 1973, it was returning the people of the east to their home, not ripping them away from it. Today, Tadoule Lake is the only community within the Seal River watershed and one of the most northerly and isolated communities in Manitoba. Like the O-Pipon-Na-Piwin Cree Nation, the Sayisi Dene are at the heart of the fight to protect the land to which they fought so hard to return.

Seal River lies far enough north that it has thus far escaped Manitoba's drive for dams and hydropower. The motivating force behind the establishment of the Seal River Watershed Alliance was a man named Ernie Bussidor, who was born the year the Duck Lake community was uprooted, and who served multiple times as Sayisi Dene elected chief and councilor. He died in January 2024, mourned deeply by his community, but he lived just long enough to see an agreement signed a week or so earlier between the SRWA member nations and the governments of Manitoba and Canada, setting up a feasibility assessment for a potential Seal River national park reserve and IPCA and directing Manitoba to make interim land withdrawals to forestall further mining claims.

The land that the Seal River IPCA would protect is unusually rich in wildlife, with 48 species of mammals including moose; caribou; black, grizzly, and polar bears; and harbor seals, some of which ascend the river as much as 125 miles—hence its name. There are more than two dozen species of fish, but it is with birds that the watershed is especially blessed.

From 2021 through 2023, Land Guardians like Lianna, in cooperation with Jeff Wells and National Audubon, deployed autonomous recording units (ARUs) at 28 locations across the watershed. These sophisticated devices record even the faintest chips, calls, and songs from passing birds. Over the three years, the ARUs compiled more than 12,000 hours of recordings, which were filtered by automated sound-recognition software, although human ears and brains confirmed any rare or unusual species. The ARUs represented Western science; the choice of where to place them to best sample the watershed's birdlife depended on traditional Indigenous knowledge, informed by recommendations from elders. A previous attempt to use ARUs detected just 70 species; this time, by placing the recorders where the people who knew the land best felt they would be most useful, 102 of the estimated 250 species of birds that breed in the watershed were identified.

Those results, combined with earlier efforts using traditional techniques like aerial surveys from low-flying aircraft, paint a picture of a continentally important bird nursery. It's more than just the number of species, but the frequency and ubiquity with which many of them were detected, that makes Seal River special. For example, the calls of lesser yellowlegs were recorded by virtually every ARU listening post, suggesting that this imperiled shorebird, whose populations have declined range-wide by 60–80 percent since the 1970s, nests across almost the entirety of the watershed. And the yellowlegs were just one of two dozen species—common nighthawk, common loon, blackpoll warbler, Swainson's thrush, and more, all likewise believed to be in serious decline—that were found at the majority of test sites, evidence of the Seal River region's crucial nature for millions of boreal-nesting birds like black scoters, a species of conservation concern found there at continentally significant concentrations.

Watching over all this natural bounty are the SRWA Land Guardians like Lianna, Chaz, and Darryn. The motto behind the Land Guardians initiative, "Land Needs Guardians," may seem simple, but it is really quite profound. It recognizes that the Western ideal of "wilderness," a place apart from humanity, is not only unrealistic, but ahistoric and fundamentally unworkable. There are human footprints, fossilized in the sediments of White Sands National Park in New Mexico and mingled with the trackways of Columbian mammoths, extinct camels, dire wolves, and Harlan's giant ground sloths, that are 23,000 years old. White Sands and dozens of other archaeological sites make it clear that humans have been in the Western Hemisphere far, far longer than Western science once believed.

You cannot separate the land in the Americas—or Australia, or Southeast Asia, or Africa, or Europe—from the people who have inhabited it, shaped it, and stewarded it for eons. To a great degree, bird conservation comes down to land conservation, and what Indigenous nations in Canada are achieving at places like Thaidene Nëné and Seal River represents one of the greatest conservation victories in the history of conservation victories. It is a victory for human dignity as well.

Our last morning in Thaidene Nëné dawned cold and clear, with a cutting wind that spoke of winter on the doorstep. Fresh flocks of white-crowned sparrows, juncos, and redpolls were foraging in the fallen birch leaves by the cabins. It was easy for the guides to lure a few of us out for one last bit of fishing just a short distance from camp, where schools of Arctic grayling—among the loveliest of the far North's fish, gray torpedoes with flamboyant sailfins that glisten with blue and purple iridescence—lay in quiet eddies where the Stark River joined the lake. I've caught grayling many times in Alaska, usually smallish but pretty fish that take a fly like the trout to which they are distantly related, but these were by grayling standards behemoths, up to 20 inches long and weighing a couple of pounds, chasing barbless-hook spinners with gusto before being gently slipped back into the water.

It was a raptor day. As my companions and I cast and reeled, a steady stream of birds of prey passed overhead, making it hard to know where to keep our attention. Ospreys and bald eagles were almost always in sight, no doubt looking for an unwary grayling; a few merlins, mostly dark brown youngsters with the arrogance of teenagers everywhere, raced through, and more than once we saw an eagle or osprey swerve and roll and flash its taloned feet upwards in defense as a peregrine falcon strafed it for the sheer hell of being the fastest, most agile hunter in the sky.

All too soon we had to pack up the rods and gather up our gear, assemble at the airstrip, and climb into the Dash 7 for the flight back to Yellowknife. But as the land rolled by beneath the plane's wings, I found my perspective had shifted in important ways. In the past, as recently as a few days earlier, I'd seen it as refreshingly empty of human impact. Now, I had a somewhat clearer sense, at least to the extent that an outsider like me can have it, of the Land of the Ancestors not just as wild open space, not just (from my selfish perspective) peerless wildlife habitat on which billions of birds depend, but as a tapestry through which tens of millennia of human history—human relationships— were also woven, and whose care would increasingly be in the hands of those to whom it ultimately means the most.

Acknowledgments

The single most important acknowledgment goes to my friend and colleague Charles Duncan, who first suggested the idea for this book several years ago. "OK, so you've done a book about all the challenges facing migratory birds," Charles said after *A World on the Wing* came out. "Why don't you write a book about what's going *right* for birds?" And so I did. Thank you for seeing clearly, and perhaps presciently, how important a book about hope might be, Charles.

My most obvious debt is to the many people around the world who allowed me to drop into their lives, shadow them in the field, peer over their shoulders, and ask innumerable questions. All of them showed the patience of Job, but more importantly, all of them share a devotion to bird conservation that transcends career goals or professional duty. Almost universally they see it is a calling rather than a job, and none of us can begin to thank them sufficiently for what they're doing on behalf of birds and our shared environment.

Along the way, many people whose names did not appear in the previous pages were enormously helpful. They include another old friend and bird conservationist, Ben Olewine IV, who in turn connected me with his colleagues at BirdLife International, Richard Grimmett, senior conservation adviser, and Ian Burfield, global science coordinator, who were a starting point for many further jump-offs. In Europe and the United Kingdom, I am indebted to Laurien Holtjer in the Netherlands, head of communications for Rewilding Europe, and to Deli Saavedra in Spain, Rewilding Europe's head of landscapes, for initial discussions and putting me in touch with the right people in Romania, Ukraine, and Bulgaria.

For a better understanding of raptor conservation and persecution in the United Kingdom, and invaluable contacts there, particular thanks to my old friend Ruth Tingay, easily one of the most tireless and ferocious advocates for raptor protection in Great Britain. Ewan Weston of the Scottish Raptor Study Group was unstinting with his guidance and knowledge. Paul Morton of Birds of Poole Harbour facilitated my visit to see CJ7 and 022 and their nest. Jeremy Roberts of Cairngorms Connect gave me a deeper sense of rewilding's promises and challenges in Scotland, and I regret that last-minute circumstances forced me to cancel my planned visit there. Beyond their hospitality in hosting me at Knepp Wildlands, Isabella Tree and Charlie Burrell also made many helpful introductions on my behalf that smoothed my way enormously.

In addition to those whom I profiled or quoted in the chapters on grassland birds and sage-grouse, Olivia Cosby, codirector of Tatága (Buffalo) Research and Education Center at Aaniiih Nakoda College, Montana, helped me understand the role of bison on northern shortgrass prairie ecology, and the importance of their return to tribal lands, while Jay Carlisle of the Intermountain Bird Observatory in Idaho was generous with IBO's research on bird populations on the BOSH Project lands. A special thanks to the residents of Karval, Colorado, for so warmly welcoming me and everyone else attending the mountain plover festival. Small-town hospitality is alive and well in southeastern Colorado.

Don Lyons, director of conservation science for National Audubon's Seabird Institute, outreach instructor Sue "Seabird Sue" Schubel, and seabird sanctuary manager Paula Shannon, made it possible for me to join Steve Kress and the Eastern Egg Rock team in the middle of their very busy field season. In Hawai'i, I was particularly grateful to Lindsay Young at Pacific Rim Conservation, and to my old friend Hob Osterlund, both of whom opened many doors on Kaua'i.

I am indebted to Dr. Keith Bildstein, retired director of conservation science at Hawk Mountain, for taking a day to discuss vulture conservation at a global level, a subject few know better than Keith.

Stephen Brown and the late Shiloh Schulte at Manomet Conservation Sciences in Massachusetts, Benoit Laliberte and Eric Reed with Environment and Climate Change Canada, and Anthony Levesque in Guadeloupe all were helpful for understanding the current state of shorebird hunting in the Caribbean. Shiloh, who was a driving force in the American Oystercatcher Working Group, lost his life in 2025 in a helicopter crash in the Arctic, leaving an immense hole in North American shorebird conservation. Thanks as well to biologist Jon Altman at Cape Lookout National Seashore, North Carolina, for updated information on piping plover and American oystercatcher populations there.

I have for more than 25 years had the pleasure of being represented by one of the best literary agents in the country, Peter Matson of Sterling Lord Literistic. Peter guided me through many books, and now that he is finally (in his tenth decade!) enjoying a well-earned retirement, I am pleased to be in the very capable hands of Christopher Combemale at SLL, whose advice and guidance are proving as wise as Peter's always were. Szilvia Molnar remains SLL's ever-capable foreign rights director, the reason I have copies of my books that I cannot read.

I am proud and privileged to count W. W. Norton as my US publisher, and doubly so to have John Glusman, vice president and executive editor, as my editor. In the United Kingdom, it is a pleasure to work with Andrea Henry and the editorial staff at Picador.

My most heartfelt thanks go to my wife, Amy. How I got so lucky I do not know, but thank you, sweetie, first, last, and always.

References

One: REBOUND

5: "One swallow": Aldo Leopold, *A Sand County Almanac* (New York, NY: Ballantine Books, 1966), 19–20.

7: "The rivers from August": Councell of Virginia, *A True Declaration of the Estate of the Colonie in Virginia* (London: William Barret, 1610), 13.

8: "When passing down": Lansford W. Hastings, *The Emigrants' Guide to Oregon and California*, 1845 (Bedford, MA: Applewood Books, 1994), 99–100.

14: "a last-ditch effort": Philip Shabecoff, "Urgent Effort to Save Ducks Begins in U.S. and Canada." *New York Times*, Feb. 8, 1988. C1.

14: "realistic goal": Ibid.

Two: PAYING SUFFICIENT ATTENTION

39: "You'd get a good hawking weekend": Maurice Broun, quoted in Michael Harwood, *The View from Hawk Mountain* (New York: Charles Scribner's Sons, 1973), 89–90.

39: "thinned out": William T. Hornaday, *Thirty Years War for Wild Life* (New York: Charles Scribner's Sons, 1931), 67.

39: "kept down": Ibid.

42: "an ecological experiment": John C. Devlin, *New York Times*, April 26, 1975, p. 10.

47: "Population models predict": Audubon of Florida, "2011 Everglades Snail Kite Nesting Summary" (2011). https://fl.audubon.org/sites/default/files/audubon_prelim_evsnailkite_nestingsum_nov2011.pdf.

48: "[W]e hypothesize": Christopher E. Cattau, Julien Martin, and Wiley M. Kitchens. "Effects of an Exotic Prey Species on a Native Specialist: Example of the Snail Kite." *Biological Conservation* 143, no. 2 (2010): 513.

54: "If I'm only allowed": John Smallwood, quoted in "Something's Happening to American Kestrels," Catrin Einhorn, *New York Times*, June 5, 2023, D4.

Three: MULLET HAWKS AND THE WITCHES' WALK

70: "under suspicious circumstances": D. P. Whitfield and A. H. Fielding. *Analyses of the Fates of Satellite Tracked Golden Eagles in Scotland*. Scottish Natural Heritage Commissioned Report No. 982. Edinburgh: Scottish Natural Heritage, 2017, i.

75: "Sometime between 9 and 10 May": Royal Society for the Protection of Birds, *Birdcrime 2022*. Sandy, U.K.: 2023, 18.

75: "It would be difficult": Ibid, 19.

75: "There is no evidence": Ibid.

80: "Millions always sound": Benedict Macdonald, *Rebirding: Restoring Britain's Wildlife* (Exeter, U.K.: Pelagic Publishing, 2019), 186.

80: "Eight percent of a nation's land": Ibid, 188.

83: "if, within five years": *Grouse Moor Management Review Group: Report to the Scottish Government*. Alan Werrity, chair. Edinburgh: The Scottish Government, Dec. 2019, 58.

Four: THE NIGHTINGALES OF KNEPP

93: "a biodiverse wilderness area": Isabella Tree, *Wilding* (London: Picador, 2018), 72.

95: "It is time": Dave Foreman, quoted in David Johns, "History of Rewilding: Ideas and Practice." Nathalie Pettorelli, Sarah M. Durant, and Johan du Toit, eds. *Rewilding* (Cambridge: Cambridge University Press, 2019), 18.

96: "Risks of Pleistocene rewilding": C. Josh Donlan, Joel Berger, Carl E. Bock, Jane H. Bock, David A. Burney, James A. Estes, Dave Foreman, Paul S. Martin, Gary W. Roemer, Felisa A. Smith, Michael E. Soulé, and Harry W. Greene. "Pleistocene Rewilding: An Optimistic Agenda for Twenty-first Century Conservation." *American Naturalist* 168, no. 5 (2006): 660.

99: "Should we, perhaps": Isabella Tree, *Wilding*, 153.

107: "These trends": British Trust for Ornithology: "Turtle Dove." https://www.bto.org/understanding-birds/birdfacts/turtle-dove.

Seven: GUANO-BOMBED ON EGG ROCK

173: "Western and Eastern Egg Rock": Ralph S. Palmer, *Maine Birds* (Cambridge, MA: Bulletin of the Museum of Comparative Zoology, 1949), 292.

173: "Those six words": Stephen W. Kress and Derrick Z. Jackson, *Project Puffin: The Improbable Quest to Bring a Beloved Seabird Back to Egg Rock* (New Haven and London: Yale University Press, 2015), 29.

175: "I was pleased": Ibid, 34.

185: "Once ocean circulation": Joseph A. Stewart, Branwen Williams, Michèle LaVigne, Alan D. Wanamaker, Aaron L. Strong, Brittany Jellison, Nina M. Whitney, Diana L. Thatcher, Laura F. Robinson, Jochen Halfar, and Walter Adey. "Delayed Onset of Ocean Acidification in the Gulf of Maine." 2025. *Scientific Reports* 15, no. 1, 2039.

185: "Generally speaking": Erpur Snær Hansen, quoted in Roger Tomás, "Puffin Population Declining More Rapidly than Previously Believed." *Iceland Review*, May 22, 2023, https://www.icelandreview.com/news/puffin-population-declining-more-rapidly-than-previously-believed/

190: "ballyhoo": Kress and Jackson, 193.

Eight: ISLANDS OF SANCTUARY

210: "If you go to Attu now": Heather Renner, quoted in "Biologist Trapper Retires After Helping Transform Aleutians," Ned Rozell, University of Alaska Geophysical Institute, Nov. 22, 2017. https://www.gi.alaska.edu/alaska-science-forum/biologist-trapper-retires-after-helping-transform-aleutians

Nine: TASTES LIKE CHICKEN

224: "a single plaintive note": Alexander Wilson. *American Ornithology*, v. 5 (Philadelphia, PA: Bradford and Inskeep, 1811), 30–1.

239: "the flesh": Thomas F. DeVoe. *The Market Assistant* (New York, NY: Hurd and Houghton, 1867), 168.

239: "In the months": Ibid, 165.

Ten: PRAIRIE GHOSTS

256: "ground sluice": John Tyler, quoted in Arthur Cleveland Bent, *Life Histories of North American Shorebirds* part 2 (Washington D.C.: Smithsonian Institution, 1929), 267.
256: "My informant stated": Ibid.
256: "they don't seem": Ibid.
256: "threats to the species": U.S. Department of the Interior, U.S. Fish and Wildlife Service, *Endangered and Threatened Wildlife and Plants; Withdrawal of the Proposed Rule to List the Mountain Plover as Threatened* (Washington D.C., 2011). *Federal Register* 76:92, 27756.

Eleven: GOOD FOR THE BIRD

279: "Heath cock": Journal of William Clark, March 2, 1806. https://lewisandclarkjournals.unl.edu/item/lc.jrn.1806-03-02#n28030206.
279: "the Size of a Small turkey": Journal of William Clark, Oct. 17, 1805. https://lewisandclarkjournals.unl.edu/item/lc.jrn.1805-10-17.
279: "great abundance": Journal of William Clark, March 2, 1806. https://lewisandclarkjournals.unl.edu/item/lc.jrn.1806-03-02#n28030206.
280: "The number of Grouse": George Bird Grinnell, quoted in Charles Bendire, *Life Histories of North American Birds* (Washington, D.C.: Government Printing Office, 1892), 111.
292: "The NAWMP highlights": Kevin Doherty, David M. Theobald, John B. Bradford, Lief A. Wiechman, Geoffrey Bedrosian, Chad S. Boyd, Matthew Cahill, Peter S. Coates, Megan K. Creutzburg, Michele R. Crist, Sean P. Finn, Alexander V. Kumar, Caitlin E. Littlefield, Jeremy D. Maestas, Karen L. Prentice, Brian G. Prochazka, Thomas E. Remington, William D. Sparklin, John C. Tull, Zachary Wurtzebach, and Katherine A. Zeller. 2022. "A Sagebrush Conservation Design to Proactively Restore America's Sagebrush Biome." No. 2022-1081. Reston, VA: U.S. Geological Survey, 2.
300: "steeper and more sustained": Kristine Johnson and Russell P. Balda. "Pinyon Jay (*Gymnorhinus cyanocephalus*), version 2.0." In *Birds of the World* (P. G. Rodewald and B. K. Keeney, eds. 2020. Ithaca, NY: Cornell Lab of Ornithology). https://doi.org/10.2173/bow.pinjay.02.

Twelve: LAND OF THE ANCESTORS

316: "lands and waters": *We Rise Together*. Indigenous Circle of Experts. Government of Canada, March 2018, 5.

320: "The existing aboriginal and treaty rights": Government of Canada, Justice Laws Website. https://laws-lois.justice.gc.ca/eng/const/page-13.html#:~:text=35%20(1)%20The%20existing%20aboriginal,are%20hereby%20recognized%20and%20affirmed.&text=(2)%20In%20this%20Act%2C,and%20Métis%20peoples%20of%20Canada.

329: "The communities": May 15, 1967 letter from Van Ginkel Associates and Hedlin, Menzies and Associates Ltd. to B. Kristjanson, Manitoba Development Authority, quoted in "The Nelson River Hydroelectric Project," Know History, 2015, 33–4.

Bibliography

One: REBOUND

Abraham, Kenneth F., Robert L. Jefferies, and Robert F. Rockwell. "Goose-induced Changes in Vegetation and Land Cover between 1976 and 1997 in an Arctic Coastal Marsh." *Arctic, Antarctic, and Alpine Research* 37, no. 3 (2005): 269–75.

Anderson, Michael G. and Paul I. Padding. "The North American Approach to Waterfowl Management: Synergy of Hunting and Habitat Conservation." *International Journal of Environmental Studies* 72, no. 5 (2015): 810–29.

Arctic Goose Joint Venture. *The Greater Snow Goose: Report of the Arctic Goose Habitat Working Group*, Bruce D. J. Batt, editor. Washington, D.C. and Ottawa, Ontario: U.S. Fish and Wildlife Service and Canadian Wildlife Service, 1998.

Arctic Goose Joint Venture. "Light Goose Populations and Special Measures/Conservation Order Regulations." May 6, 2024. https://www.agjv.ca/wp-content/uploads/2024/05/AGJV-Light-Goose-CO-Talking-Points-Final-May-6-2024.pdf.

Dahl, Thomas E. *Wetlands Losses in the United States, 1780's to 1980's*. Washington, D.C.: U.S. Department of the Interior, Fish and Wildlife Service, 1990.

DeVink, Jean-Michel and Stuart Slattery. "The Great Scaup Mystery. https://www.ducks.org/conservation/waterfowl-research-science/the-great-scaup-mystery

Ducks Unlimited. "Celebrating 85 Years of Conservation: 2022 Annual Report." https://duckscdn.blob.core.windows.net/imagescontainer/landing-pages/aboutDU/AR22.pdf.

Ducks Unlimited Canada. "Pathways to Sustainability: 2022 Annual Report." https://www.ducks.ca/assets/DUC_Annual_Report-2022.pdf.

Fox, Anthony D. and Jesper Madsen. "Threatened Species to Super-abundance: The Unexpected International Implications of Successful Goose Conservation." *Ambio* 46, no. Suppl 2 (2017): 179–87.

Jefferies, Robert L., Andrew P. Jano, and Kenneth F. Abraham. "A Biotic Agent Promotes Large-scale Catastrophic Change in the Coastal Marshes of Hudson Bay." *Journal of Ecology* (2006): 234–42.

Jefferies, Robert L., R. F. Rockwell, and Kenneth F. Abraham. "Agricultural Food Subsidies, Migratory Connectivity and Large-scale Disturbance in Arctic Coastal Systems: A Case Study." *Integrative and Comparative Biology* 44, no. 2 (2004): 130–9.

Lefebvre, Josée, Gilles Gauthier, Jean-François Giroux, Austin Reed, Eric T. Reed, and Luc Bélanger. "The Greater Snow Goose *Anser caerulescens atlanticus*: Managing an Overabundant Population." *Ambio* 46 (2017): 262–74.

Madsen, Jesper, James Henty Williams, Fred A. Johnson, Ingunn M. Tombre, Sergey Dereliev, and Eckhart Kuijken. "Implementation of the First Adaptive Management Plan for a European Migratory Waterbird Population: The Case of the Svalbard Pink-footed Goose *Anser brachyrhynchus*." *Ambio* 46, no. Suppl 2 (2017): 275–89.

Merrill, Loren, J. M. Levengood, J. Conner England, J. M. Osborn, and Heath M. Hagy. "Blood Parasite Infection Linked to Condition of Spring-migrating Lesser Scaup (*Aythya affinis*)." *Canadian Journal of Zoology* 96, no. 10 (2018): 1145–52.

Mlodinow, Steven G., Thomas B. Mowbray, Fred Cooke, and Barbara Ganter. "Snow Goose (*Anser caerulescens*), version 2.0." In *Birds of the World*, Paul G. Rodewald and N. D. Sly, eds. 2024. Ithaca, NY: Cornell Lab of Ornithology. https://doi.org/10.2173/bow.snogoo.02.

North American Bird Conservation Initiative. "The State of the Birds, United States of America, 2025." stateofthebirds.org/2025

Pearce, J. M., J. Dooley, V. Patil, T. L. Sformo, B. L. Daniels, A. Greene, and J. Leafloor. "Arctic Geese of North America." NOAA Technical Report OAR ARC (2022), https://doi.org/10.25923/txnp-hb02.

Reed, Austin, Jean-François Giroux, and Gilles Gauthier. "Population Size, Productivity, Harvest and Distribution." In *The Greater Snow Goose: Report of the Arctic Goose Habitat Working Group*. Arctic Goose Joint Venture Special Publication. Washington, D.C. and Ottawa, Ontario: U.S. Fish and Wildlife Service and Canadian Wildlife Service, 1998.

Rollins, Brigit. "In the Dirt: An Introduction to Sodbuster." National

Agricultural Law Center. April 1, 2021. https://nationalaglawcenter.org/in-the-dirt-introduction-to-sodbuster/

Tozer, Douglas C., Annie M. Bracey, Giuseppe E. Fiorino, Thomas M. Gehring, Erin E. Gnass Giese, Greg P. Grabas, Robert W. Howe, Gregory J. Lawrence, Gerald J. Niemi, Bridget A. Wheelock, and Danielle M. Ethier. "Increasing Marsh Bird Abundance in Coastal Wetlands of the Great Lakes, 2011–2021, Likely Caused by Increasing Water Levels." *Ornithological Applications* 126, no. 2 (2024): duad062.

University of Nebraska Press/University of Nebraska-Lincoln Libraries-Electronic Text Center, *The Journals of the Lewis and Clark Expedition*, April 13, 1805. https://lewisandclarkjournals.unl.edu/item/lc.jrn.1805-04-13#n11041311.

U.S. Department of Agriculture Farm Service. "Conservation Reserve Program Fact Sheet." Feb. 2022. https://www.fsa.usda.gov/Assets/USDA-FSA-Public/usdafiles/FactSheets/2019/conservation-reserve_program-fact_sheet.pdf.

U.S. Department of the Interior. "Interior Department Announces More Than $50.6 Million for Wetland Conservation Projects and National Wildlife Refuges." Sept. 13, 2023. https://www.doi.gov/pressreleases/interior-department-announces-more-506-million-wetland-conservation-projects-and

U.S. Fish and Wildlife Service. "Waterfowl Population Status, 2024." U.S. Department of the Interior, Washington, D.C. 2024. https://www.fws.gov/sites/default/files/documents/2024-08/waterfowl-population-status-report-2024.pdf.

U.S. Fish and Wildlife Service, "Final 2022–23 Frameworks for Migratory Bird Hunting Regulations." *Federal Register*, July 15, 2022. https://www.federalregister.gov/documents/2022/07/15.

Vickery, Peter. *Birds of Maine*. Princeton, NJ: Princeton University Press, 2021.

Wisz, Mary S., Mikkel P. Tamstorf, Jesper Madsen, and Martin Jespersen. "Where Might the Western Svalbard Tundra be Vulnerable to Pink-footed Goose (*Anser brachyrhynchus*) Population Expansion? Clues from Species Distribution Models." *Diversity and Distributions* 14, no. 1 (2008): 26–37.

Two: PAYING SUFFICIENT ATTENTION

Allen, J. A. "Notes on the Natural History of Portions of Dakota and Montana Territories, Being the Substance of a Report to the Secretary of War on the Collections Made by the North Pacific Railroad Expedition of 1873, Gen. D. S. Stanley, Commander." In *Proceedings of the Boston Society of Natural History*, vol. 17 (1874): 33–86.

Bedichek, Roy. "The Golden Eagle in Texas." *Southwest Review* 32, no. 4 (1947): 392–8.

Bednarz, James C. and Jean-François Therrien. "The Full Annual Cycle of the American Kestrel: State of the Knowledge, Information Gaps, and Conservation Needs." *Journal of Raptor Research* 57 (2):125–30.

Bildstein, Keith L. "A Brief History of Raptor Conservation in North America," in *The State of North America's Birds of Prey*, Keith L. Bildstein, J. Smith, and Ernesto Ruelas, eds. Washington, D.C.: Nuttall Ornithological Club and American Ornithologists' Union Series in Ornithology No. 3 (2008): 5–36.

——. "Raptors as Vermin: A History of Human Attitudes Towards Pennsylvania's Birds of Prey." *Endangered Species Update* 18, no. 4 (2001): 124–8.

Blus, Lawrence J. "DDT, DDD, and DDE in Birds," in *Environmental Contaminants in Biota: Interpreting Tissue Concentrations*, 2nd ed., W. Nelson Beyer and James P. Meador, eds. Boca Raton, FL: CRC Press (2011): 425–44.

Broun, Maurice. "The Hawk Migration During the Fall of 1934, Along the Kittatinny Ridge in Pennsylvania." *The Auk* 52, no. 3 (1935): 233–48.

Cade, Tom J., James H. Enderson, Carl G. Thelander, and Clayton M. White. *Peregrine Falcon Populations: Their Management and Recovery*. Boise, ID: The Peregrine Fund, 1988.

Cava, Jenna A., Andy D. Richardson, Eugene A. Jacobs, and Robert N. Rosenfield. "Breeding Range Expansion of Taiga Merlins (*Falco columbarius columbarius*) in Wisconsin Reflects Continental Changes." *Journal of Raptor Research* 48, no. 2 (2014): 182–8.

Darby, Philip C., David J. Mellow, and Miranda L. Watford. "Food-handling Difficulties for Snail Kites Capturing Non-native Apple Snails." *Florida Field Naturalist* 35, no. 3 (2007): 79–85.

Donsker, David B. "Mississippi Kites in New Hampshire." *New Hampshire Bird Records* 27, no. 2 (2009): 34–9.

Furmansky, Dyana Z. *Rosalie Edge: Hawk of Mercy*. Athens, GA and London: University of Georgia Press, 2009.

Hornaday, William T. *Wild Life Conservation in Theory and Practice*. New Haven: Yale University Press, 1914.

Johnson, Jeff A., Alexandra Stock, Paul Juergens, Brian Mutch, and Christopher J. W. McClure. "Temporal Genetic Diversity and Effective Population Size of the Reintroduced Aplomado Falcon (*Falco femoralis*) Population in Coastal South Texas." *Journal of Raptor Research* 55, no. 2 (2021): 169–80.

Keddy-Hector, Dean P., Peter Pyle, and Michael A. Patten. "Aplomado Falcon

(*Falco femoralis*)." In *Birds of the World*, Paul G. Rodewald, ed. 2020. Ithaca, NY: Cornell Lab of Ornithology. https://doi.org/10.2173/bow.aplfal.01.

Lear, Linda. *Rachel Carson: Witness for Nature*. New York: Henry Holt and Co., 1997.

Marks, Jeffrey S., Paul Hendricks, and Daniel Casey, eds. *Birds of Montana*. Arlington, VA: Buteo Books, 2016.

Martinico, Breanna L., George K. Sage, Megan C. Gravley, Sandra L. Talbot, Ryan P. Bourbour, Angus C. Hull, Bruce A. Haak, Allen M. Fish, and Joshua M. Hull. "Population Genetics and Phylogeography of North American Merlins (*Falco columbarius*) in the Post-DDT Era." *Ibis* (2023): 1–13.

Newton, Ian. "Invited Commentary: Fifty Years of Raptor Research: Transcript of a Plenary Address Presented at the Raptor Research Foundation 50-year Anniversary Conference, Cape May, New Jersey, 17 October 2016." *Journal of Raptor Research* 51, no. 2 (2017): 95–106.

Pául, María Luisa. "The Bald Eagle Became the National Bird Thanks to One Man." Dec. 25, 2024. https://www.washingtonpost.com/nation/2024/12/20/bald-eagle-national-bird/

Petty, S. J., D. I. K. Anderson, M. Davison, B. Little, T. N. Sherratt, C. J. Thomas, and Xavier Lambin. "The Decline of Common Kestrels *Falco tinnunculus* in a Forested Area of Northern England: The Role of Predation by Northern Goshawks *Accipiter gentilis*." *Ibis* 145, no. 3 (2003): 472–83.

Poli, Caroline, Ellen P. Robertson, Julien Martin, Abby N. Powell, and Robert J. Fletcher Jr. "An Invasive Prey Provides Long-lasting Silver Spoon Effects for an Endangered Predator." *Proceedings of the Royal Society B* 289, no. 1977 (2022): 20220820.

Ratcliffe, Derek A. "The Status of the Peregrine in Great Britain." *Bird Study* 10, no. 2 (1963): 56–90.

Roalkvam, Rune. "How Effective Are Hunting Peregrines?" *Journal of Raptor Research* 19, no. 1 (1985): 27–9.

Rolek, Brian W., Leah Dunn, Benjamin Pauli, Alberto Macias-Duarte, Brian Mutch, Paul Juergens, Tim Anderson, Chris N. Parish, Jeff A. Johnson, Brian Millsap, Christopher J. W. McClure. "Long-term Demography of a Reintroduced Population of Endangered Falcons." *Global Ecology and Conservation* 38 (2022): e02226.

Seeler, David. "Atlantic Region: Fall 2022." *North American Birds* (2023). https://wp.me/p8iY2g-f0w.

Slabe, Vincent A., James T. Anderson, Brian A. Millsap, Jeffrey L. Cooper, Alan R. Harmata, Marco Restani, Ross H. Crandall et al. "Demographic

Implications of Lead Poisoning for Eagles across North America." *Science* 375, no. 6582 (2022): 779–82.

Souder, William. *On a Farther Shore: The Life and Legacy of Rachel Carson.* New York: Crown Publishers, 2012.

Sutton, George Miksch. "The Status of the Goshawk in Pennsylvania." *The Wilson Bulletin* 43, no. 2 (1931): 108–13.

———. "Notes on a Collection of Hawks from Schuylkill County, Pennsylvania." *The Wilson Bulletin* 40, no. 2 (1928): 84–95.

US Fish and Wildlife Service. Division of Migratory Bird Management. "Final Report: Bald Eagle Population Size: 2020 Update." December 2020. Washington, D.C. https://www.fws.gov/sites/default/files/documents/2020-bald-eagle-population-size-report.pdf.

Warkentin, Ian G., N. S. Sodhi, R. H. M. Espie, Alan F. Poole, Lynn W. Oliphant, and Paul C. James. "Merlin (*Falco columbarius*)." In *Birds of the World*, S. M. Billerman, ed. 2020. Ithaca, NY: Cornell Lab of Ornithology. https://doi.org/10.2173/bow.merlin.01.

Warren, Benjamin H. *Report on the Birds of Pennsylvania*, 2nd ed. Harrisburg, PA: E. K. Meyers, State Printer, 1890.

Three: MULLET HAWKS AND THE WITCHES' WALK

Bird-Halton, Stephanie. "Drop in Numbers of Nesting Hen Harriers in 2024." Sept. 16, 2024. https://naturalengland.blog.gov.uk/2024/09/16/drop-in-numbers-of-nesting-hen-harriers-in-2024/

Border, Jennifer A., Dario Massimino, and Simon Gillings. "Potential Future Distribution and Abundance Patterns of Common Buzzards *Buteo buteo*." British Trust for Ornithology Research Report 107. Thetford, Norfolk, 2018.

Carter, Ian. "The Red Kite Reintroduction: 30 Years On." *British Birds* 112 (August 2019): 422–6.

Ewing, Steven R., Cathleen E. Thomas, Nigel Butcher, Blánaid Denman, David J. T. Douglas, David I. K. Anderson, Guy Q. A. Anderson, James Bray, Steve Downing, Ronan Dugan, Brian Etheridge, Will Hayward, Fiona Howie, Staffan Roos, Mark Thomas, Jenny Weston, Jennifer Smart, and Jeremy D. Wilson. "Illegal Killing Associated with Gamebird Management Accounts for up to Three-quarters of Annual Mortality in Hen Harriers *Circus cyaneus*." *Biological Conservation* (2023): 110072.

Fielding, Ann, Paul Haworth, Phil Whitfield, David McLeod, and Helen Riley. *A Conservation Framework for Hen Harriers in the United Kingdom.* No. 441. Peterborough, U.K.: Joint Nature Conservation Committee Report, 2011.

McKie, Robin. "'It's Incredible, The Place Just Swarms with Birdlife': Inside England's Biggest Bird Sanctuary." *The Guardian*, Feb. 1, 2025. https://www.theguardian.com/environment/2025/feb/01/its-incredible-the-place-just-swarms-with-birdlife-inside-englands-biggest-bird-sanctuary

Murgatroyd, Megan, Stephen M. Redpath, Stephen G. Murphy, David J. T. Douglas, Richard Saunders, and Arjun Amar. "Patterns of Satellite Tagged Hen Harrier Disappearances Suggest Widespread Illegal Killing on British Grouse Moors." *Nature Communications* 10, no. 1 (2019): 1094.

Orta, Jaume, Guy M. Kirwan, Peter F. D. Boesman, Jeffrey S. Marks, Ernest F. J. Garcia, and Christopher J. Sharpe. "Hen Harrier (*Circus cyaneus*), version 1.0." In *Birds of the World*, J. del Hoyo, A. Elliott, J. Sargatal, D. A. Christie, and E. de Juana, eds. 2020. Cornell Lab of Ornithology, Ithaca, NY. https://doi.org/10.2173/bow.norhar1.01.

Parliament of Scotland. "Wildlife Management and Muirburn (Scotland) Bill (As Introduced)." https://www.parliament.scot/-/media/files/legislation/bills/s6-bills/wildlife-management-and-muirburn-scotland-bill/introduced/bill-as-introduced.pdf.

Redpath, S. M., Arjun Amar, Adam Smith, Des BA Thompson, and Simon Thirgood. "People and Nature in Conflict: Can We Reconcile Hen Harrier Conservation and Game Management?" In *Species Management: Challenges and Solutions for the 21st Century*, John Baxter and Colin A. Galbraith, eds. Natural Heritage of Scotland (2010): 335–50.

Royal Society for the Protection of Birds. *Birdcrime 2023*. Sandy, U.K.: 2024.

———. *Birdcrime Report 2021*. Sandy, U.K.: 2021.

———. *Birdcrime Appendices 2021*. Sandy, U.K.: 2021.

Roy Dennis Wildlife Foundation. "White-tailed Eagle Reintroduction in Southern England. https://www.roydennis.org/white-tailed-eagle-reintroduction-in-southern-england/

———. "White-tailed Eagles in the South West." Nov. 134, 2024. https://www.roydennis.org/category/latest-news/

Thompson, Patrick S., David JT Douglas, David G. Hoccom, Jeff Knott, Staffan Roos, and Jeremy D. Wilson. "Environmental Impacts of High-output Driven Shooting of Red Grouse *Lagopus lagopus scotica*." *Ibis* 158, no. 2 (2016).

Van der Wal, René, Aletta Bonn, Don Monteith, Mark Reed, Kirsty Blackstock, Nick Hanley, Des Thompson, Martin Evans, and Isabel Alonso. "Broad Habitats Ch. 5: Mountains, Moorlands and Heaths." In *The UK National Ecosystem Assessment Technical Report*. Cambridge: UK National Ecosystem Assessment, UNEP-WCMC, 2011. 105–60.

Weston, Phoebe. "White-tailed Eagle Chick Hatches in England for First Time in 243 Years." *The Guardian*, July 18, 2023. https://www.theguardian.com/environment/2023/jul/18/white-tailed-eagle-chick-born-in-england-for-first-time-in-243-years

Whitfield, D. Philip and Alan Fielding. "Analyses of the Fates of Satellite Tracked Golden Eagles in Scotland." Scottish Natural Heritage, 2017, Commissioned Report No. 982.

Williams, Sophie-lee, Sarah E. Perkins, Roy Dennis, James P. Byrne, and Robert J. Thomas. "An Evidence-based Assessment of the Past Distribution of Golden and White-tailed Eagles Across Wales." *Conservation Science and Practice* 2, no. 8 (2020): e240.

Four: THE NIGHTINGALES OF KNEPP

Barkham, Patrick. "Officially Extinct Butterfly 'Making a Comeback' in UK." *The Guardian*, July 8, 2022. https://www.theguardian.com/environment/2022/jul/08/officially-extinct-butterfly-large-tortoiseshell-making-a-comeback-in-uk

———. "Dutch Rewilding Experiment Sparks Backlash as Thousands of Animals Starve." *The Guardian*, April 27, 2018. https://www.theguardian.com/environment/2018/apr/27/dutch-rewilding-experiment-backfires-as-thousands-of-animals-starve

British Trust for Ornithology: Bird Facts. Red-backed Shrike. https://www.bto.org/understanding-birds/birdfacts/red-backed-shrike

———. Nightingale. https://www.bto.org/understanding-birds/birdfacts/nightingale

Buckley, Cara. "Amid the Graves, Letting Nature Take Its Course." *New York Times*, Nov. 30, 2024, Section A, p.1.

Burns, F., S. Mordue, N. al Fulaij, P. H. Boersch-Supan, J. Boswell, R. J. Boyd, T. Bradfer-Lawrence, P. de Ornellas, A. de Palma, P. de Zylva, E. B. Dennis, S. Foster, G. Gilbert, L. Halliwell, K. Hawkins, K. A. Haysom, M. M. Holland, J. Hughes, A. C. Jackson, F. Mancini, F. Mathews, A. McQuatters-Gollop, D. G. Noble, D. O'Brien, O. L. Pescott, A. Purvis, J. Simkin, A. Smith, A. J. Stanbury, J. Villemot, K. J. Walker, P. Walton, T. J. Webb, J. Williams, R. Wilson, R. D. Gregory. *State of Nature 2023*. The State of Nature partnership, 2023. https://www.stateofnature.org.uk

Caird, Jo. "When Doves Cry." *BBC Wildlife*, December 2024.

Carver, Steve, Ian Convery, Sally Hawkins, Rene Beyers, Adam Eagle, Zoltan

Kun, Erwin Van Maanen et al. "Guiding Principles for Rewilding." *Conservation Biology* 35, no. 6 (2021): 1882–93.

Cornelissen, Perry, Nico Beemster, and Hans-Erik Kuypers. "Vegetatie, Vogels, Grote Herbivoren en Recreatie in de Oostvaardersplassen." June 2018. Amersfoort, Netherlands: Staatsbosbeheer. https://www.staatsbosbeheer.nl/-/media/oostvaardersplassen/oostvaardersplassen-beheer/20172018-jaarrapportage-monitoring-oostvaardersplassen.pdf.

Crees, Jennifer J., Victoria A. Oxley, Danielle C. Schreve, and Samuel T. Turvey. "Challenges for Incorporating Long-term Baselines into Biodiversity Restoration: A Case Study of the Dalmatian Pelican (*Pelecanus crispus*) in Britain." *Ibis* 165, no. 2 (2023): 365–87.

Crompton, John L. "Implications of the Rise and Decline of Golf." National Parks and Recreation Association, June 25, 2020.

Ejrnæs, Ditte Dalsgaard, Bernard Olivier, Elisabeth Suzanna Bakker, Perry Cornelissen, Rasmus Ejrnæs, Christian Smit, and Jens-Christian Svenning. "Vegetation Dynamics Following Three Decades of Trophic Rewilding in the Mesic Grasslands of Oostvaardersplassen." *Applied Vegetation Science* 27, no. 3 (2024): e12805.

External Advisory Committee for the Management of the Oostvaardersplassen. "Advies Beheer Oostvaardersplassen: Kaders Voor Provinciaal Beleid Provincie Flevoland." April 2018. Amersfoort, Netherlands: Staatsbosbeheer. https://www.staatsbosbeheer.nl/-/media/oostvaardersplassen/oostvaardersplassen-beheer/201804-advies-beheer-oostvaardersplassen-commissie-van-geel.pdf.

Foreman, Dave. *Rewilding North America*. Washington and London: Island Press, 2004.

Gow, Derek and Coral Edgcumbe. "A History of the White Stork in Britain." *British Wildlife* 36, no. 2: 230–8.

Heydon, M. J., D. Pouget, S. Gray, G. Wagstaff, M. E. M. Ashton, and E. Andison. "Beaver Reintroductions in England: 2000-2021." York, U.K.: Natural England, 2021.

Hilty, Jodi A., Charles C. Chester, Pamela A. Wright, and Kelly Zenkewich. "Uniting Hearts and Lands: Advancing Conservation and Restoration across the Yellowstone to Yukon Region." *Frontiers in Conservation Science* 4 (2024): 1264460.

Horton, Helena. "Nature in England at Risk as Amount of Land 'Effectively Protected' Falls to 2.93%." *The Guardian*, Oct. 3, 2024.

ICMO2. "Natural Processes, Animal Welfare, Moral Aspects and Management of the Oostvaardersplassen." Report of the Second International Commission on Management of the Oostvaardersplassen (ICMO2). November 2010. The Hague/Wageningen, Netherlands. Report 039. https://www.staatsbosbeheer.nl/-/media/oostvaardersplassen/oostvaardersplassen-beheer/2010nov-icmo2-rapport-oostvaardersplassen-en.pdf.

Kopnina, Helen, Simon Leadbeater, and Paul Cryer. "Learning to Rewild: Examining the Failed Case of the Dutch 'New Wilderness' Oostvaardersplassen." *International Journal of Wilderness* 25, no. 3 (2019): 72–89.

Mayall, Elouise, Lucy Groves, Rosalind Kennerley, Michael Hudson, and Aldina Franco. "Demographic Consequences of Management Actions for the Successful Reintroduction of the White Stork *Ciconia ciconia* to the U.K." *Bird Conservation International* 33 (2023): e47.

Pettorelli, Nathalie, Jos Barlow, Philip A. Stephens, Sarah M. Durant, Ben Connor, Henrike Schulte to Bühne, Christopher J. Sandom, Jonathan Wentworth, and Johan T. du Toit. "Making Rewilding Fit for Policy." *Journal of Applied Ecology* 55, no. 3 (2018): 1114–25.

Popper, Deborah E. and Frank J. Popper. "The Great Plains: From Dust to Dust." *Planning* 53, no. 12 (1987): 12–18.

Soulé, Michael and Reed Noss. "Rewilding and Biodiversity: Complementary Goals for Continental Conservation." *Wild Earth* 8 (1998): 18–28.

Stanbury, Andrew J., Dawn E. Balmer, Mark A. Eaton, Philip V. Grice, Nicole Z. Khan, Murray J. Orchard, and Simon R. Wotton. "The Status of the UK Breeding European Turtle Dove *Streptopelia turtur* Population in 2021." *Bird Study* 70, no. 4 (2023): 183–94.

Weston, Phoebe. "'We Make Nature Here': Pioneering Dutch Project Repairs Image After Outcry Over Starving Animals." *The Guardian*, June 21, 2022. https://www.theguardian.com/environment/2022/jun/21/pioneering-dutch-rewilding-project-oostvaardersplassen-works-to-rebuild-controversial-reputation-aoe

Five: FROM THE CARPATHIANS TO THE DELTA

Anthes, Emily. "Nature is Often a Casualty of War. *New York Times*, April 19, 2022, Section D page 1.

Claudino-Sales, Vanda. Danube Delta, Romania. In: *Coastal World Heritage Sites*. Coastal Research Library, vol. 28 (2019). Springer Dordrecht. https://doi.org/10.1007/978-94-024-1528-5_14.

De Bont, Raf. "Extinct in the Wild: Finding a Place for the European Bison, 1919–1952." In *Spatializing the History of Ecology*, 163–84. Routledge, 2017.

Gómez-Baggethun, Erik, Marian Tudor, Mihai Doroftei, Silviu Covaliov, Aurel Năstase, Dalia-Florentina Onără, Marian Mierlă et al. "Changes in Ecosystem Services from Wetland Loss and Restoration: An Ecosystem Assessment of the Danube Delta (1960–2010)." *Ecosystem Services* 39 (2019): 100965.

IUCN World Heritage Outlook. (2020). Danube Delta 2020 Conservation Outlook Assessment. https://worldheritageoutlook.iucn.org/

Kiss, J. Botond, C. Alexandru-Cătălin Doroşencu, Vasile Alexe, and E. Mihai Marinov. "Data Regarding Fluctuations in the Great White Pelican (*Pelecanus onocrotalus* Linnaeus 1758) Population in the Danube Delta (Romania) Between 1950–2016." *Oltenia. Studii şi comunicări. Ştiinţele Naturii* (2019): 129–40.

Kuemmerle, Tobias, Kajetan Perzanowski, Oleh Chaskovskyy, Katarzyna Ostapowicz, Lubos Halada, Andriy-Taras Bashta, Ivan Kruhlov, Patrick Hostert, Donald M. Waller, and Volker C. Radeloff. "European Bison Habitat in the Carpathian Mountains." *Biological Conservation* 143, no. 4 (2010): 908–16.

Ledger, S. E. H., C. A. Rutherford, C. Benham, I. J. Burfield, S. Deinet, M. Eaton, R. Freeman, C. Gray, S. Herrando, H. Puleston, K. Scott-Gatty, A. Staneva, and L. McRae. *Wildlife Comeback in Europe: Opportunities and Challenges for Species Recovery*. (2022) Final report to Rewilding Europe by the Zoological Society of London, BirdLife International and the European Bird Census Council. London, UK: ZSL.

Mansourian, Stephanie, Neli Doncheva, Kostadin Valchev, and Daniel Vallauri. "Lessons Learnt From 20 Years of Floodplain Forest Restoration: The Lower Danube Landscape." (2019) WWF-France.

Marinov, Mihai, Alexandru-Cătălin Doroşencu, Vasile Alexe, Lucian-Eugen Bolboacă, Liliana Ene, and Botond J. Kiss. "Bird Species of the Danube Delta Biosphere Reserve (Romania) – First Checklist." *Scientific Annals of the Danube Delta Institute* (2023), vol. 28.

Perzanowski, Kajetan and Wanda Olech. "A Future for European Bison *Bison bonasus* in the Carpathian Ecoregion?" *Wildlife Biology* 13, no. 1 (2007): 108–12.

Pucek, Zdzisław, Irina P. Belousova, Małgorzata Krasińska, Zbigniew A. Krasiński, and Wanda Olech. "European Bison: Status Survey and Conservation Action Plan." Gland, Switzerland and Cambridge: IUCN, 2004.

Rewilding Europe. "Rewilding Breathes New Life into Danube Delta Lakes and Communities." May 14, 2020. https://rewildingeurope.com/news/rewilding-breathes-new-life-into-danube-delta-lakes-and-communities/ (Accessed 1/8/24.)

———. "Rewilding Efforts Boost Natural Water Flow Further in the Ukrainian Danube Delta." Feb. 2, 2022. https://rewildingeurope.com/news/rewilding-efforts-boost-natural-water-flow-further-in-the-ukrainian-danube-delta/ (Accessed 1/8/24.)

Terraube, J., J. Andevski, F. Loercher, and J. Tavares. "Population Estimates for the Five European Vulture Species Across the Mediterranean: 2022 update." (2022) The Vulture Conservation Foundation, Koninklijke Burger's zoo b.v. Antoon van Hooffplein 1, 6816 SH Arnhem. Netherlands.

Tokarska, Małgorzata, Cino Pertoldi, Rafał Kowalczyk, and Kajetan Perzanowski. "Genetic Status of the European Bison *Bison bonasus* After Extinction in the Wild and Subsequent Recovery." *Mammal Review* 41, no. 2 (2011): 151–62.

Ukrainian Nature Conservation Group. "44% of the Most Valuable Natural Areas of Ukraine are Covered by War." https://uncg.org.ua/en/most-valuable-natural-areas-of-ukraine-covered-by-war/ (Accessed 1/8/24.)

United Nations Environment Programme – World Conservation Monitoring Centre. *The Benefits of Ecosystem Restoration: An Analysis of Five European Restoration Initiatives.* UNEP-WCMC, Cambridge, U.K. (2022), 53 pp.

Vasile, Monica. "From Reintroduction to Rewilding: Autonomy, Agency and the Messy Liberation of the European Bison." *Environment and History* (2022): 1–26.

Vislobokova, Innessa A., Alexey V. Lopatin, Konstantin K. Tarasenko, and Reinhard Ziegler. "An Unexpected Record of an Extinct Water Buffalo *Bubalus murrensis* (Berckhemer, 1927) in the Last Glacial in Europe and its Implication for Dispersal Pattern of This Species." *Quaternary International* 574 (2021): 127–36.

WWF. "Back After 250 Years: 17 European Bison Reintroduced in the Romanian Carpathians." Press release, May 18, 2014.

Six: RESCUING THE UNLOVELY

Andevski, Jovan, ed. *Vulture Conservation in the Balkan Peninsula and Adjacent Regions.* Skopje, North Macedonia: Vulture Conservation Foundation and Frankfurt Zoological Society, 2013.

Arkumarev, Volen. "Reinforcement of the Egyptian Vulture Population in Bulgaria: Integrated Report on the Release of Captive-bred and Wild Egyptian Vultures in the Eastern Rhodopes, Bulgaria in 2024." Sofia, Bulgaria: Bulgarian Society for the Protection of Birds, 2024.

Arkumarev, Volen, Vladimir Dobrev, Ivaylo Klisurov, Ivelin Ivanov, Rusko Petrov, Nikolay Arabadziev, Steffen Oppel, and Stoyan C. Nikolov. "Develop and Pilot a Restocking Strategy for the Egyptian Vulture on the Balkans. Integrated Report on the Release of Captive-bred Egyptian Vultures in the Eastern Rhodopes in 2018 Under Action C3 of the LIFE project 'Egyptian Vulture New LIFE'." Sofia, Bulgaria: Bulgarian Society for the Protection of Birds, 2018.

Botha, André J., Jovan Andevski, Chris G. R. Bowden, Masumi Gudka, Roger J. Safford, José Tavares, and Nick P. Williams. "Multi-species Action Plan to Conserve African-Eurasian Vultures." Convention on the Conservation of Migratory Species of Wild Animals (CMS) Raptors MOU Technical Publication No. 5. CMS Technical Series No. 35. 2017. Abu Dhabi, United Arab Emirates: Coordinating Unit of the CMS Raptors MOU.

Burnett, L. Joseph, Kelly J. Sorenson, Joseph Brandt, Estelle A. Sandhaus, Deborah Ciani, Michael Clark, Chandra David, Jenny Theule, Susie Kasielke, and Robert W. Risebrough. "Eggshell Thinning and Depressed Hatching Success of California Condors Reintroduced to Central California." *The Condor* 115, no. 3 (2013): 477–91.

Clark, William S., David A. Christie, and Guy M. Kirwan. "White-rumped Vulture (*Gyps bengalensis*)." In *Birds of the World*, J. del Hoyo, A. Elliott, J. Sargatal, D. A. Christie, and E. de Juana, eds. 2020. Ithaca, NY: Cornell Lab of Ornithology.

Cook, Sophie E., Rhys E. Green, Eva Lieberherr, Christopher GR Bowden, Muhammed Jamshed Iqbal Chaudhry, ABM Sarowar Alam, S. Bharathidasan, Vibhu Prakash, Abhishek Ghoshal, and Ishana Thapa. "Current Policies in Europe and South Asia Do Not Prevent Veterinary Use of Drugs Toxic to Vultures." *Ecological Solutions and Evidence* 5, no. 2 (2024): e12357.

Dobrev, Dobromir, Rigas Tsiakiris, Theodora Skartsi, Vladimir Dobrev, Volen Arkumarev, Kalliopi Stara, Anton Stamenov, Nikos Probanos, Theodoros Kominos, Antonia Galanaki, Elzbieta Kret, Ben Hallmann, Bratislav Grubač, Goran Sušić, Saša Marinković, Irena Hribšek, Stefan Skorić, Hans Jerrentrup, Vedran Lucić, Sven Kapelj, Georgi Stoyanov, Sylvia Zakkak, Hristo Hristov, Stoycho Stoychev, Lavrentis Sidiropoulos, Taulant Bino, and Dimitar Demerdzhiev. "Long-term Size and Range Changes of the Griffon Vulture

Gyps fulvus Population in the Balkans: A Review." *Bird Conservation International* 32, no. 2 (2022): 206–21.

Frank, Eyal and Anant Sudarshan. "The Social Costs of Keystone Species Collapse: Evidence from the Decline of Vultures in India." *American Economic Review* 114, no. 10 (2024): 3007–40.

Galligan, Toby H., Krishna P. Bhusal, Khadananda Paudel, Devendra Chapagain, Ankit B. Joshi, Ishwari P. Chaudhary, Anand Chaudhary, Hem S. Baral, Richard J. Cuthbert, and Rhys E. Green. "Partial Recovery of Critically Endangered *Gyps* Vulture Populations in Nepal." *Bird Conservation International* 30, no. 1 (2020): 87–102.

Government of India, Ministry of Environment, Forest, and Climate Change. 2020. "Action Plan for Vulture Conservation in India, 2020–2025." https://save-vultures.org/wp-content/uploads/2020/11/20-11-India-National-Vulture-Action-Plan-2020-25.pdf.

Green, Rhys E., I. A. N. Newton, Susanne Shultz, Andrew A. Cunningham, Martin Gilbert, Deborah J. Pain, and Vibhu Prakash. "Diclofenac Poisoning as a Cause of Vulture Population Declines Across the Indian Subcontinent." *Journal of Applied Ecology* 41, no. 5 (2004): 793–800.

Ivanov, Ivelin, Emilian Stoynov, Georgi Stoyanov, Elena Kmetova–Biro, Jovan Andevski, Hristo Peshev, Simeon Marin et al. "First Results From the Releases of Cinereous Vultures (*Aegypius monachus*) Aiming at Re-introducing the Species in Bulgaria: The Start of the Establishment Phase 2018–2022." *Biodiversity Data Journal* 11 (2023).

Kane, Adam, Ara Monadjem, H. K. Ortwin Aschenborn, Keith Bildstein, André Botha, Claire Bracebridge, Evan R. Buechley, Ralph Buij, John P. Davies, Maria Diekmann, Colleen T. Downs, Nina Farwig, Toby Galligan, Gregory Kaltenecker, Chris Kelly, Ryno Kemp, Holger Kolberg, Monique L. MacKenzie, John Mendelsohn, Msafiri Mgumba, Ran Nathan, Aaron Nicholas, Darcy Ogada, Morgan Pfeiffer, W. Louis Phipps, Matteuns D. Pretorius, Sascha Rösner, Dana G. Schabo, Gabriel Lita Shatumbu, Orr Spiegel, Lindy J. Thompson, Jan A. Venter, Munir Virani, Kerri Wolter, and Corinne J. Kendall. "Understanding Continent-wide Variation in Vulture Ranging Behavior to Assess Feasibility of Vulture Safe Zones in Africa: Challenges and Possibilities." *Biological Conservation* 268 (2022): 109516.

Mallord, John W., Krishna P. Bhusal, Ankit B. Joshi, Bikalpa Karki, Ishwari P. Chaudhary, Devendra Chapagain, Deelip C. Thakuri, Deu B. Rana, Toby H. Galligan, Susana Requena, Christopher G. R. Bowden, and Rhys E. Green. "Survival Rates of Wild and Released White-rumped Vultures (*Gyps bengalensis*), and Their Implications for Conservation of Vultures in Nepal." *Ibis* (2024).

Nepalese Department of National Parks and Wildlife Conservation and Nepalese Department of Forests and Soil Conservation. "Vulture Conservation Action Plan (2023-2027)." 2023. Babar Mahal, Kathmandu, Nepal. https://dnpwc.gov.np/media/publication/Vulture_Conservation_Action_Plan_2023-2027.pdf.

Oaks, J. Lindsay, Martin Gilbert, Munir Z. Virani, Richard T. Watson, Carol U. Meteyer, Bruce A. Rideout, H. L. Shivaprasad, Shakeel Ahmed, Muhammad Jamshed Iqbal Chaudhry, Muhammad Arshad, Shahid Mahmood, Ahmad Ali, and Aleem Ahmed Khan. "Diclofenac Residues as the Cause of Vulture Population Decline in Pakistan." *Nature* 427 (2004): 630–3.

Oppel, S., V. Dobrev, V. Arkumarev, V. Saravia-Mullin, K. Bashmili, T. Bino, A. Bounas, A. Chardin, D. Dobrev, K. Duro, E. Kapsalis, E. Kret, M.-P. Marchant, S. Nakev, N. Petrovski, H. Papaioannou, G. Popgeorgiev, L. Selgjekaj, T. Skartsi, A. Stamenov, S. Stoychev, M. Topi, D. Vavylis, M. Velevski, Z. Vorpsi, J. Weston, E. Xeka, X. Xherri, E. Yordanov, and S. C. Nikolov. "Long-term Conservation Efforts at Flyway Scale Can Halt the Population Decline in a Globally Endangered Migratory Raptor." *Animal Conservation* 27, no. 3 (2024): 374–85.

Oppel, Steffen, Vladimir Dobrev, Volen Arkumarev, Victoria Saravia, Anastasios Bounas, Elzbieta Kret, Theodora Skartsi, Metodija Velevski, Stoycho Stoychev, and Stoyan C. Nikolov. "Assessing the Effectiveness of Intensive Conservation Actions: Does Guarding and Feeding Increase Productivity and Survival of Egyptian Vultures in the Balkans?" *Biological Conservation* 198 (2016): 157–64.

Prakash, Vibhu, Debbie J. Pain, A. A. Cunningham, P. F. Donald, Nithin Prakash, Ashok Verma, R. Gargi, S. Sivakumar, and A. R. Rahmani. "Catastrophic Collapse of Indian White-backed *Gyps bengalensis* and Long-billed *Gyps indicus* Vulture Populations." *Biological Conservation* 109, no. 3 (2003): 381–90.

Rewilding Rhodopes. "Deer Releases Continue to Strengthen Circle of Life in the Rhodope Mountains." May 30, 2024. https://rewilding-rhodopes.com/news/deer-releases-continue-to-strengthen-circle-of-life-in-the-rhodope-mountains/

Terziev, Nikolay, Volen Arkumarev, Dobromir Dobrev, and Aton Stamenov. "Anti-poison Dog Unit Operation in Bulgaria (2016–2020)." (2021) Technical report under action C4 of the LIFE Project *Conservation of Black and Griffon Vultures in the Cross-border Rhodope Mountain* (LIFE14 NAT/NL/000901). BSPB, Bulgaria. 49 pp.

Velevski, Metodija, Stoyan C. Nikolov, Ben Hallmann, Vladimir Dobrev, Lavrentis Sidiropoulos, Victoria Saravia, Rigas Tsiakiris, Volen Arkumarev, Antonia Galanaki, Theodoros Kominos, Kalliopi Stara, Elzbieta Kret, Bratislav Grubač, Emanuel Lisičanec, Thanos Kastritis, Dimitris Vavylis, Mirjan Topi, Bledi Hoxha, and Steffen Oppel. "Population Decline and Range Contraction of the Egyptian Vulture *Neophron percnopterus* in the Balkan Peninsula." *Bird Conservation International* 25, no. 4 (2015): 440–50.

Vulture Conservation Society. "Years of Reintroduction Efforts Compromised: Four Cinereous Vultures Illegally Poisoned in Bulgaria." March 15, 2022. https://4vultures.org/blog/years-of-reintroduction-efforts-compromised-four-cinereous-vultures-illegally-poisoned-in-bulgaria/

Weidensaul, Scott. "In Africa, Conservationists Are Racing to Fend Off an Unfolding Vulture Catastrophe." *Living Bird* (Spring 2021): 68–75.

Weston, Jenny, Victoria Saravia-Mullin, and Stoyan C. Nikolov. "Egyptian Vulture Online Conference 2022: An Overview of the Outcomes and Perspectives for Further Work." *Vulture News* 83, no. 1 (2023): 1–13.

Seven: GUANO-BOMBED ON EGG ROCK

Arnold, Jennifer M., Stephen A. Oswald, Ian C. T. Nisbet, Peter Pyle, and Michael A. Patten. "Common Tern (*Sterna hirundo*), version 1.0." In *Birds of the World*, S. M. Billerman, ed. 2020. Ithaca, NY: Cornell Lab of Ornithology. https://doi.org/10.2173/bow.comter.01.

BirdLife International. Species Factsheet: Atlantic Puffin *Fratercula arctica*. 2024. https://datazone.birdlife.org/species/factsheet/atlantic-puffin-fratercula-arctica.

———. *European Red List of Birds*. Luxembourg: Publications Office of the European Union, 2021.

Dutcher, William. "Results of Special Protection to Gulls and Terns Obtained Through the Thayer Fund." *The Auk* 18, no. 1 (1901): 76–104.

Gochfeld, Michael and Joanna Burger. "Roseate Tern (*Sterna dougallii*), version 1.0." In *Birds of the World*, S. M. Billerman, ed. 2020. Ithaca, NY: Cornell Lab of Ornithology. https://doi.org/10.2173/bow.roster.01.

Hansen, Erpur Snær. Stofnvöktun Lunda 2020–2022. Lokaskýrsla til Umhverfisstofnunar. 2023.

Hatch, Jeremy J., Michael Gochfeld, Joanna Burger, and Ernest F. J. Garcia. "Arctic Tern (*Sterna paradisaea*), version 1.0." In *Birds of the World*, S. M.

Billerman, ed. 2020. Ithaca, NY: Cornell Lab of Ornithology. https://doi.org/10.2173/bow.arcter.01.

Jones, Holly P. and Stephen W. Kress. "A Review of the World's Active Seabird Restoration Projects." *The Journal of Wildlife Management* 76, no. 1 (2012): 2–9.

Kress, Stephen W., Paula Shannon, and Christopher O'Neal. "Recent Changes in the Diet and Survival of Atlantic Puffin Chicks in the Face of Climate Change and Commercial Fishing in Midcoast Maine, USA." *Facets* 1, no. 1 (2016): 27–43.

Kress, Stephen W. "The Use of Decoys, Sound Recordings, and Gull Control for Re-establishing a Tern Colony in Maine." *Colonial Waterbirds* (1983): 185–96.

Lowther, Peter E., Antony W. Diamond, Stephen W. Kress, Gregory J. Robertson, Keith Russell, David N. Nettleship, Guy M. Kirwan, David A. Christie, Christopher J. Sharpe, Ernesto F. J. Garcia, and Peter F. D. Boesman. "Atlantic Puffin (*Fratercula arctica*), version 1.0." In *Birds of the World*, S. M. Billerman, ed. 2020. Ithaca, NY: Cornell Lab of Ornithology. https://doi.org/10.2173/bow.atlpuf.01.

NatureScot. "Numbers of Puffins at One of the UK's Largest Colonies Have Increased by Around a Third Since 2017." June 13, 2024. https://www.nature.scot/puffin-numbers-increase-isle-may

Podolsky, Richard H. and Stephen W. Kress. "Factors Affecting Colony Formation in Leach's Storm-Petrel." *The Auk* (1989): 332–6.

Spatz, Dena R., Lindsay C. Young, Nick D. Holmes, Holly P. Jones, Eric A. VanderWerf, Donald E. Lyons, Stephen Kress, Colin M. Miskelly, and Graeme A. Taylor. "Tracking the Global Application of Conservation Translocation and Social Attraction to Reverse Seabird Declines." *Proceedings of the National Academy of Sciences* 120, no. 16 (2023): e2214574120.

Vickery, Peter D. *Birds of Maine*. Princeton, NJ: Princeton University Press, 2020.

Eight: ISLANDS OF SANCTUARY

Ainley, David G., Thomas C. Telfer, Michelle H. Reynolds, and André F. Raine. "Newell's Shearwater (*Puffinus newelli*), version 1.0." In *Birds of the World*, Paul G. Rodewald, ed. 2020. Ithaca, NY: Cornell Lab of Ornithology. https://doi.org/10.2173/bow.towshe2.01.

Athens, J. Stephen. "*Rattus exulans* and the Catastrophic Disappearance of Hawai'i's Native Lowland Forest." *Biological Invasions* no. 11 (2009): 1489–1501.

Australian Government Department of the Environment. "Macquarie Island: From Rabbits and Rodents to Recovery and Renewal." 2014. https://www.dcceew.gov.au/sites/default/files/env/pages/f47bc054-b46d-40f2-85a5-7825525bfb48/files/fs-macquarie-island.pdf.

Byrd, G. Vernon and Thomas C. Telfer. "The Laysan Albatross on Kaua'i." *'Elepaio*, 41, no. 1 (July 1980): 1–3.

Corlett, Eva. "Urban Forests Create Birdlife Boom in New Zealand's Cities." *The Guardian*, May 20, 2022. https://www.theguardian.com/world/2022/may/20/urban-forests-create-birdlife-boom-in-new-zealands-cities

DIISE. The Database of Island Invasive Species Eradications. Island Conservation, Coastal Conservation Action Laboratory UCSC, IUCN SSC Invasive Species Specialist Group, University of Auckland, and Landcare Research New Zealand. 2018. http://diise.islandconservation.org

Fernández, Patricia, David J. Anderson, Paul R. Sievert, and Kathryn P. Huyvaert. "Foraging Destinations of Three Low-latitude Albatross (Phoebastria) Species." *Journal of Zoology* 254, no. 3 (2001): 391–404.

Hernández-Montoya, Julio C., Luciana Luna-Mendoza, Alfonso Aguirre-Muñoz, Federico Méndez-Sánchez, Maria Félix-Lizárraga, and J. M. Barredo-Barberena. "Laysan Albatross on Guadalupe Island, México: Current Status and Conservation Actions." *Monographs of the Western North American Naturalist* 7, no. 1 (2014): 543–54.

Holmes, N. D., B. S. Keitt, D. R. Spatz, D. J. Will, S. Hein, J. C. Russell, P. Genovesi, P. E. Cowan, and B. R. Tershy. "Tracking Invasive Species Eradications on Islands at a Global Scale." In *Island Invasives: Scaling Up to Meet the Challenge*. C. R. Veitch, M. N. Clout, A. R. Martin, J. C. Russell, and C. J. West, eds. Occasional Paper SSC no. 62. Gland, Switzerland: IUCN 2019. 628–32.

Howell, Steve N.G. and Kirk Zufelt. *Oceanic Birds of the World*. Princeton, NJ, and Oxford: Princeton University Press, 2019.

Kroodsma, David, Joanna Turner, Cian Luck, Tim Hochberg, Nathan Miller, Philip Augustyn, and Stephanie Prince. "Global Prevalence of Setting Longlines at Dawn Highlights Bycatch Risk for Threatened Albatross." *Biological Conservation* 283 (2023): 110026.

Lyte, Brittany. "Even Bird Lovers Glad Night Football Is Returning To Kauai."

Honolulu Civil Beat, Sept. 21, 2017. https://www.civilbeat.org/2017/09/brittany-lyte-even-bird-lovers-glad-night-football-is-returning-to-kauai/

Madeiros, Jeremy. "Review of 2023 Cahow Nesting Season." Sept. 10, 2023. https://www.nonsuchisland.com/blog/review-of-2023-cahow-nesting-season

Maly, Kepā, Benton Keali'i Pang, and Charles Pe'ape'a Makawalu Burrows. "Pigs in Hawai'i, from Traditional to Modern." https://www.eastmauiwatershed.org/wp-content/uploads/2013/01/Puaa-cultural-fact-sheet-04.03.pdf.

McArthur, Nikki, Ian Flux, and Annette Harvey. "State and Trends in the Diversity, Abundance and Distribution of Birds in Wellington City." Wellington, NZ: Greater Wellington Regional Council, 2023.

McKenzie, Pete. "New Zealand Exults in Revival of the Kiwi, a National Icon." *New York Times*, Dec. 5, 2023.

Miles, Kathryn. "The Long Way Home." *Audubon*, Winter 2023: 20–7.

Mini, Anne E., Dominic C. Bachman, Josh Cocke, Kenneth M. Griggs, Kyle A. Spragens, and Jeffrey M. Black. "Recovery of the Aleutian Cackling Goose *Branta hutchinsii leucopareia*: 10-year Review and Future Prospects." *Wildfowl* 61, no. 61 (2013): 3–29.

Mlodinow, Steven G., Peter Pyle, Thomas B. Mowbray, Craig R. Ely, James S. Sedinger, Robert E. Trost, Kyle A. Spragens, and Michael A. Patten. "Cackling Goose (*Branta hutchinsii*), version 2.0." In *Birds of the World*, N. D. Sly, Paul G. Rodewald, and B. K. Keeney, eds. 2024. Ithaca, NY: Cornell Lab of Ornithology. https://doi.org/10.2173/bow.cacgoo1.02.

Osterlund, Hob. *Holy Mōlī*. Corvallis, OR: Oregon State University Press, 2016.

Parkes, John and Penny Fisher. "Review of the Lehua Island Rat Eradication Project 2009." Pacific Cooperative Studies Unit Technical Report 195. Honolulu, HI: University of Hawai'i at Mānoa, Department of Botany, 2017.

Podolsky, Richard H. "Effectiveness of Social Stimuli in Attracting Laysan Albatross to New Potential Nesting Sites." *The Auk* 107, no. 1 (1990): 119–24.

Pratt, H. Douglas. "Avifaunal Change in the Hawaiian Islands, 1893–1993." *Studies in Avian Biology* 15 (1994): 103–18.

Raine, André F., Eric A. Vanderwerf, Mele Khalsa, Jennifer Rothe, and Scott Driskill. "Update on the Status of the Avifauna of Lehua Islet, Hawai'i, Including Initial Response of Seabirds to Rat Eradication." Pacific Cooperative

Studies Unit Technical Report 203. Honolulu, HI: University of Hawai'i at Mānoa, Department of Botany, 2021.

Reynolds, Michelle H. and George L. Ritchotte. "Evidence of Newell's Shearwater Breeding in Puna District, Hawaii." *Journal of Field Ornithology* (1997): 26–32.

Robinson, Susan A. and Geoffrey R. Copson. "Eradication of Cats (*Felis catus*) from Subantarctic Macquarie Island." *Ecological Management and Restoration*. 15 (2014)

Roy, Eleanor Ainge. "No More Rats: New Zealand to Exterminate All Introduced Predators." *The Guardian*, July 25, 2016. https://www.theguardian.com/world/2016/jul/25/no-more-rats-new-zealand-to-exterminate-all-introduced-predators

Schwanecke, Gianina. "Bringing Kiwi Back to the Capital: A National Taonga Returns to Wellington." RNZ, June 27, 2024. https://www.rnz.co.nz/national/programmes/countrylife/audio/2018944556/bringing-kiwi-back-to-the-capital-a-national-taonga-returns-to-wellington

Simons, Theodore R. and Cathleen N. Bailey. "Hawaiian Petrel (*Pterodroma sandwichensis*), version 1.0." In *Birds of the World*, Alan F. Poole and Frank B. Gill, eds. 2020. Ithaca, NY: Cornell Lab of Ornithology. https://doi.org/10.2173/bow.hawpet1.01.

Sincock, John L. and Gerald E. Swedberg. "Rediscovery of the Nesting Grounds of Newell's Manx Shearwater (*Puffinus puffinus newelli*), with Initial Observations." *The Condor* 71, no. 1 (1969): 69–71.

Smith, Laurel. "Kīlauea Point National Wildlife Refuge's New Predator Exclusion Fence." Aug. 5, 2023. https://www.fws.gov/story/2023-08/pacifics-largest-predator-exclusion-fence

Slotterback, John W. "Band-rumped Storm-Petrel (*Hydrobates castro*), version 1.1." In *Birds of the World*, Alan F. Poole, ed. 2021. Ithaca, NY: Cornell Lab of Ornithology. https://doi.org/10.2173/bow.barpet.01.1.

Spatz, Dena R., Nick D. Holmes, David J. Will, Stella Hein, Zachary T. Carter, Rachel M. Fewster, Bradford Keitt, Piero Genovesi, Araceli Samaniego, Donald A. Croll, Bernie R. Tershy, and James C. Russell. "The Global Contribution of Invasive Vertebrate Eradication as a Key Island Restoration Tool." *Scientific Reports* 12, no. 1 (2022): 13391.

Storlazzi, Curt D., Edwin P. L. Elias, and Paul Berkowitz. "Many Atolls may be Uninhabitable Within Decades Due to Climate Change." *Scientific Reports* 5 (2015): 14546.

U.S. Department of Justice. "Hawaiian County Agrees to Pay Restitution and Modify Operations to Resolve Endangered Species Act and Migratory Bird Treaty Act Violations." Sept. 10, 2010. https://www.justice.gov/opa/pr/hawaiian-county-agrees-pay-restitution-and-modify-operations-resolve-endangered-species-act

U.S. Fish and Wildlife Service. Species Report for Band-rumped Storm-petrel (*Oceanodroma castro*). Portland, OR: Pacific Islands Fish and Wildlife Office, Pacific Islands Interior Region, 2021.

Walther, Michael. *Extinct Birds of Hawai'i*. 2nd ed. Honolulu, HI: Mutual Publishing, 2016.

Watson, J. S. "Feral Rabbit Populations on Pacific Islands." *Pacific Science* 15 (1961): 591–3.

Wilmshurst, Janet M., Terry L. Hunt, Carl P. Lipo, and Atholl J. Anderson. "High-precision Radiocarbon Dating Shows Recent and Rapid Initial Human Colonization of East Polynesia." *Proceedings of the National Academy of Sciences* 108, no. 5 (2011): 1815–20.

Wood, K. R., Eric A. VanderWerf, Chris Swenson, Maya LeGrande, Heather Eijzenga, and Ronald L. Walker. "Biological Inventory and Assessment of Lehua Islet, Kauai County, Hawaii." Honolulu, HI: U.S. Fish and Wildlife Service, Pacific Island Office 2004.

Young, Lindsay C., Eric A. Vanderwerf, David G. Smith, John Polhemus, Naomi Swenson, Chris Swenson, Brent R. Liesemeyer, Betsy H. Gagne, and Sheila Conant. "Demography and Natural History of Laysan Albatross on Oahu, Hawaii." *The Wilson Journal of Ornithology* 121, no. 4 (2009): 722–9.

Zeillemaker, C. Fred and C. John Ralph. "First Breeding Record of Laysan Albatross on Kauai." *'Elepaio* 38, no. 5 (1977): 51–8.

Nine: TASTES LIKE CHICKEN

Altman, Jon and Chelsey Stephenson. "Shorebird Monitoring and Management at Cape Lookout National Seashore: 2022 Annual Report." Hackers Island, NC: National Park Service, 2022.

American Oystercatcher Working Group and National Fish and Wildlife Foundation. *Business Plan for the Conservation of the American Oystercatcher*. Oct. 26, 2008. https://www.manomet.org/wp-content/uploads/2018/03/NFWF_AMOY_BusinessPlan.pdf.

BirdLife International. "New Report Reveals Plummeting Migratory Shorebird Populations Globally." Oct. 28, 2024. https://www.birdlife.org/news/2024/

10/28/press-release-new-report-reveals-plummeting-migratory-shorebird-populations-globally/#:~:text="While%20many%20of%20these%20shorebirds,a%20third%20in%20recent%20decades

Blankinship, David R. and Kirke A. King. "A Probable Sighting of 23 Eskimo Curlews in Texas." *American Birds* 38, no. 6 (Nov.–Dec. 1984): 1066–7.

Buchanan, Graeme M., Ben Chapple, Alex J. Berryman, Nicola Crockford, Justin JFJ Jansen, and Alexander L. Bond. "Global Extinction of Slender-billed Curlew (*Numenius tenuirostris*)." *Ibis* (2024).

Elliott-Smith, Elise and Susan M. Haig. "Piping Plover (*Charadrius melodus*), version 1.0." In *Birds of the World*, A. F. Poole, ed. 2020. Ithaca, NY: Cornell Lab of Ornithology. https://doi.org/10.2173/bow.pipplo.01.

Gratto-Trevor, C. L. and S. Abbott. "Conservation of Piping Plover (*Charadrius melodus*) in North America: Science, Successes, and Challenges." *Canadian Journal of Zoology* 89, no. 5 (2011): 401–18.

Gretton, Adam, Alexander K. Yurlov, and Gerard C. Boere. "Where Does the Slender-billed Curlew Nest, and What Future Does it Have?" *British Birds* 95, no. 7 (2002): 334–44.

Hansen, Birgita, Richard Fuller, Douglas Watkins, Danny Rogers, Robert Clemens, Mike Newman, Eric Woehler, and Daniel Weller. *Revision of the East-Asian Australasian Flyway Population Estimates for 37 Listed Migratory Shorebird Species*. Melbourne: BirdLife Australia, 2016.

Hecht, Anne and Scott M. Melvin. "Population Trends of Atlantic Coast Piping Plovers, 1986–2006." *Waterbirds* 32, no. 1 (2009): 64–72.

Leger, Isabelle. "Plovers in a Dangerous Time: Endangered Bird May be Making a Comeback on N.B. shores." CBC News, Jan. 19, 2025. https://www.cbc.ca/news/canada/new-brunswick/piping-plovers-population-fledglings-pairs-kouchibouguac-nb-birds-1.7432265#:~:text=Abbott%20says%20Environment%20Canada%2C%20which,pairs%20found%20in%20New%20Brunswick

Massachusetts Audubon. "Piping Plovers Enjoy Another Record Nesting Year in 2024." Dec. 20, 2024. https://www.massaudubon.org/news/press-room/2024/piping-plovers-enjoy-another-record-nesting-year-in-2024

Massachusetts Division of Fisheries and Wildlife. "Guidelines for Managing Recreational Use of Beaches to Protect Piping Plovers, Terns, and Their Habitats in Massachusetts." April 21, 1993. https://www.mass.gov/doc/guidelines-for-managing-recreational-use-of-beaches-to-protect-piping-plovers-terns-and-their/download

Peterson, Kurt. "Drawing a Line in the Sand: Off-Road Vehicle Use on National Seashores." *Ocean and Coastal Law Journal* 23 (2018): 231–80.

Saunders, Sarah. "A Hopeful Future: Another Record-Breaking Season for Great Lakes Piping Plovers." Sept. 5, 2024. https://gl.audubon.org/news/hopeful-future-another-record-breaking-season-great-lakes-piping-plovers

Smith, Paul A., Adam C. Smith, Brad Andres, Charles M. Francis, Brian Harrington, Christian Friis, R. I. Guy Morrison, Julie Paquet, Brad Winn, and Stephen Brown. "Accelerating Declines of North America's Shorebirds Signal the Need for Urgent Conservation Action." *Ornithological Applications* 125, no. 2 (2023): duad003.

U.S. Fish and Wildlife Service. March 2020. "Piping Plover (*Charadrius melodus*) Five-Year Review: Summary and Evaluation." East Lansing, MI: Michigan Field Office, and Hadley, MA, Northeast Region.

———. 2012. "Comprehensive Conservation Strategy for the Piping Plover (*Charadrius melodus*) in its Coastal Migration and Wintering Range in the Continental United States." East Lansing, MI.

Walters, Jeffrey R., Ashley A. Dayer, Stephen J. Dinsmore, Matthew H. Godfrey, C. J. Gratto-Trevor, E. N. Trent, and Stanley R. Riggs. *Evaluating Past and Present Management of Beach-nesting Wildlife Species at the Cape Hatteras National Seashore*. 2020. American Ornithological Society.

Ten: PRAIRIE GHOSTS

Boyce, Andy J., Hila Shamon, Kyran E. Kunkel, and William J. McShea. "Grassland Bird Diversity and Abundance in the Presence of Native and Non-native Grazers." *Avian Conservation and Ecology* 16, no. 2 (2021).

Derner, Justin D., Bob Budd, Grady Grissom, Emily J. Kachergis, David J. Augustine, Hailey Wilmer, J. Derek Scasta, and John P. Ritten. "Adaptive Grazing Management in Semiarid Rangelands: An Outcome-Driven Focus." *Rangelands* 44, no. 1 (2022): 111–18.

Dreelin, R. Andrew, Andy J. Boyce, and Holly P. Jones. "Keystone Effects of Prairie Dogs (*Cynomys* spp.) on Grassland Birds: Current Knowledge and Future Directions." *Conservation Science and Practice* (2024): e70004. https://doi.org/10.1111/csp2.70004.

Dreitz, Victoria J., Lani T. Stinson, Beth A. Hahn, Jason D. Tack, and Paul M. Lukacs. "A Large-scale Perspective for Managing Prairie Avifauna Assemblages Across the Western U.S.: Influences of Habitat, Land Ownership and Latitude." *PeerJ* 5 (2017): e2879; DOI 10.7717/peerj.2879.

Dreitz, Victoria J. and Fritz L. Knopf. "Mountain Plovers and the Politics of Research on Private Lands." *BioScience* 57, no. 8 (2007): 681–7.

Grissom, Grady and Tim Steffens. "Case Study: Adaptive Grazing Management at Rancho Largo Cattle Company." *Rangelands* 35, no. 5 (2013): 35–44.

Knopf, Fritz L. and M. B. Wunder. "Mountain Plover (*Charadrius montanus*), version 1.0." In *Birds of the World*, Alan F. Poole, ed. 2020. Cornell Lab of Ornithology, Ithaca, NY. https://doi.org/10.2173/bow.mouplo.01.

National Audubon Society. "Audubon Conservation Ranching's 2023 Impact Report for Audubon Certified Bird-Friendly Lands." https://media.audubon.org/2024-02/AudubonCertifiedBirdFriendlyImpactReport.pdf.

Robbins, Jim. "Culling and Concerns." *New York Times*, April 4, 2023, D1.

———. "Establishing A New Home For Bison to Roam." *New York Times*, Jan. 10, 2023, D8.

U.S. Department of Agriculture National Agriculture Statistics Service. *2017 Census of Agriculture*, United States Summary and State Data vol. 1. Part 51. Washington, D.C., April 2019.

World Wildlife Fund. "Plowprint Report 2023." https://files.worldwildlife.org/wwfcmsprod/files/Publication/file/6wlbsmxokc_PlowprintReport_2023_final.pdf.

Eleven: GOOD FOR THE BIRD

Boone, John D., Chris Witt, and Elisabeth M. Ammon. "Behavior-specific Occurrence Patterns of Pinyon Jays (*Gymnorhinus cyanocephalus*) in Three Great Basin Study Areas and Significance for Pinyon-juniper Woodland Management." *PLoS One* 16, no. 1 (2021): e0237621.

Coates, Peter S., Brian G. Prochazka, Michael S. O'Donnell, Cameron L. Aldridge, David R. Edmunds, Adrian P. Monroe, Mark A. Ricca, Gregory T. Wann, Steve E. Hanser, Lief A. Wiechman, and Michael P. Chenaille. "Range-wide Greater Sage-Grouse Hierarchical Monitoring Framework—Implications for Defining Population Boundaries, Trend Estimation, and a Targeted Annual Warning System." No. 2020-1154. Reston, VA: U.S. Geological Survey, 2021.

Dusek, Robert J., Christian A. Hagen, J. Christian Franson, David A. Budeau, and Erik K. Hofmeister. "Utilizing Hunter Harvest Effort to Survey for Wildlife Disease: A Case Study of West Nile Virus in Greater Sage-Grouse." *Wildlife Society Bulletin* 38, no. 4 (2014): 721–7.

Halka, Jeremy R., Robert A. Miller, and Jay D. Carlisle. "Integrated Monitoring in Bird Conservation Regions (IMBCR): Final Report on 2018–21 Bird

Surveys on the Bruneau-Owyhee Sage-Grouse Habitat (BOSH) Project." Boise, ID: Boise State University, 2024.

Holmes, Aaron L., Jeremy D. Maestas, and David E. Naugle. "Bird Responses to Removal of Western Juniper in Sagebrush-steppe." *Rangeland Ecology and Management* 70, no. 1 (2017): 87–94.

Innes, Robin J. and Kris Zouhar. Fire Regimes of Mountain Big Sagebrush Communities. (2018) In *Fire Effects Information System*. U.S. Department of Agriculture, Forest Service, Rocky Mountain Research Station, Missoula Fire Sciences Laboratory. https://www.fs.usda.gov/database/feis/fire_regimes/mountain_big_sagebrush/all.html. (Accessed April 8, 2024.)

Miller, Richard F., Robin J. Tausch, E. Durant McArthur, Dustin D. Johnson, Stewart C. Sanderson. "Age Structure and Expansion of Piñon-juniper Woodlands: A Regional Perspective in the Intermountain West." (2008) Res. Pap. RMRS-RP-69. Fort Collins, CO: U.S. Department of Agriculture, Forest Service, Rocky Mountain Research Station.

Olsen, Andrew C., John P. Severson, Brady W. Allred, Matthew O. Jones, Jeremy D. Maestas, David E. Naugle, Kate H. Yates, and Christian A. Hagen. "Reversing Tree Encroachment Increases Usable Space for Sage-grouse During the Breeding Season." *Wildlife Society Bulletin* 45, no. 3 (2021): 488–97.

Olsen, Andrew C., John P. Severson, Jeremy D. Maestas, David E. Naugle, Joseph T. Smith, Jason D. Tack, Kate H. Yates, and Christian A. Hagen. "Reversing Tree Expansion in Sagebrush Steppe Yields Population-level Benefit for Imperiled grouse." *Ecosphere* 12, no. 6 (2021): e03551.

Redmond, Miranda D., Frank Forcella, and Nichole N. Barger. "Declines in Pinyon Pine Cone Production Associated with Regional Warming." *Ecosphere* 3, no. 12 (2012): 1–14.

Reinhardt, Jason R., Jason D. Tack, Jeremy D. Maestas, David E. Naugle, Michael J. Falkowski, and Kevin E. Doherty. "Optimizing Targeting of Pinyon-juniper Management for Sagebrush birds of Conservation Concern While Avoiding Imperiled Pinyon Jay." *Rangeland Ecology & Management* 88 (2023): 62–9.

Rowland, Mary M., Lowell H. Suring, Matthias Leu, Steven T. Knick, and Michael J. Wisdom. "Sagebrush-associated Species of Conservation Concern." In *Sagebrush Ecosystem Conservation and Management*, Steven E. Hanser, Matthias Leu, Steven T. Knick, and Cameron L. Aldridge, eds., 46–68. Lawrence, KS: Allen Press, 2011.

Schroeder, Michael A., Jessica R. Young, and Clait E. Braun. "Greater Sage-

Grouse (*Centrocercus urophasianus*), version 1.0." In *Birds of the World*, Alan F. Poole and Frank B. Gill, eds. 2020. Ithaca, NY: Cornell Lab of Ornithology. https://doi.org/10.2173/bow.saggro.01.

Tack, Jason D., Joseph T. Smith, Kevin E. Doherty, Patrick J. Donnelly, Jeremy D. Maestas, Brady W. Allred, Jason Reinhardt, Scott L. Morford, and David E. Naugle. "Regional Context for Balancing Sagebrush- and Woodland-dependent Songbird Needs with Targeted Pinyon-juniper Management." *Rangeland Ecology & Management* 88 (2023): 182–91.

U.S. Department of the Interior. "Greater Sage-grouse Rangewide Planning Draft Resource Management Plan Amendment and Draft Environmental Impact Statement." Vol. 1 (March 2024). DOI-BLM-WO-2300-2022-0001-RMP-EIS. Cheyenne, WY: Bureau of Land Management.

———. "Bruneau-Owyhee Sage-grouse Habitat Project (BOSH) Final Environmental Impact Statement." (2018) DOI-BLM-ID-B000-2014-0002-EIS. Boise, ID: Bureau of Land Management.

U.S. Fish and Wildlife Service. Species Status Assessment Report for Gunnison Sage-grouse (*Centrocercus minimus*). Version: April 20, 2019. Lakewood, Colorado.

Twelve: LAND OF THE ANCESTORS

Australian Government. "Indigenous Protected Areas." https://www.dcceew.gov.au/environment/land/indigenous-protected-areas (Accessed Feb. 20, 2024.)

Ball, Jeffery, Chris Smith, Frank Baldwin, and Stuart Slattery. "Seal River Estuary and Knife River Delta: Report on 2013–15 Waterfowl Surveys." April 10, 2020. Ducks Unlimited Canada, Oceans North Canada, and the Manitoba Government. https://boreal.ducks.ca/wp-content/uploads/2020/09/seal-knife-river-waterfowl-survey-report.pdf.

Bussidor, Ila and Üstün Bilgen-Reinart. *Night Spirits*. Winnipeg, MB: University of Manitoba Press, 1997.

Carlson, M., J. Wells, and D. Roberts. *The Carbon the World Forgot*. Seattle, WA, and Ottawa, ON: Boreal Songbird Initiative and Canadian Boreal Initiative, 2009.

Courtois, Valérie. "Celebrating a Milestone: Indigenous Leaders Take Over Large Conservation Campaign." June 22, 2023. https://www.borealconservation.org/stories-1/iliassumesleadershipofibcc

Cowan, Carolyn. "Award-winning, Indigenous Peace Park Dragged into Fierce Conflict in Myanmar." May 15, 2023. *Mongabay*. https://news.mongabay.

com/2023/05/award-winning-indigenous-peace-park-dragged-into-fierce-conflict-in-myanmar/

Government of British Columbia. "Government of Canada, British Columbia and the First Nations Leadership Council Sign a Historic Tripartite Nature Conservation Framework Agreement." Nov. 3, 2023. https://www.canada.ca/en/environment-climate-change/news/2023/11/government-of-canada-british-columbia-and-the-first-nations-leadership-council-sign-a-historic-tripartite-nature-conservation-framework-agreement.html.

Government of Canada. "Project Finance for Permanence: Support for Indigenous-led Conservation Initiatives." Dec. 12, 2024. https://www.canada.ca/en/environment-climate-change/services/nature-legacy/about/project-finance-for-permanence.html.

Indigenous Circle of Experts. *We Rise Together*. March 2018. https://publications.gc.ca/collections/collection_2018/pc/R62-548-2018-eng.pdf.

Łutsël K'é Dene First Nation. "Dënesųłiné Fishing Knowledge of the East Arm of *Tu Nedhé* (Great Slave Lake)." (2002) Report submitted to Department of Fisheries and Oceans, Hay River, NT.

Martin, Katia Liénafa Thibault. "Beyond the Conflict: The Reconstruction of the O-Pipon-Na-Piwin First Nation Community in Manitoba." *Geography Research Forum*, 30 (2010): 50–65.

Parks Canada. "A New National Park in the Yukon Being Explored by the Gwich'in Tribal Council, the First Nation of Nacho Nyak Dun, and the Governments of Canada and Yukon." April 22, 2024. https://www.canada.ca/en/parks-canada/news/2024/04/a-new-national-park-in-the-yukon-being-explored-by-the-gwichin-tribal-council-the-first-nation-of-nacho-nyak-dun-and-the-governments-of-canada-and-.html.

Schuster, Richard, Ryan R. Germain, Joseph R. Bennett, Nicholas J. Reo, and Peter Arcese. "Vertebrate Biodiversity on Indigenous-managed Lands in Australia, Brazil, and Canada Equals That in Protected Areas." *Environmental Science and Policy* 101 (2019): 1–6.

Swan, David. *Natural Abundance: An Evaluation of Species Richness in the Seal River Watershed*. (February 2022) Winnipeg, MB: Canadian Parks and Wildlife Society—Manitoba. https://cpawsmb.org/wp-content/uploads/2022/05/Natural-Abundance-Species-Richness-in-the-Seal-River-Watershed.pdf.

Thorassie, Stephanie, Carrie Gray, Ernie Bussidor, Johnny Clipping, Jordan Stensgard, Lianna Anderson, Jina Cook, Mandy Wallman, Chaz Collier, Darryn Yassie, Cameron Bighetty, Linda Inglis, Shakayla Antsanen, Cole

Cook, Simon Duck, DJ Thorassie, Calvin Clipping, Trevin Baker, Sadie Dumas, Ronnie Moise, Raymond Ellice Jr., Kyle Clipping, Stephan Inglis, Lizette Moise, Mike Duck, Sandy Clipping, Brian Yassie, Jordan Cutlip, Kohl Barrault, and Jeff Wells. *Birdsongs of Seal River: A Bird Survey Summary.* (2024) New York: National Audubon Society and Winnipeg, MB: Seal River Watershed Alliance.

United Nations Development Programme (UNDP). "Łutsël K'é Dene First Nation, Canada." (2002) *Equator Initiative Case Study Series.* New York, NY.

Wells, Jeff, David Childs, Frederic Reid, Kevin Smith, Marcel Darveau, and Valerie Courtis. *Boreal Birds Need Half: Maintaining North America's Bird Nursery and Why it Matters.* (2014) Seattle, WA, Memphis, TN, and Stonewall, MB: Boreal Songbird Initiative, Ducks Unlimited, and Ducks Unlimited Canada.

Wright, D. F., E. J. Ambrose, D. Lemkow, and G. F. Bonham-Carter, eds. *Mineral and Energy Resource Assessment of the Proposed Thaidene Nene National Park Reserve in the Area of the East Arm of Great Slave Lake, Northwest Territories.* (2013) Geological Survey of Canada, Open File 7196. doi:10.4095/292447, 2013.

Index

abundance mapping, 107
ACE (Ashepoo, Combahee, and Edisto) Basin, 245–46
aerial surveys, 241, 332
Africa, 110–11, 147–49, 152–55, 162
Agricultural Research Service, USDA, 296–97
Alakaʻi Swamp, 198
Alaska, 2, 21, 25, 26, 27, 28–29, 39, 50, 209–10
Alaska Maritime National Wildlife Refuge, 209–10
Albania, 152, 153, 156
albatrosses, 172, 175, 198, 211–19
   black-footed albatrosses, 211, 212, 217
   Laysan albatrosses, 211–15, 217
Aleutian cackling geese, 210
Aleutian islands, 209–10
alpine swifts, 127
Alto Fragua Indi Wasi National Park, 317
American bison, 97, 115–16, 273–74
American butterfish, 183–84, 189–90
American golden-plovers, 222, 224
American goshawks, 36–39
American kestrels, 39, 52–54, 57, 103
American Ornithologists' Union, 37, 171
American Oystercatcher Recovery Initiative, 240–41
American Prairie in Montana, 102–3
American Prairie rewilding project, 275
American rewilding, 102–4
American Samoa, 200
American woodcock, 222
Andean condor, 149
Anderson, Lianna, 327–33
Angelov, Ivaylo, 157–62
annual grasses, 280–83, 289, 290, 294
anti-poisoning canine units, 150–52

aplomado falcon, 45–46
Appalachian Mountains, 50
apple snails, 46–49
Appleton, Tim, 60
Archipelago Research and Conservation (ARC), 199–207
Arctic terns, 166, 169, 179–80
Arda River, 157–63
Arizona, 46, 50, 149, 276, 279
Arkumarev, Volen, 152–57
artificial nests, 19, 60, 159, 174–77, 216
Asia Development Bank, 242
Atlantic Canada, 49, 238
Atlantic coast, 239
Atlantic Flyway Shorebird Initiative, 242–43
Atlantic herring, 183, 185, 187
Atlantic puffins, 167–92
audioluring, 172, 178–79, 213
Audubon North Carolina, 233
Audubon of Florida, 47
aurochs, 86, 91–92, 115, 118
autonomous recording units (ARUs), 207, 332
Averson Canyon, 262–64
avian influenza, 26–27, 62, 186
avian poxvirus, 198

Baffin Island, Canadian Arctic, 22
Băile Herculane, 123–24
Bake Oven Knob, 39
Bald Eagle Protection Act, 39
bald eagles, 31–32, 33–36, 39, 41, 43–45, 55, 176
Balkan Mountains, 145–62
Bambrick, Mya, 62–63
Bangladesh, 146
Barbados, 244
Barking Sands, Kauaʻi, 217
barn owls, 59

Barren Lands First Nation, 327
bar-tailed godwits, 221
Barton, Harry, 112
Bates Hole, WY, 280
bats, 94
Batumi, Republic of Georgia, 32
bearded vultures, 125, 150, 160
beavers: European beavers, 93
Bednarz, Jim, 41
bendiocarb, 70
Benz, Seth, 31–32
Bermuda petrels, 199
Bern Convention, 102
Białowieża Forest, 115
Biden, Joe, 29, 55, 192, 296
Bilgen-Reinart, Üstün, 330
Bipartisan Infrastructure Law of 2021, 293
Bird Conservancy of the Rockies (BCR), 252–54, 259–60, 263, 265–66, 268
Birdcrime report, 66, 71–72, 75
BirdLife International, 242
BirdLife Malta, 199
bird populations, 1–3
   American kestrels, 52–53
   Atlantic puffins, 185–86
   boreal zone, 312
   ducks, 15–16
   geese, 19, 21–22
   greater sage-grouse, 286, 299–300
   mountain plovers, 256
   oystercatcher, 240
   pinyon jays, 300–301
   piping plovers, 233
   shorebirds in North America, 222–23
   turtledoves, 108
   vultures, 146–48, 152
   waterfowl, 7, 9–12, 24–29
Birds of Poole Harbour, 56–64
birds of prey. *See* Hawk Mountain Sanctuary, PA
bison
   American bison, 97, 115–16, 273–74
   Caucasian bison, 115
   European bison, 100, 114–23, 145, 163
bitterns: least bitterns, 17
black-bellied plovers, 222, 224
Blackburn Head, 78
black-footed albatrosses, 211, 212, 217
black guillemots, 166–67, 175, 181
black scoters, 312, 333
Black Sea, 32, 127–29, 132
black vultures, 49
Blanchard, Dylan, 214–18

blue grama, 254, 260–61, 265
Bolsón tortoises, 96
Boone, John, 301–2
Bora, Paula, 131–32
Boreal Songbird Initiative, 311–12
Bosnia-Herzegovina, 150
Boyce, Andy J., 303
Breeding Bird Survey (BBS), 52, 60, 214, 301
Brennan, Lyra, 229, 236–38
Brewer's sparrows, 277, 299
British Columbia, 319, 325
British Trust for Ornithology (BTO), 58–60, 107
Broun, Maurice, 33, 38–39
Brown, Bracken, 31, 55
Brown, Harper, 169–71
brown kiwis, 209
brown pelicans, 34–35
Bruneau-Owyhee Sage-grouse Habitat (BOSH Project), 290–94, 297–98, 302–5
buff-breasted sandpipers, 222, 244
buffleheads, 6
Bulgaria, 143–65
Bulgarian Society for the Protection of Birds (BSPB), 143–45, 150, 154–62
bulrush marshes, 21, 23
Bulwer's petrels, 210
bunchgrasses, 280–81, 289
Bureau of Land Management (BLM), 285–86, 292–93, 296
Burrell, Charles, 89–94, 99–113
Bush, George H. W., 14
Bussidor, Ernie, 331
Bussidor, Ila, 330
Bussidor, Ronnie John, 331
Butcher, Greg, 268–69
butterflies, 94
buzzards, 57–59, 82
Bylot Island, Nunavut, Canada, 23

Cade, Tom, 42–44
cahow, 199
Cairngorms Connect, 101
Cairngorms National Park, 101–2
California, 7–8, 26, 27, 35, 45, 52, 287
California condor, 149
Camache, Carlos Molina, 133–41
Camp-10, 330–31
Canada, 25, 50, 51–52, 96, 173, 174, 226, 259, 306–34
Canada geese, 6–7, 18–27
Canadian Arctic, 20–26

Canadian Boreal Conservation Framework (CBCF), 311–12
Canadian Wildlife Service, 24, 175, 329–30
canals, 132
Cape Breton Island, Nova Scotia, 324–25
Cape Cod, MA, 225–29
Cape Hatteras National Seashore, NC, 232–33, 240
Cape Lookout National Seashore, 233
Cape May, NJ, 52
Cape vulture, 148
captive breeding, 19, 110–11, 146–47
cardinals, 195
Carey's Secret Garden, 56, 62
Caribbean, 244, 246–47
carnivores, 95, 101–2, 117–18, 164
Carolina parakeets, 10
Carpathian Mountains of Romania, 100, 114–42
Carpathian ponies, 100
carrion for vultures, 101, 126, 146–48, 157, 159–60, 164
Carson, Rachel, 33–35, 44
cathartid vultures, 149
Catholique, Iris, 323–24
Catholique, Pierre, 309
cats, 198, 201–3, 206, 208, 213–15, 240
Cattau, Chris, 47–48
cattle
    Heck cattle, 92–93
    Tauros cattle, 100
Caucasian bison, 115
Caucasus Mountains of Russia, 115
Ceaușescu, Nicolae, 118, 132
cemeteries, 103
Central Grasslands Roadmap Initiative, 259
Cerna River valley, 124–27
certification initiatives, 272–73
Cerulli, Jen, 314
chaining, 301
cheatgrass, 280–81, 289, 294
Cheile Corcoaiei (Corcoaia Gorge), 126
chestnut-collared longspurs, 265
Cheviot Hills, 82
Chevron deference, 29
Chihuahuan Desert, 53, 96
China, 107, 112, 221
Christmasberry tree, 215
Christmas Bird Counts, 1, 52–53
Churchill River Diversion (CRD), 329
cinereous vultures, 100, 124–25, 149–50, 158–63

ciscoes, 311
Clark, William, 18–19, 279
Clean Water Act, 29
climate change, 28–29, 49, 53, 188–90, 223, 297, 301
Coastal Waterbirds Program, 228
Collier, Chaz, 327–33
Colombia, 317
colonial seabirds, 26–27, 172, 186, 217
Colorado, 248–75
Colorado Birding Trail, 266
Colorado Division of Wildlife, 252
Colville River delta, North Slope of Alaska, 26
commercial fishing, 191–92
common eiders, 181, 183
common goldeneyes, 6
common mergansers, 6
common murres, 167
common myna, 195
common nighthawks, 263, 264, 332
common terns, 26, 166–81
condors
    Andean condor, 149
    California condor, 149
Congress, 9, 12–17, 32, 268
conifers, 281–304
Connecticut warblers, 312
Connelly, Jack, 284–85
conservation easement, 253–57
Conservation Ranching program, 259–60, 272
Conservation Reserve Program (CRP), 13
convergent evolution, 149
Cook, Preston, 32
Cooper's hawks, 34, 38, 41, 44, 53
cordgrass, 21, 23, 245–46
cores, 95–96, 101
Cornell University, 42–43
corridors, 95–96, 101
Cotswold Wildlife Park, 110–11
Cousins, Emily, 314
cranes: sandhill cranes, 22, 266, 297
Cree community of South Indian Lake, 329
creeping thistle, 94
crossbills: white-winged crossbills, 312
curlews
    Eskimo curlew, 8, 222, 242–44, 245
    long-billed curlews, 266
    slender-billed curlews, 222, 242
Curley Community Center, 237–38
Cutler, ME, 173

Dalmatian pelicans, 112, 130–31, 140
Danube Delta, 100, 101, 127–42
Danube Delta Transboundary Biosphere Reserve, 129–30
Darling, J. N. "Ding," 37
Davis, John, 252–55, 269–70
Davis, Russell, 248–75
Davis, Steve, 257
Davis Mountains, 40
DCR-1339, 176
DDT, 3, 33–35, 41–44, 46, 58, 136
decoys, 8, 9, 24, 172, 178–79, 191, 203, 213
Deepwater Horizon oil spill, 14–15
deer
    fallow deer, 91, 93, 100, 105, 133, 145, 163–64
    red deer, 91–93, 105, 133, 145, 164
    roe deer, 92, 93, 100, 105, 164
    white-tailed deer, 45, 105–6, 164
Defenders of Wildlife, 233
Dehcho First Nation, 324
Délı̨nę, 312–13
Dena Kayeh Institute, 325
Dene K'éh Kusān, 325
Deng, Ke Coco, 169–71
Deninu Kųę First Nation, 322
Dennis, Roy, 60, 64
Deveaux Bank, 245–47
Device, Elizabeth, 69
Device, Jennet, 65, 69
diamond mining, 318
diclofenac, 125, 146–50
disease, 26–27, 58, 101, 125–26, 147, 197–98
diversionary feeding, 79
Dobrev, Dobromir, 161–63
dogs, 147, 150, 152, 162, 201, 213, 226, 228, 231–32
domestic livestock, 86, 125–26, 283
Domogled Valea Cernei National Park, 124
Dorset, England, 56–64
doves
    spotted doves, 196
    zebra doves, 196
Downing, Steve, 65–66, 69, 72–77, 81, 199
Drasovean, Anghel, 119–23
dredge spoils, 246
Dreitz, Victoria, 252, 256–57, 267, 273
drought, 7, 9–12
Drugă, Marina, 131, 134, 137–39
Drury, William, 174–76

Duck Lake, 329–30
ducks, 5–17, 27–29
Duck Stamp, 10
Ducks Unlimited (DU), 16–17, 26, 311–12, 326
Duffy, Carol Ann, 65
Duluth, MN, 55
Dunne, Pete, 312–13
Dust Bowl, 7, 9–10, 16, 50
Dymond, Ben, 77–79

eagles
    bald eagles, 31–32, 33–36, 39, 41, 43–45, 55, 176
    golden eagles, 39–40, 45, 58, 64, 70, 81–83
    white-tailed eagles, 56–57, 63–64, 70, 98, 130, 135–37
Earth First!, 95
East Asia–Australasian Flyway (EAAF), 221, 242
Eastern Egg Rock, 166–92
eBird data, 107, 300
Edéhzhíe Protected Area, 324
Edge, Rosalie, 37–38
Egyptian vultures, 125, 150–62
eiders: common eiders, 181, 183
electrical pylons, 154–55, 162, 163
Elwood, Liv, 56–64
Emergency Conservation Committee, 38
emperor goose, 27
Endangered Species Act (ESA), 43, 204, 226, 249, 279, 285, 288–89, 296
England, 53–54, 56–84, 85–113
Enzoe, Pete, 306–9, 314–18
Ermakov Island, 133
Eskimo curlew, 8, 222, 242–44, 245
Essex, England, 107
Ethiopia, 155
Eurasian black vultures, 124–25
Eurasian goshawks, 53–54, 58, 82
Eurasian hobbies, 58, 108
Eurasian kestrels, 53
Eurasian lynx, 102
Eurasian sparrowhawks, 54
Europe, 24, 85–113, 122–27, 136–37, 149–50, 152–55
European Association of Zoos and Aquaria, 155
European beavers, 93
European bison, 100, 114–23, 145, 163
European Breeding Bird Atlas, 123
European Commission, 154
European rabbits, 210

European Red List, 186
European Union, 125–26
European vultures, 126, 145–46, 158–59
Exmoor National Park, 64
Exmoor ponies, 88, 93, 100

Fair Isle in the Shetlands, 64
falcons
    aplomado falcon, 45–46
    peregrine falcons, 31, 34, 41–44, 58, 174
fallow deer, 91, 93, 100, 105, 133, 145, 163–64
Farm Bill, 12–13
farmland birds, 89–90, 119–20
Farne Islands, 58, 186
fences, 202–3, 207, 214–18, 297–98
First Nation of Nacho Nyak Dun, 325
First Nations communities, 309–33
First Nations Leadership Council, 325
fledging rates, 187, 238
flightless ibises, 197
Florida, 33–34, 46–49
Florida apple snails, 46–47
flycatchers: gray flycatchers, 299–300
flyways, 10, 21, 24, 26, 45, 221, 222, 242–43, 245
Food Security Act of 1985, 12–13
Foreman, Dave, 95–96
Forest of Bowland, 68, 69–74
Forestry and Land Scotland, 101
Forestry England, 64
Fort Belknap Indian Reservation, 273–74
Foundation Conservation Carpathia, 100
foxes: red or Arctic foxes, 209–10
France, 34, 102, 136
Fresh Kills Park, Staten Island, NY, 103
Frontier Lodge, 314–17

Gallagher, Seth, 268–75
gallinules, 17
Game and Wildlife Conservation Trust, 72
geese, 5–8, 10, 18–27, 98
    Aleutian cackling geese, 210
    Canada geese, 6–7, 18–27
    emperor goose, 27
    pink-footed geese, 24
    Ross's geese, 25, 26
    snow geese, 7, 20–27, 223
    white-fronted geese, 24, 27
Geltsdale Nature Reserve, 75–78
Germany, 34, 59, 102
Glorious Twelfth, 67

gnatcatchers, 2
godwits
    bar-tailed godwits, 221
    Hudsonian godwits, 221, 222, 244
golden eagles, 39–40, 45, 58, 64, 70, 81–83
goldeneyes: common goldeneyes, 6
golden jackals, 135–37, 150
golf courses, 103–4
goshawks
    American goshawks, 36–39
    Eurasian goshawks, 53–54, 58, 82
Gramlich, Frank, 176
Granholm, Cathy, 213–14
grasshoppers, 54
grassland birds, 2, 250–75
gray flycatchers, 299–300
gray mullet, 63
gray wolves, 95–96
Great Bear Lake, 312
great black-backed gulls, 171, 176, 178–81
Great Britain, 34, 59, 85, 89–90, 107, 113, 131, 186
Great Duck, 181
greater sage-grouse, 278–305
great horned owls, 40, 42, 180
Great Hurricane of 1938, 224
Great Island, Newfoundland's Witless Bay, 175
Great Lakes, 7, 17, 28, 43–44, 224, 226, 238
Great Plains, 11–12
Great Slave Lake, 306–27
great white pelicans, 130, 140
grebes
    pied-billed grebes, 17
    red-necked grebes, 312
Greece, 112, 150, 152, 153, 154, 156, 161
Green, Penny, 106–13
Green Balkans Federation, 145, 155, 160
green glaciers, 282, 300
Griffiths, Tim, 287–90
griffon vultures, 124–27, 149–50, 152, 155, 156, 157, 159–62
Grinnell, George Bird, 9, 280
Grissom, Grady, 260–75
grouse/grouse moors, 66–84: red grouse, 67, 68, 79, 82
Grouse Moor Management Group, 83
grouse-shooting industry, 80–84
Grupo de Ecología y Conservación de Ilas, 217

Guadalupe Island, 217
Guadeloupe, 244
guillemots: black guillemots, 166–67, 175, 181
Gulf of Maine Research Institute, 184–85
Gulf of Maine Seabird Working Group, 187
Gulf of Mexico, 224, 239
gull-billed terns, 233
gulls
   great black-backed gulls, 171, 176, 178–81
   laughing gulls, 166
Gwaii Haana National Park Reserve, 316
Gwich'in Tribal Council, 325
Gyps vultures, 148–49

habitat conservation plan (HCP), 205, 236–38
habitat diversity in Danube Delta, 130–31
habitat management protocols, 259. *See also* conservation easement
habitat restoration, 13–14, 292–94
habitat variety, 265
hack boxes, 42
Haida Gwaii, British Columbia, 316, 319
Hall, Minna, 9
Haltonlea Fell, 78
Hanna, Dave, 214–18
Hanson, Harold C., 18–19
Harbor Princess (tour boat), 182
harriers. *See* hen harriers
Harwood, Michael, 39
Hawai'i, 193–219
Hawaiian honeycreepers, 196–98
Hawaiian petrels, 200–207, 216–17
Hawai'i Department of Land and Natural Resources, 210
Hawk Mountain Sanctuary, PA, 30–55
Hawk Ridge Bird Observatory, MN, 55
hawks, 30–55: Cooper's hawks, 34, 38, 41, 44, 53
Hebrides, 82
Heck, Lutz, 92
Heck cattle, 92–93
Hemenway, Harriet, 9
hen harriers, 64–84
Henry, Jim and Nancy, 191
herbivores, 92, 93, 99–101, 106, 164, 210
Hidden Valley Nature Center, Jefferson, ME, 327–28
highly pathogenic avian influenza (HPAI), 26–27

Hoagland, Jerry, 296–97
hobbies: Eurasian hobbies, 58, 108
Hog Island, 176, 187
Hog Island Audubon Camp, ME, 172–75, 190, 327–28
Honeycreepers: Hawaiian honeycreepers, 196–98
hoopoes, 135
Hornaday, William T., 39–40
horses
   Konik horses, 92, 99, 100, 133, 145
   Przewalski's horse, 100
   Yakutian horses, 97
horseshoe crabs, 223
Hudson Bay, 23–24, 221, 327, 330
Hudsonian godwits, 221, 222, 244
hydroelectric power, 329
hydrology, 127, 132

Iaynes, Marvin, 133–42
Iberian highlands, Spain, 100
Ibises: flightless ibises, 197
Iceland, 185–86
Idaho, 281, 284–305
Illinois, 51
India, 146–47
Indigenous Circle of Experts (ICE), 316
Indigenous Leadership Initiative (ILI), 315–16, 325–26
Indigenous Protected and Conserved Areas (IPCAs), 306–34
Inga people of Caquetá, 317
International Boreal Conservation Campaign (IBCC), 311–16
International Union for the Conservation of Nature, 222–23
InterTribal Buffalo Council (IBC), 274
Iowa, 11, 51
Ireland, 57, 59, 64, 67, 70, 89
island apple snails, 47–48
Isle of May, 186
Isle of Rum, 64
Isle of Wight, 56, 64
Israel, 156
Italy, 99, 102
Izoceño-Guaraní people of southern Bolivia, 317

jackals: golden jackals, 135–37, 150
Jackson, Derrick Z., 173
James Bay, 23–24
James Campbell National Wildlife Refuge, O'ahu, 217
Jewell, Sally, 285–86

Jones, Howard, 66–72
Jordan, 154–56
Jordan Valley, OR, 303–4
Josan, Cătălin, 131–32
juniper trees, 281–83, 287–89, 290, 297, 299–304

Kaa-Iya del Gran Chaco National Park, 317
kākās, 209
Kallick, Steve, 313–15, 319
Kansas, 249, 274, 279
Karakachan ponies, 100
Karval, CO, 257–58, 268–75
Karval Community Building, 268–69
Karval Mountain Plover Festival, 258, 268–69
Kaska Dena, 325
Kauaʻi, 193–219
Kauaʻi creeper (ʻakikiki), 198
Kauaʻi Endangered Seabird Recovery Project (KESRP), 199, 216
Kauaʻi Island Utility Cooperative (KIUC), 204
Kauaʻi ʻōʻō, 198
Kaufmann, Elizabeth, 234–36
Kawaikini Peak, 198
Kelly, Arden, 169–71
Kennerly, William, 189–90
Kent, England, 107
kererūs, 209
Kermadec petrels, 218
kestrels
  American kestrels, 39, 52–54, 57, 103
  Eurasian kestrels, 53
Key, John, 209
Kielder Forest, England, 53
Kīlauea Point National Wildlife Refuge, 213–19
killdeer, 223–24
kites, 46–52
  Mississippi kites, 50–52
  red kites, 57, 59–60, 82
  snail kites, 46–49
kiwis: brown kiwis, 209
Knarsdale Moor, 75, 78
Knepp Wildland, 85–113
Konik horses, 92, 99, 100, 133, 145
Kovan-Kaya, 157, 160–61
Kresna Gorge, Bulgaria, 150
Kress, Stephen W., 167–92
krill, 187
kulan, 100

Labrador, 49, 239
Lake District National Park, 74
Lake Tohopekaliga (Toho), 47–49
Lancashire, 64–65, 70
Lancaster Castle, 65
landbirds, 198
lark buntings, 255, 265
laughing gulls, 166
Laysan albatrosses, 211–15, 217
Leach's storm-petrels, 166, 181, 213, 217
lead poisoning, 45
least bitterns, 17
least terns, 227
Lee, Forrest B., 18–19
Lehua Islet, 210–11
leks, 278–79, 282, 293–98
Leopold, Aldo, 5
Lesser Antilles, 243–44
lesser Hawaiian petrel, 198
lesser yellowlegs, 222–23, 244, 312, 332
Lewis, Meriwether, 18, 279–80
licensing system, 82–84
LiDAR, 105
Light Goose Conservation Order, USFWS, 25–26
local extinctions, 57, 125
Lockhart, Felix, 318
Lockhart, Joe, 309
London, England, 57
long-billed curlews, 266
long-eared owls, 59, 109
longspurs: chestnut-collared longspurs, 265
loons: Pacific loons, 308–9
Louisiana, 49
Lovelace, Rob, 261–62
Lower Danube Green Corridor, 132–33
Ludwig, Sonja, 72–73
Łutsël Kʼé Dené First Nation (LKDFN), 309–24
lynx: Eurasian lynx, 102

Macdonald, Benedict, 79–80, 118
Machias Seal Island, 173–87
Macquarie Island, 208
Mad River Decoys, Vermont, 191
Madzharovo, Bulgaria, 157, 160–63
Maine, 19–20, 50, 166–92, 232, 240
Maine Audubon, 232
Maine Birds (Palmer), 172
Maine Department of Inland Fisheries and Wildlife, 171
Manitoba, 326–33
Manitoba Hydro, 329
Mantinicus Rock, 181

marine food chains, 188
Maritimes, 49
market hunting, 7–11, 21, 24–27, 222, 224, 249
marsh birds, 17
Martinique, 244
Maryland, 239
Massachusetts, 5–6, 9, 50, 103, 180, 220–39, 241
Massachusetts Audubon (Mass Audubon), 228–39
Matinicus Rock, 173, 178
Maui Bird Conservation Center, 198
Mauna Loa volcano, 201
meadowlarks: western meadowlarks, 263–66
medusahead, 280–81, 289, 294
megafires, 283
Meng, Heinz, 41–42
mergansers: common mergansers, 6
merlins, 31, 49–50, 58, 238
Mexico, 14, 21, 49
Miculescu, Vali Petru, 119–21
Midway Atoll, 212–19
migration, 31, 33, 55, 111, 130, 155–56, 221, 242–44, 245–46
Migratory Bird Conservation Fund, 10
Migratory Bird Hunting Stamp, 10
migratory bird joint ventures, 14
Migratory Bird Treaty Act (MBTA), 9, 14–15, 40, 204–5
Mi'kmaw (L'nu), 324–25
Mirick, Steve and Jane, 51
mirror boxes, 178
Mississippi kites, 50–52
Mississippi River valley, 50, 53
Mitchell, Mike, 213–14
Moldova, 99, 118, 129–30
mongooses, 198, 201
Montana, 102–3, 273–75, 303
Montezuma National Wildlife Refuge, 43–44
Moorland Association, 80
moorlands, 64–84
Moosman, Crys, 214–15
Morgan, Ken, 253
Morris, Tina, 44
mosquitoes, 197–98, 282
mountain plovers, 248–75
Mount Auburn Cemetery, Cambridge, MA, 103
mudflats, 23–24, 221, 223
muirburn, 83
Mulvey, Grace, 230–34

murres: common murres, 167
Muscongus Bay, 167, 181
musk oxen, 100, 306–8
myna: common myna, 195
myxomatosis, 58

Nā Pali Coast, 195–216
National Association of Audubon Societies (NAAS), 37–38
National Audubon Society, 259–60, 311. *See also* Project Puffin
National Fish and Wildlife Foundation (NFWF), 241–42, 268
National Park and Recreation Association, 103–4
national parks, defined, 71
National Parks England, 80
National Park Service, 233
National Trust, Farne Islands, 58
National Wildlife Refuge (NWR) system, 10
Native Americans in Philanthropy, 274
Natural Resources Conservation Service (NRCS), 274, 287–89, 303
Nature Conservancy, 191, 274
Nature Conservation Centre Eastern Rhodopes, 157
NatureScot, 82–84, 101
nature tourism, 80, 157, 195–96
Nebraska, 279
Negru, Robert, 138–42
Nelson, Harvey K., 14
Nelson River, 329
Nepal, 146–47
Nesterenko, Mykhailo, 138
Netherlands, 91–92, 99, 100
Nettleship, David, 175, 177, 188
Nevada, 301
New Brunswick, 173, 238
Newell's shearwaters, 200–202, 204–7, 216–17
New England, 240
Newfoundland, 49, 175, 177, 181
New Hampshire, 50, 51
New Jersey, 43, 52, 239
Newmarket, NH, 51
New Mexico, 50, 96, 279
Newton, Ian, 54
New World vultures, 149
New York, 49, 50, 239–40
The New Yorker (magazine), 33–35
New York Times (newspaper), 14, 42–43, 54
New Zealand, 208–9

Nieuw Land National Park, 98–99
Nigeria, 154–55
nighthawks: common nighthawks, 263, 264, 332
night-herons, 180
nightingales, 106–8, 112–13
Night Spirits (Bilgen-Reinart), 330
Ni Hat'ni Dene (Watchers of the Land), 323–24
Nihokū Ecosystem Restoration Project, 215–19
Nitah, Steven, 319–24
North American boreal forest, 307–33
North American Waterfowl Management Plan (NAWMP), 13–15, 27, 292–93
North American Wetlands Conservation Act (NAWCA), 14–15, 17, 27, 242
North Carolina, 49, 50, 233, 238, 240
North Dakota, 19, 274
Northeast Canyons and Seamounts Marine National Monument, 191–92
North Edisto River, 245
northern pintails, 6, 27–28
Northlands Denesuline First Nation, 327
North Lookout at Hawk Mountain Sanctuary, 30–32, 35–36, 54–55
North Macedonia, 150, 152, 154, 156
North Pennines National Landscape, 74
North Slave Métis Alliance, 321
Northumberland, 58, 60, 74–75, 186
Northwest Territories, 243, 306–26
Northwest Territory Métis Nation, 321–22
North York Moors, 71
Norton, Arthur H., 172–73
Norway, 63–64, 136
Noss, Reed F., 95–96, 101
Nothman, Lane, 314
Nova Scotia, 52
Noyce, Bob, 177
NSAIDs. *See* diclofenac
Nuu-chah-nulth First Nation, 320
NWT Our Land for the Future, 326

Oʻahu, 198, 217
Obama, Barack, 191–92, 256
Okeson, Lance, 293–98
Oklahoma, 249, 274, 279
Old Hump Ledge, 181
Olsen, Andrew C., 299
Ontario Ministry of Natural Resources, 23–24

Oostvaardersplassen, Netherlands, 92–93, 98–99
Operation Artemis, 66
O-Pipon-Na-Piwin Cree Nation, 327–29
Oregon, 279, 281, 287, 292
Orkney Islands, 82
ospreys, 34–35, 39, 44, 56–64
Osterlund, Hob, 193
Outer Banks of North Carolina, 232–33
oversand vehicles (OSVs), 226–28, 232–33, 236
owls, 58–59, 109
    barn owls, 59
    great horned owls, 40, 42, 180
    long-eared owls, 59, 109
    tawny owls, 59, 109
Owyhee County, ID, 290–97
oystercatchers, 239–42, 246–47

Pacific Cooperative Studies Unit, University of Hawaiʻi at Mānoa, 216
Pacific golden-plovers, 224
Pacific loons, 308–9
Pacific Rim Conservation (PRC), 191, 214–17
Pacific Rim National Park, Vancouver Island, British Columbia, 320
Pacific Seabird Group, 192
Pakistan, 146
Palmer, Ralph S., 172, 174–75, 190
parakeets
    Carolina parakeets, 10
    rose-ringed parakeets, 195–96
parasitic jaeger, 313
Pârâul Alb (White Creek), 122
Parks Canada, 320–22, 325
Partnerscapes, 274
Partners for Fish and Wildlife program, USFWS, 293
passenger pigeons, 10
Pawnee National Grasslands, Weld County, CO, 256
Peak District National Park, 71
Pearson, Gilbert, 37
pelicans
    brown pelicans, 34–35
    Dalmatian pelicans, 112, 130–31, 140
    great white pelicans, 130, 140
Pennsylvania, 30–55
peregrine falcons, 31, 34, 41–44, 58, 174
Peregrine Fund, 42
pesticides, 33, 53, 58, 148, 150. *See also* DDT
Petit Manan, 181

petrels
  Bermuda petrels, 199
  Bulwer's petrels, 210
  Hawaiian petrels, 200–207, 216–17
  Kermadec petrels, 218
  Leach's storm-petrels, 166, 181, 213, 217
  lesser Hawaiian petrel, 198
  storm-petrels, 200–204
  Tahiti petrels, 200
Pew Charitable Trusts, 311, 316, 326
Pheasants Forever, 290, 293
Philadelphia vireos, 312
Phillips County, MT, 274
pied-billed grebes, 17
pigeons: passenger pigeons, 10
pigs, 201, 215
pink-footed geese, 24
pintails: northern pintails, 6, 27–28
pinyon jays, 300–303
pinyon pines, 289, 299–303
piping plovers, 223–39, 242
Pleistocene rewilding, 96–98
plovers
  American golden-plovers, 222, 224
  black-bellied plovers, 222, 224
  mountain plovers, 248–75
  Pacific golden-plovers, 224
  piping plovers, 223–39, 242
Plymouth, MA, 227–28
Plymouth Long Beach, 227–28
pocket gophers, 260–61, 265, 267
Podolsky, Richard, 181, 213, 214
poisoning, 37, 45, 70, 125, 147–52, 154
ponies
  Carpathian ponies, 100
  Exmoor ponies, 88, 93, 100
  Karakachan ponies, 100
Poole Harbour, 56–64
poʻouli, 198
Pough, Richard, 37
power lines, 207
Prague Zoo, 155
Prairie Coteau, 12
prairie dogs, 248–71
prairie pothole region of the northern Great Plains, 11–12, 15, 27–28, 29, 52
Predator Free 2050, 209
predators, 12, 20, 68, 102, 110, 147, 177, 198–218, 237, 240–41
Princeville, HI, 213–14
project finance for permanence (PFP), 326

Project Puffin, 167–92
Project Puffin (Kress), 173
Przewalski's horse, 100
puffins: Atlantic puffins, 167–92
punt guns, 8–9, 25
Pyron, Jason, 293–98

Quicksilver Mountain, 294–95

rabbits: European rabbits, 210
Raine, André, 199–207, 210–11, 216
Raine, Helen, 199–200
Ramsar Treaty, 98
Ranchers Stewardship Alliance, 274–75
Rancho Largo Cattle Company, 260–67
raptors, 30–55, 56–84, 130
rats, 208–10
razorbills, 181
Rebirding (Macdonald), 79–80, 118
red-backed shrikes, 90, 111, 118, 122–23
Redcliff Island *(Tthegéré Nué)*, 315
red deer, 91–93, 105, 133, 145, 164
red grouse, 67, 68, 79, 82
red kites, 57, 59–60, 82
red knots, 221, 222, 244
Red List of imperiled birds, IUCN, 186
red-necked grebes, 312
red or Arctic foxes, 209–10
reed beds, 130, 132
Reid, Fritz, 313–15
reinforcement program for vultures, 155
reintroduction programs, 3, 7, 41–46, 63–64, 110–12, 117–21, 150–51
renewable energy development, 283
residential and industrial development, 283
Resources Legacy Fund, 313
rewilding, 86–113, 114–27
Rewilding Europe, 99–102, 117, 138, 158
Rewilding Rhodopes Foundation, 145, 158, 163–64
Rewilding Romania, 117–27
Rewilding Ukraine, 131–42
Reynolds Creek watershed, 296–97
Rhodope Mountains of Bulgaria, 100, 143–65
Rizza, Theresa, 167–71
Road to Recovery (R2R), 3, 287
Robbins, Chandler S., 214
Rocky Mountain Bird Observatory. *See* Bird Conservancy of the Rockies (BCR)

Rocky Mountains, 52
roe deer, 92, 93, 100, 105, 164
Romania, 114–42, 150
Roşca-Buhaiova Scientific Reserve, 130–31
roseate terns, 166, 169, 179–80
rose-ringed parakeets, 195–96
Ross's geese, 25, 26
Roy, Robert, 51
Royal Society for the Protection of Birds (RSPB), 58–59, 66, 68, 70–79, 81, 144
Roy Dennis Wildlife Foundation, 56, 64, 110
RSPB Scotland, 101
Ruckelshaus, William, 35
ruddy turnstones, 222
Rüppell's vulture, 148
rural land abandonment, 10, 95, 119–20
Russia, 102, 141
Rutland Water Nature Reserve, 60–62
Ryder, Brandt, 253–54, 260, 265–66

Sackett v. EPA, 29
Sadler Hill, 69
sagebrush habitats, 276–305
sage-grouse: greater sage-grouse, 278–305
Sage-Grouse Initiative (SGI), 287–89, 303
Sahtú Dene community of Déline, 312–13
A Sand County Alamanac (Leopold), 5
sandhill cranes, 22, 266, 297
Sand Hills, NE, 282
sand lance, 185, 189
sandpipers
 buff-breasted sandpipers, 222, 244
 semipalmated sandpipers, 223
 stilt sandpipers, 222
Saskatoon, Saskatchewan, 50
Sat Bătrân, Romania, 117–18
satellite tags, 70–75, 79, 111, 243
Saudi Arabia, 154–55
Save Our Shearwaters (SOS), 205
Sayisi Dene First Nation, 327–31
Scalp Act, 36
Scandinavia, 34, 102, 199
Scarborough, ME, 232
scaup, 28–29
Science (journal), 1–3, 287
scoters: black scoters, 312, 333
Scotland, 56–64, 65–67, 74, 80–84, 89, 101–2, 111, 186

Scottish Natural Heritage, 70, 82–83
Scottish Society for the Prevention of Cruelty to Animals (SSPCA), 83
Scussett Beach State Reservation, 229–38
Seabird Institute, National Audubon Society, 167–91
Seabird Restoration Database, 191
seabirds, colonial, 26–27, 172, 186, 217
seabirds of Eastern Egg Rock, 166–92
seabirds of Hawai'i, 193–219
Seagull Beach, Yarmouth, MA, 229–38
Seal River Watershed Alliance (SRWA), 327–33
sea temperature changes, 183–87
seawater pH, 184–85
semipalmated sandpipers, 223
sentinel poisoning, 148
shearwaters, 175, 199–206, 216–17
 Newell's shearwaters, 200–202, 204–7, 216–17
 wedge-tailed shearwaters, 210–11
Sheep Creek, 298
shooting swamps, 244
shorebirds, 8, 24, 220–47
shrikes: red-backed shrikes, 90, 111, 118, 122–23
Siberia, 96–97
Silent Spring (Carson), 33–35
Silver City Range, 294–95
Silver Lake, Rochester, MN, 18–19
Simescu, Ioan, 118–21
slender-billed curlews, 222, 242
slender-billed vultures, 146, 147, 149
small-scale farming, 119–20
Smithsonian Conservation Biology Institute, 273
Smithsonian Migratory Bird Center, 238, 273, 303
snail kites, 46–49
snipe: Wilson's snipe, 222
Snowdrift. *See* Łutsël K'é Dené First Nation (LKDFN)
snow geese, 7, 20–27, 223
social attraction techniques, 172, 178–81, 191, 193, 197, 202–3, 207, 208, 213–18
Soda Fire of 2015, 281
Sodbuster, 13
Sofia, Bulgaria, 143–65
songbirds, 2, 8–9, 108, 111, 122–23
Soulé, Michael E., 95–96, 101
South America, 52, 180, 247
South Asia, 146–48
South Carolina, 243–45

South Dakota, 274
South Downs National Park, 101
Southern Environmental Law Center, 233
Southern Indian Lake, 329
Southern Uplands, 82
South Georgia Island, 208
South Indian Lake, 328
Spain, 59, 73, 125, 136, 149–50, 158
Spanish Peaks, 266
sparrowhawks: Eurasian sparrowhawks, 54
sparrows
    Brewer's sparrows, 277, 299
    vesper sparrows, 299
sport hunting, 15–16, 67, 107–8, 222–23, 243–44
spotted doves, 196
Stancu, Alexandra, 131–32
Stark Lake *(Tthe Kálįka Tué)*, 317–18
"State of Nature" report, 89
State of the Birds report, 29
Staatsosbeheer, 98
stilt sandpipers, 222
St. Lawrence River, 21, 23
Stocks Reservoir, 72
stopover sites, 28, 221, 243
storks: white storks, 85–86, 109–12, 128, 153
storm-petrels, 200–204
Storrington, 109
Stoychev, Stoycho, 143–65
Studen Kladenets Reserve, 163–64
Sudan, 162
Suffolk, England, 107
Sulina channel, 129, 132
Suriname, 244
Sussex, England, 85–113
Sutton, George Miksch, 36–37
Svalbard archipelago, 24, 185
Swainson's thrushes, 312, 332
Swampbuster, 13
swans, 2–3, 7, 14: trumpeter swans, 7
Sweden, 59
Swedish Lapland, 99–100
swifts: alpine swifts, 127

Tadoule Lake, 327–31
Tahiti petrels, 200
tape-playback, 137
Țarcu Mountains, 117–22
Tarutino Steppe, 100, 130
Tataru Island, 133
Tauros cattle, 100
tawny owls, 59, 109

Teetł'it Gwinjik (Peel River) watershed, 325
telemetry, 69, 148, 154, 162–63, 299
Tennessee, 49
Tennessee warblers, 312
terns
    Arctic terns, 166, 169, 179–80
    common terns, 26, 166–81
    gull-billed terns, 233
    least terns, 227
    roseate terns, 166, 169, 179–80
Terziev, Nikolay, 150–52, 159
Texas, 39–40, 46, 49
Thaidene Nëné Indigenous Protected and Conserved Area, 306–34
Thayer, Abbott, 171
Thelon Wildlife Sanctuary, 307–22
Thomas, Mark, 58–59, 66, 68–69, 71, 75, 79, 84
Three Cs approach, 95–96
thrushes: Swainson's thrushes, 312, 332
Timișoara, Romania, 117
Toombs, Ted, 263–64
Torishima, 212
tortoises: Bolsón tortoises, 96
translocation, 41–42, 63–64, 176–81, 208, 216–19
Tree, Isabella, 89–94, 99–112
Tribal Buffalo Lifeways Collaboration, 274
Trump, Donald J., 15, 29, 192, 286, 296
trumpeter swans, 7
Ts'udé Nilįné Tueyata Indigenous protected area, 324
tubenoses, 200–203
tūis (Australian honeyeaters), 209
Turkey, 156
turkey vultures, 49, 149
turnstones: ruddy turnstones, 66
turtledoves, 106–9

Ukraine, 117, 127–42
Ultima Frontiera, 131–42
Union of Bulgarian Hunters and Anglers, 163
United Kingdom, 20, 24, 26, 32–33, 53–54, 56–84, 85–87, 89, 99, 106, 107–8, 111–12, 120, 123, 185–86. *See also* Royal Society for the Protection of Birds
United Utilities, 73–74
University of Florida, 47–48
University of Montana, 273
University of Toronto, 23–24

Ursuța, Sebastian, 117–28
USDA Wildlife Services, 210
US Environmental Protection Agency (EPA), 1, 29, 35
US Fish and Wildlife Service (USFWS)
  Atlantic Flyway Shorebird Initiative, 242
  Canada goose, 18–19
  duck numbers, 12
  Kaua'i Island Utility Cooperative (KIUC), 204
  listing mountain plovers, 256
  listing piping plovers, 226
  listing sage-grouse, 285–86, 296
  Nihokū Ecosystem Restoration Project, 216
  Plymouth, MA, 228
  Project Puffin, 170–71
  rats on Kaua'i, 210
  reintroduction program, 42–45
  report to Congress, 9
  sagebrush habitats, 292
  snow goose hunting restrictions, 24–25
  wetland losses, 29
US Forest Service, 286
US Geological Survey (USGS), 283
US Supreme Court, 29

Vera, Frans, 91–93, 98–99
Veracruz, Mexico, 52
VerCauteren, Tammy, 263–64
Vermont, 50
vesper sparrows, 299
The View from Hawk Mountain (Harwood), 39
vireos, 2, 308, 312
Virginia, 165, 239, 243
vultures, 100–101, 124–27, 143–65
  bearded vultures, 125, 150, 160
  black vultures, 49
  Cape vulture, 148
  cathartid vultures, 149
  cinereous vultures, 100, 124–25, 149–50, 158–63
  Egyptian vultures, 125, 150–62
  Eurasian black vultures, 124–25
  European vultures, 126, 145–46, 158–59
  griffon vultures, 124–27, 149–50, 152, 155, 156, 157, 159–62
  Gyps vultures, 148–49
  New World vultures, 149
  Rüppell's vulture, 148
  slender-billed vultures, 146, 147, 149
  turkey vultures, 49, 149
  white-backed vultures, 148
  white-rumped vultures, 146, 147, 149
vulture safe zones (VSZs), 147–48
Vylkove, Ukraine, 128, 141

Waddington Fell, 65–66, 69
Wadhurst Park, 110
wading birds, 8, 130
Wai'ale'ale volcano, 198
Waipa, Jen, 214–18
Wales, 57–64, 89
warblers, 2, 308, 312, 313
  Connecticut warblers, 312
  Tennessee warblers, 312
warbling (Japanese) white-eye, 196
Warner Mountains, 287–88
Warsaw Zoo, 110
Washington, 279
Washington, DC, 51, 165
Washington Post (newspaper), 127
waterbirds, 26, 112, 132, 205, 228–29, 246
water buffalos, 138–39
waterfowl, 2–3, 5–29
Waterfowl Breeding Population and Habitat Survey, 10–11
waterfowling, 15–16
Weald to Waves initiative, 101, 111
wedge-tailed shearwaters, 210–11
Weissburg, Casey, 271–72
Wellington, New Zealand, 209
Wells, Jeff, 312–13, 327–28, 332
Wente, Maggie, 313–16
We Rise Together report, 316, 324
Western Association of Fish and Wildlife Agencies, 292
Western Egg Rock, 171, 176
western meadowlarks, 263–66
West Nile virus, 282
West Virginia, 50
wetlands, 7, 9, 12–17, 28–29, 46, 48–49, 89, 118, 130, 227, 242, 245
whimbrels, 243–47
White, Connor, 290–97, 303–4
white-backed vultures, 148
white-fronted geese, 24, 27
white-rumped vultures, 146, 147, 149
White Stork Project, 109–12
white storks, 85–86, 109–12, 128, 153
white-tailed deer, 45, 105–6, 164
white-tailed eagles, 56–57, 63–64, 70, 98, 130, 135–37
white-winged crossbills, 312

wildfires, 29, 161, 280–81, 286, 294, 326–28
Wilding (Tree), 89
Wildlife Management and Muirburn Bill, 83
Wilson, Alexander, 224
Wilson's snipe, 222
wind turbines, 125, 162, 266, 269
Wineinger-Davis Ranch, 248–75
Wingate, David, 199
Winnipeg, Manitoba, 51
Wisconsin, 51
wisent. *See* European bison
Witches' Walk, 64–65, 69
Witless Bay, Newfoundland, 175
wolves, 95–96, 101–2, 162: gray wolves, 95–96
Woodbourne, 244
Wood Buffalo National Park, 309, 320
woodcocks: American woodcocks, 222
Working Lands for Wildlife program at NRCS, 287–88
World Wildlife Fund (WWF), 121, 132–33, 259, 274
Wrangel Island, 26

WWF-Romania, 117
Wyoming, 274, 280, 283

Yakutian horses, 97
Yassie, Darryn, 327–28, 333
Yellowknife, Canada, 311, 326
Yellowknives Dene First Nation, 322
yellowlegs: lesser yellowlegs, 222–23, 244, 312, 332
Yellow Sea, 221
Yellowstone National Park, 95–96, 102, 325
Yellowstone to Yukon Conservation Initiative (Y2Y), 95–96, 325
Yemen, 162
Yorkshire Dales, 74
Young, Lindsay, 217
Yukon, 95–96, 325

Zaporizhzhia plant, Ukraine, 127–28
zebra doves, 196
zebra mussels, 28
Zimov, Sergey and Nikita, 97
Zipperer, Katie, 269
Zoeller, Camryn, 169–71

Scott Weidensaul is one of the most respected natural history writers in the US, and the author of nearly thirty books. He is an active field researcher specializing in bird migration, co-director of Project Owlnet and co-directs Project SNOWstorm, studying the migration of snowy owls. He has received numerous awards, including the Audubon Award for Environmental Writing, and has been honored as a prestigious fellow of the American Ornithological Society. Weidensaul is a highly sought-after speaker at universities, museums and birding festivals. His book *Living on the Wind: Across the Hemisphere with Migratory Birds* was a Pulitzer Prize finalist. *The Return of the Oystercatcher* is his latest book.